HINDU GODDESSES

Beliefs and Practices

LYNN FOULSTON AND STUART ABBOTT

sussex
ACADEMIC
PRESS

BRIGHTON • PORTLAND

1 2 4 6 8 10 9 7 5 3

First published 2009 in Great Britain by
SUSSEX ACADEMIC PRESS
PO Box 139
Eastbourne BN24 9BP

and in the United States of America by
SUSSEX ACADEMIC PRESS
920 NE 58th Ave Suite 300
Portland, Oregon 97213–3786

British Library Cataloguing in Publication Data
A CIP catalogue record for this book is available from the British Library.

Library of Congress Cataloging-in-Publication Data
Foulston, Lynn.
Hindu goddesses : beliefs & practices / Lynn Foulston and Stuart Abbott.
p. cm.
Includes bibliographical references and index.
ISBN 978-1-902210-43-8 (alk. paper)
1. Goddesses, Hindu. 2. Worship (Hinduism) I. Abbott, Stuart.
II. Title.
BL1216.F68 2009
294.5'2114—dc22
2008020443

Mixed Sources
Product group from well-managed
forests and other controlled sources
www.fsc.org Cert no. SGS-COC-2482
© 1996 Forest Stewardship Council
FSC

Typeset by SAP, Brighton & Eastbourne.
Printed by TJ International, Padstow, Cornwall.
This book is printed on acid-free paper.

Contents

Part II **Practices**

List of Illustrations

The colour plates are after page 148.

Divali, purchased in New Delhi in 2000. Photographer: Lynn Foulston.

The chapter heading logo – the *Sri yantra* or *Sri cakra* – is a two-dimensional diagram that represents the essence of the goddess in visual form.

Preface and Acknowledgements

Why do we need another book about Hindu Goddesses, you might be wondering? Perhaps the fact that there are so many to choose from indicates a deep fascination with, arguably, the world's oldest living goddess tradition. The many types of book, anthropological studies, ethnographies, textual analyses, etc. that focus on a particular goddess are reflective of the rich diversity of this tradition. For every assertion made about goddess worship, the observant reader will discover that the opposite might also be claimed. This makes constructing lectures about Hindu goddesses challenging, to say the least, but never dull. There always seems to be so much to say, but never enough time to say it in. This book is an attempt to provide the undergraduate student or simply the interested reader with an overview of what we understand by Hindu Goddesses, in terms of the beliefs and practices associated with them. Hopefully, even if you have read other books on the subject – and if not I suggest you do – you will find something in this book (story, goddess, temple, or idea) that you had not already encountered. If this is your first foray into the wonderful world of Hindu goddesses, I hope that this book will encourage you to find out more.

With regard to this project there are many people whose help must be acknowledged. I would like to start with the late Professor David Kinsley, referred to by Rachel Fell McDermott as the 'father' of Kali studies in North America. I would like to go further and call him the 'father' of Hindu goddess studies worldwide. I know that his pioneering work, which was accessible to so many, is the reason why many scholars became interested in Hindu goddesses; it is certainly so in my case. He has much to do with my engagement in goddess studies and consequently you will find reference to his work throughout.

I am deeply indebted to Dr Jeaneane Fowler, who tirelessly waded through early drafts of much of this book offering very constructive and creative suggestions. I would like to thank Rachel Fell McDermott for offering advice on my trip to experience Durga Puja in Kolkata in 2002. It was she who connected me with Hena Basu who worked during this time as my research assistant, offering translation assistance, companionship and valuable insights into this most amazing festival. In connection with this visit I would like to thank my good friends Ashis and Bandana Chakravartti who accommodated and fed me between my visits to the 32 *pujas* that Hena took me to. Some of the photographs used in this book are those that I regularly use in my teaching and were supplied by Jayanta Roy. He enabled me to gain a sense of the elements of worship in Kolkata that I was unable to see for myself. I was helped considerably in Orissa by Niranjan Mohapatra, who worked with me as translator and research assistant, selflessly giving up his free time to do so. In Colavandan I was assisted principally by Dr P. Sarveswaran, previously at the Madurai Kamaraj University, but now retired.

I would like to thank Stuart for helping me complete this book by writing the chapter on Tantrism, which is a special interest to him, and contributing to the chapter on worship. Unfortunately for him, he was also recruited to carry out some of the less glamorous tasks such a proof-reading and indexing. I hope that he will go on to write more in the future. My colleague, David Norcliffe, was also kind enough to read through a late draft looking for errors and omissions.

Anthony Grahame, Editorial Director of Sussex Academic Press, has again been supportive in this endeavour with his constructive advice and, more importantly, his unfailing patience as this work has taken so long to come to fruition. Last, but not least, I would like to thank my husband Graham who has supported me throughout, especially for his stoical tolerance of my distracted behaviour and the piles of books and papers that seem to gravitate around me when I write and his willingness to 'test out' the book by being the first one to read the whole draft.

Despite all the help and assistance provided, any errors and omissions contained in this work remain my responsibility.

LYNN FOULSTON
UNIVERSITY OF WALES, NEWPORT
January 2009

Introduction

The Goddess pervades the world and everything in it. In every living being, in the rivers that water the land, in the land itself, in the smallest blade of grass or the tiniest insect. Beyond and above, within and without, nothing exists or stirs in the cosmos that is not infused with the power of the Goddess.

Who is the Mother Goddess? She is called Amba (the Mother), Durga (the Divine Warrior), Kali (the Dark One) and Laksmi (the Bringer of Wealth and Happiness). The goddess in Hinduism is also called Sakti (pronounced Shakti), an abstract term for power and energy, which has become one of her names as well as describing her deepest essence. The bewildering array of terms for her is interchangeable as are some of the goddesses themselves since many names are indications of the aspects of the Mahadevi (lit. Great Goddess), an all-encompassing form of female divinity.

Who or what is a Hindu Goddess?

Hindu goddesses are many and varied and it is by no means an easy task to trot out a few lines providing a neat definition of who or what they are. If you happened to be walking down a street in Kolkata (Calcutta), Delhi or Mumbai (Bombay) and decided to ask someone you met about Hindu goddesses, you might well be surprised by their answer. More than likely, they would claim that there are 330 million goddesses! Confusion would almost certainly furrow your brow as you consider the implication of this statement. Moreover, you would perhaps wonder whether you are supposed to take this statement literally. The simple answer to this is yes *and* no! From a certain perspective, it would be just as true to say that there is only one goddess, Sakti, who represents power and energy. However, to dwell on this interpretation would be to dismiss the many thousands of goddesses that are worshipped by the majority of the population. Even in small settlements, there can be many different shrines and temples dedicated to individual goddesses. According to the research of Pauline Kolenda, in a village settlement in Uttar Pradesh, northern India, a population of five thousand worshipped no less than one hundred goddesses.[1] So one reason for the estimate of 330 million is an indication of how popular and important goddesses are. Each goddess has her own origin myth, her own iconography and her own style of worship. Many are only worshipped in one hamlet or village (commonly referred to as local or village goddesses) whereas others have many representations that are worshipped in a particular region of India (commonly referred to as regional goddesses). If all the goddesses in the myriad temples and shrines in every hamlet, village, town and city were counted up, it is unlikely that they would number 330 million. However, there might be many millions. The point here seems to be that there might be any number of goddesses because power and energy, which they represent, are limitless. This is an idea that we will return to in chapter 1.

Not all goddesses reside in local settlements. If you are ever lucky enough to visit the ancient city of Madurai in Tamilnadu, you could not help but be impressed by the magnificent temple that fills the centre of the city. The Minaksi (fish-eyed goddess) temple, with its four soaring temple towers (Tam. *gopurams*), dominates the city in terms of its sheer size, beauty and as the centre that draws to it thousands of pilgrims and tourists alike. Throughout India, goddesses, much more widely than male deities, are the mainstay of daily religious life. However, goddesses are most prolific in local settlements and since "there are about half a million villages in India and four-fifths of the population live in them"[2] their importance should not be underestimated.

Goddesses – an aspect of divinity

The other reason for saying that there are 330 million goddesses – of which the same can be said for male deities – is that this is such an unimaginably large number that it indicates infinity. In other words, there can be an infinite number of goddesses and gods because metaphysically they represent opposite aspects of one all-encompassing entity, referred to as Brahman. Brahman is neither female nor male but is simply beyond gender and indeed is beyond description or comprehension by humans. Nevertheless, much has been written about Brahman, for it is viewed as the source of the cosmos and everything in it. The only way that we, as mere mortals, can talk about Brahman is to say what it is not. Therefore, in texts such as the *Upanishads* that encompass wide and varied discussions on the nature of Brahman and our relationship to it, Brahman is referred to as *neti – neti* "not this – not this".[3] So where do the 330 million gods and goddesses fit in if Brahman is beyond gender? All the gods and goddesses may be viewed as emanations of Brahman representing the many facets of Ultimate Reality that are ordinarily beyond human comprehension. The gods and goddesses provide mortals with the chance to form a meaningful relationship with the divine even though ultimately it is beyond any sort of personalization. Since Brahman is eternal and infinite, surely there can also be infinite emanations in the form of the many and varied gods and goddesses.

So, getting back to the statement of the person we met in Kolkata, Delhi or Mumbai, they gave us a great deal of information in their simple statement that there are 330 million Hindu goddesses, but they might well be unaware of the complexity of their claim. On one hand, we have the idea that Hindu goddesses represent energy and power, which is just one facet, albeit an important one, of Brahman. Goddesses appear across India in anthropomorphic (human) form with sophisticated theologies, but they also appear in very simple forms, such as a rock or a tree decorated with red vermilion paste, often with dramatic silver eyes attached. This diversity of form and thought still leaves us with a problem, how to simply and easily define what a Hindu goddess is?

Goddess worship – a legacy from the past?

Perhaps we should start with the past. The practice of conceiving of the earth as a Mother Goddess, who provides the means of survival for her children, is an extremely ancient one. Many early civilizations, especially those based on agriculture, ordered their lives around the changing seasons, making periodic offerings to the earth. The Mother Goddess was often represented as the ultimate genetrix, source of fertility, as the discoveries of numerous female statues with accentuated breasts, belly and vagina indicate. In the same respect, the earth that yielded the crops necessary for life was perceived as the womb of the goddess bringing forth food. This primordial mother has many different names and forms, such as Isis and Hathor in ancient Egypt, Ishtar in Mesopotamia, and Greek and Roman goddesses such as Gaia, Athene and Aphrodite to name but a few.[4] It is perhaps no wonder that artefacts found at prehistoric settlements in ancient India have included many female figurines that may be suggestive of a cult of goddess worship.

The Indus Valley Civilization (c.2500 BCE – c.1500 BCE) was highly sophisticated and flourished when civilization in Britain was approaching the Iron Age (c.1000 BCE). The major cities of the Indus Valley, Harappa and Mohenjo-daro, were large and well organized with brick-built houses on planned streets. The houses had two or more storeys with a number of rooms arranged around a courtyard. Perhaps the most impressive and unexpected feature of these houses was the inclusion of a bathroom that drained into a sewer system running under the streets to soak-pits, prompting Arthur Basham to comment: "No other ancient civilization until that of the Romans had so efficient a system of drains."[5] The cities of Harappa and Mohenjo-daro were arranged around a central feature assumed to be a great bath, a feature that has perhaps prevailed in the huge water tanks commonly found in or near many Hindu temples.

What are of most interest to us are the many artefacts found in the houses that may point towards a predominant goddess cult. However, we should be cautious in assuming that this cult is the pre-cursor of goddess worship in India today. Undoubtedly there may be links but goddess worship as it is today has evolved over a vast period of time, born of many influences. Until the language of the Indus Valley Civilization, found on many seals, is finally deciphered we can only speculate about the significance and meaning of the statuettes and scenes depicted on the seals. Scholars assume that goddess worship was prevalent because in practically all the houses of Mohenjo-daro and Harappa terracotta female figurines were found. Many had smoke-blackened headdresses suggesting that they may have been used for ritual purposes[6] while most found in Mohenjo-daro were painted with red slip, a symbol of menstrual blood perhaps.[7] Although male figures were also found, those depicting females were significantly more predominant. The female figurines were of two types, some were polished and finely fashioned, perhaps made for the middle classes or the elite, whereas the majority were crudely made, prompting Basham to conclude that "effigies were mass produced by humble potters to meet popular demand" and further infers that they were used for goddess worship.[8] It would certainly be tempting to equate the mass-produced figurines with the contemporary local goddesses who are similarly reproduced for popular religion; however, to do so would be to jump to conclusions too readily.

More intriguing than the figurines are the many seals containing the as-yet un-deciphered writing of the Indus people and a variety of pictures. Some scholars have concluded that the pictorial inscriptions on the Indus Valley seals are further proof that a goddess cult existed. On one seal, in particular, there appears to be a female figure with a tree or plant issuing from her womb. This image is perhaps suggestive of a "Mother Goddess as the genetrix and source of all vegetation".[9] This is a notion that has attracted many scholars; Bhattacharyya, for instance, proposes that this seal "may be regarded as the prototype of the Earth Mother Sakambhari of the Puranas from whose body grow the life-sustaining vegetables."[10] Another seal appears to depict a female character, this time in a tree, being worshipped, it is generally surmised. However, what is not clear is whether the characters on the seals and the figurines are depictions of the same entity. Furthermore, a number of ring shaped stones, perhaps symbolizing the *yoni* (female generative organ), and those of a phallic nature, have also added to the idea that a mother cult was a significant element of Indus Valley religion. The dilemma of what this evidence really means will not be solved until the Indus Valley script is finally deciphered. Until that day, any speculations that scholars might care to make about the Indus Valley evidence must remain exactly that, speculation.

While many ancient cultures have clearly had a belief in the power of a Mother Goddess, very few of those belief systems are still in existence. What is fascinating about Hinduism is that it has an ongoing tradition of goddess worship which, in the twenty-first century, is no less vital and alive. Goddess worship as it is today has evolved from many different influences, and, since the Hindu tradition rarely eradicates beliefs but assimilates them, there must remain elements of Indus Valley religion in goddess worship as it is practiced today.

In this book, I have drawn together lots of different ideas about Hindu goddesses, focusing on the beliefs about them and the variety of practices that are involved in their worship. **Part I – Beliefs** – looks at the theoretical importance of Hindu goddesses, starting with an examination of goddesses as Sakti, divine power and energy in chapter 1. You might probably find this first chapter difficult, but the ideas outlined in it underpin goddess worship and, therefore, need to be addressed first. In teaching courses on Hindu Goddesses, I have found it beneficial for students to read this introductory chapter first, and to read it again after some or all of the other chapters. Chapter 2 brings together the various ways that goddesses have been represented in textual sources from the *Vedas* (the earliest written sacred texts) to the later goddess-centred *Puranas*, with chapter 3 examining Brahmanical and local mythology. Part I ends with a scrutiny of the importance of goddesses in Tantrism, an esoteric and much misunderstood aspect of Hinduism (chapter 4). **Part II – Practices** – investigates the various religious practices addressed to Hindu goddesses, from daily worship (chapter 5), important goddess festivals (chapter 6) and places of pilgrimage (chapter 7) to some of the more modern aspects of goddess worship (chapter 8). In particular, the last chapter examines the politicization of the divine through the worship of Bharat Mata, the continued worship of the living goddess (Kumari) in Nepal, an examination of the rise to fame of Santosi Ma (the Mother of Satisfaction) and the recent manufacture of two new goddesses. What we have attempted to do within the pages of this book is to convey the multiplicity of Hindu goddesses, the varied and sometimes contradictory expression of beliefs concerning them and the rich diversity of their ritual practice, which is brought together here in its many fascinating forms.

Part I
Beliefs

1 *Sakti* – The Divine Feminine

How is one to define divine power, especially the power behind mani-festation? What would a suitable name be for the dynamism of the world or the energy that enables the world, as we know it, to function? The word used by Hindus is s*akti* (pronounced *shakti*). *Sakti*, is defined in Monier-Williams' Sanskrit dictionary as "power, ability, strength, might, effort, energy, capability" and "capacity for, power over".[1] *Sakti* then, in its most abstract sense, is the energetic principle of Ultimate Reality, conceptualized as primordial power, but is also personified by the myriad goddesses that are an integral part of Hindu religious expres-sion. The term *sakti* has wide connotations, being used to indicate the dynamic aspect of the divine or, on a more mundane level, to advertise the supremacy of a certain brand of Indian washing powder or car battery, among other consumer goods! Leaving aside the merits of Indian cleaning products, this discussion is concerned with what *sakti* really means in a religious context.

The feminine term *sakti* cannot be separated from the goddesses who are personifications of the deepest level of divine power and energy. Hence, they are referred to in many ways: Mahadevi (Great Goddess), as the creator and nourishment of the world, is the Mother Goddess or, indeed, simply individual goddesses, Parvati, Kali or Laksmi. All are expressions of *sakti* in either its cosmic or its more mundane forms. Each expression or form of the divine feminine symbolizes either an aspect of the multifarious character of power and energy or, in simplistic terms, one particular facet of it. For instance, the goddess Uma represents the power of wisdom, which is demonstrated when she appears in the *Kena Upanisad* bestowing *brahma-vidya* (knowledge of Brahman) on Indra.[2] In her more complex forms, the divine feminine is given many names,

Devi (Goddess), Sakti (Power/Energy), Parasakti (Supreme Power), Adyasakti (First or Primordial Power) or Mulaprakrti (Primordial Matter). Although the naming and terminology of the many different goddesses may seem overly complex, in reality the names/terms/epithets are generally interchangeable. The reason that the divine feminine needs so many names is that they convey different aspects of her nature. If you consider the implications of the terms *power* and *energy*, you realize that the nuances of such terminology cannot be conveyed in a few words. Both power and energy take on many different forms as for instance the power or energy in a nuclear power plant is significantly different from the power of a small battery; for though both may be power they are of different types. In the same way, some aspects of the divine feminine more explicitly convey or reveal the meta-physical or cosmic nature of *sakti* whereas others convey individual powers such as love or protection.

A conceptual understanding of *sakti*

In order to appreciate fully the conceptual notion of *sakti* that is advanced in the *Sakta* texts (those in which the goddess is the primary deity) it is first important to be aware of the fundamental Hindu ideas on which *Sakta* beliefs are based. The most important idea is the concept of an Absolute or Ultimate Reality, most commonly referred to as Brahman, a term without gender.

The religious tradition that arose as a refinement and culmination of the *Vedas* (the earliest sacred texts) is referred to as *Vedanta*, meaning "end of the *Veda*". The philosophical texts of this period, the *Upanisads*, formulated some of the most fundamental and profound religious ideas that are the basis of many aspects of later Hindu thought. One such idea is the concept of a correspondence between God, referred to as Brahman or Ultimate Reality, and the totality of all cosmic manifestation. The all-encompassing nature of Brahman gave rise to the theory that everything, whether divine or human, was in its essence the same – thereby, estab-lishing a connecting factor, the *atman* or permanent essence, in all life; hence, *Chandogya Upanisad* 3. 14. 4 asserts: "This self (*atman*) of mine that lies deep within my heart – it contains all actions, all desires, all smells, and all tastes; it has captured this whole world; it neither speaks nor pays any heed. It is *brahman*. On departing from here after death, I will become that."[3] The earlier *Upanisadic* texts offered a vision of Ultimate Reality that could be neither described nor known, except through intuitive knowledge (*jnana*). The overriding characteristic of the *Upanisads* was monistic, emphasizing the identity between the unmanifest Brahman and the individual soul or *atman*. Since Brahman was considered neither male nor female, it was not surprising that, at that point, there was an absence of any emphasis on the divine feminine. However, the later *Upanisads*, in particular the *Svetasvatara*, provided a more accessible depiction of the Absolute, giving credence to the manifest (*saguna*) aspect of Brahman, without, however, negating the underlying unity between the essence of Brahman and the essence of the manifest world. In the *Svetasvatara Upanisad*, Brahman was portrayed as the manifest Lord or Isvara, making a theistic relationship possible, and indeed desirable, between deity and devotee.

Gradually, an increase of literature with a predominantly theistic standpoint appeared, the most important being the epics – the *Mahabharata* and the *Ramayana* – and a range of texts concerned primarily with myth and legend – the *Puranas* – that asserted the supremacy of individual deities. This period is generally referred to as the Classical period of Hinduism. The *puranic* texts built on the unifying foundation established in the *Upanisads*, but tended to express the supremacy of a particular god, equating him in his unmanifest (*nirguna*) form with Brahman. In this context, the myriad deities of the Classical period were considered aspects or manifestations of Brahman, the Ground of Existence. While the majority of *puranic* texts predominantly offered a male deity, most commonly Visnu or Siva, as the supreme manifestation, a variety of *Sakta Puranas*, those dedicated to the goddess, and two texts in particular – the *Devi-Mahatmya*[4] and the later *Devi-Bhagavatam* – asserted the supremacy of the divine feminine. Although in most *puranas* the goddesses were presented primarily as the consorts of the gods, they were also closely associated with three significant principles – energy (*sakti*), primary matter (*prakrti*) and illusion (*maya*) – thereby establishing a relationship between female divinity and creative power.

In the *Kurma Purana*, the goddess Sri or Laksmi was mythologically presented as appearing at the churning of the ocean of milk, a myth examined in chapter 3. The text makes clear that she is subordinate to Visnu as he is described as taking "possession of her (as his consort)".[5] However, though Visnu is clearly in a position of supremacy, Laksmi, significantly, functions as the means of Visnu's power, described as "that great Sakti (potency) of my form".[6] A variety of goddesses were considered to represent *sakti*, but in contrast to the views presented in the *Sakta Puranas* they were always considered a part of, or subject to, the will of their consorts. It would appear that, despite the fact that an individual goddess was addressed by the name Sakti, *sakti* as a quality was possessed by both male and female deities, with an overt identity between female divinity and cosmic energy yet to be established.

Two texts, the earlier *Devi-Mahatmya* (*c.* 500–600 CE) and the later *Devi-Bhagavatam* (*c.* 1100–500 CE), changed the way that the divine feminine was perceived. The *Devi-Mahatmya*, originally a section of the *Markandeya Purana*, was most influential in establishing the all-inclusive nature of feminine power. The importance of this text, and its uniqueness, are apparent in its independence from the parent text. Thomas Coburn comments that while there are very few complete manuscripts of the *Markandeya Purana*, those of the *Devi-Mahatmya* are countless.[7] The recitation of the text is still an integral part of goddess worship, where, according to Coburn, it forms a part of "daily liturgy in temples of Durga".[8] The goddess did not appear as a consort of a male god representing his power, but was conceived of as an independent power in her own right. The most important facet of this conceptual shift in emphasis was the gradual identification of the goddess, as cosmic power, with the Absolute, Brahman.

Cosmic power abounds throughout the world. Its energy and vitality power the circular motion that makes the seasons change and the world to evolve from its creation to its periodic dissolution. Everything emanates from Brahman the Ultimate Reality. Therefore, Brahman encompasses all that we see and all that we do not see. Ultimately for Hindus the divine is not simply male, but is female also. However, all duality, including the discrimination between male and female, is undifferentiated during periods of unmanifestation and apparent only when manifestation occurs and the cosmos is born anew. A vital aspect of Brahman is the energy that makes the act of creation and dissolution possible in a practical sense. The Devi (Goddess) or Mahadevi (Great Goddess) so carefully outlined in the *Devi-Mahatmya* leaves the reader in no doubt of the fluidity of her character. She is the personification of all aspects of energy, being simultaneously creative, preservative and destructive.

> By you this universe is borne, by you this world is created. By you it is
> protected, O Devi and you always consume it at the end. O you who are
> (always) of the form of the whole world, at the time of creation you are
> the form of the creative force, at the time of sustentation you are of the
> form of the protective power, and at the time of the dissolution of the
> world, you are of the form of the destructive power. You are the supreme

Sakti – *The Divine Feminine*

knowledge as well as the great nescience, the great intellect and contemplation, as also the great delusion, the great devi as also the great asuri. (*Devi-Mahatmya* 1. 75–77)[9]

This verse makes it clear that the all-encompassing Goddess in the text represents all aspects of power and energy, both positive and negative, as she is described as goddess (*devi*) and demoness (*asuri*). Devi originated at a time of cosmic crisis and, consequently, her role seems very similar to that of Visnu in his many incarnations (*avataras*). Just as Visnu promises to manifest himself in order to protect the cosmic balance of positive and negative energies, Devi, too, promises to return if needed.[10]

The *Devi-Mahatmya* was the first, but is not the only text, to offer an all-inclusive concept of female divinity and equating it with the principle of Ultimate Reality. The later *Devi-Bhagavatam* presents a *Sakta* response to a variety of *puranic* strands of thought. According to Cheever Mackenzie Brown, its original parts were written as a *Sakta* response to the *Bhagavata Purana*.[11] The *Devi Gita*, which comprises *skandha* (book) 7, chapters 30–40 of the *Devi-Bhagavatam*, is based on the style of the *Bhagavad Gita*, but is presented from a *Sakta* perspective. The ninth *skandha*, according to Brown, is almost a verbatim copy of the '*Prakriti Khanda*' of the *Brahmavaivarta Purana*, which Brown describes as "a kind of encyclopedia of goddesses", associating them with primary matter (*prakrti*).[12] The *Devi-Bhagavatam* also encompasses a version of the *Devi-Mahatmya* and retells a number of *puranic* myths. Of significance is the retelling of the Devi's initial appearance, from the original version in the *Devi-Mahatmya*, in which she is born from the combined power of the gods. In the *Devi-Bhagavatam*, no such male intervention is acknowledged as the Devi appears by her own volition from a blinding light in response to the gods' devotion and propitiation of her. According to Brown, the appearance of the Goddess parallels the myth of Uma Haimavati in the *Kena Upanisad* (3) a "lustrous power revealed in scripture" and the self-manifestation of Siva's fiery linga (phallic symbol), which is related in the *Siva Purana* (*Vidyeshvara Samhita* 1. 7) and the *Linga Purana* (1. 17).[13]

The text is more metaphysically orientated than the earlier *Devi-Mahatmya*, frequently eulogizing the conceptual goddess who is presented as the power behind the functions of the *trimurti*, the triad of deities – Brahma, Visnu and Siva – who are responsible for the periodic creation, preservation and dissolution of the universe respectively.

That Goddess is Eternal and Ever Constant Primordial Force. . . .

She is the source of Brahma, Visnu and the others and all of these living beings. Without Her force, no body would be able even to move their limbs.

That Supreme Auspicious Goddess is the preserving energy of Visnu, is the creative power of Brahma, and is the destroying force of Siva. (*Devi-Bhagavatam* 3.30. 28–30)[14]

It is also significant that in the *Devi-Bhagavatam*, the Great Goddess is explicitly shown to be independent of any male authority and control. Indeed, in the previous verses the gods are subject to her will, being completely reliant on her power. The goddess/es of the *Devi-Bhagavatam* are repeatedly portrayed as eternal, the basis of everything, and identical with Brahman. The goddess herself clearly states: "When everything melts away, i.e. there comes the Pralaya or general dissolution, then, I am not female, I am not male, nor am I hermaphrodite. I then remain as Brahma with Maya."[15]

The Goddess's associations with maya *and* prakrti

In the *Narada Purana*, the goddess, called variously Uma, Laksmi, Bharati, Girija, Ambika, Durga, etc., as well as being referred to as Sakti, is also depicted as Visnu's *maya*.[16] Similarly, in the *Kurma Purana*, Sri is described as Visnu's beloved Maya, "the Infinite, by whom this Universe is sustained", and Visnu states "it is through her that I fascinate this entire Universe".[17] When the goddess is linked with *sakti* and *maya*, she embodies the power of illusion, encompassing ignorance (*avidya*) and knowledge (*vidya*), and is thereby presented with a dual personality. She creates the illusory nature of the world but, more importantly, is also the means of liberation from it.

From the Classical period onwards, the goddesses, whether as consorts of the gods, or as independent entities, were consistently revealed as having an intimate relationship with illusion (*maya*) and primary or primordial matter (*prakrti*). The conceptual understanding of *maya* and *prakrti* are important throughout Hinduism, not just in connection with the divine feminine. Both *maya* and *prakrti* in many contexts have rather negative connotations, but when they are associated with the goddess, they become positive powers. Let us first examine *maya*. According to the philosophy of Sankara's *Advaita Vedanta*: "*Maya* is the principle of illusion . . . it is beginningless and endless and in itself has no reality. It acts as a kind of veil over the real essence of things, the *Atman*, and represents error in true perception. As such, it is very close in meaning to ignorance, *ajnana* or *avidya*. Indeed, as far as Sankara was concerned, these terms were synonymous."[18] For Sankara, *maya* had wholly negative implications, in that it prevented the individual from seeing the identity between Brahman and the Self (*Atman*), fooling them into incorrectly perceiving the world around them as real. This wrong belief led to attachment to the material world, a path leading away from liberation (*moksa*) rather than toward it. By contrast, in *Sakta* thought, *maya* was perceived as a positive creative force, a necessary tool for the goddess to wield and one that was not separate from her essential nature.

> I imagine into being the whole world, moving and unmoving, through the power of my Maya,
> Yet that same Maya is not separate from me; this is the highest truth.
> From a practical point of view, Maya is regarded as self-evident.
> In reality, however, it does not exist – only the supreme exists, in an absolute sense.
> I, as Maya, create the whole world and then enter within it,
> Accompanied by ignorance, actions and the like, and preceded by the vital breath, O Mountain [Himavan, the god to whom she is speaking].
> How else could souls be reborn into future lives?
> They take on various births in accord with modifications of Maya. (*Devi Gita* 3. 1–4)[19]

The Goddess explains the nature of *maya* as non-existent, though what she means is that from the perspective of Brahman, the Absolute, *maya* could be said to be unreal because it is constantly changing. In contrast, Brahman, or in this case the Goddess, is eternal and unchanging but because of her *maya*, her power of illusion, she is able to bring the world into being. The world is both real and unreal because it exists but is "not what it appears to be",[20] for when the individual soul attains enlightenment, the world no longer has any substance. In the *Sakta* view, there is a more intimate relationship between the Goddess and the world as she not only creates it but enters into it. Therefore, despite the fact that many of the ideas advanced in the *Devi-Bhagavatam*, and the *Devi Gita* in particular, are strongly influenced by *Advaita* philosophy, they represent a more positive view of the world and its creation. Hence, Cheever Mackenzie Brown comments: "For Saktas with their affirming cosmological orientation, Maya is basically a positive, creative, magical energy of the Goddess that brings forth the universe, rather than a deceiving power that ensnares individuals in the false realm of the world and hinders their enlightenment – a common Advaita interpretation of Maya."[21] *Maya* enables the Goddess, who in reality is beyond conception, to provide accessible forms of herself, with which her devotees can interact, for the *Sakta* texts, despite being metaphysically based, promote devotion (*bhakti*) as a means to liberation. Therefore, in sharp contrast to *Advaita Vedanta*, the physical body is not considered disgusting but is "an exceptionally powerful vehicle for spiritual transformation".[22] On perhaps a more mundane level, the Goddess periodically uses her *maya* simply to delude the demons (*asuras*). Clearly, *maya* is a very complex notion, which can represent the power to deceive, or as an intrinsic facet of the Goddess, the power of creation and liberation.

Another important aspect of the Goddess's character (that is inseparably linked with *sakti* and *maya*) is her association with *prakrti* (primordial matter), the principle underlying the manifest world. In order to gain an understanding of *prakrti* it is necessary to examine the school of thought from which it originated. *Sankhya* is perhaps the oldest school of philosophical thought. The ideas and concepts outlined by its thinkers are an integral facet of Hindu thought, both ancient and modern. *Sankhya* envisaged everything as originating from two principles, consciousness (*purusa*) and primordial matter (*prakrti*), principles that according to K. Guru Dutt: "In one form or another, underlie the entire mythology of India".[23] He goes on to claim that *purusa* and *prakrti* are: "At the bottom of the Tantrik and Puranic notion of the generation of the Universe by the union of male and female principles symbolized as Shiva and Shakti."[24] According to Classical *Sankhya* philosophy, *purusa* or *purusas*, represented the individual souls, that were activated by the proximity of *prakrti*. *Prakrti* was the source of and the means of manifestation of the material world in which the individual souls were trapped, or more correctly considered themselves to be trapped. *Prakrti*, or material nature essentially consisted of three attributes (*gunas*), *sattva* (purity, goodness, the illuminating principle), *rajas* (activity, passion, the energetic principle) and *tamas* (darkness, inertia, dullness). Although each soul or *purusa* was identical, the distinct character of each individual was dependent on the distribution of the three *gunas*. For instance, a learned and spiritual holy man would have more *sattva* than *rajas* and *tamas* whereas a lazy, wicked person is considered to have an abundance of *tamas*. In the context of *Sankhya* philosophy, *prakrti* was a binding force and one that must be overcome before the individual soul could be liberated. However, *prakrti* was an essential principle of manifestation as without it *purusa* is inert.

The divine feminine in her various forms came to be closely identified with *prakrti* alongside *sakti* and *maya*. Each are integral aspects of her character and in this respect, *prakrti*, like *maya*, loses its negative overtones. For as Klaus Klostermaier observes: "In contrast to other Hindu philosophies that diminish or deny the reality of matter over spirit, Sakta texts emphasize the non-difference between matter and spirit and the reality of *maya* as creative power, not as illusion. Sakti is 'Adya-Prakrti,' original matter, 'Mula-Prakrti,' the root of nature."[25] The Goddess as *prakrti* and *sakti* manifests herself, by her *maya*, into three powers. Just as all that is manifest is composed of three qualities, the goddess in her higher manifest forms becomes Mahalaksmi representing *sattvic* power, Mahasarasvati, who represents her *rajasic* power and Mahakali, representing her dark and destructive *tamasic* power. However, in reality the Goddess is beyond the distinctions of *prakrti* and the *gunas*, literally beyond human conception. Her appearance in the world is to offer a source of liberation to the souls, who in essence are no different from her own being, offering them an object of devotion and a source of knowledge that can lead them beyond the physical world that surrounds them.

Sakti manifested as the Mahadevi or Great Goddess

The most significant development in the worship of *sakti* as the divine feminine was the conception of a Great Goddess or Mahadevi. One way this idea is conveyed in a number of the non-*Sakta puranas* is that a particular goddess is depicted as the source of all other goddesses. In the *Brahmavaivarta Purana*, for example, the primary goddess of this text, Radha, is herself described as being one-fifth of *prakrti*, along with Durga, Laksmi, Sarasvati and Savitri: "By the desire of the self-willed Krsna to create, The goddess Mulaprakrti suddenly became manifest; By his command she became fivefold through division in the act of creation; Or rather, out of consideration for her devotees, she assumed a form for their sake."[26]

The text goes on to explain that all female beings, including local goddesses and mortal women, are, to various degrees, parts of Radha, as *prakrti*. All these forms are simply parts of the one energetic source, in this case referred to as Mulaprakrti, the primordial material source of the universe. The text further states specifically that the village goddesses are fractions (*kalas*) of *prakrti*; therefore all are aspects of one reality.[27] However, in the *Brahmavaivarta Purana*, though the goddess is considered the source of all other feminine beings she is still considered an aspect of, and subject to, her male partner. This idea is explicitly shown in the following verse, which rather interestingly emphasizes the divine nature of diametrically opposed feminine forms: "The Lord divided his female form too into many beings, such as beautiful and ugly, quiet and turbulent, white and black in complexion etc."[28]

Although the *puranic* goddesses embody the power of creation and illusion that binds the unenlightened to the eternal cycle of birth, death and rebirth (*samsara*), they are nevertheless presented as submissive to their male partners. It was not until the relatively later texts that a concept arose which posited the suggestion that the various goddesses were aspects of one, all-encompassing power, *sakti*, the energetic principle or creative force that enabled Brahman to manifest itself, but was simultaneously personified as the Mahadevi, or Great Goddess.

The *Puranas* are not the only textual sources to lead toward a more metaphysical conception of a Great Goddess; *Tantric* texts have also been influential (see chapter 4). As Tracy Pintchman claims: "It is in Tantric treatises arising outside the Vedic-Brahmanical tradition that the most fully and systematically articulated conception of *sakti* as a cosmogonic and cosmological capacity identified as omnipresent and omnipotent goddess develops."[29] The concept of a Great Goddess, representing *sakti*, the power of the universe, and on an equal footing with the male principle, Siva, is fundamental in *Tantrism*. Guleri explains: "The account of Sakti as given in the Tantras proves that Saktitattva is divided into two parts. First the *mayasakti* which consists of the *gunas*, second the *cittasakti* which is above the *gunas* and thus in the form of bliss. By *mayasakti* this vast world is created."[30] In addition to their elevated status, many *Tantric* goddesses have a distinctly unorthodox nature, encouraging the partaking of impure substances and accepting blood sacrifices. This unorthodox nature is also evident in *Sakta* texts; in particular, it is a characteristic of the Devi (Goddess) of the *Devi-Mahatmya*, who, among other unorthodox attributes, has a fondness for alcohol.

The idea of a Great Goddess was articulated most fully in the mythology of the *Devi-Mahatmya* (examined in chapter 2). This most significant and popular goddess text offers a vision of a supremely powerful Goddess whose deepest essence is the basis of all other goddesses. Implicitly, she is the basis of all power. Although she was created by the combined powers of the gods, the powerful female that the gods produced, immediately established herself as a powerful entity in her own right. Created to perform the deeds that the gods could not achieve for themselves, she soon established her own significant might and power. Conceptualized as the Great Goddess or Mahadevi, her role as a cosmic protector is the basis of the text's mythological narrative. The *Devi-Mahatmya* implies that all goddesses are in reality one being. The various consorts of the *puranic* texts are drawn together to form one cosmic power. This idea is advanced as the Devi (Goddess) of the text is constantly addressed by different names, which point to her multifarious powers. Whether she is called Ambika (the Mother) or Candika (the Violent and Impetuous One) underlying her various forms, which represent different aspects of her character, she is simply Sakti. Also in the *Devi-Mahatmya*, but more explicitly stated in later *Sakta* texts, is the idea that all feminine forms, including that of the human woman, belong to her. Thus, Stella Kramrisch commenting on the Devi of the *Devi-Mahatmya* declares:

> While the host of celestial women and the swarms of sevenfold "great mothers of the universe," of "divine mothers," and the group of "seven mothers" or Saktis, that is, powers envisaged as female, float across time and space, rising and falling, the "Great Goddess," or Devi, is known in innumerable shapes yet remains totally herself. She addresses herself to mankind. She is elegant in the consciousness of her power, whatever her appearance; a woman of fashion, created, like everything else, exclusively by herself. She created the universe, she is its very substance, Prakrti. So vast is her power that she draws into herself all her forms and thus stands alone.[31]

The later *Devi-Bhagavatam* is more explicit in its conceptual understanding of a Great Goddess who is cosmic power, and from whom, all other forms unfold. As well as the title Mahadevi, she is also called Adyasakti (Primordial Power). An important facet of the Mahadevi is that she encompasses both benign and terrible aspects. This idea is explicitly conveyed in the *Devi Gita* portion of the *Devi-Bhagavatam*, when the Devi reveals her cosmic form to the gods, in much the same way as Krsna revealed his cosmic form in the *Bhagavad Gita*:

> They beheld that Cosmic Body of the Great Goddess, that form beyond all other forms.
> The sky is its head, the moon and sun its eyes.
> The cardinal directions are its ears, the Vedas its speech, the wind its breath, so it is proclaimed;
> The universe is its heart, they say; the earth its loins, so it is thought. (*Devi Gita* 3. 23–4)[32]

The following verses continue in the same manner, clearly stating that the Devi encompasses everything. As the gods look on, the appearance of the Devi changes as her terrible aspect is revealed. What the gods' then witness makes them swoon:

> Such was the massive form that the best of gods beheld,
> With its thousands of blazing rays, licking with its tongue,
> Producing horrible crunching sounds with its teeth, spewing fire from its eyes,
> Holding various weapons, heroic in stature, making mush of Brahmans [priests] and Ksatriyas [warriors] for its food. (*Devi Gita* 3. 35–6)[33]

Having experienced all aspects of the Devi's cosmic form, the gods plead with her to resume her beautiful appearance. In this respect, their preference for her auspicious aspect perhaps parallels the Devi's human devotees, many of whom feel most comfortable with her beautiful and auspicious forms. The essentially benign goddesses, some of whom will be examined shortly, represent the manifest forms of Devi's auspicious aspect, her power of wisdom, nourishment and liberation. However, the manifestations of Devi's terrible aspect are just as important and are evident in the goddesses who accept blood sacrifices and who periodically restore the *dharmic* balance in the cosmos. In many myths the angry aspect of Devi or of individual goddesses, represents a positive force. The power of anger is a catalyst of transformation, which in many instances is necessary to overcome a formerly invincible foe. For example, consider the appearance of Kali at the climax of the battle between Devi and the *asuras* (demons):

> They saw the Devi, smiling gently, seated upon the lion on a huge golden peak of the great mountain.
> On seeing her, some of them excited themselves and made an effort to capture her, and others approached her, with their bows bent and swords drawn.
> Thereupon Ambika became terribly angry with those foes, and in her anger her countenance then became dark as ink.
> Out from the surface of her forehead, fierce with frown, issued suddenly Kali of terrible countenance, armed with a sword and a noose. (*Devi-Mahatmya* 7. 3–6)[34]

Kali is a transformation and extension of the Devi's anger, a force that separates from her, becoming a goddess in her own right. This transformation, of which anger is the catalyst, not only produces an individual goddess considered to be anger personified, but also provides an injection of power substantial enough to defeat two formerly invincible demons.

Although there is clearly a notion in the later *puranic* texts of a Mahadevi or Great Goddess who is the underlying essence of all goddesses, individual goddesses retain their own mythology. Therefore, Hindu goddesses need to be understood on two levels. They are individuals in that they have their own iconography and a mythology that in many cases is individual to themselves. However, each goddess is a manifestation of cosmic power (*sakti*) and, as such, they all have the same underlying essence. It is this combination of individuality and cosmic correspondence that allows the Goddess to be both available and yet beyond human conception, to live among her people despite being their ultimate source.

The most visible expression of *sakti* is in the personification of the many goddesses representing the most perceptible side of Hinduism. The huge amount of Hindu goddesses can be divided into roughly two types, Brahmanical, orthodox or pan-Indian goddesses and local goddesses. The first group, referred to as pan-Indian, are generally known across India and are in the main Brahmanical, though some do have some unorthodox tendencies. These goddesses generally have well-developed mythologies, are given textual credence, and are most often found anthropomorphically presented in temples, large and small. Local goddesses, on the other hand, may only be known in a single village or hamlet and, despite the fact that they may have a known story of origin, are seldom found in any written sources. They are represented in many different ways from a tree or a stone to an anthropomorphic form in small and large temples. Local goddesses are often referred to as village goddesses but personally, I prefer the term *local* because these goddesses are found in towns as well as villages.

Pan-Indian goddesses as personifications of *sakti*

The pan-Indian goddesses are the most well-known expressions of the divine feminine in India and beyond. Since the recent popularization of all things Indian, the West has also become aware of the most popular Hindu deities. Laksmi, the pan-Indian goddess representing the power of good fortune and wealth, or Sarasvati, the goddess of learning and wisdom, have become recognizable outside India. However, by far the most famous Hindu goddess is Kali, often erroneously referred to as the goddess of death and destruction. I say erroneously referred to as such because, though Kali may have a finger in these pies she represents a far wider power that includes liberation and protection. Obviously there are significant differences between goddesses like Laksmi and Sarasvati and goddesses such as Kali and Durga. In Hindu thought, all deities are aspects of the one Brahman, the origin of everything, including the negative aspects of life. There is no single concept of an all-benevolent god or goddess and a separate power of evil. There are, of course, demons that often clash with the gods in Hindu mythology but the demons have also emanated from Brahman. For the moment, it is sufficient to understand that, whatever goddesses appear to be on the outside, underneath they represent divine power or energy. Therefore, the pan-Indian goddesses can be divided into roughly two groups. On one hand, there are those goddesses that personify the essentially benign aspects of power or energy such as devotion, wisdom, love or compassion, etc. In contrast to the essentially benign goddesses are those who are best described as essentially fierce. These goddesses personify the more dynamic powers of protection and the destruction of evil, they require that their devotees face up to their fears and in return offer the salvific power of liberation. An important point to bear in mind is that the groups are *essentially* benign and *essentially* fierce. The benign goddesses are not wholly benign: there can be fierce elements to their characters. Likewise, the fierce goddesses have a benign side to their personalities. The dual nature of the goddesses highlights the dualism and opposition that is a characteristic of divine power (*sakti*) or indeed any power or energy. For instance, the power of fire necessary to maintain life can and does at times destroy life. Similarly, the power that made creation possible is the same power that will periodically destroy, or perhaps more correctly dissolve, life – transforming it into an unmanifest state once more.

Essentially benign goddesses

The numerous aspects of the divine feminine show the infinite facets of her nature. The essentially benign goddesses reward their devotees with divine grace. Among these orthodox goddesses are Radha the lover of Krsna, Gauri the golden one, Sita the devoted and faithful wife of Rama, Sarasvati the goddess of wisdom and learning and Laksmi the goddess of good fortune and wealth. Generally, these goddesses are very beautiful and pleasing to look at. They are eminently approachable, coaxing the devotee to form a close and loving relationship with the divine. In a very gentle way, the essentially benign goddesses show the devotee how to follow their *dharmic* path, helping them to overcome obstacles along the way. These goddesses above all offer the devotee the power of love and grace and there need not be any apprehension on the part of the devotee in approaching them.

The majority of the essentially benign goddesses are the consorts of various gods. In this role, they represent their husband's power as his *sakti*. They are generally portrayed significantly smaller than their husband and often shown in a subservient role, such as Laksmi who is often depicted rubbing Visnu's feet. In their role as wife, the benign goddesses convey many paradigmatic features such as support and faithfulness, often representing the supreme devotee. In this respect, they are conceived of as ideal role models for Hindu women in general. Having made some general points about the essentially benign goddesses, let us take a closer look at just a few of them.

Sri-Laksmi (Goddess of Fortune)

The goddess Sri or Laksmi is now widely known as the goddess of wealth and prosperity. She is the *sakti* and consort of Visnu and they represent the ideal couple according to *puranic* tradition. Laksmi is governed by, and subservient to, her husband while he provides her with strength and a solid base. In classical iconography Laksmi is always represented as a significantly smaller figure than her husband and in their most common representation is shown massaging his feet as he reclines on the body of Sesa, the cosmic snake. However, Laksmi has not always been associated with Visnu and "in the early centuries preceding and following the Christian era Sri-Laksmi appears to have been worshipped in her own right, quite unallied with any other sectarian cult and, as such, was worshipped by the people of all sects alike".[35] Furthermore, as an aspect of the Mahadevi, Laksmi is considerably more than Visnu's subservient wife. For instance, in the following verse from *Visnusmriti* 99. 4, the Earth goddess Bhudevi praises Laksmi:

> Thou art repose (final liberation), the highest among the four objects of human pursuit; thou art Laksmi; thou art a support (in danger); thou art Sri; thou art indifference (the freedom from all worldly pursuits and appetites which is the consequence of final emancipation); thou art

victory; thou art beauty (*saundaryam*); thou art splendour (of the Sun and the moon personified); thou art reknown; thou art prosperity; thou art wisdom; thou art power of expression; thou art purifier.[36]

Although the names Sri and Laksmi are now used interchangeably for the same goddess, often referred to as Sri-Laksmi, they were formerly the names of two individual goddesses. They first appear as distinct goddesses in the *Sri Sukta*, a hymn appended to the fifth book of the *Rg Veda*.[37] In the early Vedic period, *laksmi* and *sri* were terms rather than goddesses. The word *laksmi* referred to a mark, sign or token, with *sri* meaning material prosperity. These early ideas and meanings were retained in the nature of each goddess as the following hymn clearly shows:

Invocation to Goddess Laksmi

1. Jatavedas [Agni the fire god] is implored on behalf of the sacrificer to invoke Laksmi, who is *hiranyavarna*, *hiranmayi*, 'radiant as gold', *harini*, 'reddish yellow', who is bedecked with a necklace of gold and silver, *suvarnarajatasraja*, *candra*, 'radiant as the moon.'
2. The presence of Laksmi, who is firm and steady, '*anapagamini*', bestows gold, milch cattle, horses and human-beings.

Invocation to Goddess Sri

3. *Sri* is the lord of all creatures '*isvari*' and has the best of horses, *asvapurna*; she is seated on the middle of the chariot, *rathamadhya*; she is delighted by the roaring of the elephant, *hastinadapramodini*.
4. She is dressed in gold, *hiranyaprakara*; she is moist *ardra*; she is seated on a lotus *padmesthita* and she has the colour of lotus *padmavarna*; she is lustrous like fire *jvalanti*.
5. Goddess *Sri* is bountiful *udara*; she is honoured by all the divinities; she appears like a lovely lotus *padmanemi*; she is radiant as the moon *candra*. Goddess *Sri* is resorted to so that Alaksmi [ill-luck] may be removed.
6. Goddess *Sri* is resplendent as the sun *adityavarna*; through the austerities of *Sri* the Bilva tree was born; the goddess is prayed (*sic*) so that through her favour the Bilva fruits may dispel Alaksmi.
7. *Sri* is implored to bestow fame and prosperity.
8. *Sri* is prayed (*sic*) for banishing *abhuti* – want, *asamrddhi* – poverty and Alaksmi, who is characterised by dirty qualities of hunger and thirst *Ksutpipasamala*.
9. Goddess *Sri* is perceptible through odour, *gandhavara*; ever abundant in harvest *nityapusta*; she lives in cowdung *karisini*.
10. Sri is prayed (*sic*) for conferring food and cattle.

11. Kardama 'mud, mire, slime' is referred to as the illustrious progeny of Sri. Kardama is invoked to abide along with his mother Sri, who is described as *padmamalini*.
12. Ciklita 'mire, ooze', another son of Sri is prayed (*sic*) to dwell in the abode of the invoker in company with his mother Sri.

Invocation to Goddess Laksmi

13. Goddess Laksmi is described as *ardra* 'moist', she is bedecked with lotus flowers *puskarini*; she is slim and slender *yasti*; she is like the sun in splendour *surya*. She is radiant as gold *hiranmayi, hemamalini, suvarna*.
14. She is *ardra* – moist; she is bedecked with lotus flowers *puskarini*; she wears a garland of lotus flowers *padmamalini*. She has the brilliance and splendour of the moon *candra* and abundance personified *pusti*. She is of golden colour *hiranmayi, pingala*.
15. Laksmi is firm and steady *anapagamini*, through her grace the invoker attains gold and cattle etc.[38]

Clearly, Sri was closely associated with fertility and vegetation as she is described as living in cow dung (*karisini*) and "ever abundant in harvest" as in verse nine. Even though both Laksmi and Sri are described as moist (*ardra*) in verses four and thirteen, scholars believe that verses thirteen to fifteen were added later when the two goddesses were one. Although Sri-Laksmi's association with fertility has been overshadowed somewhat by her role as goddess of wealth and prosperity, in her later iconography and ritual worship its importance remains.

It was not until the period of the *Brahmanas* and the early *Upanisads* that the character of the two goddesses fully merged into one. There are various myths providing the origins of Sri-Laksmi. The *Satapatha Brahmana* describes her as the daughter of Prajapati in contrast to the *Mahabharata* that in one verse describes her as the daughter of Brahma and in another as one of Daksa's daughters who was given in marriage to Dharma. By far the most well-known origin myth of Sri-Laksmi is her appearance at the churning of the milk ocean (examined in detail in chapter 3). There are various versions of this myth, one of which, in the *Padma Purana*, suggests that the goddess already existed before the ocean was churned. The later versions of the myth make a connection between Laksmi and Visnu after the goddess appears as one of the precious things that appeared when the ocean of milk was churned. However, in early versions of the myth, such as that found in the *Adiparvan*, (The Beginning) of the *Mahabharata* (1. 16. 35), Sri or Laksmi emerges as an independent character. Another interesting account of Laksmi that appears in the *Santiparvan* (The Peace), book twelve of the *Mahabharata*, depicts her living with the demons (*asuras*) because at the time they behaved righteously, reading the scriptures and performing the sacrifices, as was their duty. However, when the *asuras* became unreligious and neglectful of their duties, Laksmi left them – going instead to the god Indra – taking with her prosperity and wealth: "Formerly I lived with the Asuras on account of their being full of truth and merit. Seeing, however, that the Asuras have assumed adverse natures, I have left them and wish to live in you."[39] Notice that the goddess says that she wants to live *in* Indra not with him. Therefore, Laksmi transfers her powers of prosperity from the *asuras* to Indra (the king of the gods). The myth suggests that prosperity is not only financial and material, but is also spiritual as well. As her association with Visnu developed, later versions of this myth depict her arriving before Indra driving Visnu's chariot and accompanied by Garuda (with the talons and beak of a bird of prey and the body of a man), a creature associated most readily with Visnu.

Before her association with Visnu, an early and very popular representation of Laksmi was that of Gaja-Laksmi. Seated on a lotus and flanked by two elephants whose upraised trunks showered her with water, Laksmi appeared on coinage and on the walls of many ancient caves and temples. Elephants, as well as being associated with royalty and kingship are also symbolic of rain and fertility. Therefore, the Gaja-Laksmi image was interpreted, according to Jan Gonda, as, "the fertilizing of the female being representing, or connected with, the earth or the fields by rain clouds; clouds were often represented by elephants".[40] By the Gupta period, Sri-Laksmi was firmly established as the consort of Visnu, though she was previously connected with other gods. In the *Sri-Sukta* she was associated with Jatavedas (an epithet of Agni the god of fire). Both Sri and Laksmi were at one time the wives of Purusa and were associated with Kubera (king of the *yaksas* – vegetation spirits), and the gods Dharma and Indra. However, the most significant association was with Visnu in which Sri-Laksmi, most often simply called Laksmi, has remained as his *sakti* or power. As power, Laksmi, as well as being an individual personality, is an aspect of the Mahadevi representing prosperity, well-being, royal power and illustriousness, the qualities through which she manifests herself.

Laksmi's association with Visnu has led to the conception of her as supreme creative power in the *Pancaratra* School (see chapter 4). As the power of Visnu, Laksmi actively creates the world while Visnu looks inertly on. His role is "that of an inactive architect" whose plan, Laksmi effortlessly activates.[41] The *Laksmi Tantra* clearly elevates Laksmi from the role of subservient wife to an equivalent of Brahman for the goddess claims:

> The universe is produced from me (as a 'mode' of myself), hence I am called Prakrti. I am the (only) shelter to be resorted to and I destroy the misfortunes of the pious.
> I listen to the lamentations (of devotees) and gladden the world with my virtues. I inhere in all beings (*saye*) and take delight in (*rame*) the virtuous. I am ever worshipped by the gods and am the embodiment of Visnu. Beholding these attributes of mine, the learned in the Vedas and Vedantas, who know how to relate attributes to their possessor, extol me as Sri. The same Myself am eternal, manifested in all and ever existent.[42]

Sarasvati (The Flowing One)

Sarasvati, the goddess who personifies the power of wisdom and learning is one of the few currently worshipped goddesses whose development can be traced from the *Vedic* period. Her name, meaning "the watery" or "the flowing one" underlies her origin as a sacred river, originally one of seven sacred rivers, all of which were considered feminine. Unlike the river Ganges, or Ganga Ma as she is affectionately called, the Sarasvati river no longer exists, though it is still believed to flow as a mythical underground river. Connections between the divine and water or rivers in India have been important in the development of the idea that India itself is a sacred place. It emphasizes the interconnection between the physical and the divine, especially as the sacred rivers, in Hindu mythology, are said to flow from the realm of the gods. The life-giving property of water is suggestive of divine grace being poured onto the land, as David Kinsley says of Sarasvati: "Her association with Soma in some texts and with water in general suggests that Sarasvati is identified with the underlying sap of vitality necessary for all living things, that she nourishes life and promotes fertility."[43]

In the *Vedas*, Sarasvati was a relatively unimportant river deity but the reference to *Vedic* sacrifices made on the riverbank meant that Sarsvati became associated with sanctity. After the *Vedic* period, and especially during the Classical period, there can be seen a diminishing of Sarasvati's associations with the sacred river and an emphasis on her role as the goddess of wisdom and learning. Today Sarasvati's sphere of influence is much wider than it was originally since she has taken over the powers of goddesses who are no longer significant powers themselves. Most notably, she absorbed into her character the qualities that were formally attributed to the *Vedic* goddess Vac, the goddess of speech. Speech plays a very important part in Hinduism as Alain Daniélou points out: "Speech is the power through which knowledge expresses itself in action. Sarasvati is the source of 'creation by the word', which runs parallel to the visible 'creation in terms of forms'."[44] Sacred speech complemented Sarasvati's associations with learning and wisdom and she eventually became known as the Mother of the *Vedas* and subsequently one of her many names is Vedagarbha (womb or source of the *Vedas* or Knowledge). Consequently, Sarasvati became the consort of Brahma, the God of Creation and the keeper of the *Vedas*. As the energy of Brahma, Sarasvati enables him to carry out his creative function. However, even though she is the consort of Brahma, Sarasvati is usually worshipped alone since her popularity has risen and his has declined.

There are many reminders of Sarasvati's cosmic associations in her symbolism and iconography. For instance, she is depicted with a white complexion representing purity. Her vehicle, a swan, represents spiritual transcendence, as does the lotus on which she is usually portrayed sitting or standing. Hence Kinsley comments: "She floats above the muddy imperfections of the physical world, unsullied, pure, beautiful. Although rooted in the mud (like man rooted in the physical world), the lotus perfects itself in a blossom that has transcended the mud."[45] The lotus, representing transcendence of the manifest world, more than any other symbol reminds the devotee that through the goddess's purifying power of sacred knowledge, liberation (*moksa*) can be achieved.

Parvati (She who is Born of a Mountain)

Parvati, like many other goddesses in the Hindu pantheon, came to prominence in the Classical period. Although she is an important goddess as the wife of Siva, she has very little independent history. Described as the daughter of Himavan (the Himalayas) she is generally considered the reincarnation of Siva's first wife Sati. Sati immolated herself because her father excluded her husband from his great sacrifice (a myth explored in chapter 3). After Sati's withdrawal from the world Siva also withdrew into a prolonged state of asceticism and meditation, which meant that his creative aspect was being neglected. Therefore, Parvati's main function was to marry Siva and bring him into the realm of the householder, to involve Siva in the manifest world. There are various detailed accounts of Parvati's attempts to win Siva as a husband. When her beauty and charm failed to rouse him from his meditation, Parvati tried the path of the ascetic. Eventually, after a prolonged period of severe ascetic practice, Parvati's devotion to Siva secured him as her husband. Parvati represents the ideal devotee, an important facet of her character because it associated her with Siva's divine grace. Therefore, Kinsley comments: "The implication is that Parvati, in subtle form, resides within every human being. She is awakened by means of devotion to Siva, which expresses her most essential nature."[46] In iconography and later texts, the couple are most often depicted discussing religious philosophy or making love. Parvati in her subtle nature represents the creative power of the cosmos, which is essential as a counter-balance to the destructive nature of Siva. She is important as the polar opposite of Siva with the power to quieten his destructive nature. Hence, David Kinsley claims Parvati "is portrayed as a patient builder, one who follows Shiva about, trying to soften the violent effects of her husband. She is a great force for preservation and reconstruction in the world and as such offsets the violence of Shiva."[47]

However, as with other goddesses, Parvati also has a dual nature. She is a devoted follower of Siva but as Siva's *sakti* she has ultimate power. It is only through Parvati as *sakti* that Siva can accomplish his full capability. The interdependence of their metaphysical relationship is portrayed in the Ardhanaisvara image in which Parvati as Sakti occupies the left side of the body while Siva occupies the right side. The Ardhanaisvara image represents Parvati's cosmic character of power and Siva as consciousness. Nevertheless, elsewhere Parvati is represented with a mundane character as different images and texts place emphasis on different sides of Parvati's nature depending on the point they are trying to make, as Wendy Doniger O'Flaherty contends: "Parvati may act more like her mortal counterparts (totally subservient to Shiva) or more like her immortal alter ego (totally dominant over Shiva)."[48] Although Parvati is often depicted significantly smaller than Siva, seated on his lap, the *puranic* texts also reveal the other side of her complex character. The inherent nature of Parvati can be seen in the description of her in the *Kurma Purana*, which describes her cosmic form, being both frightful and frightening in that it is so awe inspiring.

> It was ablaze with thousands of flames in clusters resembling hundreds of world-destructive conflagrations (at the end of the world). It was terrible due to its curved fangs and was irresistible. It was embellished with clusters of matted hair.

It wore a crown and was holding a mace, a conch, a discus and an excellent trident in its hands. The terrible form was frightening everyone.

(Simultaneously) it was tranquil, charming-faced and gentle and possessed of infinite wonders. It was bedecked with the limbs (crescents of the moon) and lustrous like a crore of moons.

It was bedecked in coronets, it wielded a mace in its hands and was ornamented with anklets. It wore divine garlands, garments and was besmeared with divine scents and unguents.

It held a conch and a discus. It had a pleasing appearance and three eyes and it wore an elephant's hide as its robe. It was stationed both within and without the Cosmic Egg. It was both inside and outside of everything.

It was endowed with all *Saktis*, was extremely pure (white), omniformed, eternal, its lotus-like feet were revered by gods Brahma, Indra, Upendra (Visnu) and prominent Yogins.

It had hands and feet all round, had eyes, heads and faces in all directions. He saw that Supreme Goddess standing before enveloping the universe.[49]

Here, at the request of her father, Himavan, Parvati allows him to experience the full glory of her cosmic form, which is representative of cosmic energy. These verses are an excellent example of the way in which the duality of *sakti* energy can be experienced 'simultaneously'. She is at once the power of total destruction and the power of perfect peace. She is hideous but beautiful, being human-like and yet unimaginable. Parvati in her cosmic form encompasses everything; she is within and without her creation.

Although Parvati most readily fits into the essentially benign goddess category, there is one aspect of Parvati that sets her apart from Sarasvati and Laksmi, her connections with the essentially fierce goddesses Durga and Kali. In some mythology, Kali is said to be the embodied anger of Parvati. W. J. Wilkins sees this as a clear example of her great power for he says: "It is when she appears as Durga, Kali etc., that she manifests divine power, and exhibits a very different spirit from that which appears in her as Parvati."[50] Perhaps due to her associations with Durga and Kali, it may be noted that Parvati seems to have a closer affiliation with the Great Goddess, Mahadevi. Among the essentially benign pan-Indian goddesses, Parvati certainly has the widest associations. The majority of local goddesses – most often Durga or Kali but other goddesses too – according to their devotees are forms of Parvati. In this respect, Parvati seems to bridge the divide between the benign and fierce aspects of *sakti* and between the pan-Indian and local representations of that cosmic power.

Essentially fierce goddesses

The essentially fierce goddesses, especially the two that are examined here, Durga and Kali, represent the more dynamic personifications of *sakti* energy. In many cases, the *sakti* or power of the essentially benign goddesses is subtle whereas that of the essentially fierce goddesses is blatant. They are clearly powerful in their own right and seem to delight in showing off that power. In a general sense, both Durga and Kali represent the power of protection. While Durga conforms outwardly to the Brahmanical ideal of womanhood, Kali is firmly on the outside of what is generally accepted as orthodox. Her unwholesome appearance and strange practices have led many to misunderstand her completely. Consequently, Kali is the most grossly misrepresented Hindu goddess. Portrayed in films such as *Indiana Jones and the Temple of Doom* as the goddess of death and destruction, her positive and subtle attributes have been conveniently discarded in favour of her more dramatic characteristics. However, Hindu goddesses cannot simply be taken at face value, a point that will become eminently clear as this exploration of Hindu goddesses progresses. Durga hovers on the edge of acceptability, but is becoming more accepted as her less orthodox traits are submerged or smoothed over.

Durga (The One who is Beyond Reach)

It is probable that the goddess Durga originally had non-Aryan tribal associations, especially with those in mountainous regions and perhaps with a particular tribe called the *Sabaras*. One of the main reasons for this supposition is Durga's clearly unorthodox tendency of the consumption of intoxicants, drinking blood and eating meat. Another reason to assume that Durga was originally a tribal or village goddess is the link with fertility evident within her worship, ritual and in some myths. She is linked with a goddess of vegetation, Sakambhari in the *Devi-Bhagavatam* (VII 28. 46–80) as it is Sakambhari who slays the demon Durgama and consequently becomes known as Durga. The association between fertility and battle imagery has led Narenda Bhattacharyya to conclude that the myths of the many battles with demons that Durga has are really nature myths as the goddess of vegetation overcomes the demons representing drought.[51] As well as the identification of Durga with plants and fertility is the importance of animal sacrifice and the gift of her devotees' blood, a practice plainly referred to in the *Devi-Mahatmya*: "Now abstaining from food, and now restraining in their food, with their minds on her and with concentration, they both offered sacrifices sprinkled with blood drawn from their own bodies."[52]

Durga is clearly linked to a much older tradition than her Brahmanical origin myths would indicate. Perhaps at one time she was a village goddess, who, for some reason became popularized. She was apparently well known by the medieval period, after the sixth century. This is most probably due to the variety of myths ascribed to her. In the *Skanda Purana* she is said to be the embodied wrath of Parvati. However, by far the most popular account of her origin is in the *Devi-Mahatmya*, which casts her as a warrior goddess. Durga's role in slaying a previously invincible demon, celebrating the victory of good over evil, is celebrated every year at the *Durga Puja* festival (described in detail in chapter 6). The *Devi-Mahatmya* establishes that Durga and her emanations, such as Kali and Candika, are all aspects of the Great Goddess, Mahadevi, who is synonymous with Brahman, the Ultimate Reality and power of all. Durga is perhaps the most important aspect of the Mahadevi in this text and consequently we are left in no doubt of her divine nature: "You are the sole substratum of the world, because you subsist in the form of the earth. By you, who exist in the shape of water, all this (universe) is gratified, O Devi of inviolable valour!"[53]

In the *Devi-Mahatmya*, Durga is said to have emanated from the combined fiery powers (*tejas*), of all the gods, in their desperation after they were constantly defeated by the demons (*asuras*):

Then from Visnu's face, which was filled with rage,
Came forth a great fiery splendor (*tejas*), (and from the faces) of Brahma and Siva.
And from the bodies of the other gods, Indra and the others,
Came forth a great fiery splendor, and it became unified in one place.
An exceedingly fiery mass like a flaming mountain
Did the gods see there, filling the firmament with flames.
That peerless splendor, born from the bodies of the gods,
Unified and pervading the triple world with its lustre, became a woman.[54]

The verses show that Durga is explicitly regarded as the incarnate strength of the gods and, therefore, represents cosmic energy. She originated at a time of cosmic crisis and consequently Durga's role seems to be very similar to that of Visnu when he takes on various incarnations (*avataras*) in order to protect the cosmic balance, she too promises to return, if needed: "Thus O King, the adorable Devi, although eternal, incarnating again and again, protects the world."[55] Could this be an indication that at this time a new goddess was needed to fulfil a need in the people that goddesses like Sarasvati, Laksmi and Parvati could not fill?

One of the most interesting facets of Durga's character is her independence and her challenge to the stereotypes of women presented in the Hindu law books (*Dharma-sastras*). In the character of Durga, *sakti* is ever present and visible. Durga does not depend on a male consort and successfully manages male roles herself. In battle, for instance, she does not fight with male allies; if she needs assistance she tends to create female helpers, like Kali, from herself. Her role as *sakti* also differs from that of the benign goddesses, as she does not empower the male deities. This is an important facet of her character as the embodiment of divine power as David Kinsley observes: "Unlike the normal female, Durga does not lend her power or *sakti* to a male consort but rather *takes* power from the male gods in order to perform her own heroic exploits. They give up their inner strength, fire, and heat to create her and in so doing surrender their potency to her."[56]

A good example of this tendency can be found in an episode of the *Devi-Mahatmya* in which Visnu is in a deep sleep because he is pervaded by Durga in the form of Mahamaya, "Great Illusion". Only when Devi leaves his body is Visnu able to continue with his own function as preserver of the cosmos. Although not stated explicitly, in the *Devi-Mahatmya* Durga is equated with Brahman because she encompasses within herself all the functions of creation, preservation and dissolution. Hence Kinsely states: "Durga's association or identification with *sakti, maya*, and *prakrti* lends to the great demon-slaying goddess an immediate, tangible dimension."[57] However, Durga also operates on a personal level as she promises to respond to her devotees who propitiate her in the correct manner. In this form, she is like a mother to her children, attending to their well-being. In the literature regarding Durga, we can clearly see three roles ascribed to her. She is *Sakti*, Cosmic Energy that is seen in her dynamic warrior form. She is also *maya* – she creates the world in a state of delusion, she plays with her creation in a divine *lila* (game). However, she is also able to bestow divine knowledge on her devotees if she so wishes: "You are the primaeval maya, which is the source of the universe; by you all this (universe) has been thrown into an illusion, O Devi. If you become gracious, you become the cause of final emancipation in the world."[58]

The way in which Durga is depicted is very interesting, especially when compared to other fierce goddesses such as Kali. Durga is portrayed as a beautiful golden warrior goddess with ten or a thousand arms. In her mythology, her enemies usually want to win her as their bride, but her looks do not belie her excellence in battle. Compared to goddesses like Kali she looks more akin to the benevolent goddesses, Laksmi, Parvati and Sarasvati. However, Durga has not lost her non-Aryan habits of accepting blood sacrifices and her consumption of alcohol in her Candika aspect: "Candika, the Mother of the worlds, quaffed a divine drink again and again, and laughed, her eyes becoming red."[59] Durga manages to combine Brahman acceptability without compromise to her independent and less constrained (*devi*-like) origin. Although she has entered the Hindu pantheon as the wife of Siva, she remains essentially independent. Consequently, the essential nature of Durga is far more explicit and potent than can be easily ascertained for goddesses like Sarasvati, Laksmi and Parvati. It would appear that Durga is the embodiment of both the benevolent and the terrible aspects of goddesses combining the two within herself.

Kali (The Black One: The Power of Time)

Portrayed holding a sword and a severed head, her protruding tongue dripping with blood, the goddess Kali depicts an aspect of *sakti* that cannot be ignored. Kali is perhaps the most fascinating and is certainly the most famous Hindu goddess, despite being the most misunderstood. Kali provided a morbid fascination for early western writers who had never before encountered such an unconventional aspect of feminine divinity. Accordingly, early statements about Kali clearly articulate the writers' contempt, such as that of E. Osborn Martin, who states: "The 'black' manifestations of Siva's consort culminate in the portrayal of Kali, the horrible goddess of blood. Human invention or imagination, however depraved and brutalised, cannot equal elsewhere the terror of this conception of deity."[60] Martin also concludes: "She drinks the blood of her victims. She lives in an orgy of horror."[61] Ironically, one contemporary scholar, Rachel Fell McDermott, who has studied Kali in Bengal for a number of years, made an important discovery about the conception of Kali by ordinary Bengalis. After McDermott had delivered a paper about the interpretation of Kali by western scholars, an Indian scholar explained: "Kali is simply Ma, the all-compassionate Mother. If there is a part of the goddess which represents death, it is a part not readily noticed or emphasized by the majority of her votaries. Even Kali's iconographic depiction is so familiar to people that it fails to inspire thoughts about the inevitability of destruction."[62] While it is important to remember that those who look on Kali may not see her as horrible or terrifying, her iconographical features suggest that she is a more complex character than simply the "all-compassionate Mother", for Kali, more than any other goddess, expresses the duality of *sakti* energy within her very being. Not surprisingly, Kali is perhaps the most important goddess within *Saktism* and *Tantrism* since for them she is the ultimate personification of cosmic energy. Thus, Alain Daniélou remarks: "In the hierarchy of manifestation, Kali stands as the highest, the most abstract, aspect of duality."[63]

It is certainly not difficult to see why Kali represents cosmic power since her outward form is fearsome and her ability to destroy the forces of evil is unquestionable. In the wider duality of *sakti* energy, Kali can clearly be seen as a polar opposite of the essentially benign goddesses mentioned earlier. Kali brings the devotee face to face with danger and death, which are as much a part of the cosmic totality as love and peace, symbolized by other goddesses.

Kali's origins seem most definitely to be tribal as she is still worshipped on the fringes of orthodox society, for example in the cremation grounds as was recommended by the *Manasara-silpasastra* written around the sixth to eighth centuries CE. This text advocates that her temples should be built near the cremation grounds, far from villages and towns.[64] She is closely associated with many village goddesses and is also worshipped with a daily blood sacrifice in her most important place of worship, the Kalighat temple in Kolkata (formerly known as Calcutta). Although Kali now has a legitimate place within the Hindu pantheon, as Kinsley points out, she still elicits mixed reactions among the Hindu populace: "Kali's associations with blood sacrifice (sometimes human), her position as patron goddess of the infamous Thugs, and her importance in Vamacara Tantric ritual have generally won for her a reputation as a creature born of a crazed, aboriginal mind."[65]

Kali is a post-*vedic* deity and little significant mention is made of her until her appearance in the *Devi-Mahatmya* (7. 6ff.). Interestingly, Kali does not become a popular subject of Bengali literature until relatively late and, indeed, was "overshadowed by such goddesses as Manasa, the snake goddess and Sitala the goddess of smallpox", a surprising fact considering that she has been most popular there for some time.[66] The main mythology of Kali, produced under Brahmanical influence, asserts that she first appeared on the battlefield as a manifestation of Durga's anger or forcefulness. Kali has a terrifying appearance that strikes fear into her enemies.

> Thereupon Ambika became terribly angry with those foes, and in her anger her countenance then became dark as ink.
> Out from the surface of her forehead, fierce with frown, issued suddenly Kali of terrible countenance, armed with a sword and a noose.
> Bearing the strange skull-topped staff, decorated with a garland of skulls, clad in a tiger skin, very appalling owing to her emaciated flesh, with gaping mouth, fearful with her tongue lolling out, having deep-sunk reddish eyes and filling the regions of the sky with her roars, and falling upon impetuously and slaughtering the great asuras in that army, she devoured those hosts of the foes of the devas.
> Snatching the elephants with one hand she flung them into her mouth together with their rear men and drivers and their warrior-riders with bells.
> Taking likewise into her mouth the cavalry with the horses, and the chariot with its driver, she ground them most frightfully with her teeth. (*Devi-Mahatmya* 7. 5–11)[67]

This episode is told to show that Kali is the ultimate destroyer of evil. In another important battle, recounted in the *Devi-Mahatmya*, Kali is essential to the destruction of one particular demon, Raktabija. This demon had a special power by which whenever he was wounded, his blood would produce more demons. Although Durga and her *saktis* had no trouble wounding the demon, they could not destroy him. Therefore, Kali, who is referred to as Camunda (an epithet of Kali given because she killed the demons Canda and Munda) was petitioned to drink his blood.

> Then Kali drank Raktabija's blood with her mouth. Then and there he struck Candika with his club.
> The blow of his club caused her not even the slightest pain. And from his stricken body wherever blood flowed copiously, there Camunda swallowed it with her mouth. The Camunda devoured those great asuras who sprang up from the flow of blood in her mouth, and drank his (Raktabija's) blood. (*Devi-Mahatmya* 8. 57–60)[68]

Kali's iconography points back to these appearances in which Kali's character is firmly established as a potent energy capable of destroying the forces that threaten cosmic stability. Her custom of accepting blood sacrifices clearly symbolizes her destruction of the demon Rajtabija. In her left hands she holds a sword and a severed head. These symbols show that she is the destroyer of evil, but her sword is also used to cut the ties of bondage that tether her devotees to the world and so effect their liberation. Therefore, Ajit Mookerjee points out: "She is there for swiftness, for immediate and effective action, for the direct stroke, the frontal assault that carries everything before it. Awe-inspiring, determined and ruthless, she destroys evil force."[69]

Kali is described in the *Tantras* and other texts as being fearsome and hideous to look at. This original representation can still be found in the many iconographic images of Kali though popular art has toned down her ferocity, presumably in an effort to make her more palatable. It is the original representations that we should keep in mind while discussing the symbolism of Kali. She is most usually pictured in the cremation ground or battlefield with the signs of destruction all around her. She stands on the prone body of Siva who is as lifeless as a corpse, or, not completely lifeless if they are represented in the act of *viparitarati* (sexual intercourse with the female in the dominant position). Around her neck is a garland of skulls and around her waist a skirt made of human hands. She appears to be laughing as her protruding tongue drips the blood of her victims. Kali holds in her left hands a severed head and a blood-stained sword; her right hands are making the gestures of 'fear not', and that of granting boons. Her three eyes seem to stare menacingly at whoever looks at her.

Despite the overwhelmingly fierce overtone of this image of Kali, when the symbolism is examined in more detail the benevolent side and the inherent duality of Kali can be experienced. She stands on the lifeless body of Siva for two reasons; the first is as a symbol that she, as the personification of *sakti*, is the energetic principle of the cosmos, he as consciousness is inert in isolation. The other concept symbolized by the union of Kali and the prone figure of Siva is her role as creatrix of the manifest world, since from the union of Siva–Sakti arises manifestation. Thus, the *Niruttarva-Tantra* says: "When Nirguna Kali becomes Saguna She is engaged in viparitarati",[70] that is to say, when the unmanifest (*nirguna*) becomes manifest (*saguna*), it springs from the union of consciousness and energy (Siva and Sakti).

The skulls around Kali's neck and the severed head that she holds aloft are both symbolic of her power to destroy evil. However, the sword that Kali holds is not just for the destruction of evil but also to sever the many ties that bind the egotistical person to this world, a point explained beautifully by Alain Daniélou: "It is through the destruction of all that appears to us desirable and by facing what appears to be most fearful, namely the power of time, of death, that we can become free from bondage and attain the aim of our existence, the limitless supreme bliss of non-existence."[71] Kali forces her devotees to face their fears and to learn to subjugate their egos in order to transcend this life. Therefore, Kali is shown as having the power to grant liberation to her devotees, a power reinforced by her right-handed gesture of conferring boons and assuring her devotees not to fear. Providing that the devotees can approach Kali as children, as Siva did, and prostrate themselves before the goddess, then she will protect and cherish the child-like devotees (*sadhakas*).

Kali is conceptualized as Daksinakali, south-facing Kali, south being the direction associated with death. Here is a further inference that Kali is the goddess who tackles death head on and, ultimately, has the power to conquer it. So, rather than simply being the goddess of death as she is so often mistakenly portrayed, Kali's iconography has many profound meanings. Below is a table outlining each feature of Kali's image and the meaning of each facet. It is based on the most popular image of Kali, in which she is standing upon the chest of Siva in the cremation ground.

Iconographical feature	Meaning
name (Kali)	black; time; power of time; power of dissolution
black colour	formlessness; *nirguna* nature in which all contradictions merge
nakedness	symbolizes reality unveiled
three eyes	power over the past, present and future
unbound hair	unleashed power and non-conformity to the norms of society
protruding tongue	sexual gratification; consumption of forbidden/polluted substances
garland of skulls	heads of demons – restoration of *dharma* (also represent the Sanskrit letters – power of creation; domination of form)
four arms	complete circle of creation and dissolution
right hands	fear not *mudra* (hand gesture) grant boons/favours *mudra*
left hands	sword – cuts the ties of this life destruction of ignorance severed head – false consciousness
skirt of arms	arms – deeds, actions destruction of the devotees' *karma*

standing on Siva	unity in duality
	dynamic aspect of Siva/Sakti duality
cremation ground	reduces all worldly concerns to ashes

Kali is most dramatically associated with death in the extreme form of Smasana Kali, the goddess of the burning *ghat* or cremation ground. In this form, she is closely associated with *Tantrism* and the extreme ascetics, *Aghoris*, who subdue their ego by existing within the precincts of the cremation ground. By conquering their aversion to death and the repulsion at being forced to live on the remains of others, the *Aghoris* hope to take the boon of liberation offered by Kali. Smasana Kali is perhaps the most feared form of Kali, especially by ordinary Indians, many of whom would be afraid to venture into her temple at the cremation ground. However, by seeing only the terrifying aspect of Kali, only one dimension of her duality is being comprehended. When the totality of Kali's manifest form is appreciated she no longer appears frightening, hence Daniélou stresses: "Beyond death, beyond existence, there is a supreme stage which is absolute joy. Kali is fearful only relatively, from the point of view of existence and worldly enjoyment. When, in the course of man's spiritual adventure, the relative is transgressed, his individuality dissolves into the primordial infinite joy."[72]

Kali is important as a liberating force. However, the way to liberation through Kali is quite different than through other goddesses. Kali brings her devotee face to face with the horror and uncertainty of life. Rather perceptively David Kinsley comments: "Kali puts the order of dharma in perspective, perhaps puts it in its place, by reminding Hindus that certain aspects of reality are untamable, unpurifiable, unpredictable, and always a threat to society's feeble attempts to order what is essentially disorderly: life itself."[73] In no other goddess are there found such striking polarities of character and so many symbols that point towards the totality of ultimate reality. Whatever her appearance, Kali's devotees look to her as a Mother. She enables them to face up to their innermost fears of death and disorder and by overcoming their fears they progress further on the path to *moksa*. Therefore, according to Kinsley: "Depending on where one is in one's spiritual pilgrimage, then, Kali has the power either to send one scuttling back to the womb of *dharma* or to provoke one over the threshold to *moksa*. In either role, she might be understood as the mother who gives her children shelter."[74]

Local goddesses as personifications of *sakti*

Local goddesses that abound in India's villages and towns are the life-blood and vitality of Hinduism. The myriad shrines and temples adorned with carvings or sandal-paste and vermilion, punctuate the rural landscape of India, offering a readily available spiritual sanctuary. Although the huge, ornate temples of the cities with their beautifully decorated images (*murtis*) cannot fail to inspire wonder and awe, it is to the simple goddess shrines that the majority of the Hindu population are drawn on a daily basis. Wonder and awe are fine on occasion, but what people need most often is their own simple deity – in many places, this is a goddess – whom they know intimately.

There are an estimated half a million villages in India that are inhabited by the majority of the population. It is in these villages and assorted local settlements that the greatest profusion of goddess worship takes place. There are some gods worshipped alongside the female deities but in comparison, their importance is minimal. The local goddesses may be peculiar only to one settlement or may be known throughout a whole region. In my own experience, the "goddess collectives" of Khurdapur (a cluster of villages) in Orissa and Colavandan (a small town) in Tamilnadu encompassed both local and regional deities.[75] Furthermore, a local goddess may have a variety of forms and characteristics in one settlement, making generalizations or any sort of categorization particularly difficult. In some instances, the local goddesses may have different names but similar characteristics. Conversely, a group of goddesses may share the same or a strikingly similar origin myth. Goddess worship at a local level embraces ritual, worship, and iconography, rather than philosophy and metaphysics. There is usually a variety of goddesses and other deities within each settlement, the number generally dependent on population size. The various castes, within the settlement, would have their own deities; this applies particularly to the scheduled castes or *dalits* (formerly untouchables) who generally have a separate hamlet within the village.

The local goddesses are often not represented anthropomorphically as their symbol is perhaps a stone, a tree or a water pot. In one south Indian village, a goddess called Kunna-kanadi (eye-mirror) is represented by a brass pot filled with water and a mirror propped against it.[76] Many goddesses have their site of worship at the foot of a tree or are represented by the tree itself. What is clear is that there is no standard representation of each deity as a goddess may be given different symbols in various villages in India. Goddesses are not necessarily known in the surrounding villages or goddesses may have similar characteristics but different names. However, certain characteristics do seem to be widespread and typify these goddesses. The majority of the local goddesses have *devi*-like tendencies. They are independent and wild in nature. This *devi*-like behaviour is very prominent at many of the village festivals, which may include animal sacrifice.

To the vast number of Indians, the local deities are more important than the deities of the Hindu pantheon. In one study, there is evidence that the villagers did not know many of the most important Hindu deities, e.g. Siva and Visnu.[77] The scholar admits that his sample of villagers was mostly men, but did include literate and non-literate subjects. However, many villages do have shrines and festivals for Brahmanical deities, but they are often known by different names, for instance Siva in Madurai in south India is called Sundaresvara. The local population may also place an emphasis on different characteristics than would be common in orthodox Hinduism; perhaps this was why the main deities were not recognized in the village.

Local goddesses are concerned with the issues that are important to their devotees. While goddesses such as Durga and Kali are fighting demons and restoring cosmic order, local goddesses protect their caste group, communicate the whereabouts of lost cattle and find suitable jobs and husbands for their supplicants. They represent a different aspect of *sakti*, which is grounded in the mundane, a readily available power source for the inhabitants of the settlement that they reside in. One of the most widespread forms of the local goddess is as the goddess of smallpox. Although smallpox has now been eradicated, the goddesses remain popular, being more concerned with other infectious diseases now (see chapter 8). In south India, she is called Mariyamman, and in the north and especially Bengal, she is called Sitala. Variations of these names are found from place to place. There are no standard representations of the goddess. In some villages, such as Siana in Rajasthan, she is represented in anthropomorphic, human form as opposed to being represented as a stone or a water pot as she is in some other villages. If an epidemic does sweep through the village then the sickroom becomes the temple of the goddess. The affliction of disease is viewed by the villagers in a number of ways. In some cases, it is thought that the disease is the invasion of demons into the village; on the other hand, the goddess herself is thought to be the source of it. At times, the onset of the disease is considered a manifestation of the goddess's wrath because her worship has not been carried out in a satisfactory manner. However, the disease is also considered to be the goddess making herself manifest in the village. Under these circumstances, the disease is regarded as the 'grace' of the goddess.[78] The function of the local goddesses, especially those associated with disease, bears strong similarities to the role of the goddess Kali who makes her devotees face up to a broader view of reality.

Local goddesses are often treated as though they have no relationship to the Brahmanical goddesses, nor to the conception of *sakti* that all goddesses personify. I am unsure why there is an apparent dilemma here. My encounter with a number of local Hindu goddesses has left me in no doubt that there is some relationship between pan-Indian and local goddesses. While it is true that local goddesses cannot simply be considered the local equivalents of pan-Indian goddesses, there is, nevertheless, a basic comprehension that all goddesses represent divine power and, furthermore, that between all goddesses there is some underlying correspondence. According to textual sources, local goddesses are just as much manifestations of the Great Goddess as are the Brahmanical, pan-Indian goddesses. The *Brahmavaivarta Purana*, and the *Devi-Bhagavatam*, both express the idea that all goddesses spring from one reality. Although Radha (consort of Krsna) is only one of many goddesses associated with *prakrti*, in the following verse she is considered an essential part of reality, as the text states: "This is the fifth Prakriti and she is denominated as Radha. Every female in every Universe is sprung from a part of Sri Radha or part of a part."[79] In fact, the pan-Indian goddesses themselves have numerous manifestations, a point emphasized in the *Kurma Purana* in the chapter in praise of Parvati, the *Sahasra-Nama* of Parvati. Here, one epithet of the goddess is Ekanekavibhagastha, meaning, "stationed in one as well as in many divisions".[80] It is likely that the often used phrase, "all the mothers are one", may have its genesis in these basic correlations.

In local settlements, there is generally interplay between the pan-Indian and local goddesses, in which attempts may be made to Brahmanize, Sanskritize, or Hinduize, a local goddess. This process reduces a goddess's overtly local characteristics, such as the acceptance of animal sacrifice and, instead, moulds her character to resemble more closely those of pan-Indian or Brahmanical deities. One part of this process has been termed "spousification"[81] in which an independent goddess is ritually married, either temporarily, annually or – if fully Hinduized – permanently, to an established god, usually Siva. Conversely, some pan-Indian goddesses have been localized, being endowed with names and forms that are more popular, with their myths relating them to the local settlement or area.

There seems to be an intimate relationship between local deities and their devotees: they know each other well as their lives are inextricably entwined. While the pan-Indian deities may be considered more intrinsically pure, and certainly more orthodox, they remain at the periphery of local life, paid homage to when required but not necessarily sharing the daily lives of the masses. It is local goddesses, therefore, that are most important in the daily workings of Hinduism. The day-to-day concerns of the population are most readily addressed to the goddesses close by. They are always ready to concern themselves with the problems of their devotees, no matter how trivial, and they have the power necessary to rectify them. Therefore, local goddesses personify the most immediate and accessible aspect of *sakti*, a world away from the metaphysical workings of *sakti* on the cosmic plane.

2 Goddesses in Textual Sources

One of the most enriching yet frustrating aspects of the study of Hinduism is its huge body of religious writing. The fledgling scholar is confronted by a vast array of sacred literature that presents confusing and often conflicting ideas. Because Hinduism is such an ancient religion, its textual heritage has been compiled over considerable time. Most importantly, the sacred books of the Hindus do not replace each other but instead have built up into an extensive mass of sacred knowledge. While none of the texts should be dismissed simply because they do not all agree with one another, there are some texts that are considered more sacred and important than others, particularly in Brahmanical or orthodox Hinduism. The oldest written texts are the *Vedas* or *Veda samhita*, hymn collections thought to have been composed between 1200–1000 BCE. The *Vedas*, of which there are four, their related commentaries and the later *Upanisads*, constitute the most sacred writings of the Hindus. Referred to as "that which has been heard" (*sruti*) these texts represent basic "truth" or "revelation" and form the basis of orthodox, brahmanical Hindu belief. Another, larger, corpus of literature is referred to as *smrti* "that which is remembered" and constitutes "tradition". The *smrti* texts are numerous and varied comprising of:

- The law books and codes of law such as the *Laws of Manu* (*Manusmrti*) and the *Dharma-sastras* that offer moral codes and rules of conduct.
- "History" (*Itihasa*) that includes the hugely popular and important epic poetry of the *Mahabharata*, "The Great (*maha*) Story of the Bharatas", containing the *Bhagavad Gita* (*Song of the Lord*),

perhaps the most famous Hindu scripture and the *Ramayana* "The Tale of Rama".

- The "Ancient (Books)" (*Puranas*) that offer creation stories and the mythologies of many deities.

Alongside these texts are the many sectarian treatises including *Tantric* and *Sakta* writings which, though not subscribed to by some people, are still regarded as sacred literature.

Goddesses in the *Vedas*

The oldest written sources in which Hindu goddesses are mentioned are the *Vedas* or "Books of Knowledge". The *Vedas* comprise:

- The Royal (*Rg*) Knowledge (*Veda*), the oldest written text is a collection of hymns, in which numerous deities – many associated with natural phenomena and abstract notions – are praised.
- The Knowledge of Ritual (*Yajur Veda*), which only mentions those deities who are connected with sacrifice.
- The Knowledge of Songs (*Sama Veda*).
- The Knowledge of Incantations (*Atharva Veda*) the latest of the *Vedas*.

Most of our knowledge of *Vedic* goddesses comes from the *Rg Veda* and the less frequently translated *Atharva Veda*. It is primarily from these sources that the following discussion on some of the most important *Vedic* goddesses is taken. However, this confines our investigation to goddesses and attitudes acceptable to the orthodox upper classes, for as Lynn Gatwood has pointed out, "most statements about Vedic religion are based upon the written record, which is silent regarding the religious practices of the non-literate majority of the population."[1] This is true of all the literary portrayals of the goddesses examined in this chapter; the majority represent orthodox, Brahmanical conceptions of the divine.

At first glance, the *Vedic* goddesses seem to have had little importance, as there were hardly any female deities of any consequence. Few goddesses had any hymns dedicated solely to them and of these, Usas, goddess of the Dawn, was the most often praised. While some scholars begin with the generalization that *Vedic* goddesses had little importance, another scholar, V. S. Guleri, has quite astutely commented: "The number of female deities, and good and evil spirits having separate hymns, or parts of hymns or incidentally mentioned in the Rgveda is more than the number of male deities". This point, Guleri concludes: "is an evidence to disprove their unimportance."[2] The *Vedic* goddesses, it seems, though they may not have been as famous as Indra and Agni, subtly pervaded the *Vedic* religious world view, personifying such important roles as Mother Earth (Prthivi), Mother of the Gods (Aditi), Night (Ratri), and Dawn (Usas). Perhaps we should not be so quick to dismiss the importance of the *Vedic* goddesses, even though many of them disappeared into obscurity at the end of the *Vedic* period when religious ideas became more philosophical and less theistic. However, the qualities that the goddesses of the *Rg Veda* embodied have reappeared in later Hinduism in various forms and in the characteristics of other goddesses.

Usas (Dawn)

Usas, the 'remover of darkness' or 'bringer of light' who personifies the Dawn, is the *Vedic* goddess that we know most about. She is the only goddess who has twenty hymns written in praise of her and is mentioned over three hundred times in other hymns.[3] Usas is, according to Gatwood, "the sole female deity personified as vividly as the Vedic gods".[4] Interestingly, Usas is also important as an independent goddess who, though she is often described as the wife or consort of the Sun (Surya),[5] is addressed separately from him. She is most consistently portrayed as a beautiful, young, regal maiden riding across the sky in a chariot drawn by purple and white horses. She is welcomed and praised as a benevolent goddess who brings with her the light that stirs humankind at the start of each new day.

Usas is the daughter of the Sky/Heaven (Dyaus)[6] and the sister of the Night (Ratri). She occupies a place, according to Guleri: "between the end of night and the rise of the sun" and "reflects the destruction of ignorance and the appearance of knowledge".[7] She is clearly an important goddess who is superior to many male deities, though she receives no share of the sacrifice.[8] She is most often appealed to for protection against evil forces and to bestow wealth, health and happiness. Usas stimulates activity in plants, animals and people, encouraging them to perform acts of worship. While she is envisaged as beautiful and youthful, perhaps being reborn each day, she is also ancient[9] because she has appeared each morning, for as long as anyone can remember. Usas' ability to be simultaneously young and old points to an association with passing time. David Kinsley takes this line of reasoning further when he claims: "She is also petitioned to grant long life, as she is a constant reminder of people's limited time on earth (7. 77). She is the mistress or marker of time."[10] This is an important facet of Usas' character that I shall return to shortly.

One important and intriguing incident mentioned in a number of *Rg Vedic* hymns involves the king of the gods and wielder of the thunderbolt, Indra's destruction of Usas' chariot. As N. N. Bhattacharyya rightly says, the poet who details the confrontation clearly admires Indra's heroism:[11]

8. And this heroic deed of might thou, Indra, hast achieved,
That thou didst smite to death the Dame, Heaven's Daughter, meditating ill.
9. Thou, Indra, Mighty One, didst crush Usas, though Daughter of the Sky.
When lifting herself up with pride.
10. Then from her chariot Usas fled, affrighted, from her ruined car.
When the strong God had shattered it.
11. So there this car of Usas lay, broken to pieces, in Vipas [the name of a river],
And she herself fled far away. (*Rg Veda* 4. 30. 8–11)[12]

The same event is mentioned in three other hymns in praise of Indra.[13] At first glance, the incident appears to be a power struggle in which Indra's supremacy is unmatched. Bhattacharyya goes as far as to describe this episode as the "rape of Ushas".[14] He concludes, along with D. D. Kosambi, that the story revolves around tribal rivalries, surmising that Usas might have been "borrowed from a pre-Vedic religion of the Mother Goddess".[15] Gatwood follows Bhattacharyya's line of reasoning but sees in the overthrow of Usas, perhaps the "only independent Vedic goddess",[16] the need for a major male deity to flex his divine muscles and put her in her place. Gatwood claims: "In Ushas, however, there is the first indication of the later spousifying process whereby a Devi-like deity becomes somehow out of control, in competition with men, and in need of male chastisement."[17] The verses that report the downfall of Usas allude to two reasons why Indra should attack her chariot, namely that she was "meditating ill" and that she was "lifting herself up with pride".[18] The idea that Usas was full of pride supports Gatwood's thesis, that Indra felt it was his duty to 'take her down a peg or two', so to speak. However, the other claim, that she had some evil intent, seems completely out of character for a goddess who is constantly praised for her benevolence. This statement is not explained nor indeed alluded to in any other hymns.

Now, we need to return to the previously made point that Usas represents time or passing time. This idea is evident in more than one hymn, such as in the following verses:

> 10. The divine and ancient ushas, born again and again, and bright with unchanging hues, wastes away the life of a mortal, like the wife of a hunter cutting up and dividing the birds.
> 11. She has been seen illuminating the boundaries of the sky, and driving into disappearance the spontaneously-retiring (night). Wearing away the ages of the human race, she shines with light, like the bride of the Sun. (*Rg Veda* 1. 92. 10–11)[19]

Renate Söhnen offers a convincing argument suggesting that Indra's attack on Usas represents his power to conquer time.[20] Usas, as the power of time, necessarily "wears away" the lives of mortals propelling them towards old age and death. Indra, by smashing the chariot of Usas, symbolically stops the degenerative power of time that comes with each successive dawn. Thereby, he establishes his position of supremacy. Similar ideas appear in other hymns praising Indra as he slays the demon Vrtra, and is able to stop the flow of a river.[21] Perhaps there is an element of truth in each of these arguments. Certainly, Indra remains an enduring presence whereas Usas eventually disappeared during the post-*Vedic* period.

Aditi (Mother of the gods)

Aditi is the mother of a variety of important gods, such as Indra, Varuna and Mitra. Although she is clearly and consistently associated with motherhood, she is a rather nebulous deity. There are no hymns addressed solely to Aditi and, according to Kinsley, despite being "mentioned nearly eighty times in the Rg-Veda, it is difficult to gain a clear picture of her nature".[22] Her name, (A) diti, means '(un) bound', '(un) binding', '(un) limited', or freedom, the opposite of *diti* meaning 'bound'. The rather abstract nature of this goddess, coupled with the meanings of her name, has led Guleri to claim:

> 'Aditi' literally means 'unbound' or 'unlimited', it seems to be a name for the invisible the infinite which surrounds us on all sides and also stands for the endless expanse beyond the earth, the clouds and the sky.

It is in the immense substratum of all that is here and also beyond. Here we have the anticipation of a universal all-embracing, all-producing nature itself, the immense potentiality of the Prakriti of Samkya Philosophy.[23]

Various verses in the *Rig Veda* allude to Aditi's unlimited nature, for instance: "Not Being, Being in the highest heaven, in Aditi's bosom"[24] and *Rg Veda* 8. 101. 15 in which Aditi is called "the navel-centre of Immortality".[25] Although these instances support Guleri's assumptions, it is difficult to know how far he is relying on hindsight, making Aditi correspond to the later idea of feminized primordial matter, *Prakrti*. Nevertheless, it is an attractive idea for surely there are suggestions contained within the *Vedic* hymns that may have informed later philosophical speculation.

What we do know about Aditi is that she was a benevolent goddess who was petitioned for protection and was often associated with sustenance. For instance, Aditi was identified with the primordial cow, her milk being associated with the vitality of *soma* (an intoxicant that represented the sap of life).[26] P. K. Agrawala describes Aditi as: "The Great Mother *par excellence* of Rgvedic religion".[27] He claims that Aditi was often assigned the title Mahi Mata or *Magna Mater*.[28] As the mother of Varuna, the guardian of "the regulating force of the cosmos"[29] (*rta*), Aditi also protects the eternal cosmic law.

In later *Vedic* thought, Aditi became closely associated with sacrifice, particularly in the *Yajur Veda*. She was identified with the sacrificial animal in the horse sacrifice (*asvamedha*) and, during the *soma* sacrifice, the opening and closing offerings were made to her.[30] The *Yajur Veda* also associated Aditi with Prthivi, goddess of the Earth. Aditi eventually became a goddess of minor importance. She was characterized as the wife of Visnu in the *Vajasaneyi Samhita* and in the later *puranic* texts is the wife of Kasyapa, the sage.[31]

Prthivi (Earth)

Vedic religion, like many other ancient belief systems, conceived of the earth as female. Prthivi, though she has only one hymn dedicated solely to her, is most often encountered paired with the Sky god, Dyaus. Together they are universal parents of the gods and all that flourishes on earth. Interestingly, as a pair they are sometimes referred to as mother, for example: in *Rg Veda* 10. 64. 14 "The Mothers, Heaven and Earth, those mighty Goddesses, worthy of sacrifice, come with the race of Gods."[32] The literal meaning of the word Prthivi is "The Broad One" in reference to her expansive nature, which, as Guleri points out, "is obvious to the human vision."[33] However, apart from the conception of extensiveness, it is Prthivi's identity with fertility and maternal protection that is most common in the *Rg Veda*. Alongside the conception of Prthivi as a cow – an animal that not only gives milk, but also fuel in the form of dung for cooking etc. – her maternal and protective nature is beautifully evoked in the following *Vedic* funeral hymn:

> 10. Betake thee to the lap of the Earth the Mother, of Earth far-spreading, very kind and gracious.
> Young Dame, wool-soft unto the guerdon–giver, may she preserve thee from Destruction's [Nrriti's] bosom.
> 11. Heave thyself, Earth, nor press thee downward heavily: afford him [the corpse] easy access, gently tending him.
> Cover him as a mother wraps her skirt about her child, O Earth. (*Rg Veda* 10. 18. 8–10)[34]

Few *Vedic* goddesses play a significant part in the writings of the *Yajur Veda*, though Prthivi and Sarasvati are prevalent. In the case of Prithivi, various episodes explain the characteristics of the earth, such as natural fissures and the growth of vegetation. The deities in the *Yajur Veda* are also those associated with sacrifice, prompting Guleri to remark: "No other Veda represents Prthivi so closely connected with sacrifice as this Veda does. In the Rgveda the invocation of Prthivi was limited to the prayers and praises while in the Yajurveda she is one of the most important factors of the sacrifices."[35]

Prthivi represents the sacrificial altar and the place of the sacrifice and, in this respect she is, perhaps, the foundation on which the sacrificial ritual rests. Possibly because of her all-encompassing, maternal and accommodating nature, Prthivi, the Earth remained an important female deity. She is one of the very few *Vedic* goddesses who did not disappear in the post-*Vedic* period. As Kinsley points out: "Prthivi persists in later Hinduism and becomes associated with the god Visnu. She is often called Bhudevi (the goddess of the earth)."[36] The goddess Sita, whose name means "furrow", later absorbed some of Prthivi's characteristics.[37] Although Sita was a minor deity in the *Rg Veda*, she later became the consort of Rama, one of Visnu's most enduring incarnations.

Ratri (Night)

The goddess Ratri personifies the night and is often described as the sister of Usas, the Dawn. Ratri is characterized as a benevolent goddess who provides rest, offering protection from the perils of the night. Rather than being the blackness of night, Ratri is envisaged as a starlit night, in which the stars represent her eyes.[38] The one hymn in the *Rg Veda* that is dedicated solely to Ratri clearly denotes her motherly and protective nature:

1. With all her eyes the Goddess Night looks forth approaching many a spot:
She hath put all her glories on.
2. Immortal, she hath filled the waste, the Goddess hath filled height and depth:
She conquers darkness with her light.
3. The Goddess as she comes hath set the Dawn her Sister in her place:
And then the darkness vanishes.
4. So favour us this night, O thou whose pathways we have visited
As birds their nest upon the tree.
5. The villagers have sought their homes, and all that walks and all that flies,
Even the falcons fain for prey.
6. Keep off the she-wolf and the wolf; O Urmya, keep the thief away;
Easy be thou for us to pass.
7. Clearly hath she come nigh to me who decks the dark with richest hues:
O Morning, cancel it like debts.
8. These have I brought to thee like kine. O night, thou Child of Heaven, accept
This laud as for a conqueror. (*Rg Veda* 10. 127)[39]

Along with Usas, Ratri represents the passing of time and the cosmic order (*rta*) in which day follows night and vice versa, prompting Kinsley to comment: "Together they illustrate the coherence of the created order: the ordered alternations of vigor and rest, light and dark, and the regular flow of time."[40]

In the *Ratri Khila*, a hymn appended to the *Rg Veda*, the poetic language used to praise Ratri clearly expands on her benevolent character. Perhaps more importantly, as Thomas Coburn has demonstrated, some of the sentiments expressed in this hymn surface again in accordance with the Devi in the later *Devi-Mahatmya*. For instance, in the following verses of the *Ratri Khila* 4. 2 v. 3–4, the portions in italics indicate significant overlaps in the two texts:

3. I take refuge in *the night, the mother, the resting-place of all creatures,* *(Who is) auspicious (bhadra) blessed, black, the night of all the world,*

4. Occasioning rest, drawing (things) in, garlanded with the planets and constellations.
I take refuge in *auspicious (siva) night*; *O auspicious one,* may we obtain what is best.
O Agni, may your splendor abide in my invocations.[41]

While there is no direct succession between the goddess Ratri and the later conception of an all-encompassing Devi or Mahadevi, the underlying importance of the *Vedic* goddesses should not be dismissed. It would appear that some of the ways in which *Vedic* goddesses were clearly viewed have been taken up and developed at a later date. As far as the goddess Ratri is concerned, in the *Yajur Veda,* her importance waned. The gods Mitra and Varuna were considered the cause of day and night and, according to Guleri: "In the later period the day was regarded as belonging to the gods and the night to the Asuras. It is on account of the Asuras taking shelter in the darkness of the night after stealing the wealth of the gods."[42]

Vac/Vak (Speech)

The goddess Vac is the personification of Speech and as such is an important *Vedic* deity despite the fact that she disappeared after the *Vedic* period. In *Vedic* religion, the spoken word was particularly important as the medium "heard" by the seers and written in the form of hymns in the *Rg Veda,* and in the invocations and ritual words spoken by the priests during sacrifices. The perfected utterance of the priest was the axis on which a successful sacrifice rested. Vac is mentioned often in the *Vedas,* but one particular hymn, addressed to her, has remained an important aspect of goddess theology. Although there are isolated references elsewhere in the *Vedic* texts that tentatively suggest a correlation between power and the divine feminine, in a *Vedic* hymn referred to as the *Devi Sukta,* Vac's power seems unequivocal:

1. I travel with the Rudras and the Vasus, with the Adityas and All-Gods I wander.
I hold aloft both Varuna and Mitra, Indra and Agni, and the Pair of Ashvins.

Goddesses in Textual Sources

2. I cherish and sustain high-swelling Soma, and Tvashtar I support, Pushan and Bhaga.
I load with wealth the zealous sacrificer who pours the juice and offers his oblation.
3. I am the Queen, the gatherer-up of treasures, most thoughtful, first of those who merit worship.
Thus Gods have stablished [sic] me in many places with many homes to enter and abide in.
4. Through me alone all eat the food that feeds them, – each man who sees, breathes, hears the word outspoken.
They know it not, but yet they dwell beside me. Hear, one and all, the truth as I declare it.
5. I, verily, myself announce and utter the word that Gods and men alike shall welcome.
I make the man I love exceedingly mighty, make him a sage, a Rishi, and a Brahman.
6. I bend the bow for Rudra that his arrow may strike and slay the hater of devotion.
I rouse and order battle for the people, and I have penetrated Earth and Heaven.
7. On the world's summit I bring forth the Father: my home is the waters, in the ocean.
Thence I extend o'er all existing creatures, and touch even yonder heaven with my forehead.
8. I breathe a strong breath like the wind and tempest, the while I hold together all existence.
Beyond this wide earth and beyond the heavens I have become so mighty in my grandeur. (*Rg Veda* 10. 125)[43]

Clearly, Vac represents divine power, described by one scholar as, "the sole principle of creative energy".[44] There is certainly no indication here that Vac is simply the power, or deeds of, a consort. She is presented as an individual, bestowing her power on gods and humans alike. Although Vac is associated with the power of speech in this hymn, her power or energy appears implicitly transcendent. Bhattacharyya believes that this hymn was a later interpolation, though he describes its content as "a rudimentary conception of an all-pervading female principle".[45] The importance of this particular hymn is not lost on other scholars. Thus, Coburn comments, "in general studies of the rise of Saktism, *vac* as a concept, and RV 10. 125 in particular, are cited almost without exception".[46]

In later *Vedic* thought, Vac was associated with the creator god Prajapati and, according to Kinsley: "There are also hints that it is through Vac, or in pairing with her, that Prajapati creates."[47] However, Kinsley goes on to say that: "This is different from the role of *sakti* in later Hindu philosophic schools, in which the male counterpart of *sakti* tends to be inactive."[48] An element of Vac's powerful nature evolved into a more developed theology, despite the fact that Vac herself eventually disappeared. Vac's most important characteristics were assimilated within the personality of Sarasvati who, despite being a river goddess in the *Vedas*, eventually became the goddess of Wisdom and Learning, often referred to as Mother of the *Vedas*.

Indrani (Indra's wife)

One of the reasons that *Vedic* goddesses are often dismissed as largely unimportant is that a group of them are simply wives of the gods. Very little is known of these goddesses except their names, which leads Bhattacharyya to comment: "They are mere shadowy reflections of the gods with but little independent power. Hardly anything about them is mentioned but their names, which are simply formed from those of the gods with the feminine suffix *ani*."[49]

Indrani, the wife of Indra, is perhaps the most famous of these goddesses. We are able to learn something of her nature through the one hymn that is dedicated to her.[50] The composer of the hymn has addressed it to Saci Paulomi, though it is clearly concerned with Indrani. The goddess is addressed as "Shaci", a term used elsewhere in the *Rg Veda*, but not as a title. Griffith defines the term *saci* as "act" or "exploit", describing the hymn as metaphorically praising Indra's "glorious acts".[51] The hymn is interesting in that it reveals something of Indrani's nature. She appears triumphant in the hymn as she says: "I have subdued as conqueror these rivals, these my fellow wives, That I may hold imperial sway over this Hero [Indra] and the folk."[52] Indrani also claims in two of the verses that she is victorious over Indra and that he is now "submissive" to her will.[53] The idea that Indrani represents "Indra's deeds of power deified", a statement made by S. K. Das,[54] is significant because it is suggestive of the position of goddesses in later textual sources, especially those in the *Puranas*, who represent their consort's power. It is a point that has not escaped Kinsley as he says of the *Vedic* consorts: "It is important to note their existence in light of subsequent Hindu mythology, in which many of the most important goddesses are consorts of well-known Hindu gods, and also in light of the later Hindu concept of *sakti*."[55] Das concludes that in *Rg Veda* 3. 60. 2 *saci* is not mere blind physical force, but denotes "skill or ability" implying conscious intellectual faculty (*prajna*).[56] He notes that, though "the term Saci originally meant nothing more than 'help or friendly assistance', she came to be invested, even in the hymns of the earlier books of the Rgveda, with the character of an intelligent divine principle."[57]

Nirrti (Destruction, Disorder)

All the goddesses encountered so far have been benevolent, being most frequently approached for protection and succour. The goddess Nirrti is contrasted sharply with these goddesses as she represents disorder. There are no hymns in the *Rg Veda* addressed solely to Nirrti, but she is petitioned in a number of hymns to stay away from the worshipper. For instance in *Rg Veda* 10. 59, four of the ten verses end with the invocation: "Let Nirrti depart to distant places".[58] The reason for the worshipper's aversion to Nirrti is that this goddess personifies destruction and disorder the antithesis of the order created in the sacrifice. According to S. K. Lal: "Nirrti represents the anarchic forces of chaos in the universe. She is a deity of destruction, decay, evil and misfortune."[59] During the *Vedic* period she was feared, especially for her power to disrupt sacrifices and, consequently, rites for her appeasement were undertaken before each sacrifice.[60]

Although Nirrti is an indistinct figure in the *Rg Veda*, she appears more frequently, and is described in more detail, in the *Atharva* and *Yajur Vedas*. In the *Atharva Veda*, Nirrti is offered a share of the sacrifice in return for the protection of cattle.[61] Nirrti is also petitioned to send those who die to heaven, to the realm of order rather than disorder.[62] In the *Yajur Veda*, Nirrti's real form is described as being black, though she also has other forms, such as "golden-locked", according to one verse.[63] A certain duality seems inherent in the goddess and in the attitude towards her. This prompts Guleri to claim: "The treatment of Nirrti in the Yajurveda is a contradictory one. On one hand she is praised, while on the other hand she is asked to run away from the sacrifice."[64] Although the later *Vedic* literature provided a more detailed picture of Nirrti, she became largely unknown in the post-*Vedic* period. However, the goddess Alaksmi, who later personified ill-luck and misfortune in *puranic* literature, appears to have incorporated many of Nirrti's characteristics into her own personality.[65]

Goddesses in the *Mahabharata*

Described by Alf Hiltebeitel as "Hindu India's national epic",[66] the *Mahabharata*, a poem of 100,000 verses written between *c.* 500 BCE and 400 CE, is an important textual source in the understanding of Hindu thought. It falls into the category of history (*itihasa*) though its content often represents legend rather than actual historical events. Nevertheless, its impact and value should not be underestimated for as Will Johnson claims: "Even the most tentative approach uncovers in the text many, if not all, of those key assumptions, tensions, and questions – mythological, theological, and soteriological – that converged, precisely during the period of the Mahabharata's crystallization, to form the great and variegated religious culture subsequently labelled 'Hinduism'."[67]

The focus of the *Mahabharata* is the restoration of the balance of *dharma* culminating in a huge and significant battle between two sets of cousins, the Pandavas and the Kauravas or Kurus. The battle, in which Krsna the incarnation (*avatara*) of Visnu plays a crucial part, heralds the beginning of the Dark Age (*kali yuga*), in which we now live. Alongside the story of this epic battle are woven stories about various gods and goddesses, who contribute, either directly or indirectly, to the events that lead to the final confrontation. Here are just a few significant encounters with goddesses, both benign and terrible.

The mortal form of Ganga

The *Mahabharata* is well known by many people in India and abroad following its television serialization. One of the enduring images from the series was the beautiful goddess Ganga (a personification of the river Ganges) throwing her newborn infants into the river. Why would an essentially benign goddess do such a thing? One of the early myths of the *Mahabharata* lets us in on her secret.

This story, like many, starts on the celestial plane where Ganga lives with the other gods.[68] One day a noble king who had earned a place in heaven by performing "a thousand Horse Sacrifices and a hundred Horse Race Festivals" was visiting Brahma's court.[69] Ganga, his daughter, was present and when a sudden gust of wind blew her skirt up, all the other gods looked away except the king, who could not take his eyes from Ganga's beauty. As a punishment, Brahma declared that he would return to the mortal world, once more taking on a human form. Ganga began to feel sorry for the king, wondering what she could do to help him. As she left the court, she encountered the Vasus, a group of eight minor celestial gods. They told Ganga that they had inadvertently disturbed the meditations of the sage Vasistha, who then cursed them to be born as humans. The Vasus pleaded with Ganga to help them. If she would take a mortal form and give birth to them, she could then free them from their punishment by throwing them in the river, thus releasing them back to the celestial realm. Ganga chose the king who had so openly admired her to be the earthly father of the Vasus. Her stipulation to the Vasus was that the king should be left with a son who, though he was virile, would not have any offspring of his own. The Vasus readily agreed.

Ganga took the form of a mortal and appeared to King Samtanu from the river Ganges, "a beautiful woman who blazed with loveliness, like Sri the lotus goddess come to earth. Her body was flawless, her teeth impeccable, and celestial ornaments adorned her."[70] King Samtanu was completely enamoured of this strange and beautiful woman and asked her to become his wife. This, she readily agreed to but with certain conditions. Ganga said:

> "I shall be your obedient queen, O lord of the earth. But if perhaps I do something, whether it pleases or displeases you, O king, I must never be stopped nor harshly spoken to. If you will act thus I shall live with you sire. But once you stop me or scold me, I shall surely forsake you".[71]

The king was overjoyed, wondering what this woman could possibly do to displease him. The couple lived very happily for some time. The king "begot on her eight sons who resembled immortals. And each son as soon as he was born she threw into the water; and saying 'I do you a favour', she drowned each in the river Ganges. It did not please King Samtanu, but he dared not say a word lest she forsake him."[72] The king could not understand how his wife could kill her children so easily. When her eighth son was born, Ganga unexpectedly started to laugh. The king, who had so far held his tongue, could remain silent no longer and pleaded with his wife not to kill their son, demanding to know how and why she had killed the others. Ganga gave King Samtanu his son and explained who she was and why she had killed his other sons, releasing them from their earthly bondage.

Her task was now completed so she withdrew herself back to the world of the gods, but assuring the king that their son, Gangadatta (Gift of the Ganges) would be strong, noble and virtuous. Indeed, later in the *Mahabharata*, this son, known as Bhisma, and the uncle of the embodiment of goodness, the Pandavas, is instrumental in the forthcoming battle.

There are other stories concerning the goddess Ganga but in this myth she is presented as benevolent, even in the act of killing her own children. Many passages in the *Mahabharata* are instructive in nature. The story of Ganga's mortal form is no exception for it shows us that mere mortals cannot easily fathom the actions of the gods. One action or attribute of a deity may seem destructive but may in fact be salvific, as was the case with Ganga and the Vasus.

The creation of Mrytu (Death)

The creation of a goddess whose sole purpose in the world is the destruction of the creatures that inhabit it is perhaps the most touching goddess myth related in the *Mahabharata*. It is also, according to Alf Hiltebeitel, "one of the oldest (if not the oldest) Indian myths about a goddess in her destructive aspect".[73] This particular myth, which describes the creation of the goddess Mrtyu (Death), is told to help alleviate the suffering of Yudhisthira – the eldest of the Pandavas, and son of the god Dharma – who mourns his nephew's death during the great battle. It is repeated in at least two books of the *Mahabahrata*, in the seventh, the book of Drona (*Dronaparvan*) and in the twelfth, the book of Peace (*Santiparvan*), with minor differences between the two accounts. Of the two, the version in the *Dronaparvan* is considered the oldest. In both cases, the appearance of the goddess Mrtyu is prompted by the earth's inability to cope with an ever-growing population:

> 38. In the beginning of the creation, the Grandsire Brahma created all beings. Then that highly powerful one, seeing that the beings of his creation suffered no decay,

> 39. Fell into thinking, O king, as to how he should cause their destruction. Meditating long over the subject, he then failed to find out any means of destruction, O ruler of earth. (*Dronaparvan* 52. 38–9)[74]

Having created the world, including all its creatures, Brahma had not considered the problem of overpopulation. Because he could not find a solution to the problem that he himself had created, he became angry. His anger manifested itself in the form of fire that started to destroy everything in the world, both animate and inanimate. In a reversal of roles, Siva (the destroyer or dissolver) approached Brahma (the creator) begging him to stop his destructive emissions.

Goddesses in Textual Sources

17. When that high-souled god had thus extinguished that fire of his wrath, there came out from the various outlets of his sense-organs, a female figure.

18. She was dark and red and tawny and her tongue, countenance and eyes were red, and she was adorned with two shining ear-rings and various other brilliant ornaments.

19. Coming out of his body, she betook to the southern quarter, and she smilingly cast glances at those two lords of the universe.

20. Then Brahma, that controller of the creation and destruction of the world, called her by the name of Death. And, O ruler of men, he said to her: "Slay these beings of my creation.

21. You are the offspring of the wrath I harboured for the destruction of the universe. Therefore, kill you all these creations including the learned and the idiot (*Dronaparvan* 53. 18–21)[75]

According to Hiltebeitel: "Such a description leaves little doubt that although *Brahma* addresses her as *Mrtyu* ("Death"), a goddess with a *Vedic* past, she is here just as much a reflection of the goddesses *Durga* and *Kali*, at a point where these latter, or at least their prototypes, are breaking into the literary tradition."[76] Whoever this goddess is, her burden is heavy as, quite simply, Mrtyu must clear up Brahma's mess. What is most interesting about this story is Brahma's apparent lack of concern for the creatures of the world. Admittedly, he never intended them any harm, but appears to have had no compunction in ordering Mrtyu to kill them. In contrast, she, who has been assigned the role of "harbinger of death", is distraught at the prospect of arbitrarily killing the creatures of the earth, she "began to wail aloud helplessly in plaintive voice", and Brahma caught the tears that fell from her eyes.[77] Mrtyu repeatedly resists the role for which she has been created and practices severe ascetic penances for billions of years in the hope that she might be excused from her fate. The goddess was concerned that she would be committing a sin and that the creatures of the earth would despise her. Sadly, she has no choice but to bring death to the world, but because of her penances she is able to make her touch of death less random: "Let covetousness, anger, animosity, malice, dissentions and folly and shamelessness and other stern passions tear to pieces the frames of corporeal beings."[78] In a final ironic twist to this tale, Brahma declares that the tears shed by the goddess in her distress for the creatures of the world shall become the diseases that will help to usher in their deaths. A new goddess of death and disease was born in this story – one who, despite Brahma's assurances that she would accrue no sin from her actions, was destined to be maligned and misunderstood in her later destructive incarnations. The heavy burden that she was made to bear has been passed on to the other goddesses, especially Kali, who now shoulder her weighty load. Thus, despite the fact that one of the final verses of this chapter claims: "Creatures destroy themselves. Death does not destroy anyone, armed though she is with the mortal dart. Therefore, the wise, knowing death to be unavoidable being ordained by Brahma, never lament for those who are dead."[79]

The worship of Durga

The *Mahabahrata* presents us with two important and interesting hymns addressed to the goddess Durga. In this early period, Durga is clearly the goddess of victory in battle, for each time she is invoked it is for protection. The first invocation to be examined is missing from the earliest (Kashmiri) manuscripts and has been relegated to an appendix by the critical edition. However, Madeleine Biardeau considers this hymn, which appears in book four, chapter six of Roy and Dutt's translations, to be in its rightful place, though it may have been a later inclusion.[80] The context of the hymn is the arrival of the five Pandavas and their wife Draupadi at the kingdom of King Virata. They have been living in exile in the forest for twelve years and must now spend a year in hiding if they are to re-take the kingdom that was lost in a fateful dice game. Biardeau considers the Pandavas' year in hiding, spent in King Virata's court, as a period of preparation or initiation (*diksa*), after which time they are able to confront their cousins, an act that precipitates the battle, the climax of the *Mahabharata* story.[81] Therefore, Yudhisthira's invocation of the goddess seems fitting, as does Arjuna's (third Pandava – son of Indra) invocation later, on the eve of the great battle. Having established the context of Durga's praise, we need to examine what the hymns tell us about the goddess. In the *Virataparvan*, chapter 6, the goddess, who is praised principally as Durga, clearly has a variety of forms and attributes. The goddess is identified as the one who substituted herself for the baby Krsna and was subsequently dashed against a rock by his evil uncle Kamsa. Kamsa had heard a prophecy that Krsna would herald his downfall. The goddess is praised as the slayer of demons (*asurus*) and the rescuer of her worshippers (v. 5). She is described as beautiful, being decorated with many ornaments and holding weapons. She is a virgin goddess (v. 15), who has slain the demon Mahisa (v. 16) and consequently she represents victory in battle, as the names Jaya and Vijaya suggest (v. 17). In contrast to her benevolent and beautiful aspect, the goddess is also called Kali and Mahakali, and, as such, is described as being fond of wine, meat, and animal-sacrifice, making her home in the Vindhya Mountains (v. 18) She is also directly addressed as Durga (vs. 20 and 26) and is lauded as the greatest refuge (v. 21). The goddess is pleased with Yudhisthira's devotion and shows herself, promising the Pandavas victory in their battle and, through her grace, the ability to remain hidden during their thirteenth year in exile (vs. 29 and 35).

This hymn is mirrored, according to Biardeau,[82] by Arjuna's petition for victory, which is perhaps the more important of the two, and recommended to him by Krsna, *Bhismaparvan* 23. This hymn to the goddess (Devi-*stotra*), according to Klaus Klostermaier, "does not appear as an improvisation for the situation. It looks like an established, well-known hymn for such occasions."[83] The hymn provides one of the first encounters with the idea of an all-encompassing goddess, one with many names and forms, who is 'identical with Brahman'. Clearly, Durga is established as a goddess of war, particularly victory in battle, for Arjuna praises her with these words: "O fierce one, O giver of victory, O victory's self! ... O thou that bearest an awful spear, O thou that holdest a sword and a shield ... I bow to thee that art fond of battle! ... I praise thee. O great goddess! let victory always attend me through thy grace on the field of battle!"[84] However, the goddess revealed in this hymn is considerably more as she is praised as: "the *Vedas*, the *Srutis*, and the highest virtue! . . . propitious to Brahmanas engaged in sacrifices . . . knowledge of the past . . . ever present in the sacred abodes erected to thee ... the science of Brahma among sciences ... sleep of creatures from which there is no waking!"[85] Finally, Arjuna praises the goddess thus:

> Thou art the unconciousness, thou the sleep, thou the illusion, the modesty, thou beauty of (all creatures)! Thou art the twilight, thou art the day, thou art *Savitri*, and thou art the mother! Thou art contentment, thou art growth, thou art light! This is thou that supportest the Sun and Moon and that makes them shine! Thou art the prosperity of those that are prosperous! The *Siddhas* and the *Charanas* behold thee in contemplation![86]

Durga finally appears and assures Arjuna that victory belongs to the Pandavas. Many of the implicit sentiments of this hymn were later taken up and woven into a more explicit conception of the goddess, with Durga the buffalo slayer a key character. Furthermore, Biardeau points out that rather than the goddess being involved in the fighting, "it is Siva who invisibly precedes Arjuna onto the field of battle".[87] However, this is not strictly true, as the examination of another goddess, Kala-ratri, will show.

The goddess Kala-ratri (Death-night) in the Sauptikaparvan

While Siva may play an integral part in the great battle, and Durga may be the goddess who is worshipped to secure victory, the goddess Kala-ratri (Death-night) also has her share of the action. In stark contrast to the vision of Durga formerly presented, the goddess Kala-ratri appears at the height of a post-battle killing spree. The context of her appearance is the slaughter of the Pandava's followers who had taken up residence in the Kuru or Kaurava's camp, which is empty following their defeat. However, Asvatthaman, whose father (Drona) was tricked into surrender by the Pandavas, was determined to avenge his father's death. At night, which was against the rules of war, he crept into the camp, and infused by the power of Siva, he attacked and killed many of the Pandava followers. At the height of his frenzied attack the goddess appeared:

> Then chanting, there appeared before them a black-skinned
> Woman, the Night of all-destroying Time, [Kalaratri]
> Whose mouth and eyes were the colour of blood,
> Whose garlands and unguents were just as crimson,
> Who wore a single blood-dyed garment, and
> Held in her hands a noose.
>   They saw horses,
> Elephants and men, bound by terrible cords,
> Driven by her as she carried away
> All kinds of hairless spirits roped together
> With the great warriors, divested of their arms.
> On other nights, the greatest of those warriors
> Had seen her in their dreams, leading the sleepers
> Away – and Drona's son forever killing them.
> Ever since the war between the Kuru
> And Pandava hosts began, they had dreamt
> Of that baleful goddess, and of Drona's son. (*Sauptikaparvan* 8. 64–7)[88]

In distinction to the goddesses we have examined so far – even the goddess Mrtyu (Death) who appeared benevolent, calm and peaceful – the goddess Kala-ratri bursts, unannounced, into the middle of the massacre. Although her appearance may be a later inclusion, she seems to represent and personify the horror of the battle. Whereas Durga, in her hymns of praise might be said to personify the nobility and victory of winning a battle, Kala-ratri personifies the negativity of war, laying its unpleasantness bare. Guleri describes Kala-ratri's appearance as "a graphic description of Kali",[89] which to some extent it is. A further association with Kali in her transcendent form might be inferred from Jacques Scheuer's description of Kala-ratri as "Destin" (Destiny) and "cours du Temps" (the course of Time)[90]. These are two important aspects of Kali's character, especially in her *Tantric* associations with the *Dasamahavidyas* (ten forms of transcendent knowledge), detailed in chapter 4.

In general, goddesses do not represent a significant part in the *Mahabharata*, though their mythology is found throughout the text. We find there many incarnations of the goddess and, perhaps, the beginnings of ideologies yet to be fully developed. As we work our way chronologically through Hindu sacred scripture the importance of the goddesses increases. Consequently, the next section examines goddess sources in which the idea of 'Goddess' as divine power and energy is at the forefront.

Goddesses in the *Devi-Mahatmya*

There are various *Puranas* that include sections in praise of goddesses, such as (*Vamana Purana* 17–21 and 51–6; *Varaha Purana* 21–8 and 90–6; *Kurma Purana* I. 11–12 and the *Harivamsa* II. 2–4 and 22).[91] However, by far the most famous and influential is the *Sri Durga Saptasati*, *Candi Path*, or *Devi-Mahatmya* as it is most popularly known, already mentioned in chapter 1. The importance of this text, from a *Sakta* perspective, cannot be overstated for, as Cheever Mackenzie Brown claims:

> The Great Goddess, or Maha-Devi as she is known in India, burst onto the Hindu religious stage in the middle of the first millennium of the Christian era. Prior to that time there were many goddess traditions in India. But it is in the *Devi-Mahatmya* (c.AD [sic] 500–600) of the *Markendeya Purana* that the various mythic, cultic and theological elements relating to diverse female divinities were brought together in what has been called the "crystallization of the Goddess tradition".[92]

The *Devi-Mahatmya* was the first goddess-centred text to establish the all-inclusive nature of feminine power. It is a text that is loved and known by the populace, but is equally revered for its goddess theology by scholars of Hinduism. The mythological account of the struggle between the Great Goddess (Mahadevi) and the demons, the key events in the text, has informed the iconography of many goddesses, especially Durga. Although the Mahadevi is addressed by many names, and appears in many forms in the *Devi-Mahatmya*, it is Durga who is most closely associated with this particular conception of the divine feminine. Her connection with the cental events of the text is immortalized in the portrayal of her slaying the demon Mahisasura. This particular episode is so well known that very few Hindus, if any, could not relate it.

Various battles between the Devi and the demons constitute the heart of the *Devi-Mahatmya*, but take place within a larger frame story. A king and a merchant, we are told, approach Medhas the sage seeking to know why they still feel attachment and affection for those who have treated them badly and cast them out. Medhas proceeds to explain that: "Men are hurled into the whirlpool of attachment, the pit of delusion, through the power of Mahamaya (the Great Illusion), who makes the existence of the world possible."[93] The sage then proceeds to explain the power of the Goddess through the retelling of three stories. The first one starts by establishing the supremacy of the Goddess, and her status as Mahadevi, in two important ways. It retells the story of Madhu and Kaitabha, two *asuras* who emerged from the dirt in Visnu's ear and attacked Brahma. In the original version, Visnu tricked the demons by his own power and killed them, earning him the title Madhusudana (Slayer of Madhu), used throughout the *Mahabharata*;[94] but in the *Devi-Mahatmya* the goddess, Yoganidra (Yogic sleep), is the key player as she prevents Visnu from waking up. It is only when Yoganidra withdraws herself from Visnu that he is able to wake and fight the demons. The goddess as Mahamaya (Great Delusion/Illusion) helps him further by deluding the demons and giving Visnu the advantage needed to kill them. Interspersed with this narrative are verses in praise of the Goddess, leaving the reader in no doubt that she represents the all-encompassing power of *sakti* in all its forms. Brahma praises her thus:

> Whatever and wherever anything exists, whether it be real or unreal, O you who have everything as your soul,
> Of all that, you are the power (*sakti*); how then can you be adequately praised?
> By you the creator of the world, the protector of the world, who (also) consumes the world (i.e., lord Visnu)

Is (here) brought under the influence of sleep (*nidra*); who here is capable
of praising you?
Since Visnu, Siva and I have been made to assume bodily form
By you, who could have the capacity of (adequately) praising you? (*Devi-Mahatmya*, 1. 63–5)[95]

Having established that the Great Goddess (Mahadevi) is the source of
all power, the *Devi-Mahatmya* goes on to the main events, the battle
with two demons Sumbha and Nisumbha and their associates and, most
famously, the killing of the buffalo demon, Mahisasura.

In a reproduction of the mythology of Visnu's incarnations
(*avataras*) that appeared when cosmic *dharma* or equilibrium was
threatened, the Devi was produced by the combined power of the *devas*,
specifically to dispatch the demons that are threatening the gods and,
more importantly, to uphold the equilibrium of power between the
positive forces represented by the gods (*devas*) and the negative forces
represented by the demons (*asuras*). How, then, had the *asuras* become
so powerful? In a situation that is replayed many times in Hindu
mythology, the demons had won their power through their severe
penances and austerities. What is clear in Hindu tradition is that anyone
can win the favour of a particular deity through the build-up of inner
heat or power, referred to as *tejas*. If an individual or group creates
enough *tejas* it can seriously disrupt the equilibrium between positive
and negative forces, indicating that power and energy are not static but
continually fluctuate. To remedy this situation, some *puranic* stories tell
of divine nymphs (*apsarasas*) being sent down to earth to disrupt the
ascetic practices of the holy men whose austerity (*tapas*) has accumulated too great a store of power. The events in the *Devi-Mahatmya* are
precipitated by a similar event. Through boons given by the god
Brahma, in response to the power of certain demons, the demons
became invincible – vulnerable only to the power of a woman. The
restoration of power to the gods, therefore, necessitated the help of a
supreme warrior goddess.

Once created by the power of the gods, the Devi was the epitome of
beauty and awesome power. At once captivating to look at, but frightening to behold, she stalked the battlefield standing on top of her lion
mount: "She (the Devi) gave out a loud roar with a defying laugh again
and again. By her unending, exceedingly great, terrible roar the entire
sky was filled, and there was great reverberation. All worlds shook, the
sea trembled."[96]

This vision of the divine feminine dispelled all previous conceptions of what a goddess is. Although conventionally beautiful her behaviour from the outset was unorthodox. Her great power was emphasized by her many arms that wielded the weapons given to her by the gods who created her:

> Then he saw the Goddess, filling the triple world[97] with her radiance,
> Causing the earth to bow down at the tread of her feet, scratching the sky with her diadem,
> Making all the nether regions tremble at the sound of her bowstring,
> Standing (there) filling all the directions with her thousand arms.
> Then there began a battle between the Goddess and the enemies of the gods. (*Devi-Mahatmya* 2. 36–8)[98]

Although the Devi had been born from the combined power of the gods, once created she remained in command of herself: independent in her own right, she never returned to her source.

The Devi immediately engaged the armies of Mahisasura in battle. A key aspect of this battle is her engagement of two demons, Sumbha and Nisumbha. This event along with the later Mahaisasura battle are to be found in other texts, but in the *Devi-Mahatmya* they are re-written with a decidedly *Sakta* bias. For instance, the original version of the slaying of Sumbha and Nisumbha is slightly different in that their killing was originally ascribed to an ancient regional goddess, Vindhyavasini, the sister of Krsna-Gopala.[99] However, the elaborate nature of the *Devi-Mahatmya*'s version of this myth makes it clear that the text is not simply dealing with a regional goddess but with a universal one, who is the source of all power, a point beautifully demonstrated by Devi when Sumbha accuses her of relying on help to kill his brother, Nisumbha (see the *Saptamatrika* section of chapter 4). The goddess's response is:

> The Devi said: I am alone in the world here. Who else is there besides me?
> See O vile one, these Goddesses who are but my own powers, entering into my own self!
> Then all those, Brahmani and the rest, were absorbed into the body of the Devi. Ambika alone then remained.
> The Devi said: The numerous forms which I projected by my power here–those have been withdrawn by me, and (now) I stand alone. Be steadfast in combat. (*Devi-Mayatmya* 10. 4–5)[100]

Mistakenly thinking that a female would be no match for them, the *asuras* attacked her but soon discovered that this was no ordinary

Goddesses in Textual Sources

woman. Even though they hurled their weapons at her by the thousand she very easily destroyed them. The Devi, who during this episode was called by many names, was initially a force by herself but as she sighed during her struggle with the demon troops, she created an army of her own. Her breaths became her assistants that, in turn, attacked the *asuras* with "axes, javelins, swords and pikes".[101] The *Devi-Mahatmya* offers a vivid picture of the Devi's strength and the carnage that accompanied the destruction of Mahisasura's army:

> Then the Devi killed hundreds of asuras with her trident, club, showers of spears, swords and the like, and threw down others who were stupefied by the noise of her bell; and binding others with her noose, she dragged them on the ground. Some were split in two by the sharp slashes of her sword, and others, smashed by the blows of her mace, lay down on the ground; and some severely hammered by her club vomited forth blood. (*Devi-Mahatmya* 2.55–8)[102]

The killing of Mahisasura's army established the Devi's credentials as the supreme warrior, leading also to the climax of this text, the slaying of Mahisasura himself. Having seen his armies destroyed the buffalo demon sent his chief attendants to kill the goddess. These great warriors were also dispatched by the Devi, who was named variously – Ambika (Mother) Bhadrakali (Fierce Kali) and Candika (Violent and Impetuous One) – indicating her various attributes.

Eventually only the Devi and Mahisasura were left to face each other in mortal combat,[103] the latter a formidable force in his buffalo form:

> Mahisasura, great in valour, pounded the earth with his hooves in rage, tossed up the high mountains with his horns, and bellowed terribly.
> Crushed by the velocity of his wheeling, the earth disintegrated, and lashed by his tail, the sea overflowed all round.
> Pierced by his swaying horns, the clouds went into fragments. Cast up by the blast of his breath, mountains fell down from the sky in hundreds.
> Seeing the great asura swollen with rage and advancing towards her, Candika displayed her wrath in order to slay him. (*Devi-Mahatmya* 3.25–8)[104]

During the ensuing battle, Mahisasura changed into numerous animal forms. As the Devi attacked one form, he changed into another. At the climax of the episode, Devi was described as drinking a divine drink until she became intoxicated, her eyes red, laughing aloud – clearly an unorthodox depiction. The goddess mimicked the *asura's* mood. When he was "swollen with rage" she, too, drew on the strength of anger before the battle commenced. In Hindu mythology, both Brahmanical and local, anger is often a necessary emotion to cause an injection of power sufficient enough to overcome a difficult obstacle. Thus, just before the final blows were struck, Devi became intoxicated – a parallel to Mahisasura, who was intoxicated with his own strength and valour. Eventually the *asura* reverted to the form of a buffalo and it was at this point that Candika finally captured him. As he emerged in human shape from the mouth of his buffalo form, the Devi decapitated him:

> Having spoken thus and springing up, she mounted the great Asura.
> Having struck him with her foot, she beat him with her spear.
> Then he, struck with her foot, came forth out of his own mouth,
> Completely hemmed in by the valour of the Goddess.
> That great Asura, who had come forth halfway fighting, was felled by the Goddess,
> Who had cut off his head with a great sword. (*Devi-Mahatmya* 3. 37–9)[105]

One of the most familiar images of the goddess Durga, representing one aspect of divine energy (*sakti*), is of this great, divine, female warrior effortlessly killing a buffalo-headed demon, her beauty and incredible strength shining forth as she deals the deathblow with her trident. Although the text offers the first conceptualization of an all-inclusive feminine divine force – Mahadevi or simply Devi – it is the slaying of Mahisasura that has captured the hearts and minds of the Hindu population. In Bengal, skilled craftsmen work all year creating huge tableaux of the ten-armed Durga dealing the final blow to Mahisasura's buffalo form just as he tries to escape from it. Richly decorated and displayed in temporary pavilions (*pandals*), the Durga images compete with each other in terms of beauty and splendour. This is the heart of the *Durga Puja* festival (detailed in chapter 6), during which the myths of Devi's many valorous deeds are recited.

At the end of the text, Devi explained the benefits of her worship, promising to return when she was needed. The king and the merchant duly worshipped the goddess and she finally appeared to them and granted their wishes. Two types of knowledge were bestowed on them: the king wished for an imperishable kingdom and a return to life, but the merchant chose the supreme knowledge of realization that removes the attachment of "I" and "mine" and so gained liberation (*moksa*).[106] Devi in the *Devi-Mahatmya* is able to amply supply both.

Goddesses in the *Sakta Puranas*

The *Sakta Puranas* are whole texts in which the Goddess is the supreme deity. Although the individual *Puranas* may give her different names, she is generally conceived of as "Mother of the universe" the "Supreme Reality" who is described in her manifested and unmanifested forms.[107] Texts that are available in printed form are the *Devi Purana*, the *Mahabhagavata Purana*, the *Kalika Purana*, the *Devi-Bhagavata Purana*, and of these four, only the last two have been translated into English. The *Puranas* were probably written to spread *Saktism* and, according to R. C. Hazra, who has undertaken an extensive study of them, they deal with how Devi is to be conceived of.[108] Although there are remnants of *Vedic* deities such as the Earth Mother, Prthivi, contained in Devi's character, generally her over-riding personality, which is pleased with blood-sacrifice and liquor, is non-*Vedic*. Hazra maintains that the forms of Devi found in the *Sakta Puranas* are based on popular aboriginal goddesses, many of whom had a fierce warrior nature or were deities associated with vegetation. He claims:

> We do not know the number and names of the female deities originally worshipped by these aboriginal tribes, and among the Sakta deities of the Puranas and Tantras there are certainly some who owe their origin to the deification of abstract ideas; but it admits of little doubt that many of the Sakta deities of the Puranas and Tantras, viz., Uma, Kausiki, Vindhyavasini, Durga, Candi, Kali, Kalika, Camunda, Kamakhya, Sakambhari and others, were modelled on the popular ones, especially those associated with mountains, viz., Himalaya and Vindhya.[109]

The *Devi Purana* is the earliest of the *Sakta Puranas*, probably written, according to Hazra, during the latter part of the sixth century CE in Bengal.[110] The *Devi Purana* is most often absent from the lists of eighteen *puranas* or minor (*upa*) *puranas*, possibly because of its *Tantric* character at a time when this form of worship was not acceptable. Hazra poses the idea that an earlier *Kalika Purana* existed that is now lost, but that this did not have a *Tantric* nature. However, the existing *Kalika Purana*, and the *Mahabhagavata Purana*, do contain many *Tantric* ideas. They are perhaps included because they were written much later, when those ideas were more widely accepted.

Although the *Devi Purana* does not mention the *Devi-Mahatmya*, it does include a different version of the Mahisa myth. In chapters 4–9 and 13–20 the goddess Uma is described as Yoganidra and Adyasakti who came to earth and rode on a lion consisting of all the gods and goddesses. In this form, she was known as Vindhyavasini, because she created the illusion of herself as a virgin girl in the Vindhya Mountains. She attracted the demon, Ghora, who had grown too powerful and was threatening the power balance between the gods and demons. When Ghora assumed the form of a buffalo (*mahisa*), the goddess killed him, being known thereafter as the killer of Mahisa.[111] Interestingly, the Goddess in this text most often appears as Vindhyavasini who, at the time, had a famous temple in Tamluk. Analogous is the goddess Kamakhya, whose important temple in Assam (see chapter 7) features most prominently in the later *Sakta Puranas*.

The *Mahabhagavata Purana* is, according to Hazra, a "comparatively late work" which was probably written during the tenth and eleventh centuries of the Christian era, in or near to Bengal.[112] Its opening verses present Devi as Adyaprakrti who created the world of her own accord. She is often depicted as the wife of Siva, referred to in the text as Sambhu. However, the text clearly portrays Devi as the source or creator of Brahma, Visnu and Siva (the *trimurti*). She created *Purusa* and stimulated it to create the gods from its three manifest components, *rajas* (the energetic nature of Brahma), *sattva* (the purity of Visnu), and *tamas* (the destructive nature of Siva).

The author of the *Mahabhagavata Purana* was undoubtedly influenced by *Tantra*, as is clear in its inclusion of *Tantric* forms of goddess worship and of its account of Sati, who appears in a much more forceful incarnation than she does in other texts. To a certain extent the author tried to combine *Vedanta* and *Tantrism* as at one point Devi says: "O Samkara, the Agama [Tantric texts] and the Veda are my two hands with which I sustain the whole universe consisting of stationary and moving objects."[113] The *Mahabhagavata Purana* contains the oldest account of the *Dasamahavidyas*, ten forms of the goddess who represent supreme knowledge (examined in chapter 4). Their inclusion is bound up in the account of Sati's immolation, an important myth in each of the *Sakta Puranas*, which is detailed in the next chapter. On first appearance in most myths, the goddess Sati falls most readily into the category of pure, benign goddesses. However, this is only one side of her inherently dualistic nature, for according to the Sati myth in the *Mahabhagavata Purana*, she was anxious to go to her father's sacrifice although she had not been invited. She tried unsuccessfully to persuade her husband, Siva, to give his permission for her to go. However, when her supplication failed, Sati decided to remind Siva exactly who she was. What is most significant in this account is that her fierce aspect represents Sati's power, and this is presented initially as the goddess Kali. Confronted by her fierce form, Siva tried to turn away from her but she produced other forms until the *Dasamahavidyas*, ten forms of transcendent knowledge, surrounded him:

> Seeing the goddess with her lips trembling with anger and her eyes blazing like the conflagration at the end of an aeon, Siva closed his eyes. Suddenly she displayed her terrible teeth in her fierce mouth and laughed. Observing this, Siva became afraid and trembled with an averted face. With much difficulty he reopened his eyes and beheld a terrible form. Abandoning her golden clothes, Sati's skin became discoloured. She was nude with dishevelled hair, a lolling tongue and four arms; her black body was covered with sweat. Decorated with a garland of skulls, she was exceedingly fierce and had a frightful roar. On her head was a crescent moon and a crown as luminous as the rising sun. In this terrific form blazing with her own effulgence, she roared and stood in all her glory before Siva. Bewildered with fright, Siva forsook her and trembling with an averted face, he fled in all directions as if deluded.[114]

The *Mahabhagavata Purana* clearly shows that within her meek and accommodating exterior Sati, as the personification of *sakti*, also contains the contrasting aspect of terrible cosmic force. Sati's representation of her most powerful aspect is considerably less pure – her body "covered with sweat", "wearing a garland of skulls" – than her pure, benign form. Sati shows that although she most often *chooses* to present herself as the consort of Siva, content to carry out his wishes, in reality *she is* the power underlying the entire cosmos, subject to the will of no one, and encompassing all duality.

The Kalika Purana

The *Kalika Purana*, a text compiled in the middle of the ninth century, was written in Assam to "popularize the cult of *Sakti*, particularly the mother goddess Kamakhya"[115] (see chapter 7). However, the text clearly begins, and emphasizes throughout, that the goddess takes many forms. Therefore, in the second verse of the *Purana*, the writer asserts: "Let that Maya protect you; (She is) Visnumaya [one of the 16 names of Durga, according to Shastri] because of her alluring charm of all the living beings, who like the sun dispels the darkness of ignorance (*avidya*) from the mind of the ascetics, who is the cause of their salvation, and destroys the evil desire in the pure mind of the people."[116]

The vision of the divine feminine presented in the *Kalika Purana* is a more positive one than that of those in which a male deity is the principal god. Like other *puranas* it is "encyclopaedic in contents and exhaustive in treatment of subjects".[117] Shastri points out the importance of the *puranic* texts, which he says are, "the philosophy of life to the people of their time . . . The *Puranas* are always popular with the masses of this subcontinent because they are accessible and intelligible to one and all, because they disseminate knowledge to the people of all strata of the society through popular myths and legends, which directly appeal to the human heart."[118]

The nature of goddess worship in the *Kalika Purana* is not uniform and no special system is advanced. There are many passages concerned with ritual and the procedure for worship. It is perhaps most famous for its chapter on animal and human sacrifice, an aspect of worship that will be examined in chapter 5. There is also a concrete picture of the goddess, of her forms, and her mythology, which accompany the less tangible, more philosophical passages. In this text, the goddess is most often in the form of Kamakhya, though it is also at pains to provide her cosmic perspective. The text claims:

> Kamakhya is Mahamaya herself, who has always been praised to be the fundamental form (cause); though she is known by different names according to her manifestation in different seats (*pithas*) in reality she is the same. (*Kalika Purana* 58. 52)[119]
>
> Mahamaya is called Kamakhya by gods and men because of her coming to the mountain (Nilakuta) for enjoying sexual pleasure.
>
> Just as a man is called parasol bearer (*chatri*) when he carries a parasol (over his head), and a person is called bather (*snapaka*) when he bathes (people) the same way the Goddess is called Kamakhya i.e. that is the etymology of the name Kamakhya.
>
> She is Kamada when moves [sic] hither and thither sitting on the lion. She who takes her shape at will, likes to sit sometimes on the white ghost, at other times on the red lotus and still at other times on the back of the lion. When the Goddess stands on the red lotus the lion stands in front of her. (*Kalika Purana* 58. 54–5, 59–60)[120]

The red lotus represents Brahma, the white ghost is Siva and the lion stands for Visnu. Whereas other *Sakta* texts, such as *Devi-Mahatmya* and the *Devi-Bhagavatam*, stress that Sakti is the power behind the gods, the *Kalika Purana* implies that Brahma, Visnu and Siva (the *trimurti*) are symbolic representations that the goddess either stands on or rides upon. More overtly the text goes on to claim that: "The Goddess is one and everything together, the *Primordial* cause of the Universe and is also the embodiment of the world, she is always upheld by Brahma, Visnu and Siva."[121]

The Devi-Bhagavatam Purana

By far the largest and perhaps the most comprehensive *Sakta Purana* is the *Devi-Bhagavatam*, compiled five to ten centuries after the *Devi-Mahatmya*.[122] Although the "inspirational seed"[123] of the *Devi-Bhagavatam* was, according to Cheever Mackenzie Brown, the *Devi-Mahatmya*, the later text "represents a justification or vindication of the Goddess tradition, as well as an elaboration of it".[124] In the final chapter, the text is said to have originated in half a verse (*sloka*) that emanated from Devi and was then expanded by Brahma into the twelve books that comprise the 18,000 verses of the *Devi-Bhagavatam*. The text was apparently written to "satisfy the Sakti worshippers"[125] and as a *Sakta* response to the *Vaisnava Bhagavata Purana* and the *Bhagavad Gita*. There are striking similarities between Visnu's incarnations (*avataras*) that periodically appear to restore cosmic *dharma* and the many epic battles between Devi and the demons, after which power is restored to the gods. Kinsley describes the Goddess of the *Devi-Bhagavatam* as "a female version of Visnu",[126] except for her association with primal material nature (*prakrti*), illusion (*maya*) and ignorance (*avidya*). Lalye adds that the various forms taken by the Goddess in order to conquer the demons are characterized by the three *gunas* (*sattva*, the illuminating principle; *rajas*, the energetic principle; and *tamas*, darkness, inertia, dullness), the three attributes of material nature, representing potential and kinetic energy.[127]

Perhaps the most fundamental concern in the *Devi-Bhagavatam* is, according to Kinsley, "to demonstrate that the supreme deity in the universe is a goddess to whom all male deities are subordinate".[128] This argument is made through philosophical treatises and often in the re-writing of well-known myths with a decidedly *Sakta* bias; some being blatant whereas others advance their points in a subtle manner. In one verse the author says: "O Mother! When Thou dost will to create this visible Universe, Thou createst first Brahma, Visnu and Mahesvara [Siva] and makest them create, preserve and destroy this universe; but Thou remainest quite unattached to the world."[129] In another, Devi herself skilfully and directly reminds the gods that they are totally dependent on her, putting them in their place when they become too full of their own importance. The Goddess says: "Through My Grace you have obtained victory in the battle. Know verily, that it is I that make you all dance like inert wooden dolls as My mere instruments. You are merely My functions. I am the Integral Whole. I give sometimes victory to you and sometimes victory to the Daityas [demons]."[130]

An important part of the *Devi-Bhagavatam* are chapters 30–40 in book seven, referred to as the *Devi Gita* (*Song of the Goddess*). It was written as a *Sakta* alternative to the famous *Bhagavad Gita*, the teachings of Krsna. In the same way that Krsna explained his relationship to the world and revealed his cosmic identity to Arjuna in the *Bhagavad Gita*, the Goddess also explains that as Mahamaya she is the source of creation and she too reveals her cosmic form. The following nine verses are said to contain the essential teachings of the *Devi Gita*. They also represent a type of *mantra* which, if repeated daily, "is viewed as a quick and potent means to bring the presence of the Goddess directly into one's life, providing the same worldly and spiritual benefits as other more complex forms of worshiping and meditating upon the Devi".[131]

1. We know you as Mahalaksmi, we meditate on you as the Sakti of all.
May the Goddess inspire the knowledge and meditation of ours.
2. Hail to her in the form of the Cosmic Body; hail to her in the form of the Cosmic Soul;
Hail to her in the Unmanifest State; hail to her in the form of the glorious Brahman.
3. Through her power of ignorance (avidya and maya), she shows herself as the world, like a rope appearing as a serpent, wreath, and the like.
Through her power of knowledge (vidya), she dissolves the world back into herself. We glorify her, Ruler of the Universe (Bhuvaneshvari).
[The Goddess describes her power known as Maya.]
4. [Maya is variously called] knowledge, illusion, matter, nature, energy, or the unborn.
Those versed in Saiva works call it intelligence.
5. From a practical point of view, Maya is regarded as self-evident.
In reality, however, it does not exist—only the supreme exists, in an absolute sense.
[The Goddess outlines the basic spiritual practices for realizing the supreme unity of Self, the Goddess, and Brahman.]
6. [My sacred syllable Hrim] transcends the distinction of "name" and "named", beyond all dualities.
It is whole, infinite being, consciousness and bliss. One should meditate on that reality within the flaming light of consciousness.

7. Fixing the mind upon me as the Goddess transcending all space and time,
One quickly merges with me through realizing the oneness of the soul and Brahman.
8. Just this Brahman is immortal; in front is Brahman, behind is Brahman, on the right and the left;
It extends above and below. The whole universe is just this Brahman, the greatest.
9. Like clarified butter hidden in milk, knowledge dwells in every being;
One should stir continuously, using the mind as the churning stick.[132]

The ideas presented in these verses are not new. The first verse, for example, is in the form of the Gayatri *mantra* that appeared in the *Rg Veda* 3. 62. 10, and represents a way of summoning the Goddess.[133] The verses draw on ideas formulated in the *Upanisads* (the Brahman-Atman synthesis) and make allusions to renowned philosophical ideas (Sankara's famous rope appearing as a snake analogy in *Advaita Vedanta*). However, they consistently place the Goddess at the heart of those ideas. The Goddess is identical with Brahman; as Mahamaya, she is the source of ignorance about the reality of the world, but she also offers the knowledge to gain liberation (*moksa*).

The Goddess is clearly presented in the *Devi-Bhagavatam* as the supreme power of the universe, the Adyasakti. Her many names provide a glimpse of her multifarious nature. She is Mahamaya (Power of Illusion), Devesi (Ruler of the Gods), Paramesvari (Supreme Ruler); as well as these grand incarnations she is also Kumari (Virgin or Maiden), Ramaniyangi (Beautiful of Limb), but one of her most abiding forms in the *Devi-Bhagavatam* is Bhuvanesvari (Ruler of the Universe).[134] The *Devi-Bhagavatam* provides a kind of encyclopaedic mix of goddess mythology, ritual practice and metaphysical discussion. The Goddess that emerges in the text represents all-inclusive feminine power. However, unlike the rather lofty and inaccessible conception of Brahman, the Goddess, mainly through her heroic deeds, remains engaged with the world for, as Lalye points out: "The Devi combines in Herself the qualities of the kind, the heroic and the prophetic and thus becomes the grand saviour of mankind."[135]

In this chapter, we have only examined a few of the many goddesses that pervade Hindu sacred textual literature. Clearly the goddesses in these sources are numerous and varied. Their respective popularity ebbs and flows like a tide, which sees various goddesses becoming popular while others fall away into obscurity. By looking at the sources in a chronological order we can detect a development of sorts: as goddesses, in general, appear to become more popular, culminating in significant power in the later *Sakta* texts. Although they have not been dealt with in this chapter, *Tantric* texts, beliefs and practices, also represent an important influence in the popularity and the way in which Hindu goddesses have been regarded. *Tantric* ideas and modes of worship have become integrated in many textual sources and patterns of belief mostly, but not only, in association with *Sakta* religion. However, we should not lose sight of the fact that textual sources only offer us one piece of the jigsaw; the deities of the majority of the population – who are in many cases, goddesses – do not appear in written form, their religion being based instead on oral tradition. Although some of the goddesses we have examined are not orthodox and may well have originated from non-Aryan sources, they are still largely presented in more palatable, orthodox or Brahmanical forms.

3 Goddess Mythology

Most cultures are rich in both religious and secular mythical stories that are part of ancient tradition and historical folklore. Hinduism is no exception. Like other cultures, Hinduism has its tales of brave heroes, beautiful maidens, evil demon kings, and legends that recount the unbelievable and miraculous. It is the Classical period of Hinduism that is particularly rich in such myths, contrasting with the more philosophical and speculative material of the *Upanisads*. A rich and varied mythology also abounds in the *Puranas* and in such myths deities are graphically portrayed as entities in their own right despite the fact that they are ultimately aspects of one transcendent Absolute. Goddesses are no exception, and the stories and legends of their origins and their many deeds have been transmitted as much orally as in the rich literature that is a component of the Hindu canon. Brahmanical mythology makes the lofty orthodox goddesses accessible to the whole population. Those with access to textual sources are able to read for themselves the exploits of the many gods and goddesses that make up the Hindu pantheon. Those who cannot read the texts of Hinduism have access through storytellers and, more recently, through film and television. A voracious appetite exists in India for the regular television dramatizations of the Indian epics. Passing through villages on a balmy Indian night, it is quite common to see a village community huddled round the communal television set enjoying the current episode of the *Ramayana* or the *Mahabharata*. All eyes are glued to the screen, following the heroes that are loved so dearly, replaying the dramas the audience know so well. For the majority of the Indian people, mythology constitutes their religious knowledge and experience; it is the main source of information about their gods and goddesses. Many myths have a number of versions and local mythology, in particular, is often adapted to include links to a certain community or a geographical location.

Brahmanical mythology

It is the great epics, the *Ramayana* and the *Mahabharata*, and the many *Puranas*, which relate the stories of India's myriad gods and goddesses. Filled with tales of epic battles fought between gods and demons, and the struggles of individual deities to gain recognition and power, the Brahmanical myths humanize the orthodox deities of Hinduism, making them more accessible to the general populace. Through Brahmanical mythology, ordinary people can relate their own experiences to those of the gods and goddesses. It allows them to understand their characters, their strengths and weaknesses. For instance, through the stories in the *Devi-Mahatmya*, it is easy to identify with the anger of the goddess as well as her satisfaction at conquering the demons (*asuras*) that threaten cosmic order. The *Puranas* inspire wonder as the goddess Sri or Laksmi appears from the milk ocean or marvel as Parvati reveals her celestial, all-encompassing form to Himavat. Through Brahmanical mythology, the reader or listener can sympathize with emotional pain, such as that which Siva experienced when his beloved Sati killed herself (or more correctly, withdrew herself from her body). Through such myths, then, the entire range of emotional experience is portrayed to arrest the senses of the listener or reader.

Although the majority of *puranic* texts are concerned with portraying the supremacy of particular gods, there are also many stories concerning the deeds of the goddesses. However, it was not until relatively late (*c.* 500–600 CE) that a collection of goddess myths was gathered, the earliest being the *Devi-Mahatmya*. From the vast store of Brahmanical stories circulating in India, here are just a few of the many goddess myths.

The descent of Ganga

The story of Ganga's descent from heaven to earth is narrated in many texts including the two epics, the *Ramayana* and the *Mahabharata*. The goddess Ganga was the eldest daughter of Himavat, and lived with the gods. Her descent from the abode of the gods to the abode of mortals started with the human King Sagara, whose name in Sanskrit means Ocean. Through austerity, King Sagara gained the boon of children for his two childless wives. Kesini (Saibya) had one son and his other wife,

Sumati (Vaidarbhi), had 60,000 sons,[1] for Sumati gave birth to a pumpkin gourd, which contained 60,000 seeds. The seeds were planted in pots of *ghee* (clarified butter) or milk and they became Sagara's 60,000 sons. After some time, Sagara decided to perform the *asvamedha* (horse sacrifice),[2] the greatest sacrifice he could offer the gods. As tradition dictated, Sagara released a horse to wander under the protective gaze of his 60,000 sons. However, the horse disappeared and no trace of it could be found on the earth. Sagara's 60,000 sons next searched the netherworld, entering through a huge hole. They immediately spotted the horse grazing next to the sage Kapila who was deep in meditation. Unfortunately, Sagara's sons disregarded the sage and went to get the horse, thinking that he had taken it. Angered by their lack of respect, Kapila reduced them to ashes with his fiery glance.

Sagara eventually learned of his sons' fate and sent for his grandson, Ansuman (Amsumat) – his only other son proving to be cruel and worthless. Ansuman, however, was a righteous man. Sagara sent him to look for his uncles and to bring back the sacrificial horse. In due course, Ansuman found his uncles' ashes and the white horse, still in the company of Kapila. He paid due respect to the powerful sage and in return was offered a boon. If the heavenly river Ganga could come and wash over the ashes, her salvific power would liberate the souls of the sons of Sagara. Ansuman then returned with the horse to King Sagara and helped him to complete the *asvamedha* sacrifice.

Unfortunately, despite all his efforts, Sagara died without seeing Ganga brought to earth as did Ansuman's son, Dilipa. However, Dilipa's son, Bhagiratha, gave his kingdom to the care of his minister and devoted all his attention to gaining favour from the goddess Ganga. Bhagiratha went to the Himalayas where he practised austerities for one thousand years. Pleased with his perseverance, Ganga appeared to him in her bodily form.[3] In the *Ramayana* version of this myth, Bhagiratha, rewarded for his penances by Brahma, was advised that only Siva would be able to stop Ganga destroying the world in her descent. In both versions of the myth, Bhagiratha then petitioned Siva for a further period. Siva finally agreed to break Ganga's fall and, standing on top of Mount Kailasa, he caught her in his matted locks. As a result, one of his many names is Gangadhara meaning "Bearer of the Ganges".[4] Once her destructive force had been dissipated in Siva's hair, Bhagiratha led Ganga to the hole leading to *patala* (the netherworld). She poured over the ashes of Sagara's sons and filled up the ocean.

The legend reminds the Hindu that perseverance and penance will bring reward. Hence, Benjamin Walker claims: "The name Bhagiratha is proverbial for persistence and determination, and the achievement of any difficult objective is referred to as the result of 'Bhagiratha prayatnam', the Labours or Perseverance of Bhagiratha."[5] In some mythological accounts of her descent to earth she is said to have split into seven streams as she emerged from Siva's matted locks; "three flowing to the east, three to the west, and the Bhagirathi to the south".[6]

To this day, a yearly bathing festival is held on the last day of the lunar month of *pausa* (*pausa samkranti*) on Sagara Island in the Bay of Bengal where the river Ganges meets the sea. On the island, reached only by boat, is the monastic refuge (*asram*) of the legendary saint Kapila. All types of people gather at Ganga-Sagara for the festival celebrating the liberation of King Sagara's 60,000 sons. Their freedom heralded Ganga's liberating force that now extends to the whole of India. Although it is usually deserted, once a year the island comes to life with ascetics, pilgrims, prostitutes, and hawkers of every kind. They all wait for the auspicious moment – dictated by planetary positions and announced by the festival organizers – before rushing into the water to take advantage of its healing power. Once the festival is over and everyone has drifted away, the island returns to its tranquil state until the temporary revitalization that the next festival brings.

The churning of the milk ocean

The myth of the churning of the ocean of milk appears in a number of the *Puranas* as well as the two epics, the *Mahabharata* and the *Ramayana*. It is seldom included in selections of goddess mythology though it is an occasion when the goddess Sri or Laksmi – the names being interchangeable – makes an important appearance. This myth is primarily concerned with the tortoise (*kurma*) incarnation (*avatara*) of the great god Visnu. The churning of the milk ocean was precipitated by the withdrawal from the world of good fortune, symbolized by the goddess Sri. The act of churning the milk ocean produced an incarnation of Sri, who returned her grace to the world. There are variations of this myth although the majority include the following details.

The events of the legend are caused by the curse of the sage Durvasas, either considered a part of Siva as in the *Visnu Purana* 1.9 or a great ascetic who had amassed a powerful store of heat accumulated by ascetic practices (*tapas*) as in the *Padma Purana* 4.8ff. Durvasas was given a divine garland by the goddess in recognition of his devotion to her. On meeting the god Indra, riding on his elephant, Durvasas decided to honour the god by offering him the sacred garland. Indra graciously accepted the garland, but put it on his elephant's head. However, the divine garland excited the elephant to such a degree that it slipped to the ground and he accidentally trampled on it. Durvasas was furious. Feeling that his gift had been slighted he flew into a rage and cursed Indra saying: "Since, you being endowed with the glory of the three worlds, are thinking lightly (of me), there is no doubt that your glory of the three worlds would perish."[7]

The curse of Durvasas decreed that good fortune would disappear from the world. Consequently, the goddess Sri or Laksmi withdrew herself and her power of wealth and good fortune. The result of the curse was devastating. Initially, religious practices were no longer maintained, and the land and the people diminished. The myth emphasizes that the world of humans and gods breaks down without Sri's power of good fortune. With good fortune gone, it was easy for misfortune to invade and take over the world, and the demons, called *daityas* or *danavas*, became powerful – *asuras*, of course, thrive in such a climate of religious neglect. The gods fought the demons but their *tapas* had gone and they were, therefore, powerless. In desperation, they approached the great god Brahma, asking him what they should do. Brahma suggested that they seek the help of Visnu, who told them to churn the ocean of milk to acquire the elixir of life. Visnu also told them that they must persuade the demons to help them churn the ocean using Mount Mandara as a churning stick, and the divine serpent Vasuki as the rope. Visnu, as an *avatara* in the form of a tortoise, promised to support the mountain. Coiling Vasuki around mount Mandara, the gods should pull one end of the snake while the demons should pull the other. However, Visnu promised the gods that though the demons were helping them, he would ensure that they did not get the elixir.

When the ocean of milk was churned, fourteen precious things emerged from it, including the goddess Sri:

> While the Ocean was being churned again Sri herself directly manifested herself delighting with her glance the three worlds, surpassing the splendour of all.
> All Suras, Asuras, men desired to get hold of her but nobody could approach her brilliance and power.
> Knowing her to be Sri, by her holding a lotus in her hand, Vasava and God Brahma and others, who knew her, were highly delighted.[8]

Sri brought good fortune back into the world and the elixir of life brought power back to the gods. Although the demons managed to seize the elixir of life when it emerged from the milk ocean, Visnu assumed the form of a beautiful woman, Mohini and, true to his word, he deluded the demons into giving up their prize. After the gods had fortified themselves with the elixir, power was once more restored to them.

In the version of this myth provided by the *Bhagavata Purana* an interesting emphasis is laid on the appearance of Sri (referred to in this text as Laksmi) and her power of wealth and good fortune. In the previous myth, good fortune had departed from the world as Sri disappeared. Good fortune, a necessary element of the world, was restored when Sri reappeared during the churning of the milk ocean. However, the *Bhagavata Purana* suggests that the churning of the milk ocean created the first appearance of the goddess Sri in the world, leaving us questioning the source of good fortune before her appearance:

> And thereafter was manifested goddess Laksmi, the very embodiment of Affluence (Sri), the delight of (Rama), who is (absolutely) devoted to the glorious Lord. She illumined with her splendour all the quarters (making people residing therein desirous to have affluence), even as the flash of lightning does against the crystalline reflector like mountain Sudama.[9]

The text also offers a different perspective of wealth and good fortune, albeit a subtle one. For what is particularly interesting about this verse is that the appearance of the goddess triggers the desire in humans to acquire wealth. On consideration, this desire, instigated by Sri's appearance, may not be wholly beneficial. While the power of good fortune ensures that communities thrive, that misfortune is kept at bay, and that the maintenance and observance of religious duty can proceed, it stimulates the desire for wealth among humankind, a desire that is often accompanied by adversity.

The destruction of Daksa's sacrifice and the immolation of Sati

The account of the destruction of Daksa's sacrifice is particularly old, the origin of which may be found in the *Rig Veda*.[10] Although missing from the oldest versions of this myth, the later inclusion and development of the immolation of Daksa's daughter, Sati, has become one of the most important goddess myths.

The chain of events that led to the death of Sati began in the divine realm where it was decided that Siva was in need of a wife to necessitate the continuation of creation (*Kalika Purana* 7. 5). Devi agreed to be born as the daughter of Daksa, one of the mind-born sons of Brahma, in order to become Siva's wife (*Kalika Purana* 7. 1–3). The names Mahamaya (Great-illusion) and Visnumaya (Illusion of Visnu), by which the goddess is addressed in these verses, reminds the reader of her powers of illusion, allowing her to appear in many different guises. On earth, Daksa had been praying to the goddess for a long time for which he was duly rewarded by her appearance before him:

> Kali of the black complexion is seated on a lion, she has swelling high breasts, four arms, lovely face, a blue lotus and a sword in her two hands, while the other two hands are in *varada* (bestowing boon) and *abhayada* (removing fear) pose, she is with red eyes, lovely open hair, and endowed with all virtues, she looks charming; Daksa, the lord of the people, having seen Mahamaya in the above shape started praying her [sic] by lowering his head with great pleasure. (*Kalika Purana* 8. 9–11)[11]

Although the goddess is described in this verse as Kali, her iconographical description differs from the majority of images of Kali. She is described as riding a lion and holding a blue lotus and a sword in her two hands, whereas ordinarily Kali holds a severed head and stands upon the breast of Siva. However, Kali, and indeed the goddess, can take many shapes and forms, though ultimately all forms are one.

After many lifetimes of prayer, Daksa was offered the favour by the goddess of becoming his daughter (*Kalika Purana* 8. 30):

> The goddess says:
> O lord of the people! within no time I shall be born to your wife as your daughter and then shall be the wife of Hara. [Siva]
> But whenever you become less devoted to me I shall immediately give up this body, no matter whether I remain happy or otherwise.
> O lord of the people! in every circle of creation (pratisarga) I shall be born your daughter and become the consort of Hara; this boon is granted to you.[12]

She was called Sati, grew up, and married Siva as she wished. But the myths state that Daksa did not like his son-in-law at all. Some versions say he did not like Siva's habit of wearing skulls and animal skins, which is outside the normal sphere of orthodoxy. In other versions, (*Devi-Bhagavatam* 7. 30) Daksa received a divine garland from the sage Durvasas, which he placed in his bedroom. Excited by the scent of the garland he had sexual intercourse with his wife, which defiled the garland. As a punishment for his actions, Daksa created his own downfall by harbouring bad feelings towards Siva. Either way, when Daksa organized a grand sacrifice he invited all the gods, and according to some texts all creatures, but neglected to invite Siva and his wife Sati. When she discovered her father's slight on her husband and herself Sati became very angry. She was about to curse Daksa, when she remembered the bargain she had struck with him. In face of his lack of devotion to her, Sati prepared to leave the world, which she did by her own *yoga*:

> The daughter of Daksa having given her serious thought over the matter and remembering the terrible deeds of Daksa once again flew into a rage. Then Sati, with eyes turning red in anger by adopting a posture of yoga closed all the nine doors in her body and made an indistinguished sound (*sphota*).[13]
> By that sound (*sphota*) her spirit went out from her body by breaking the tenth door.[14]
> Then the gods in the heaven having seen her (Sati) dead, with eyes full of tears, made the loud exclamation of *ha ha* in sorrow. (*Kalika Purana* 16. 47–50)[15]

The version of this myth in the *Kalika Purana* is important as it emphasizes the control of the goddess in her own destiny. In most non-*Sakta* versions of Sati's immolation, she is portrayed as a wife who throws herself onto her father's sacrificial fire because she cannot endure the insult to her spouse. The *Kalika Purana* gives prominence to the calm and logical way in which Sati, through yoga, extinguished her life in this particular incarnation. On thinking about giving up her body, Sati wondered if she had fulfilled her purpose, as she had not provided Siva with a son. She eventually concluded that her purpose was to make Siva want a woman; although she was the only woman, he would ever want or could have. Therefore, Sati promised to return again in another form to be the wife of Siva once more. It is commonly accepted that she was reincarnated as the goddess Parvati.

When Siva discovered what had happened, he flew into a terrible rage and destroyed Daksa's sacrifice, cutting off his head and replacing it with that of a goat (*Devi-Bhagavatam* 7. 30. 40). He was extremely distressed at the death of Sati and became inconsolable, putting Sati's body on his shoulder and wandering about with it "like a madman" (*Kalika Purana* 18. 37). Unfortunately, by mourning in this way he was seriously threatening the world. The other gods, Brahma and Visnu, were fearful of Siva in this state and resolved to remove Sati's body in the hope of lessening Siva's anger and grief. They entered the body and disposed of it piece by piece (*Kalika Purana* 18. 39–40) or, as is recounted in another source (*Devi-Bhagavatam* 7. 30) Visnu cut it from Siva's shoulder with his arrows or discus.

This myth has been instrumental in systematizing the many geographical places where goddesses are worshipped scattered across India. When Sati immolated herself her body was cut into pieces by the other gods in order to lessen Siva's suffering. The places where her body parts fell are now referred to as *Sakta pithas* (seats of the goddess) and as such are considered especially powerful places of goddess worship (examined in chapter 7). Although there is no decisive list of how many pieces of Sati fell to earth or their exact location, it does not seem particularly important. India is undeniably infused with the power of the goddess, and to what extent individual places are defined is less important than grasping the idea of the interconnectedness of all life that this myth expresses and promotes.

Local mythology

As well as the rich Brahmanical goddess mythology that abounds, particularly in the *puranic* texts and the epics, there is also a wealth of local mythology, a significant portion of it concerning goddesses. It comprises a wealth of stories that are passed orally, or sometimes in written form, from one generation to the next. This is by far the greatest body of information about Hindu deities, though it is an aspect of Hinduism that is often disregarded or overlooked. Some local mythology might only be known in one village relating to a specific god or goddess, whereas other stories are taken from village to village by wandering storytellers. The periodic visit of the storyteller brings, not only local mythology to a wider audience, but also Brahmanical mythology to an audience that might not otherwise have access to the written texts. Occasionally, the mythology of the most popular local goddesses is written down and sold as pamphlets in the local vernacular. The most rich and varied mythology is represented in the many myths that are recited at festivals and fairs, or simply to pass away the evenings. Local mythology is a way of explaining various circumstances, such as how a particular god or goddess came to be worshipped in a specific place. Alternatively local mythology might provide some explanation for why and how certain illnesses, most commonly diseases, came about. Those living in rural settlements would know many Brahmanical myths, although some myths of Brahmanical origin have been adapted to suit

local deities. One such example is found in the Renuka myths that identify native goddesses as incarnations of a Brahmanical figure, providing
such goddesses with a measure of orthodoxy. Similarly, many rural
myths seek to validate their deities and to localize some pan-Indian
deities, placing them firmly in the rural setting. Finally, this mythology
helps to elevate humans, generally women, who have died a premature,
violent or unjust death, to the status of goddess. The type of woman who
might be eulogized in mythology is most often one whose honour was
violated or who became a *sati* (good woman) having burned herself on
her husband's funeral pyre. The following are a collection of stories that
provide an insight into the richness and variety of local goddess
mythology.

Origin mythology

Local mythology often tells us something of the origins of local
goddesses, explaining how they came to be worshipped and, in many
cases, how they came to a particular village or town. The following
origin myths were collected from two communities in India, the village
settlement of Khurdapur[16] in Orissa and the small but ancient town of
Colavandan in Tamilnadu.[17]

In the village settlement of Khurdapur, situated about 12 km from
the state capital of Bhubaneswar, the goddess Ma Khanduala resides in
a small temple under the shade of a large banyan tree. She is represented
anthropomorphically (in human form) by a black statue with piercing
silver eyes. Until the last few years, she was represented by a rock
covered in glossy vermilion and silver eyes. She lived in a small shrine
at the base of the tree until her temple was completed. What is intriguing
about this goddess is how she had come to be worshipped there in the
first place. Ma Khanduala's mythology states that many years ago trees
covered the whole area where Khurdapur is now situated. There was no
settlement, just isolated dwellings. One night a pious man had an incredible dream. In this dream, a goddess came to him requesting that he make
a place for her to live under a small tree. The goddess told him that she
was currently in a place called Bhatarika, 40–50 km to the south. The
man complied with her wishes, placing a stone at the base of a nearby
banyan tree. The goddess approved of his choice and has lived there ever
since.

Ma Khanduala is not the only goddess to originate from outside
Khurdapur, nor is she the only goddess whose beginnings were in
Bhatarika. Also from Bhatarika is the goddess Bana (forest) Durga,

simply represented (until the 1999 cyclone in Orissa) by a mango tree adorned with a delicate flower garland and some red bangles. According to the owner of the mango grove where she resided, she was brought to Khurdapur by his great, great paternal grandfather. This man had gone to Bhatarika to immerse the ashes of a deceased relative in the deep water there. During the night, a goddess came to him in a dream and asked that he should take a small statue of her back with him and worship her. This he did, and for some time he kept this statue in his house. Eventually the goddess came to him in a dream, requesting that he move her outside. Initially unsure where to place her, he went outside and saw a small mango tree that seemed an ideal place for her to reside. In due course, it was accepted that the soul or essence of the goddess had permeated the tree, and the statue was, therefore, redundant. Bana Durga remained in the small mango tree until thirty-five years ago when she moved to the mango grove, after the destruction of her original tree.

Another type of origin myth that seems common among local deities, and even some pan-Indian deities, is the discovery of a bleeding stone. In Tamilnadu, one such myth is told in the small town of Colavandan, about fifty minutes by bus from the ancient city of Madurai. A goddess attracted attention to herself by causing a disturbance. She was secreted in a clump of bushes not far from the town, but the reason for this is unknown. For many months, anyone who passed by a certain clump of bushes was hampered in their journey, causing a good deal of consternation among those who regularly passed that way. Eventually, armed with spades and a certain amount of trepidation a party of *Pariahs* (*Dalits*) and agricultural workers set off to try to discover the source of their annoyance. Suddenly, while poking about in the bushes, the spade of one of the men struck a stone. To their amazement, blood seeped out of it. It was then that they realized that it must be a goddess. There must have been quite a commotion as the bleeding stone, representing the goddess, was brought back to their settlement. Since then, this particular deity has been worshipped as Jenakai Mariyamman (i.e. Mariyamman of the ancient town of Jenakai, now called Colavandan), eventually occupying a position in the centre of town.

Renuka myths

The priests at the Mariyamman temple in Colavandan tell another origin myth, commonly associated with the south Indian regional goddess Mariyamman, the goddess of smallpox.[18] The local mythology of Mariyamman is elaborately entwined with that of a woman called

Renuka. Renuka was originally a Brahmanical character that appears in a relatively minor incident in the *Mahabharata*, which has developed into an important local legend.[19] The Colavandan version of this myth is related to their own goddess, Jenakai Mariyamman, but the same may be repeated elsewhere. Jenakai Mariyamman was originally Renuka Devi, the wife of a Saint, Jamadakini Munivar, said to be a form of Siva. Each morning, using her great powers, Renuka would bring water from the river in a pot made of sand. One day, the god Indra flew overhead and she saw and admired his reflection in her pot of water. At that moment, the pot broke and she was then unable to remake it. Her husband was angry with her and asked his sons, in turn, to behead their mother. Only Parasurama, the youngest, followed his father's instructions, and chasing his mother to a nearby wood, he beheaded her. Parasurama then went back to his father, who offered him a boon for his obedience. Parasurama asked for his mother's life back, but when they went to restore her, they found her body but not her head. The only head to be found was a very fierce one with fangs, which they put on Renuka's body. The *Mahabharata* version of this myth corresponds with its main events although Renuka is simply restored to life. In several versions of this myth, Parasurama also cut off the head of a *Pariah* woman. When Renuka was restored to life, the Brahman head of Renuka on the untouchable body became Mariyamman and the untouchable head on the Brahman body became another goddess, Yellama.[20] The Colavandan myth in which Renuka/Mariyamman's head is replaced with a fierce one is exclusive to this particular goddess (Jenakai Mariyamman), so far as I am aware.

Other versions of the Renuka myth emphasize Mariyamman's connection with smallpox. According to one myth, there was a Saint by the name of Jamadakini and his wife called Renukai (Renuka):

Jamadakini Munivar died because of his son. Renukai became *sati* [immolated herself on her husband's funeral pyre]. While Renukai was committing *sati*, Indra showered rain [upon the fire] and she was saved, but her body was burned. Because of the burning, she had many blisters. She wore a *margosa*-leaf dress because her body needed covering. Some of the people from the lowest caste [scheduled castes, *Harijans*] noticed her and could tell that she was a Brahman. She was therefore unable to eat their [cooked] food so they offered her some raw rice powder, (Tam. *paccarici*), *jaggery* (Tam. *vellam*), tender coconut water, tamarind and a sugar drink [made of *jaggery* and spices] (Tam. *panakam*). At that time the lords from heaven, *devas*, appeared and said that if any problems, like blisters, come to the people, especially those who helped her [Renukai], they could use *margosa* leaves and the same foods that they had given her and these would cure them. All these ingredients should also be used for *abhisheka* [ritual bathing] dedicated to her.[21]

Two other stories provide accounts of the connection between the goddess Mariyamman and smallpox.[22] In one, she is associated with the wife of the sage Piruhu. When Brahma, Visnu and Siva came one day to test her reputed virtue, she turned them into children. In their anger they in turn made her beauty fade and her skin become pox marked; she then became known as the goddess of smallpox. The second myth claims that Mariyamma (Mariyamman), the wife of the poet Tiruvallar, was able to cure herself of smallpox by fanning herself with *margosa* leaves. When she was fully recovered, she was worshipped as the goddess of smallpox and people hung *margosa* leaves over their doorway in an effort to ward off the disease.

The origin of smallpox in south India

Mariyamman is not the only goddess associated with smallpox. In another south Indian myth the goddess Bhadrakali is closely related to the disease. According to this myth, Siva created a goddess called Bhadrakali (Bhadra meaning fierce) to kill the demon Daruka.[23] A long battle took place between Daruka and Bhadrakali, during which time the demon's wife, Manodari, performed austerities in order to obtain a boon from Siva to save her husband. Siva was reluctant to give the boon, but in the end he had to relent because Manodari's *tapas* (power or heat accumulated by ascetic practices) was so strong. Siva gave Manodari a few drops of sweat from his body,[24] saying: "Worry thyself not over thy husband; whenever thou art in need sprinkle a few drops of Our sweat on men, and they shall give thee the best of whatever they have."[25] In the meantime, Bhadrakali killed Daruka and in her anger, Manodari threw the sweat at the goddess. Bhadrakali was immediately stricken with smallpox. Siva, who was inadvertently the cause of the goddess's misfortune, tried to help her by creating a goblin out of his ear, called Ghandakarna. Siva sent Ghandakarna to lick off the spots from Bhadrakali's body, but as he was about to lick her face the goddess stopped him, saying: "Let those rashes on my face remain there as a sort of ornament for me. You are my brother; it is not proper, therefore, that your face should come in contact with mine."[26] When Bhadrakali had recovered from her ordeal, Manodari was brought before her. In retribution; "her limbs and ears were cut off, and her eyes blinded, and she was asked to remain with the goddess as her vassal".[27] Manodari was renamed Vasurimala or "Pox-garland", and it is she who is blamed for epidemics as she carries out Kali's bidding. The only sense that Vasurimala possesses is smell; therefore, strong-smelling food should not be cooked near a smallpox house. Although Bhadrakali is quite clearly related to the outbreak of smallpox in this myth, in her many local incarnations she is not overtly associated with disease of any sort.

Mythology that validates local goddesses

An important function of local mythology is to define the relationship between local goddesses and pan-Indian goddesses, most commonly the goddesses Parvati and Durga. Ma Mangala, a popular regional goddess in Orissa, offers a clear example of the form such associations often take. In Orissa, the goddess Mangala is considered one of the *saktis* that Durga produced during her epic struggle with the demon Mahisasura as related in the *Devi-Mahatmya*.[28] In the generally available orthodox versions of this text, Mangala is not mentioned as an epithet of the Devi. However, she is mentioned in chapter 79 of the *Devi Purana*, where twelve forms of Devi are recorded: among them is Mangala, meaning auspicious.[29] Nevertheless, the Orissan myth, reproduced and sold in pamphlets entitled *Mangala Mahapurana*, asserts the Mangala–Durga connection. It states that Ma Durga is called Mangala because one day, after she had fought with Mahisasura, she became very tired, but the demon still had plenty of energy. He dropped her in the middle of the ocean and she was helpless. Durga breathed out and gave birth to a baby girl who immediately grew into a goddess. The goddess held onto one hand of the demon while Durga held the other hand, and together they pulled him out of the ocean and killed him. Because the goddess had benefited everyone, she was called Mangala (Auspicious); Durga decreed that she should receive *puja* everywhere.[30] Their devotees consider many other local goddesses to be *saktis* produced by Durga or the Mahadevi, particularly in relation to her battle with Mahisasura.

The snake goddess Manasa's history appears to follow a familiar pattern in that her origins are most likely among the folk deities of Bengal despite later mythological accounts that claim Siva as her father. Manasa's original characteristics and origin mythology, it seems, have been adapted to suit the ideals of the higher classes. By examining the myths in the *Manasa-mangals* (devotional poetry to her) it is possible to discern the struggle of the goddess, either in terms of Brahmanical influence or by the efforts of the Bengali poets to raise her status, in trying to establish her cult as being a legitimate part of the Hindu pantheon. Manasa is the goddess of snakes but she is unusual as she is the only snake goddess (according to Stutley and Stutley) who is not a snake herself.[31] She is presented as the sister of Vasuki and the mother of Astika who was born to save the snakes from destruction in the great snake sacrifice of King Janamejaya, to avenge the death of his father who was killed by the mighty serpent Taksaka.[32]

Manasa is also mentioned in the first book of the *Mahabharata* where she is married to the sage Jarutkaru and subsequently gives birth to Astika. Her marriage to the sage is the only part of her myth which occurs in the *Puranas* and the *Manasa-mangals*. The *Manasa-mangals*, although thought to be the oldest in the *mangal-kavya* tradition, are considered to be later than the *Puranas* and in fact draw some of their material from them. The *Puranas*, on the other hand, deliberately ignore any folk myths, prompting Smith to complain: "Their accounts are almost totally purged of folk elements."[33]

Mythology that localizes pan-Indian goddesses

Local mythology also places pan-Indian, Brahmanical deities in a local context, associating them with a particular place. The goddess Kali seems very popular in local forms in Tamilnadu. Small and large settlements alike include localized forms of Kali among their village deities. The small town of Colavandan has no less than eight different forms of Kali, or Kaliyamman as she is known locally. Some of these forms allude to her centres of worship in northern India such as Kalighat (see chapter 7), whereas others are firmly rooted in south India. For instance, Vadakatti Kaliyamman, as her name Vadakatti (meaning, coming from the north or northern side) indicates, was brought to Colavandan by one of the present *pujari's* forefathers after a military trip to north India. While there, he prayed to Kali who, through her grace, allowed him to bring her essence back with him in a box. On his return the goddess was transferred to a temporary abode until her current temple/shrine was completed. Another form of Kaliyamman in Colavandan is also said to originate in north India, in Kolkata to be precise. Ujjaini Kaliyamman came from Kolkata with her *pujari's* ancestors, who were instructed by Kali to take a small cow with them and travel in a southerly direction. The goddess told them that they should settle in the place where the cow stopped and lay down. The cow walked continuously for six months until it came to the current site of this temple/shrine. Here the cow lay down and died, being subsequently buried with the goddess's shrine established above it. However, what is unclear is why this goddess is called Ujjaini Kaliyamman since Ujjain is a separate north Indian city.

Goddesses originating from humans

Two goddesses in Colavandan were originally human women. Their mythology tells the sad tale of the shattering events that necessitated their transformation into goddesses. In the origin myth of Pecciyamman at the Irulaparicami (Siva) temple in Colavandan, the transformative power of anger is the cause of a mortal woman becoming a goddess. This particular incarnation of Peycciyamman, a goddess who is popular in Tamilnadu, was originally a beautiful, pregnant, mortal woman. Her beauty was her downfall as it attracted a local king who tied her up and intended to rape her. She became so angry that a transformation took place enabling her to take him into her mouth to kill him. At this point, she became a goddess and is now iconographically represented with a demon hanging out of her mouth. Transformations of this type are common in local mythology, particularly in Tamilnadu. The transformative power of anger is a recurrent theme in goddess mythology, not just on a local level but in *puranic* mythology as well. For instance, it is only when Devi/Durga became angry, during the battle with Mahisasura, that Kali was produced, representing her personified wrath. Kali appears in a number of other textual sources as the result of the goddess's anger or as a container for the anger and subsequent power necessary to defeat an enemy.[34]

Another sort of mythology is also common in Tamilnadu and perhaps in the rest of India. The goddess Patalamman in the Ankalaparamisvari temple is unusual because she faces south, the direction associated with the abode of Yama, the god of death. According to Patalamman's origin story, four hundred years ago, a group of people came to the settlement for a bamboo folk dance and they stayed there for some time. Among the party were a brother and sister. There was a problem with the marriage of the sister and, tragically, she committed suicide by falling from a tree that stood where her shrine is now. The girl was buried at the spot where she fell and was then considered a goddess. There is no image of her, only a large altar (*palipidam*), possibly sacrificial, although blood offerings are never given to this goddess. The nature of the marriage problem was unknown but assumptions can be made, as there are a number of local goddess origin myths in which a human woman committed suicide and, because of her premature death, gained divine status. The girl's suicide probably had some connection to her defilement, either being pursued by a low-caste male, being somehow duped, wrongly accused, or losing her virtue. This type of myth, which centres on a woman becoming a goddess in death, is popular. Patalamman's shrine faces south, to the abode of Yama (the god of death), because as a divine human she has met death and overcome it.[35] Because she faced death, it is no longer a threat to her, and her regeneration as a goddess and her power are apparently drawn directly from death.

Overlooking the ocean near to the southernmost tip of India is the small red and white striped shrine of a goddess called Totakariyamman. The shrine is empty but before it are two water-filled gashes in the rock. Totakariyamman's origin myth explains the empty shrine and the significance of the rock clefts. The goddess was originally the daughter of a local ruler called Konthalapparaya. Totakari was very beautiful and a local chieftain, Kumarparaiya, fell in love with her. Kumarparaiya wanted to marry Totakari but was unable to because of their class differences, particularly since he was an untouchable. However, Kumarparaiya was undeterred and pursued Totakari as she tried to run away. She ran until she reached the place where her shrine now stands. There she came upon the home of seven *kumaris* (virgins), a place indicated by seven red marks on the rocks. The red marks are described as the betel spit of the *kumaris*.[36] A spring in the rocks here developed fire so that Totakari could immolate herself and escape from her pursuer. She jumped into the fire and was burnt. Kumarparaiya was so in love with Totakari that he wanted to burn himself with her but this act would also have defiled her. Fortunately, she had prayed to the *kumaris* and so they created another fire into which Kumarparaiya leapt. This is why there are two clefts, side by side, in the rock and an empty shrine. On the right, Totakari died and the water in the cleft is sweet. On the left is Kumarparaiya's cleft that yields salt water. This particular myth has two functions: it explains the natural phenomena of the two clefts, but also provides another example of a human becoming divine.

Sati

The handprints that adorn many of the palace gateways of Rajasthan are a chilling reminder of the many women who have ended their lives on the funeral pyre of their husbands. Sanctioned in the *Mahabharata* by the self-immolation of the royal wife Madri, and by some of the wives of Krsna, this ultimate act of self-sacrifice and the transformation of a human woman into a divine goddess is the most controversial, and perhaps for those in the West the most difficult facet of Hinduism to understand and approach objectively. The practice of *sati* is very rare, but the many myths of ancient *satimatas* (*sati* mothers) still have meaning for the women of today as the tradition and the myth-making process is still developing. Despite the fact that the practice, and indeed the glorification, of *sati* are now outlawed, according to one scholar, Lindsey Harlan, "sati veneration is a major aspect of the religious lives of Rajput women".[37]

The act of self-immolation on the funeral pyre of one's husband is, according to *stridharma* (a woman's duty), the most meritorious act a Hindu wife can perform, ostensibly for the welfare of her husband. Hence Tryambakayajvan's *Stridharmapaddhati* 42. 6–7 declares: "Just as the snake-catcher drags the snake from its hole by force, even so the virtuous wife (*sati*) snatches her husband from the demons of hell and takes him up to heaven."[38] Other verses claim that no matter how sinful a husband might be, if his wife becomes *sati* she has the power to liberate him. The term *sati* literally means "a good woman", therefore, when a wife immolates herself on her husband's funeral pyre – an act most properly termed in Sanskrit, *sahagamana* "going together with [one's husband]" or *anumarana* "following [one's husband] in death – she *becomes* a truly faithful wife (*sati*) rather than *performing sati*, a term often used in the West. India, and particularly Rajasthan and the north-west, is dotted with sacred stones, temples and shrines to *satimatas*. Local mythology honours those women who have ended their lives on their husband's funeral pyre, making it clear that a legitimate *sati*'s nature is such that she has been preparing for this moment throughout her life and signs of her fitness for this end would be apparent long before the death of her human form. She is filled with a fiery power (*sat*), indicating her inner purity. Hence, John Stratton Hawley comments: "Every time a genuine sati is enacted, it signifies the flowering of a seed of virtue sown in the woman herself, from childhood on."[39]

Although some *satimatas* are known and worshipped in cities such as Delhi and Kolkata, the majority are known only in isolated areas, seen as the protectors of individual families or caste groups. Therefore, Paul Courtright states: "This display of devotion releases a surplus of religious merit, which the *sati* distributes to her kin and community at the time of her death and afterward in the form of her continuing presence as a beneficent ancestress to her lineage."[40] When a wife becomes *sati* she benefits not just her husband in securing for him a place in heaven but, also, a larger community group, either by bestowing blessings at the time of her immolation or, by protecting them after her earthly death. One such example is Narayani Satimata, who protects a barber caste in the Ajmer district of Rajasthan. According to her temple mythology, her husband's premature death through snakebite was in order that her act of self-immolation might take place. The benefits of her self-sacrifice have been considerable as her subsequent deification has brought peace and prosperity to this region, and her temple, built at the site of her immolation, yields a constant supply of fresh water.[41] However, while *satimatas* have a powerful benevolence from the time that they vow to become *sati*, being then referred to as a *sativrata*, they also have the power to curse (*srap*) those who might try to prevent them from carrying out their vow. Local mythology also relates tales of those who have been cursed because they were responsible for the woman's position. For instance, Lindsey Harlan relates one such Rajput account:

> There was once a woman whose husband was fond of liquor. Rajputs are allowed to drink liquor. This husband, however, abused this prerogative by overindulging regularly. This caused much unpleasantness within the family. One day while inebriated he fell off a roof and died. At that time his wife took a vow of sati. Before immolating herself, she pronounced a curse that from then on no male in the family would be allowed to drink liquor.[42]

The most famous incident of *sati* happened on 4 September 1987 when an eighteen-year-old girl, Roop Kanwar, a wife of only eight months was immolated on the pyre of her dead husband. Since her death – which attracted international attention, due largely to the activism of the women's movement – fierce speculation has deliberated whether she truly became *sati* or whether her husband's family forced her onto the pyre. Although she was allegedly watched by thousands of spectators, no one tried to stop her from becoming *sati*. One account explains their inaction:

> The girl, they say, acquired *sat* – a supernatural power which is akin to a trance-like state where the woman's body burns to the touch and her eyes redden and glow. No one dared dissuade her for fear of being cursed by *satimata*. She is said to have led the procession, chanted the *gayatri mantra* and blessed people. Roop Kanwar, they say, had only raised her hands and the pyre lit itself.[43]

Another account recreates the image of *sati* that is transmitted in numerous local myths. For instance, it is claimed that in the traditional manner: "She took her husband's head in her hands as she seated herself on the pyre and submitted calmly to the flames. The force of her inner truth (*sat*) ignited the pyre, making it plain to profane eyes that she had been transformed from a human being into a goddess, a *satimata*."[44] An important aspect of this account is the belief that the true *sati* is not burned when the funeral pyre is lit, but immolates herself by her innate purity and truth.

However, accounts of Roop Kanwar's immolation are inconclusive and other reports suggest that, far from "submitting calmly to the flames" she was drugged or forced back onto the pyre as many as three times when she tried to escape. Whether Roop Kanwar's immolation is viewed as a miraculous event or a callous murder, for many people she is now a goddess, who – despite the 1987 legislation that made the 'glorification of *sati*' illegal – is an object of veneration. This worship takes the form of pilgrimage to the village of Deorala in Rajasthan, to the site of Roop's immolation. Many thousands of people ignored the illegality of their actions, flooding into Deorala to celebrate the first anniversary of her immolation. They visited her house, now a shrine, shouted ritual slogans about her glorious death and purchased composite photographs of her and her husband, taken while they were both still alive, despite the fact that a number of Roop Kanwar's male in-laws had been arrested for her murder (although they were never formally prosecuted). According to Julia Leslie: "The crude montage photograph, bought by thousands of devotees for private worship, says it all. Roop Kanwar is shown seated amidst the flames of the funeral pyre, her husband's dead body across her lap. She wears her wedding finery and an enigmatic half-smile. This is the iconography of a modern legend."[45]

Despite the sanctions employed after the death of Roop Kanwar to outlaw the veneration of *satis*, and the doubt surrounding Roop's death, occasionally modern women are still burnt on their husband's funeral pyre. On 6 August 2002, Kuttu Bai, a sixty-five-year old woman from a village in Madhya Pradesh, immolated herself with her husband. Although the police tried to stop her, the villagers pelted them with stones and prevented them from doing so. Newspaper reports suggest that Kuttu Bai planned to become *sati* when she discovered that her husband was dying. As the time of the cremation drew near, she was described as sitting on the pyre, "bejewelled and dressed in a red sari with her husband's head on her lap for a good half hour during which time the villagers came and made offerings."[46] Although this evidence suggests that Kuttu Bai had voluntarily decided to immolate herself, a later article points out: "With news spreading of a possible sati in the area, people from surrounding villages gathered around the pyre at the designated hour; rendering it practically impossible for Kuttu Bai to back out even if she wanted to".[47] Later investigations into the case throw doubt on the idea that Kuttu Bai burned herself unaided. It transpires that she did not get on with her husband, nor with her eldest son who reportedly lit the pyre. Doubt has also been cast on whether she could have climbed on top of the pyre by herself.[48] In this particular case, the authorities have made more strenuous efforts to ensure that no *sati* stone is set up to glorify Kuttu Bai's death. The most recent cases (that I am aware of) also happened in Madhya Pradesh when a 45-year-old tribal woman, Janakrani was burnt on her husband's funeral pyre, an event that prompted a new debate on the prevention of this ritual.[49] Only three weeks later, Mithlesh, a 27 year old woman tried to immolate herself on her husband's pyre in Tikamgarh district of the state.[50] However, she was unsuccessful as her family prevented her actions, suggesting that in this particular case the widow was not coerced. Only time will tell how Kuttu Bai and the others are regarded in the years to come, and whether the place of their immolation, like that of Roop Kanwar and the many other women who, over the centuries undertook the ultimate self-sacrifice, will become a place of pilgrimage – a place where a human woman was transformed into a goddess.

Mythology, both Brahmanical and local, plays an important part in the understanding of Hindu deities. Through its rich tapestry, a relationship of sorts is formed between deity and devotee. Rather than an abstract sense of the divine, the ordinary devotee builds up an image and understands something of the essence of his or her chosen deity through the medium of mythological knowledge. This is brought into encounters with divinity when the devotee approaches the divine during worship. Mythology provides a frame of reference as it were, a point of contact between two worlds. Through an appreciation of Brahmanical mythology, the devotee is able to empathize with the ongoing struggle faced by his or her gods and goddesses, who maintain the balance of the cosmos. Through local mythology, the devotee can take ownership of his or her deities, leading to an understanding of how those deities come to be part of the particular settlement. Finally, mythology often provides an explanation for the inexplicable, making some sense of what is beyond our limited knowledge, making the divine real and important.

4 *Tantrism* and Hindu Goddesses

Defining *Tantrism*

Before going on to examine *Tantric* goddesses and to explore the differences between *Tantrism* and *Saktism*, it is necessary to offer some general observations on *Tantrism* and to make some attempt at a working definition. If the start of this chapter seems a little tentative it is because to define '*Tantrism*' is a precarious task.[1] The word *Tantrism* comes from *tantra*, commonly the name of the texts of this tradition, and is derived from the root '*tan*' meaning 'to spread or expand', later indicating expansive knowledge perhaps, but originally not having any religious meaning, being associated with the loom.[2] The term '*Tantrism*' itself is the creation of western scholars by whom it was used to describe a broad body of teachings, texts and practices considered to be heterodox to the prevailing 'mainstream' practices found within the various Indian religions. As academic understanding of *Tantrism* has progressed, such a description has been brought into question, expanded upon, and subsequently much debated within scholarly circles. There are various *Tantric* worldviews found in all three of the major Indian religions – Hinduism, Buddhism and Jainism – pointing to the fact that the historical phenomenon of *Tantrism* was a trans-religious occurrence during its inception and subsequent development. As such the historical emergence of '*Tantrism*' and *Tantric* practices during the middle of the first millennium of the Common Era must be located within a pan-Indian socio-religious context, which exerted significant influence on all the major religious traditions of the time. *Tantrism*, then, cannot be viewed as a unified religious system, but instead must be understood as a varied body of scriptures, traditions, beliefs and practices. Hindu *Tantra* is essentially sectarian (*Saivite, Vaisnavite*, and *Sakta*); therefore, making generalizations about its doctrine is difficult since each sect, to a certain degree, has its own doctrine and practices. Whilst the present discussion will be limited to *Tantrism* and its relationship with goddess worship in Hinduism, it is nevertheless important to acknowledge this broader cultural milieu from which *Tantric* movements and attitudes emerged.

Despite the many problems associated with defining '*Tantrism*' there are common elements of *Tantric* belief and practice that can be identified as distinguishing traits. An important aspect of *Tantric* belief is that the Absolute is conceived of as being bipolar in nature, having both masculine and feminine aspects, denoted by the term Siva-Sakti. The masculine aspect is understood as the transcendent, unmanifest and unchanging aspect of the divine consciousness, whilst the feminine aspect is understood as being immanent, active, dynamic and the manifesting power of the Absolute. Thus Sakti is understood as the fundamental power of Ultimate Reality, she is the source of creation and destruction, the foundation of a real and existent cosmos. Ultimately *Tantrism* considers Siva and Sakti as one and the same, united they are the divine and its power and, as such, are conceived of as being inseparable, like fire and its capacity to burn.[3]

The emphasis on *sakti* found within *Tantrism* serves well as a definitional reference point in attempts to delineate the *Tantric* from the non-*Tantric* Hindu traditions. As has been demonstrated in this book some non-*Tantric* Hindu traditions share this conception of the universe as *sakti* with *Tantric* traditions, however, it is within the *Tantric* traditions that we find fully developed, systematic philosophical theologies eloquently conveying this position.[4] A primary characteristic of *Tantrism*, then, is its preoccupation with feminine divine energy and its awe inspiring potency for creation and destruction. From the perspective of an individual religious practitioner, the power of the goddess is the root of all birth and liberation and she is to be honoured and approached as such. The theological and metaphysical frameworks proposed by *Tantrism* articulate a concept of divine feminine power as the fundamental ground of manifestation and human experience. Consequently for *Tantrism*, knowledge and understanding of *sakti* is paramount and for this reason it is of importance when discussing goddess worship in India.

Tantrism, as a means of liberation, is open to all regardless of class, caste or gender. It is essentially a dynamic system, which offers the chance of liberation in one lifetime. The various sects that constitute what we call *Tantrism*, might be divided into two categories; the so called 'right' (*daksina*) and 'left' (*vama*) handed paths. The terms 'right handed' and 'left handed' have significant implications in India, the right hand being used for eating and pure tasks, while the left hand is only used for polluting and impure functions. Essentially, the rituals and practices adopted on the 'right handed' path are not very different to those encountered in Brahmanical Hinduism. In contrast, the 'left-handed' path employs techniques and practices that directly challenge the orthodox moral codes that are central to Brahmanical Hinduism, such as imbibing forbidden substances, engaging in sexual practices and flouting caste and purity rules through use of the infamous *panca-makara* or 5 Ms, five impure substances of power (meat, fish, alcohol, grain and sexual intercourse). The more extreme 'left handed' path uses the actual five Ms within its rituals, giving them both practical and symbolic importance. Forms of left handed *Tantra* such as *Kaula Tantrism* discussed below, believe that the correct use of the *panca-makara* will bestow transcendent powers on those partaking in such rituals. Within 'right handed' forms of *Tantra* such as the *Sri Vidya* tradition discussed below, the focus is not on the performance of the ritual using the *actual* substances; rather they become objects of internal contemplation and meditational focus. Not surprisingly it is the 'left handed' path that is often misunderstood and the most criticized by outsiders. Clearly these practices are spiritually dangerous and so another crucial aspect of *Tantrism*, across various sects, is the impor-tance of the guru. Since the *Tantic* texts are cryptic in nature it is crucial for the *Tantric* adept to be initiated and trained by a guru, who decides when the *sadhaka* (practitioner) is ready to take the next step in their spiritual path. The guru is held in the highest esteem, as is clear in the following verse from the (*Kaula*) *Kularnava* ('Ocean of the Heart') *Tantra*:

Just as words such as "pot," "vessel," and "jar" all mean the same object,
so too are god and mantra and guru said to be the same object.
Just as divinity is, so is the mantra; just as there is mantra, so there is the guru.[5]

Hindu *Tantrism* perceives the divine female power as taking many forms, the omnipotent Goddess is said to possess multiple powers. Conceived of as feminine deities, these various *saktis* are associated with levels of cosmic manifestation, thus within the *Tantric* pantheon are a diverse assortment of semi-divine female agents and divine goddesses who are identified as universal energies by *Tantric* practitioners (*sadhakas*). Within the *Tantric* worldview the universe is understood as the unfolding of a complex web of feminine power, which manifests as subtle energies and gross material forms. Accordingly, Hindu *Tantric* traditions conceive of the macrocosmic universe and the microcosmic human body in terms of *sakti*, ultimately both are expressions of the divine feminine power. In the recognition of the universe and the human body as expressions of *sakti*, each becomes a means of identification with absolute power, a basis for achieving a liberating unity with the divine.[6] For the *sadhaka*, the body becomes the dwelling place of deities and their powers, an idea emphasised by the *Kularnava Tantra*:

> The body is the abode of God, O Goddess; the embodied self is God, Ever-abiding Siva. Abandon ignorance as if it was old flowers offered in worship and perform worship with the contemplation "I am He".[7]

The *Tantric* practitioner aspires to transcend ordinary limited external conscious experience associated with bodily incarnation through interior contemplation on the body as a manifestation of the divine. The *Tantric* body becomes a locus of religious transformation in which the consciousness of the individual is purified until its fundamental identity with divine consciousness is realized. The individual ego is burnt up in the blazing power of divine consciousness and the practitioner experiences their essence united with the divine. On the same basis external manifestation is also an aspect of *sakti* and, therefore, imbued with sacred transformative power, resulting in the idea that external objects and substances can also become the basis for achieving religious realization. In this respect the *Kularnava Tantra* asserts:

> Drinking wine, eating flesh, carrying out the practices of one's own initiatory teaching, contemplating of the unitive experience of both "I" and "That," so the Heart yogin dwells in true happiness.[8]

For *Tantrism* the body and universal manifestation are in essence aspects of the divine feminine power. The *sadhaka* aims to awaken the divine energy found within the self, often termed *kundalini* or 'serpent energy', examined in chapter 5. To do so is to become one with the energy of divinity, thus achieving the knowledge and powers associated with the *sakti* of the deity being worshipped. As such, *Tantric* worldviews provide a functional and pragmatic, cosmological and physiological framework in which religious practitioners aim to utilize the powers or *saktis* of *Tantric* deities in order to modify the subtle energies perceived within their own body. The *sadhaka* maps the deities onto their subtle body aiming to awaken and control the *sakti* they are associated with. This process of self-deification is common to most *Tantric* traditions; an emphasis on practical methods, predominantly ritualistic and yogic is posited as a means of engaging with (predominantly female) deities with the aim of personally transforming the *Tantric* practitioner in some way. It is then through correct physical, mental and religious discipline known as *sadhana* that the practitioner may seek to condition their own being in order to win the favour of the *Tantric* goddesses.

Tantrism offers a soteriological goal for practitioners, a means by which the *sadhaka* can achieve liberation (*mukti* or *moksa*) from the endless cycle of reincarnation (*samsara*). However, whilst *moksa* is a key aim within *Tantrism* it is not the only one. A defining characteristic of *Tantrism* is its pre-occupation with the acquisition of supernatural powers (*siddhis*) for the benefit of worldly enjoyment (*bhukti*). Through identification with the various cosmic powers the practitioner is felt to gain supernatural abilities such as clairvoyance, the capability to attract people at will, the ability to say anything and have it come true and other similar miraculous and magical powers. Thus unlike some Indian traditions *Tantrism* advocates and indeed provides a means of acquiring supernatural powers which are said to bring about enjoyment, victory, wealth and love among other mundane worldly powers. Accordingly, *Tantric* deities have often been venerated as givers of power both spiritual and worldly. During the medieval period in India, these ideas made *Tantrism* an attractive form of religious practice among feudal royal rulers. Seeking worldly power and domination, royal lineages would patronize terrifying deities and their *Tantric* ritual specialists to ensure the acquisition of their power to aid in fighting wars and protecting the kingdom.[9]

Such spiritual and worldly goals are often achieved through the use of *mantras,* sacred sounds or chants felt to be imbued with power, and *yantras*, visual geometrical diagrams felt to represent or contain the essence of the divine. Within *Tantric* traditions students are only initiated into the meaning of various *mantras* and *yantras* by their guru when it is felt they are spiritually pure enough and mentally ready. Used as aids in meditational and visualization techniques, *Tantric mantras* and *yantras* have significant soteriological symbolism for the *sadhaka*. The *Kularnava Tantra* discusses the liberating power of *mantras*:

There are innumerable hundreds of thousands of mantras and they unsettle the heart of one's own divine consciousness. The one mantra obtained by the grace of the guru will provide every goal and accomplishment.

One should perform the recitation of the mantra by fixing oneself on it, with life breath coursing through it, setting it within one's consciousness, and making deep connections that form the meaning of its syllables.[10]

Tantric mantras and *yantras* are also directly identified as the divinities themselves, they are felt to be imbued with *sakti*, as forms of the energy of the deity with which the *sadhaka* can interact. The *Kularnava Tantra* affirms the importance of *yantras* in the following verses:

A yantra or diagrammatical form is said to consist [actually] of mantras; the deity has the form of mantras as well. The Goddess worshipped in the yantra, O Goddess, is pleased spontaneously.
As the body is for an embodied soul like oil for a lamp, my beloved, so likewise the yantra is the place of all divinities.[11]

As such, using *mantras* and *yantras*, the *sadhaka* projects the *Tantric* deities onto their own physical and subtle body, thereby aiming to form a direct relationship with the deity and their power. Through such procedures the practitioner aims to acquire certain characteristics, energies or 'powers' associated with the deity.[12]

Tantrism is a tangible element within Indian religion, one that advocates a direct confrontation with the orderly external world through transgression of accepted social values. Impure substances perceived as being imbued with transformative power are understood as manifestations of the fundamental female energy. Advocating a perilous and precarious path of power, the ritualized act of transgression thus has the capacity for transformation within the practitioner. The notion of religious change through heterodox ritual action is a defining trait within *Tantric* practice, whether it is taken literally or symbolically. However, the path of *Tantra* is not taken lightly for a worshipper must be prepared to submit to the terrifying but incredible enormity of absolute power. In this respect the immensity of the divine feminine power is conceived of as transformative and destructive in essence, all-consuming in its reality it destroys the individual ego of the worshipper, thus it is perceived as dangerous and terrifying in its nature. For the *Tantric sadhaka*, the non-differentiated absolute female power transcends worldly values of purity and pollution since they rest upon dualistic notions of difference and opposition, of pure and impure, of good and bad. Transgressive practices are then often allied with the worship of fierce, frightening and powerful goddess figures such as Kali, who through their transcendent and all powerful nature are able to create or destroy at will. The origins of *Tantrism* are closely associated with the worship of violent female deities who whilst embodying change and impermanence also demonstrate the redemptive and transformative power of the divine. As such the worship of goddesses and the development of Hindu *Tantric* practice are intimately related.

The historical development of *Tantrism* and *Saktism*

The relationship between *Saktism* and *Tantrism* is both intriguing and complex. The two traditions, whilst distinct, share in a number of similar characteristics regarding their conception and worship of goddess figures and the divine feminine. Both traditions share obvious similarities and at times overlap in terms of belief and practice.[13] Whilst forms of *Tantrism* are found in other Hindu sectarian traditions such as *Vaisnavism* and *Saivism*, which centre on the worship of male deities, they nevertheless preserve a cosmological understanding of manifestation as *sakti*, retaining a focus on the female aspects of the Absolute.[14] Philosophically *Saktism* and *Tantrism* share much in common, both emphasize the feminine aspects of the divine. They conceive of the dynamic manifest cosmos in terms of *sakti*, the divine feminine power, and as such both revere feminine deities as aspects and embodiments of cosmic manifestation. The importance of the powerful and dangerous aspects of *sakti* to both traditions is reflected in their shared pre-occupation with fierce and transgressive forms of the Great Goddess.

It is likely that both traditions, in part, share common origins in non-*Vedic* elements of early Indian religious practice.[15] Scholars have suggested the existence of a substratum of 'tribal' or 'folk' religious cultures which existed alongside the *Vedic* Brahmanical tradition. A key aspect of these localized forms of religious practice involved worship of non-*Vedic* village 'mother' deities who were often connected with creative and destructive powers and the bestowal of worldly benefits such as good harvests and the removal of illnesses.[16] Associated with unpredictable and often injurious elements of nature, such female deities were perceived as being both threatening and beneficent, imbued with the power to either harm or help. Representing the extreme aspects of the divine, such goddesses were deemed powerful and terrifying in their nature, thus their worship took the form of ritual propitiation in the hope that their violent natures might be appeased. As Brahmanical tradition spread, it encountered innumerable non-*Vedic* regional goddesses and there occurred an assimilation and incorporation of the myriad of female divinities into Brahmanical literature and religious practice.[17] Through this process, non-*Vedic* regional goddess figures slowly gained recognition and acceptance within the Brahmanical pantheon.[18] Scholars generally agree that the non-*Vedic* and transgressive aspects of Hindu goddess worship stem, in part, from the assimilation of non-*Vedic* tribal divinities into the Brahmanical tradition that occurred during the first millennium CE.

The developed religious traditions of *Saktism* and *Tantrism* are distinct entities, *Saktism* understood as a sectarian movement centred upon the devotional worship of the Great Goddess, as opposed to *Tantrism*, a tradition of distinctive religious praxis that traversed defined sectarian and religious boundaries. With regard to literary evidence, scholars differentiate between orthodox devotional *Puranic Sakta* materials and heterodox *Tantric* textual sources, *Tantric* literature often defining itself against orthodox praxis through engagement in heterodox modes of worship which transgressed *Vedic* purity values. The assimilation of non-*Vedic* deities and their associated symbolisms into Brahmanical traditions resulted in the evolution of new forms of religious practice of which *Saktism* and *Tantrism* are prime examples. With the rise of orthodox forms of *Saktism* there occurred a process of 'domestication' of wild goddess figures by Brahmanical cults.[19] The process (also known as Brahmanization or Sanskritization) involved fierce non-*Vedic* regional deities and their symbolisms being adapted to suit Brahmanical devotional sensibilities, particularly with regard to their observance of orthodox purity codes. As such regional deities were incorporated into wider goddess cults, becoming the objects of devotional worship by Brahmanical householder movements. For orthodox *Sakta* traditions, deities such as Kali retained their powerfully transgressive and transformative symbolisms, but were also venerated with typical modes of Brahmanical worship that adhered to traditional conventions of purity and pollution. In the development of *Tantrism*, by contrast, the process of domestication incorporated not only fierce goddesses and their symbolisms of power, but also transgressive ritual practices associated with their worship.[20] Such rites directly contravened *Vedic* notions of purity

The historical development of Tantrism *and* Saktism

and pollution, thus those *Tantric* cults which practiced them were considered heterodox to conventional Brahmanical tradition.

Such practices have their roots in cremation ground cults such as heterodox ascetic groups like the *Kapalikas*. Viewed as fearsome and dangerous figures, the skull-bearing *Kapalikas* operated on the margins of Brahmanical society.[21] Seeking liberation and the acquisition of magical powers, these early *Saiva* and *Sakta* oriented ascetic traditions were known for their practice of rituals which directly transgressed *Vedic* values of purity. Known as 'skull-bearers' due to their carrying of a skull-bowl in honour of Siva, the *Kapalikas* practiced orgiastic and ecstatic rites, which included the propitiation of fierce cremation ground spirits.[22] It is from these cremation ground traditions that later forms of systematized and domesticated *Tantrism* emerged. *Sakta* and *Saiva* oriented *Tantric* traditions were closely associated with one another, both strongly influenced by *Kapalika* cremation ground culture.[23] Philosophically both traditions understand the Absolute as possessing both masculine and feminine aspects and in this respect each gives credence to the position of the other. As such the two broad traditions are often closely affiliated with one another, frequently venerating both deities as supreme. Consequently, sub-traditions of *Tantric Saivism* and *Saktism* are differentiated only by whether they hold Siva or Sakti as supreme deity, if indeed they do make such a distinction; for instance, then a practitioner of the *Kaula* tradition may practice both *Saiva* and *Sakta* rituals. It is apparent that *Tantric Saktism* developed in relation to *Tantric Saivism*, *Tantric Sakta* traditions often viewed themselves as the supreme teaching of Siva and Sakti. Appended to lower *Saiva* doctrines, the *Sakta* teachings presented themselves as transcending the *Saiva* teachings and thus as the highest and most effective mode of *Tantric* practice.

Tantric Sakta cults are broadly classified as belonging to one of two distinct traditions, each with an emphasis on differing aspects of the Great Goddess. The first of these traditions is named *Kali-kula* or 'lineage of Kali' and is associated with terrible and fierce forms of the goddess. As forms of Kali, these overtly powerful deities were worshipped using rituals which contravened normal *Vedic* rules of purity and impurity. Significantly Alexis Sanderson traces the development of the *Tantric Kaula* veneration of Kali to early *Kapalika* cremation ground cults centred upon worship of *Yoginis*.[24] The *Kali-kula* is then generally associated with 'left handed' forms of *Tantrism*. The other tradition of *Sakta Tantrism* is known as the *Sri-kula* or 'lineage of Sri'. In contrast to the *Kali-kula*, the *Sri-kula* is associated with the worship of benign forms of the goddess and in general dispenses with transgressive rituals. The *Sri-kula* tradition tends to assert an emphasis on the mental interpretation of transgressive *Tantric* symbols rather than their practical ritual use. Thus the *Sri-kula* is generally associated with forms of 'right handed' *Tantra* and can be understood as reflecting orthodox Brahmanical concerns pertaining to purity in its interpretation of *Tantric* tradition.[25]

Tantric goddesses

The Matrkas *(Mothers)*

Before discussing overtly *Tantric* goddesses, it is useful to briefly consider an example of the earlier substratum of female deities from which it is likely such goddesses emerged. One such important grouping of goddesses were the *Matrka* or 'mother' deities who likely represent a common source for various *Tantric* goddess figures such as the *Saptamatrkas* and *Yoginis* discussed below.[26] Scholars have cautiously suggested that in the *Matrkas* there can be discerned a synthesis of earlier *Vedic* and non-*Vedic* tribal goddesses who had been worshipped in a regional and village context from a very early period. The *Matrkas* can then be understood as a form of the often nameless groups of fearsome mother deities associated with, and often perceived to be the cause of, childbirth difficulties, childhood diseases and psychological illnesses.[27] Whilst the name '*matrka*' implies motherhood, and indeed the goddesses are often depicted holding small children, it is significant that from the earliest period these figures represent dangerous and hostile deities who were in fact perceived as a threat to children. Only through successful propitiation of these violent divinities could the misfortune they sought to inflict be prevented. David Kinsley has suggested that such malevolent child-afflicting deities may have had their roots in the common conviction that women who died without children and those who died in childbirth remained in the spirit world, becoming jealous and resentful of those mothers who had children and the young themselves. To placate their jealousy such spirits were felt to covet healthy and attractive children, seeking to steal them away or harm them in some way.[28] The mythological narratives of the *Matrka* deities display powerful associations with motherhood, children and death, themes common in the descriptions of later fierce goddess.

The *Matrka* goddesses first appear as definitive groups in narrative literature from around the first century CE onwards. The *Mahabharata* contains several references to *Matrkas*, generally portraying them as dangerous and fearsome goddesses. The *Vanaparvan* (*Book of the Forest*) section of the great epic relates a story in which a group of inauspicious and terrible female divinities known as the 'mothers of the world' are sent by the gods to kill the child Karttikeya (also known as Skanda) soon after his birth. However, when they approached the child their maternal instincts prevailed and they instead nursed him. Of note is a description of one of the goddesses as thirsty for blood and angry in nature, who nevertheless vowed to guard the child like her son. Such an account demonstrates both the terrible and benign aspects of the goddess's character.[29] Thus Harper comments, "underlying the myth is a belief in the tremendous powers of various folk goddesses to nurture or destroy".[30] Elsewhere in the *Mahabharta* the *Matrkas* are described thus:

> These and many other mothers, . . . numbering by the thousands, of diverse forms, became the followers of Karttikeya. Their nails were long, their teeth were large and their lips were protruding. Of straight forms and sweet features, all of them, endowed with youth, were decked with ornaments. Possessed of ascetic merit, they were capable of assuming any form at will. Not having much flesh on their limbs, they were dark and looked like clouds in hue and some were of the colour of smoke. . . . Of inconceivable might and energy, their prowess also was inconceivable. They have their abode on trees and open spots and crossings of four roads. They live also in caves and crematoriums, mountains and springs. Adorned in diverse kinds of ornaments, they wear diverse kinds of attire and speak diverse languages. These and many other tribes (of the mothers), all capable of inspiring foes with dread, followed the high-souled Karttikeya at the command of the chief of the celestials.[31]

The references to different and darker complexions, the wearing of strange clothing and ornaments, speaking of different languages and living on the periphery of normal society is indicative that at an early stage the *Matrkas* were perceived as non-*Vedic* goddesses.[32] Kinsley states:

> It is hard to resist the conclusion that the groups of goddesses called the Matrkas in the *Mahabharata* represent the many village goddesses throughout India who are widely worshipped by the common people and who are often associated with disease or the prevention of diseases, espe-

cially those that afflict children. Such deities are not found in the Vedic pantheon but are probably indigenous to a non-Brahminic, if not pre-Aryan, religious universe.[33]

It is thus apparent that the *Matrka* deities, whilst not overtly identified as *Tantric*, nevertheless exhibit *Tantric* characteristics.[34] They were associated with the boundaries of *Vedic* society and occupied a liminal position on the margins of Brahmanical tradition perhaps representing the unknown and untamed aspects of nature. Juxtaposed with the ordered *Vedic* worldview, such deities were considered violent and threatening, powerful and dangerous. Through a gradual process of assimilation and adaptation, non-*Vedic* goddess figures such as the *Matrkas* became incorporated into the Brahmanical worldview. As evidenced by Sanskrit textual sources such as the *Puranas* and *Tantras*, the religious cults that developed around such figures were integrated alongside one another to form the broader traditions of orthodox devotional *Saktism* and heterodox *Tantrism*. In this process the untamed creative and destructive powers associated with groups of wild female deities such as the *Matrkas* came to be incorporated into the broad theological and cosmological worldviews centred upon the concept of *sakti*, as promoted by *Saktism* and *Tantrism*. Through a brief examination of the *Matrka* goddesses it becomes clear that these often inauspicious and dangerous deities provide a plausible foundation for later *Tantric* characterizations of overtly transgressive fierce goddesses.[35]

The Saptamatrkas *(Seven Mothers)*

The *Saptamatrkas* are a grouping of goddesses which emerged from the band of female deities known simply as the '*Matrkas*' or 'mothers' around the fourth century CE. As part of the developing movement of *Sakta* oriented sectarian traditions, the *Saptamatrka* deities became the religious focus of a *Tantric* cult between the fourth and sixth centuries CE. It was during this period that *Tantric* and sectarian theistic *Sakta* movements were in their ascendency, and the cult of the *Saptamtrikas* can be considered an example of the development of such traditions. As part of this process, worship of the seven mothers was also adopted and adapted for ritual use by the Brahmanical tradition, resulting in the standardization of the seven mother figures.[36] The *Saptamatrkas* first appear as a group in *puranic* literature from around the fourth century CE onwards, with a distinct iconographic tradition emerging in the following two centuries. The names of the seven goddesses included within the group differ according to various sources, with the earlier literature presenting slightly different lists of names from the later standardized iconographic depictions. The first literary mention of the group is a version of the seven mother goddesses described in the *Devi-Mahatmya*. The *Sakta* text, whilst not generally considered to be *Tantric*, nevertheless hints toward important *Tantric* ideas through its depiction of terrifying and transgressive goddesses.[37] In an important mythological account, the *Saptamatrkas* are created by the male gods to aid Mahadevi in battle. According to the narrative Sumbha and Nisumbha, two evil demon kings, having defeated the gods, are locked in a ferocious war with the Great Goddess and her hordes of fierce *Matrka* deities. When the demon armies take the upper hand, the watching gods create seven *saktis*, female versions of themselves, to aid the Goddess, at this point as Candika (the Violent and Impetuous One). The text describes their appearance thus:

> *Saktis*, having sprung forth from the bodies of Brahma, Siva, Skanda, Visnu, and Indra, and having the form of each approached Candika.
> Whatever form, ornament, and mount a particular god possessed,
> With that very form did his *sakti* go forth to fight the Asuras.
> In a heavenly conveyance drawn by swans, with rosary and waterpot,
> Came forth the *sakti* of Brahma: she is known as Brahmani.
> Mahesvari sallied forth, mounted in a bull, bearing the best of tridents,
> With great serpents for bracelets, adorned with the crescent of the moon.
> Ambika having the form of Guha (Skanda), as Kaumari went forth to fight
>   the demons, With spear in hand, having the best peacocks as her mount.
> Then the *sakti* known as Vaisnavi went forth, mounted on Garuda,
> With conch, discus, club, bow and sword in hand.
> The *sakti* of Hari who has the matchless form of a sacrificial boar
> Then came forth, bearing the body of a sow.
> Narasimhi, having the form like the man-lion, Then came forth, with
>   many a constellation cast down by the tossing of her mane.
> Then Aindri, with thunderbolt in hand, mounted upon the lord of
>   elephants, Went forth; she had a thousand eyes, just like Indra.
> Then Siva, surrounded by these *saktis* of the gods, Said to Candika: "May
>   the demons now be quickly slain by you in order to please me."
> Then from the body of the Goddess came forth the very frightening *Sakti*
>   of Candika herself, gruesome and yelping like a hundred jackals.
> And she, the invincible one, spoke to Siva, of smokey, matted locks:
> "You yourself become my messenger to Sumbha and Nisumbha"[38]

Whilst the story is clear that the seven *saktis* appear from the gods and indeed share their characteristics, they are nevertheless understood as *saktis* of the Great Goddess, not as consorts of the male deities. The fact that Siva becomes a mere messenger of Candika demonstrates the overall superiority of the divine feminine within the narrative. Furthermore, the *saktis* are later absorbed into Devi as discussed in chapter 2. It is then clear that within the *Devi-Mahtmya*, the *Saptamatrkas* are understood as forms of the Great Goddess, as powers of the supreme divine feminine.[39] Towards the end of the *Devi-Mahatmya* the *Saptamatrkas* are also presented as forms of Mahadevi in a list of the many names of the Great Goddess. After finally vanquishing her demon enemies and having proven her superiority over all, Mahadevi and her *saktis* drink the blood of the slain, becoming drunk, an event that has distinctly *Tantric* overtones. Versions of this myth are also found in later *Sakta Puranas*; Kinsley notes that the *puranic* mythological descriptions do not generally discuss the individual characteristics of each of the seven mothers, instead treating them as a collective. As such the *Saptamatrkas* were usually characterized as being ferocious in nature and as becoming drunk on the blood of their victims.[40]

With the establishment of the *Tantric Saptamatrka* cult, an iconographic tradition developed with a standard set of seven deities – Brahmani, Vaisnavi, Mahesvari, Kaumari, Varahi, Indrani and lastly the fierce goddess, Camunda, who was depicted as an independent *sakti*. Representing the cosmic cycle, Harper notes that the group always began with Brahmani, the *sakti* of Brahma the creator god, the agent of creation with whom the universe begins. In most cases the fourth and middle deity is depicted as Vaisnavi, the *sakti* of Visnu, the power of preservation within the cosmos. The group always ends with Camunda, the terrifying goddess of destruction, who was understood as a form of Kali, and as such associated with the god Siva. Harper notes that the significance and ordering of the intermediate goddess figures is now lost but would no doubt have had important esoteric symbolism.[41] The *Saptamatrkas* were then primarily understood in relation to one another as an independent group of violent and terrifying female deities.

Harper has argued that in earlier *Vedic* and non-*Vedic* cultures, groupings of seven, and in particular heptads of female deities, represented models of the transient cyclic universe, the female divinities being understood as imparters of the cosmic powers of destruction and renewal. She continues by suggesting that the developed *Saptamatrkas*, as objects of personal spiritual focus and devotion, are examples of the development of such ideas along soteriological lines. "The proto-matrikas were worshipped for annual renewal. The *Saptamatrikas* were worshipped for personal and spiritual renewal, i.e., rebirth on an entirely different plane of existence, that of non-existence."[42] As such, the *Saptamatrkas* represent systematized and refined forms of earlier *Matrka* deities; no longer were they simply understood as the cosmic powers of creation, preservation and destruction, but also as energies of the Great Goddess. As such, they represented the fundamental nature and power of Mahadevi to create, sustain and destroy the universe, the very cycle of existence. Equally for the *Tantric Sakta* practitioner, the goddesses were felt to wield the power of incarnation and liberation over all persons and were understood to be capable of liberating the religious practitioner from the endless round of reincarnation. Therefore, in a *Tantric* context:

> The Seven Mothers guide the soul of the *sadhaka* or are, in effect, the agents through which the *sadhaka* attains *moksha*. Saptamatrika icons are a visualisation of the psychosomatic experience of the intiate as well as soteriological symbols of the most ecstatic kind.[43]

From an individual perspective, the symbolism of the *Saptamatrkas* offered the devotee both an exoteric (accessible) worldview and an esoteric (secret) means of transcendence and spiritual change.

The cult offered participants not only the opportunity for religious salvation, but also a means of achieving worldly gain (*bhukti*). As such, the goddesses were worshipped as leaders of clans of less significant female deities, and were called upon as protectorates and martial deities.[44] In this respect the *Saptamatrkas* were employed as patrons by royal houses and state rulers.[45] For warring feudal kings, *Tantric* ritual performed to the female deities would invoke not only the protection of these powerful and awesome beings, but also the benefits of their terrible and destructive powers, in order to vanquish the enemy. In the cult of the *Saptamatrkas*, the nurturing and destructive qualities associated with the early *Matrka* deities were interpreted, employed and exploited for mundane ends, through a process of *Tantric* ritual practice by influential groups within society. Through identification with the goddesses, the ritual specialist, on behalf of their patron, was felt to acquire and utilize the magical and supernatural powers (*siddhis*) of the *Saptamatrkas* for worldly ends.

Closely associated with *Tantric* systems of yoga and meditation, the *Saptamatrkas* are understood as forming a *Tantric yantra* or *mandala* symbolizing the process of manifestation. Each is identified with a level of existence, a state of consciousness, and a *cakra* (energy centre of the subtle body). As symbols of the manifestation of exterior reality, the goddesses are also symbols of interior re-absorption. Harper discusses the iconographic symbolism of the deities in relation to this point:

> To pass from one Matrika to the next is to progress along the road of emancipation – a spiritual genesis beyond life, beyond rebirth, beyond time. The infants who nestle in the lap of each goddess can be interpreted as the soul of the initiate as it is reborn on each new plane. The weapons held by the goddesses symbolically wage war on the ego and bring the initiate closer to final release. . . . To reach and to surpass the seventh mother is to realize the final birth, that of non-birth, *moksha*.[46]

The *Saptamatrkas* are thus to be understood as objects of inner *Tantric* visualization through which the *sadhaka* aims at a distilling of consciousness, resulting in the knowledge of supreme identity with the highest absolute, the Great Goddess. Understood as deities of spiritual transformation, the esoteric symbolism of the *Saptamatrkas* demonstrates the developed philosophies of emancipation forwarded by *Sakta* and *Tantric* traditions.

Yoginis

Yoginis are important female figures within *Tantric* traditions. As objects of *Tantric* cults they are found as both independent goddesses and as attendants to other more powerful goddesses. *Yoginis* have been venerated by historical *Tantric* cults, but also remain important female figures within contemporary folk *Tantra*. The term '*yogini*' has a number of different meanings and connotations within Hinduism and can refer to human as well as supernatural figures. The feminine form of the masculine noun '*yogin*', the term essentially means 'a female practitioner of *yoga*', can indicate an accomplished female adept of yogic or *Tantric* practice. As such, the term has also been employed in narrative sources to describe female adepts who were associated with the acquisition of magical *siddhis* and occult sorcery. In this respect, such figures were perceived as dangerous witches or sorceresses, able to turn men into animals and bring the dead back to life.[47] Hailed as protectors of women, *Yoginis* are said to be angered if a *sadhaka* insults a woman; they are believed to be able to fly through the air and take the form of birds. Terrifying hordes of *Yoginis* are said to gather in circles in cremation grounds to perform bloodthirsty sacrifices to fierce forms of Siva and Sakti. Chanting the names of *Yoginis* is said to bring about all manner of worldly benefits, particularly in association with healing disease and childhood illnesses.[48] As powerful female deities, *Tantric* ritualists have sought to gain and utilize the extreme powers associated with *Yoginis* by performing formidable *Tantric* rituals with the aim of attracting and interacting with the deities. As such, 'left-handed' *Tantric* literature also uses the term to refer to the low-caste female consort who takes part in transgressive sexual rituals in honour of the *Yoginis*.

Historically, worship of fearsome *Yoginis* emerged from the broad regional traditions of divine and semi-divine supernatural females, both *Vedic* and non-*Vedic*, that were worshipped in India during the early centuries of the Common Era.[49] As in the case of the *Matrkas*, such female divinities were often perceived as terrifying and inimical, as existing on the boundaries of ordered society, as being powerful, dangerous and bloodthirsty.[50] Often connected with animal and nature spirits, veneration of *Yogini* figures was closely linked with the worship of *Yaksinis*, female tree spirits associated with fertility.[51] Such associations continued during the development of *Yogini* cults as evidenced in later temple images such as those at the *Yogini* temple at Hirapur in Orissa, which depicts sixty-four *Yoginis* many with animal heads.[52] These female figures traversed the realms of the supernatural and the human, of power and pollution, of purity and impurity. Embodying creative and destructive aspects of the divine, such deities were associated with the Great Goddess. Often presented in groups of eight or sixty-four, propitiation of *Yoginis* was felt to bring the worshipper worldly benefits. In the *Kalika Purana*, a list of sixty-four *Yoginis* is presented followed by the instruction "A devotee should worship all these sixty-four *yoginis* in side [sic] the *mandala* for achieving all round success in *artha* [wealth] and *kama* [pleasure]."[53]

The origins of *Yogini* cults are also associated with influential *Tantric* cremation ground traditions such as the *Kapalikas*.[54] The bloodthirsty and skull-bearing imagery associated with *Yoginis* certainly reflects such influences. *Yogini* figures were associated with 'clans' or 'lineages' of female deities known as *kula*; such 'families' of female deities became venerated as protectorates of various groups located at the fringes of ordered *Vedic* society, and as such are indicative of their role as earlier regional deities.

As a defined *Tantric* cult, *Yogini* worship emerged during the eighth century CE as part of a heterodox *Tantric* tradition known as the *Kaula* path. The *Kaula* tradition practiced a *Saiva-Sakta* form of *Tantra* in which manifestation was understood and worshipped as a form of the Great Goddess. Initiation into this esoteric form of left-handed *Tantra* involved the ritualized use of the *panca-makara*, the five transgressive power substances, which was perceived as a particularly terrifying and dangerous approach to the divine. *Kaula* literature describes how these fierce and terrifying female deities favoured those who undertook this form of *Tantric* practice. The tradition offered initiates an accelerated means of achieving spiritual liberation, as well as the swift acquisition of magical and supernatural powers (*siddhis*).[55] Such rites were performed in circles and were thus known as *cakra-puja*. During such practices the female partner was directly identified with the powerful *Yogini* deities or as the Great Goddess herself. In this respect *Yoginis* are associated with non-*Vedic* practices and ideals, and are said to punish those who observe caste distinctions during *Tantric* rituals.[56]

The *Kaula* tradition was secretive, open only to elite circles of initiates who were deemed appropriate and pure enough to take part in such dangerous and powerful rituals. As such, the path of the *Yoginis* is said to be perilous, undertaken only by those adepts and initiates valiant enough to become a *'vira'* meaning 'hero' or 'conqueror'.[57] The esoteric nature of the *Kaula* path of the *Yogini* is demonstrated in the *Kularnava Tantra* when it claims: "This treatise called the Ocean of the Heart exists within the heart of divine yoginis. I have illumined it today; and with true effort it should be kept secret."[58]

In their *Kaula* context *Yoginis* were understood as patrons of those initiated into the *Kaula* tradition, the *kula* or 'clan lineage'.[59] White suggests that initiation into the *Yogini* lineage was achieved through the ingestion of combined male and female human sexual fluids following the performance of sexual rituals with a human female who was understood as a physical embodiment of the *Yogini* goddesses. It was believed that the *Yoginis* possessed the female consort, seeking to feed on the bodily fluids of the male partner and in return bestowing enlightening spiritual powers, enabling the speedy acquisition of *siddhis* and liberation through direct union with the Absolute.[60] Having been symbolically offered to the *Yoginis* through intercourse, the combined sexual fluids were understood as clan 'essence' or 'nectar' and deemed particularly powerful and thus able to spiritually transform the initiate at an accelerated rate. Thus by becoming part of the *Tantric kula* or *Kaula* 'family' an initiate was felt to attain spiritual liberation as well as the attainment of *siddhis* associated with the terrifying *Yogini* hordes.

Yogini worship was popular around the eighth to the twelfth century CE in India.[61] Of the nine *Yogini* temples discovered to date, two are located in Orissa (north-east India). Of these, perhaps the most interesting is in the village of Hirapur discovered as recently as 1953, despite its close proximity to Bhubaneswar, the state capital. It is a squat (only 8–9 feet high) circular, hypaethral (open roofed) building with sixty niches carved around its inner walls.[62] (See plate 1). These niches and four others that surround an inner rectangular *mandapa* (inner sanctum), house black chlorite images of the *Yoginis*.[63] Sixty-four is a number closely connected with the *Yoginis* (as eight of the nine temples have sixty-four *Yoginis*), but may also link them with other groups of sixty-four, such as Bhairavas (fierce forms of Siva) and modes of sexual enjoyment.[64] The primary goddess at this temple is Mahamaya Durga (Great Illusion) and worship of her and the other *Yoginis* is still evident today. (See plate 2). The temple warden has a list of the *Yoginis* who include many of the *Saptamatrkas*, *Mahavidyas* (discussed below), along with some of the more famous fierce and benign goddesses such as Candika, Camunda, Uma, and Ambika. The *Yogini* images are rich with symbolism as each stands on a symbolic item and many have animal faces, though their bodies are wonderfully sinuous and very beautifully carved. Despite some damage to the *Yogini* images, both they and the temple are remarkably well preserved. Local people still bring offerings of coconuts, and bangles, which are placed before the *Yoginis*. (See plate 3). On one visit a new auto rickshaw had been brought to be blessed. (See plate 4). An interesting turn of events is that this temple, which was probably much feared as a place, when it was the centre of *Tantric* worship, is now becoming a tourist destination. Since 2002, signs to the temple and a small shop have appeared. It will be interesting to monitor what happens to it in the future.

The Ten Mahavidyas

Sometimes referred to as the '*Dasamahavidyas*' meaning the 'Ten Great Revelations' the *Mahavidyas* are well recognized by most Hindus and are often iconographically depicted in temples dedicated to the goddess.[65] The word '*Mahavidya*' literally means 'Great Knowledge' or 'Supreme Insight' and as such the ten *Mahavidyas* are bestowers, or personifications, of transcendent and liberating religious knowledge. The term '*vidya*' may also be understood in a variety of ways including '*sakti*' or power, as 'essence of reality', or significantly as '*mantra*', referring to the syllabic *mantras* which are identified with the essence of the deities themselves.[66] Thus the epithet '*Dasamahavidyas*' may be translated as the 'ten great *mantras*' and in this way the goddesses, in typically

Tantric fashion, are at once the *mantras,* the religious knowledge they convey, and the essence of reality itself.[67] The *Mahavidyas* symbolize or are identified with, stages and aspects of spiritual consciousness which a *Tantric* practitioner may expect to experience during their spiritual evolution. Each of the individual goddesses is associated with a particular mental perfection (*siddhi*) or mode of perception; the goddesses are perceived as blessing the *Tantric sadhaka* with the progressive advancement of higher yogic states or moods (*bhavas*).[68] In this respect the *Mahavidyas* are sometimes associated with the practice of *kundalini yoga* and the progressive opening of energy centres (*cakras*) in the subtle body of the *Tantric* aspirant.[69]

The *Mahavidyas* have been identified as a group since the tenth century CE, although some of them, such as Kali, were the focus of devotional cults in their own right prior to the early medieval period, which has continued to be to the present day.[70] As a whole, the group of ten goddesses are generally understood within textual and iconographic sources to be aspects or forms of the transcendent feminine Absolute, Mahadevi. As such, they exemplify the propensity of the Great Goddess to manifest herself in a variety of forms at various times for different reasons.[71] This trait is a common feature of a number of mythological narratives of the Great Goddess.[72] The *Mahavidyas* are a means of expressing the multi-faceted nature of Mahadevi, illustrating both her benign and terrible aspects. When associated with local goddesses they provide a way of linking the provincial deity directly with the transcendent element of the Great Goddess, thus Kinsley states: "The presence of the *Mahavidyas* in a goddess temple identifies a local or regional goddess with an all-India mythology or symbolic structure, lending her a certain prestige."[73] While they are depicted in various temples, belonging to goddesses, they seldom appear as a group in their own temple, though individually they may have their own temple. However, there is a group of temples dedicated to the *Mahavidyas* alongside the Kamakhya temple in Assam, to be discussed in chapter 7.[74]

As *Tantric* goddesses, the *Mahavidyas* are seen to bestow both religious and worldly assistance on their devotees. A practitioner may seek an insight into the higher realms of spiritual consciousness associated with the pursuit of liberation (*mukti*) or, alternatively, the acquisition of magical powers in order to achieve more mundane worldly aims or rewards (*bhukti*). In this respect, the *Mahavidyas* are also persistently associated with or, indeed, identified as, occult magical abilities (*siddhis*) that may enable the holder to achieve certain capabilities such as financial gain, attracting members of the opposite sex, power over enemies or other worldly enjoyments. The granting of worldly blessings and boons is associated with many Hindu deities, but as *Tantric* deities and expressions of spiritual transformation, the association of the *Mahavidyas* with such qualities is particularly pertinent. Kinsley elaborates on this point: "insofar as the Mahavidyas might be thought of as aspects or stages of consciousness in the spiritual quest, the association of *siddhis* with them is not surprising".[75]

Whilst the ten *Mahavidyas* are often considered as a group, each also embodies individual characteristics of their own. With the exception of Kamala and Bhuvanesvari, all are fierce goddesses exhibiting dangerous and powerful qualities. Kali, meaning 'the black goddess', is often considered the first or supreme *Mahavidya*; in some textual sources the other *Mahavidyas* are characterized as arising from Kali.[76] She represents the primal and dynamic energy (*sakti*) of the Absolute and is associated with the divine acts of creation and destruction.[77] Kali is associated with death and dissolution, ideas which the *Tantric sadhaka* fully confronts as a technique for achieving salvation and thus immortality of the self. Above the other *Mahavidyas*, Kali is presented as typifying and thus revealing the true nature of the Absolute. Kali is understood as transgressing many of the usual characteristics of Hindu wifehood: she is sexually dominant, appears naked and prefers to reside in cremation grounds rather than within society. Such transgressions denote the transcendence of social and worldly values and the freedom this brings. These are ideas that are prevalent and deemed necessary within *Tantric* practice as a means of achieving transcendent insight into ultimate reality.[78] As one of the *Mahavidyas* the goddess Kali can be understood as a liminal symbol, both occupying and traversing the very boundaries of social purity and order, and danger and pollution.

The name Tara means 'the goddess who guides through troubles'. Tara often follows Kali within the group, both sharing a prominent place and indeed common symbolisms. Like Kali, Tara is popular in Bengal with perhaps her most famous temple being at Tarapith (seat of Tara). As part of the *Mahavidya* group, the figure of Tara bears a close resemblance to Kali as she, too, expresses the dominance of the divine feminine principle over the masculine through dangerous and transgressive symbolism. Such are the commonalities between the two deities that Kinsley states of Tara: "she appears to be a variant expression of Kali, a kindred spirit, as it were, who expresses the same truths as Kali, only in slightly different form."[79] Reminiscent of Kali, Tara is associated with the principles of death and destruction, particularly fire and the cremation ground, indeed she is sometimes directly identified with the purifying and transformative powers of the cremation ground fire.[80] Iconographically Tara portrays the dominance of Sakti over Siva as she is often depicted as standing upon the corpse of Siva, or mothering him as an infant, thus the *Tara Tantra* declares:

> Standing firmly with her left foot on a corpse, she laughs loudly – transcendent. Her hands hold a sword, a blue lotus, a dagger, and a begging bowl. She raises her war cry, *hum*! Her matted tawny hair is bound with poisonous blue snakes. Thus the terrifying Tara destroys the unconsciousness of the three worlds and carries them off on her head [to the other shore].[81]

Along with her obvious shared symbolisms, Tara also exemplifies gentler aspects and qualities of the divine feminine. She is characterized as a saviour to those who are truly devoted to her, rescuing her devotees when they are in need; indeed the goddess is also known as "she who brings us to the other shore"[82] which is a common way of expressing her salvific nature. In this respect, Tara also expresses maternal, nurturing and creative qualities. [83]

The third goddess of the group is Tripura-sundari meaning 'she who is lovely in the Three Worlds'. Also known as Sodasi meaning 'she who is sixteen' and Lalita meaning 'she who is beautiful', Tripura-sundari is sometimes portrayed with Tara and Kali as a primordial power or *adisakti*, signifying a high position within the group.[84] Within devotional literature Tripura-sundari's benign aspects are often emphasized as being beautiful, pure, auspicious, fertile and beneficent; elsewhere, however, she is described as being dangerous, ferocious and wild. In her more terrifying forms she resembles and becomes identified with Kali.[85] The name Tripura-sundari is associated with a number of tripartite symbolisms, including those of her triple syllable *mantras*, the three channels of the subtle body associated with *kundalini* yoga and the three divine powers of will, knowledge and action.[86] The goddess is often identified with and depicted by her *yantra*, known as the *Sri cakra* and the *Sri vidya* mantra. Such representations are key aspects of *Tantric* conceptualization, practice and worship of the divine, thus prominent associations between Tripura-sundari and *Tantric sadhana* are evident within her character.[87] Tripura-sundari was an important *Tantric* goddess before her inclusion within the *Dasamahavidyas* and remains so today, particularly within the *Sri Vidya* tradition (to be examined below).

The name Bhuvanesvari means 'she whose body is the world' indicating her particular association with creation and the sustenance of the earth. As such, Bhuvanesvari is often identified with *prakrti*, the physical world and its elemental constituents. In mythological sources the world is said to have emerged from her. [88] Bhuvanesvari ceaselessly attends to the manifest world, conferring boons and support upon her devotees and those in need. The *Bhuvanesvari Tantra* associates her with *soma*, a mind altering drink, which during the *Vedic* period was deified because it represented the sap of life:

> With the ambrosia made from lunar essence, that is, the seed, the sacrificial offering, soma, she quenches the thirst of the world. This is why the all-powerful goddess has the moon, the cup of *soma*, as her diadem. She takes care of the three worlds and feeds them, so one of her emblems is the gesture-of-granting-boons (*vara mudra*).[89]

Bhuvanesvari is one of the two benign goddess figures within the *Mahavidyas*. Textual sources often discuss her beautiful appearance which, it is suggested, may be "understood as an affirmation of the physical world",[90] a key concept asserted by both *Sakta* and *Tantric* ideologies. In this respect the goddess is understood as the fundamental energy of manifestation, the dynamic power of renewal and replenishment. Sometimes considered as a form of Tripura-sundari in narrative sources, Bhuvanesvari is also identified with her *yantra* and *mantra* forms, particularly as part of *Tantric sadhana*. It is said devotion to the goddess of the world is rewarded by her bestowal of *siddhis* associated with material accomplishment such as the powers of attraction and control over others.[91]

Chinnamasta is 'the self-decapitated goddess', signifying her striking appearance and symbolic identity. As her name implies, the iconography of this terrifying and awe inspiring goddess is formidably powerful, indicating her dangerous and transgressive nature. The *Chinnamasta Tantra* depicts her as such:

> Her left foot in battle, she holds her severed head and a knife. Naked she drinks voluptuously the stream of blood-nectar flowing from her beheaded body. The jewel on her forehead is tied with a serpent. She has three eyes. Her breasts are adorned with lotuses. Inclined toward lust, she sits erect above the god of love, who shows signs of lustfulness.[92]

The image of a severed head is also associated with both Kali and Tara. In their cases, the head is that of a demon; in contrast, Chinnamasta offers her own head to her worshippers. Within *Tantric* ideology the symbolism of a severed head is extremely meaningful and potent; it is representative of the sacrifice of the limited egoistic self carried out by the aspirant in their bid to achieve liberation through identity with the divine. Chinnamasta is associated with the defeat and discipline of desire as signified by her standing upon Kama, the god of love. This is symbolic of the need for the aspirant to control sexual desire in order to succeed in yogic and religious disciplines; within the *Tantric* context it is extremely important for the *sadhaka* to have yogic control over sexual energies and desires prior to embarking on *Tantric* practices involving such practices in a ritualized context. In this respect Chinnamasta also signifies the creative and transformative powers of sexual vitality and desire; the goddess can then be understood to represent the sublimation of desire in order for it to be employed in a *Tantric* religious context. Her associations with sex and death are symbolic of divine creation and destruction, all typically *Tantric* themes. Chinnamasta's iconography also suggests connections with the rousing of *kundalini* energy in *kundalini yoga*.[93]

The epithet Bhairavi means 'the fierce one'. As such, the goddess embodies the terrible and destructive aspects of the divine and like many of the *Mahavidyas* she is closely associated with Siva, particularly his fierce and destructive forms. As goddess of destruction, she is associated with death, punishment, self-destructive practices and infertility in men.[94] Despite her fiercesome associations, Bhairavi's terrifying and annihilatory character are nevertheless viewed in relation to the divine acts of creation and sustenance. In this respect her destructive tendencies are honoured and respected, for without them creation and thus manifestation could not take place. As a typically fierce goddess, Bhairavi embodies fundamentally *Tantric* ideals of transgression, and as such is closely associated with non-orthodox practice. Also known as Tripura-bharavi (She who is fierce in the three worlds), the *Kalika Purana* discusses worship of the goddess: "The people of *sudra* caste and others should offer the best quality of drink to the goddess Tripurabhairavi. An adept may worship Tripurabharavi following the heterodox method."[95]

Bhairavi is said to have a number of distinctive forms, each with its own set of symbolic associations, *Tantric yantras* and *mantras*, and range of blessings.[96] Her various forms and her strong link with the cosmic cycle of creation, preservation and dissolution indicate that within her symbolism are contained all the powers of the divine, not just the power of destruction.[97]

The seventh goddess is Dhumavati, 'the widow goddess'. Kinsley notes she is barely known outside of the *Mahavidya* cult and that there is no evidence to suggest she had an independent cult of her own prior to her inclusion in the group.[98] Depicted as a widow she is representative of all that is inauspicious, the *Dhumavati Tantra* describes her in the following way:

> She appears as a woman of unhealthy complexion, restless, wicked, tall with a dirty robe and dishevelled hair. With gaps in her teeth, she looks like a widow . . . Her eyes seem cruel, her hands tremble, her nose is long. She behaves deceitfully and is sly in her looks. Insatiably hungry and thirsty, she inspires fear and is the instigator of quarrels.[99]

Associated with ugly and unappealing aspects of reality, she is said to dwell in desolate and deserted areas and is strongly associated with cremation grounds, indeed she is said to dress in clothes taken from corpses.[100] As such, Dhumavati exemplifies the transformative nature of social transgression; like Kali she is a liminal figure, embodying the inherent dangers associated with the margins of society. She exemplifies the religious and *Tantric* ideals of renunciation and non-attachment to mundane ends, instead instilling distaste for worldly affairs in her followers.[101]

The name Bagalamukhi (lit. "face of a crane") is conceived of as 'the paralyser'. The epithet possibly relates to the power of the goddess to intervene on behalf of her devotees, stopping thought and action in their enemies thus enabling control over them. Accordingly she is strongly linked to occult magical powers and the attainment of *siddhis*, more so than any of the other *Mahavidyas*.[102] Often depicted sitting upon a corpse, Bagalamukhi is also closely connected to the *Tantric* practice of *sava-sadhana* which involves the *Tantric* adherent performing rituals and meditating whilst positioned on a corpse. Deemed to be a particularly powerful *Tantric* practice, *sava-sadhana* suggests the symbiotic relationship between dissolution and creation, the corpse being indicative of the static masculine aspects of reality (Siva) and the practitioner embodying the dynamic feminine aspects (Sakti). The ritual itself is also closely associated with the attainment of *siddhis*. Kinsley suggests a number of symbolic meanings behind the iconography of the corpse, which is also found in association with a number of other *Mahavidyas* such as Kali, Tara, Chinnamasta Dhumavati and Matangi. Primary among these are the transgressive and liminal qualities associated with corpses, cremation grounds and death in general. Such qualities make these ritual items, places and concepts powerfully transformative and thus attractive to practitioners of extreme forms of *Tantric* religious practice.[103]

The ninth goddess, Matangi, is known as 'the outcaste goddess'. She is commonly associated with pollution, in particular left-over food stuffs, which are deemed especially impure within Hindu tradition. According to narrative literature, devotees of Matangi, whilst in a polluted state themselves, purposefully present their own polluted left overs to the goddess as offerings. As an embodiment of inauspiciousness and the forbidden, the goddess exemplifies the transcendence of social norms associated with *Tantric* practice. Through the offering of impure substances and practices the *Tantric sadhaka* aims to overcome worldly values regarding pollution, an indication that they have also gained mastery over the ego, which is the source of desire and aversion. Worship of Matangi allows the adherent to face, head on, the associated dangers and powers with the aim of achieving spiritual freedom as a result. Matangi is then perceived as liberating in nature, offering her devotees the chance of salvation through transcendence of pollution.[104] The association with impurity extends to her connection with outcaste groups considered to be highly polluted within Hindu society. Such social groups often fulfil jobs considered particularly polluting such as the collection of waste, handling of meat and the overseeing of cremations. These connotations of inauspiciousness and death indicate Matangi's connection with the boundaries and periphery of Hindu society, key themes in *Tantric* practice. Matangi embodies the idea of transgression and provides a prime focus for *Tantric* adherents aiming to overcome aversion to social pollution in the hope of achieving religious liberation or gaining magical powers for worldly aims.

The final goddess within the *Mahavidya* group is Kamala, meaning 'the lotus goddess'. She is almost always presented as the last goddess within the group, suggestive of an inferior place in relation to the other goddesses.[105] As the second of the benign goddesses within the group, Kamala is understood as a bestower of good fortune and abundance. Worship of Kamala is associated with worldly and material gain, as she is viewed as a being able to fulfil her devotees' mundane desires such as wealth and love. Directly identified with the goddess Laksmi or Sri, Kamala is perceived as having the most auspicious and benign qualities within the *Mahavidya* group. Like Kali, Kamala has always been a popular goddess within Hinduism and devotional cults to her existed long before her inclusion within the *Dasamahavidyas*, which scholars noted occurred relatively late.[106] Kinsley comments that her role as a

Tantric Mahavidya is strangely out of context for a goddess who is normally identified with purity, domesticity and as the spouse of Visnu. Accordingly, within *Mahavidya* literature, Kamala is not overtly identified as a consort of Visnu, indeed she is "almost entirely removed from marital and domestic contexts."[107] As a *Mahavidya*, Kamala is associated with terrifying qualities such as demon slaying. These are aspects which are generally absent in her worship outside of the *Mahavidya* context. It seems apparent that those who appropriated Kamala as a *Mahavidya* modified her character to suit their needs. The goddess is representative of normal states of consciousness and is perceived as the first step on the religious path, from which a practitioner must progress in order to experience the highest form of consciousness represented by the fearsome Kali.[108]

A *Tantric Sakta* tradition – *Sri Vidya*

Placing emphasis on the gentle and motherly forms of the Goddess, the *Sri Vidya* tradition can generally be understood as a form of 'right-handed' *Tantra* in which many of the more transgressive practices of *Kaula Tantra* have been dispensed with. Instead, such rituals are interpreted symbolically and cosmologically rather than concretely and practically. Whilst the *Sri Vidya* tradition has its historical origins in the 'left-handed' *Tantric* traditions of the *Kaula*, it has assimilated and adapted the transgressive *Kaula* teachings for its own purposes, reinterpreting heterodox *Tantric* doctrines to bring them more in line with orthodox Brahmanical ideals of purity.[109] As such the *Sri Vidya* views itself as an orthodox form of *Tantrism*, claiming to be both *Vedic* and *Tantric* in nature.[110]

Asserting the common cosmological and philosophical positions affirmed in Hindu *Tantrism*, the *Sri Vidya* cult conceives of the manifest cosmos as a form of the Goddess. As such the deity Sri represents the active and dynamic qualities of the divine Absolute. The Goddess is understood as the supreme aspect of the divine, she is Sakti who whilst maintaining constant union with her consort Siva, nevertheless remains superior to him. Within the tradition then, both feminine and masculine aspects of the Absolute are recognized, but the *Sri Vidya* cult is careful to maintain the overall pre-eminence of the Goddess. In this regard the active female aspect of the divine is understood as the independent source of the dynamic cosmic powers of creation, preservation and dissolution. Correspondingly, the static masculine aspect of the divine is comprehended as unchanging and eternal in nature. Sakti is then both the possessor of power, and the power itself and thus functions as an independent totality. For the *Sri Vidya* cult, without the dynamic power of the goddess, the masculine aspect of the divine would be inert and ineffectual, unable to create and maintain the manifest universe, thus it is the goddess that is held to be supreme above and beyond her masculine counterpart. It is through the divine feminine power that the magical and glorious process of creation may take place. Equally it is through the grace of the goddess that her devotees may partake in the honour of worshipping her, and eventually come to know her directly through religious experience of her *sakti*.

The term '*Sri Vidya*' literally means 'knowledge of the auspicious goddess Sri'. As a form of *Sakta Tantrism*, the tradition worships the beautiful and benign aspect of the Great Goddess under the names Sri, Tripura-sundari, or Lalita, one of the *Mahavidyas* discussed earlier. The *Sri Vidya* tradition is avowedly *Sakta* in orientation and *Tantric* in its practice, asserting the bountiful goddess Sri and her power as the supreme form of the divine feminine, surpassing and subsuming all other forms of the Great Goddess. In this respect, Sri is also sometimes described as having inauspicious, terrifying and fierce aspects, but such forms are considered derivative and secondary to her superlative benevolent and beautiful form. As an independent benign (*saumya*) *Tantric* goddess, the goddess Sri and her associated qualities can be directly contrasted with independent terrifying (*ugra*) female deities such as Kali.[111] Brooks notes three primary attributes of the goddess, stating; "she is royal, auspicious and subsuming. All three characteristics are manifestations of her most essential attribute: power (*sakti*)."[112] Through her associations with concepts of royalty and auspiciousness, Sri is felt to bestow upon worldly sovereigns the right to rule and is said to destroy heretical forms of religion that are anti-*Vedic*. Understood as a protectorate of kingdoms she is viewed as a loving but firm mother figure who grants the wishes of all those truly devoted to her. As a regal deity she wields her 'power' over the manifest world, imbuing it with life giving qualities. The goddess is felt to engage within worldly affairs on behalf of her devotees in order to uphold the laws of *dharma*.[113] In this respect, *Sri Vidya* directly contrasts with other forms of *Tantrism* that seek to break the laws of *dharma* through their transgressive practices.

The deity Sri is understood as manifesting herself in two forms, one 'gross' or 'physical' and the second 'subtle' as 'energy' or 'power'. The anthropomorphic figure of the goddess Sri is held to be her simplest 'material' or 'gross' form. This physically manifest aspect of the deity is the object of meditational contemplation and devotional practice by all manner of devotees of the goddess, not only those initiated into the *Sri Vidya* tradition. Such conventional forms of exterior worship are associated with outward public religious practice. In this form the goddess is worshipped and honoured with traditional *puja* ceremonies, and she is glorified in narratives such as the *Lalitasahasranama* 'the thousand names of Lalita' which vividly describes her beautiful and youthful appearance. As an object of devotional worship, the goddess Sri is widely recognized and worshipped by many Hindus and is an important member of the Hindu pantheon.

However, for initiates of the *Tantric Sri Vidya* tradition the goddess Sri is also understood as manifesting in 'subtle' form as *Tantric yantras* and *mantras*. Initiates into the goddess's cult receive the secret *yantra* and *mantra* formulas only when deemed ready by their guru. For the *sadhaka*, these tools of *Tantric* visualization are considered to be the essence and embodiment of cosmic manifestation, Sakti itself.[114] As such, they are filled with potency and transformative power which the adherent aims to utilize and identify with. These subtle forms of the goddess are of key importance to the tradition as it is through induction into these mysterious and arcane aspects of the divine that a *Sri Vidya* practitioner may experience the ultimate power of the goddess. In contrast to exterior, exoteric, forms of devotional religious practice associated with the goddess's gross form, worship using these esoteric *Tantric* forms involves the practitioner taking an individual and internalized approach to religious discipline. These powerful forms of the deity are understood as expressions of her transcendent nature, as her *sakti*. As visual and sound forms of the deity, they are felt to be the purest and highest expression of the feminine Absolute, filled with cryptic symbolism through which the *Tantric sadhaka* aims to gain insight into the true nature of reality. Through yogic visualization techniques, centred upon these subtle manifestations, the *Sri Vidya* initiate aims to internalize the subtle essence of the goddess. The practitioner aspires to wholly identify with the supreme power of the divine feminine, thus achieving the standard *Tantric* rewards of magical powers and liberation from reincarnation. As such the subtle forms hold not only worldly benefits *for* the *sadhaka*, but are also of key soteriological significance, providing a means by which the practitioner can unite with the divine feminine.

The goddess's *mantra* is known as the *Sri Vidya mantra* and consists of 'seed' syllables (such as *hrm* or *krm*), which, in themselves, do not make any literal sense. These root sounds are felt to be identical with the goddess, and are forms of her *sakti*. The *sadhaka* uses the *mantra* to transcend the manifest world through a process of ritual purification of their consciousness. The *mantra* is then employed to bring about a relationship of identification between the various aspects of the practitioner's experience. The universe, the practitioner and the deity are understood as expressions of the one true reality, Sakti.[115] When recited correctly and with appropriate understanding of its symbolic significance, the *mantra* is said to bring about the extinguishing of desire and union with the Absolute for the practitioner. The *mantra* is not then a means of addressing the goddess or requesting her help, rather it is considered to be an auspicious and powerful expression of the nature of the divine.[116]

As well as being expressed in sound, the divine feminine is also represented in the form of a diagram known as the *Sri yantra* or *Sri cakra*. The two-dimensional diagram is the visual form of the essence of the goddess, and it is felt to contain the presence of the divine. By concentrating the mind on the diagram's interconnecting triangles, the *sadhaka* seeks a connection with the goddess in this most abstract of forms. As a subtle form of the goddess, the diagram fulfils a number of functions for the *Tantric* initiate:

> The *sricakra* functions on three levels for the initiated adept: (1) it is a map of creation's divine essences projected visually; (2) it is divine power which can be become accessible to those who obtain initiated esoteric knowledge about its use; and (3) it is the real presence (*sadbhava*) of divinity, worthy of worship, admiration, and even fear because of its potential to transform one's relationship with the sacred.[117]

The *Sri cakra* is one of the most easily recognized Hindu *yantras* and is a particularly famous visual image within Hindu *Tantrism*.[118] The different levels of the *Sri yantra* diagram represent the process of cosmic manifestation and dissolution. It consists of a central dot or 'point' known as a *bindu* which is symbolic of the subtle and unmanifest Absolute prior to the beginning of the process of manifestation. It is representative of the innate potency contained within the union of Siva–Sakti. Surrounding the *bindu* are five downward pointing triangles, symbolic of Sakti and four upward pointing triangles representative of Siva. The nine triangles intersect creating forty-three triangles. The nine triangles represent the powers of creation and dissolution; the five Sakti triangles are said to represent earth, water, fire, air and space; whilst the Siva triangles are associated with four metaphysical functions of Siva. Surrounding the triangles are concentric circles filled with first eight, and then sixteen lotus petals. Encompassing the circles is a square with central openings in each of the four sides. This exterior part of the symbol, the square, is representative of the physical manifest world. The various levels are also identified with parts of the gross and subtle human body; thus as well as being a form of divine power, the *Sri yantra* is understood as a symbolic map of the various levels of macrocosm and microcosm experienced by the *Tantric sadhaka*.

As the reader will now appreciate, *Tantrism* is a rather complex form of Hinduism to do justice to in an introductory text. Yet in a study on the beliefs and practices associated with Hindu goddesses, its inclusion is crucial. Not only does it uphold and promote the more dangerous, darker side of goddess worship it also provides a highly sophisticated goddess-centred philosophy, prompting scholars such a Benjamin Walker to claim: "Tantrism contains the loftiest philosophical speculation, side by side with the grossest obscenities; the most rarefied metaphysics with the wildest superstition."[119]

This marks the end of Part I of this book, which has examined a wide variety of attitudes and beliefs about Hindu goddess that have accumulated over a vast period of time. Part II, practices, will demonstrate how these beliefs – which at times seem rather abstract or fanciful – have entered the daily lives of those we might refer to as Hindus. It is within the practices of any religious tradition that the religion truly lives. Consequently, the reader will find a rich diversity of religious ritual behaviour scrutinized in the chapters to follow.

Part II
Practices

5 Goddess Worship

In their most abstract form, goddesses represent the energy and power that is commonly referred to as *sakti*. Since no meaningful relationship can be established between the devotee and an abstract principle, the Goddess appears in the manifest world in various forms. These goddesses then become the object of devotion for the many devotees who regularly worship her. While some worship here is in her grand and lofty temples, attended by throngs of priests, the majority approach the Goddess in her more humble, localized forms. It is these shrines and small temples that provide rural India with its religious character. However, this worship is not confined to the many temples that abound in India's towns and cities; it is also an important ritual in the home, remaining unseen by the majority of India's many visitors.

Puja, which is most often performed before an image or *murti* of a deity, is generally undertaken on an individual basis, though there are times when people may join a larger congregation at a shrine or temple, most often on festival days, or in the larger temples, when the priests perform rituals at specific times. Although this chapter is concerned with goddess worship, many aspects of ritual worship are the same for the gods and goddesses. Therefore, the term deity rather than goddess will be used unless rituals performed exclusively for goddesses are being discussed. It tends to be within local worship that the ritual and devotion differs depending on the gender of the deity. Consequently, where there are differences this will be pointed out.

Another important aspect of Hindu worship that is commonly directed towards the Divine in female form is *Tantric* worship. Just as in local worship the goddess tends to dominate, in aspects of *Tantric* ritual the emphasis on the goddess is more evident than in orthodox practice. While many aspects of *Tantric* worship are meditational, seeking an identity between the worshipper and the worshipped, it is often the more extreme and marginal practices that revolve around the goddess, such as cremation ground rituals and the non-symbolic use of the *panca-makara* (five forbidden substances each beginning with 'm') discussed below.

This chapter will first examine worship as practiced in the temple and the home, providing a detailed account of some of the more important rituals, such as *abhiseka* (ritual anointing of the deity). A section on *bhakti* (loving devotion) in Bengal will highlight how goddesses, even those who appear outwardly fierce, can be the inspiration for beautifully crafted poetic works, the writing of which becomes an act of worship. Some aspects of local worship, such as snake veneration, that will not be covered in the chapter on festivals (chapter 6) will be examined and the chapter will conclude with an examination of aspects of goddess worship that are uniquely *Tantric* in nature.

Orthodox or Pan-Indian worship of the goddess

Temple worship

Although temple worship is perhaps what constitutes the most common and visible expression of theistic Hinduism, it did not become widespread until about the sixth century CE. It is most widely discussed in the later *Puranas*, which provide instruction on temple construction and ritual performance for the deity that the particular text is dedicated to. Temples provide a home or palace for the gods and goddesses where they are treated in much the same way as kings and queens might traditionally have be treated. The temple is a place where they receive their loyal subjects and their veneration. The largest temples are sprawling places usually housing a number of deities, but are generally dedicated to a particular deity, who the temple is often named after. These large temples, which have been constructed over many years by local rulers, almost represent mini towns or cities themselves. For instance, the Kalighat temple (dedicated to Kali) in Kolkata has, within its walls, stalls selling *pera*, the sweets that Kali is particularly fond of, garland sellers, and stalls selling pamphlets, pictures, books and religious trinkets. All that is needed for the worship of Kali is found in the little shops that line the inner walls of the temple.[1] It also has a series of sanctums which house various deities, a sacred fire pit, reminiscent of the *vedic* sacrificial fire pits (*homa*) and a separate sacrificial area where goats are sacrificed on a daily basis. This aspect of the temple is uncommon since animal sacrifice is only performed in a handful of contemporary temples, and certainly only those dedicated to goddesses, Kali in particular. There is a kitchen, an open hall (*mandapa*) and at the heart of the temple is the sanctum of Kali herself. The main sanctum is referred to as the *garbhagrha* "womb-house", "house of the seed" or "embryo". This small windowless room is the sacred nerve-centre of the temple; its roof points up towards the heavens and this is where the main, immovable, image (*mula murti*) is kept. This is opposed to the movable festival image (*utsava murti*) that is taken outside the temple during the main festival and is discussed below.

Unlike religious worship in the West, and Christianity in particular, the worship of deities in Hindu temples is generally an individual affair, therefore necessitating the continual coming and going of devotees to the temple. The temples housing the most popular goddesses, such as Kalighat in Kolkata, Durga in Varanasi and Minaksi in Madurai, are alive with the constant cacophony of sound. The sound of bells, drums, the blowing of conch shells and the intonations of the priests fill the temple, as a stream of people constantly visit the many sanctums to pay homage to their favourite deities. Although temples are often noisy chaotic places, some areas of the larger temples may provide spaces of quiet contemplation. However, whether noisy or tranquil, temples provide an opportunity for Hindus to come and communicate with the focus of their devotion, the gods and goddesses. In most cases their devotion is mediated by the temple priests who act as intermediaries between the worshipper and the deity, taking the offerings, giving them to the deities and returning the *prasada* (a part of the offering that has been blessed by the god or goddess) to the devotee.

Since deities should be worshipped at least once a day, *puja* is the main daily ritual carried out in the temple. Generally there are no formal services, such as might be the case in a Western church, though, there are times of the day, particularly in the larger temples, when the priests regularly perform *puja*, such as early evening and first thing in the morning. Other regular rituals include bathing and feeding the deities and times when the deities take rest periods when they are enclosed in their sanctums. At other times there is a constant stream of people coming in and out of the temple with offerings for the deities. Therefore, most temples perform *puja* many times a day, but this is carried out on demand. The core ritual of *puja*, both in the temple and in the home, is the offering of light (*arti* or *arati*) during which Sanskrit *mantras* or hymns from the *Vedas* are chanted. In some temples, the only time the devotee can really see the deity is when the priest offers the *arti* flame before the face of the goddess. Many sanctums are situated at the end of a passageway and are, therefore, rather dark. Since only the priest is allowed to enter the sanctum, the devotee is kept at a distance from the deity and can only truly take *darsana* (have sight of the deity and consequently their blessing) during *arti*.

Temple worship also provides the devotee with a temporary respite from the world. The architecture used in the building of the temple is designed to make the devotee aware that the place being entered is sacred and the further into the temple one progresses the more sacred it becomes. George Mitchell articulates this idea well as he claims: "Penetration towards the image or symbol of the deity housed in this setting is always through a progression from light into darkness, from open and large spaces to a confined and small space."[2] No where is this more evident than at the magnificent Minaksi temple in Madurai. The outermost wall that marks its sacred boundry is punctuated in the four primary directions by four huge (45–50 metres tall) tapering entrance towers (Tam. *gopurams*) that mark out the sacred precinct separating it from the rest of Madurai. (See plate 5). Each one is populated by myriads of brightly painted, carved deities who keep a watchful eye on all who enter; they also direct the eye toward the heavens. The visitor cannot help being impressed by such majestic entranceways. The wonder does not stop at the gateway to the temple as the Minaksi temple is one of the most extensive temple complexes in India, filled with a hall containing a thousand pillars and rambling corridors that encircle the sacred, golden lotus tank or pool. Although dedicated to Minaksi and her consort Sudaresvara (a localized form of Siva), this temple is also filled with other deities, many of whom have their own priests and their own forms of worship. Entry into the temple represents not only a passage from the secular world outside to a sacred world within, but on a metaphysical level it represents a journey into the self. This passage represents a journey to the heart or 'nerve centre' of the temple, the most sacred part and that which must be protected. The temple provides a means of contact between divinity and humankind and, as such, might be viewed as a place of transcendence where the purifying power of divinity infuses the devotee through the rituals performed by them while there. Because the contact between the deity and visitor to the temple can be very close, sometimes non-Hindus are excluded from entering the main sanctum area, as is the case at the Minaksi temple, while other temples may exclude non-Hindus from the temple altogether.

One occasion when communal worship is prevalent in the temple is during the many festivals celebrated in India (see chapter 6 for an account of some of the most important goddess festivals). During these events, the temple is the focus of worship, where many people gather to witness and participate in special temple rituals such as the ritual bathing of a deity in various substances (*abhiseka*). Many festivals can only be celebrated at the larger temples that have the room to store the necessary festival paraphernalia, such as the palanquins or chariots used to take the festival images of the deities in procession around the temple. Along with the more visual aspects of festival, another important aspect might be the reading of sacred texts. This is an important part of the festival as it provides the opportunity for devotees to hear the texts being spoken in the language in which whey were composed, generally Sanskrit or Tamil. It is a meritorious act to listen to a text as well as reciting it. This was considered so potent that traditionally women and those of a low caste were prohibited from hearing them.

Home worship

Worship in the home is the most consistent religious practice within an orthodox Brahman household with *puja* offered to their chosen deities at least twice a day, morning and night. In a wealthy household, there might be a separate *puja* room, kept ritually segregated from the main living areas, where a collection of *murtis* and pictures of gods and goddesses are placed. The shrine room acts as a mini temple within the home and may provide the occupants with a place of refuge and peace, which is so necessary in today's busy world. However, in most houses the home shrine is placed in a corner of the kitchen, the room in the house that is considered the most pure. It may be very small and simple with just a few pictures or images of deities, or may reflect the richness and inclusive nature of Hinduism with many deities including Jesus, Mary and images or objects from other faiths. The home shrine often provides clues as to the spiritual behaviour of the family as it may also contain religious souvenirs, such as a pot of Ganges water or a small photograph of the Kali image at Kalighat or Daksinesvar, brought back from the places of pilgrimage (chapter 7) that the family have visited.

Worship offered at the home shrine is a relatively simple and intimate affair, a part of daily practice for the pious. On the other hand, temple worship is a much more elaborate form of worship that, for some people, is practiced only on special occasions. Nevertheless, the basic rituals used to honour the deities of Hinduism are essentially the same for home or temple worship. In the home, the devotee offers *puja* directly to the chosen deities, whereas in the temple, the *puja* is performed by a priest or in some smaller temples, a *pujari* (a non-Brahman priest). The acts of worship, whether performed in the home or the temple, represent a meeting between humans and the divine.

Abhiseka: *ritual bathing and decoration of the goddess*

The ritual bathing of a deity (*abhiseka*) is one of the most frequently performed rituals in India. It ranges from the simple act of bathing a deity with milk or water, to the spectacular ceremony of bathing a whole temple with various substances (*kumbhabhiseka*) during certain festivals. Generally speaking, *abhiseka* appears to be a more obvious part of weekly goddess rituals in south India, especially Tamilnadu, than it is in the north. On a practical level, the seeming abundance of flowers and other ritual ingredients such as sandal-paste may mean that *abhiseka* is easier to perform in Tamilnadu. During research in Orissa some informants claimed that *abhiseka* is only given to male deities, with a simpler form (*majana*) being offered to goddesses. In Tamilnadu, however, there appears to be no such distinction although at temples dedicated to goddesses, a relatively simple version of *abhiseka*, primarily consisting of milk, is performed each Tuesday and Friday, the special days of the goddess. On other occasions a more lengthy and complex ritual is performed. Although it is a popular ritual, there are very few written sources to indicate the significance of the various constituents used in the *abhiseka* ceremonies, with many of the *pujaris* seemingly unsure of their importance. Fortunately, one local temple that I visited, the Pralaya Nayakiyamman temple,[3] does use a pamphlet that lists the various ingredients and the benefits they produce, although how many of them are used, would depend on the funds available or what individual devotees offer.[4] According to this pamphlet, the ingredients for *abhiseka* and the benefits they enjoy are as follows:[5]

Sandalwood oil	for happiness
Rice flour	for the removal of debt
Turmeric powder	for beauty and attractiveness
Fragrant smelling commodities	for long life
Curd, *ghee*, milk, etc.	for health
Juice of five fruits (*pancamartham*)	for salvation

Fruit mixture (mango, jackfruit, banana)	for salvation
Milk	for long life
Curd	for children
Ghee	for salvation
Light hot water	for salvation
Honey	for health
Tender coconut	for becoming a king
Jaggery juice	for a loss of enmity
Juice of sugar cane	for health
Boiled rice	for obtaining a kingdom
Sacred grass and water	for wisdom
Wood apple/*Bilva* leaf and water	for children
Holy ash	for being rich in all ways
Sandal-paste	for being showered with wealth
Adornment with dress	for a good position in life
Gingely oil	for the relief of household problems
Flowers	for seeing the god or goddess
Fruit juice, especially lemon varieties	for loss of enmity

A bright yellow cascade of turmeric water obscuring the face of the goddess and then replaced by a torrent of white milk, is an arresting sight. Afterwards the deity is decorated with flower garlands and sandal-paste. It is then presented with coconut, betel, *kumkum* (red powder), plantain, flowers and ash (referred to as *acanna*). Sweet *ponkal* is given in south India and is the usual *prasada* at the Pralaya Nayakiyamman temple. Finally, *arti* (the offering of light and prayers) concludes the ceremony. Variations of this ritual may be prevalent in other parts of India, but this series of events is common in worship of the goddesses in Colavandan, a small town in Tamilnadu.

Abhiseka is said by the informants to renew the power of the goddess, especially the *kumbhabhiseka*, a complex and lengthy ritual performed over a number of days following the refurbishment of the temple. The subsequent ritual bathing of the temple, when the *abhiseka* ingredients are poured from the top of the sanctum, is performed in order to supercharge the temple as a whole.[6] This should, theoretically, be carried out in all temples every twelve years. I say theoretically because the cost of restoring the temple, which accompanies the *kumbhabhiseka*, is in many cases prohibitive. Nevertheless, *abhiseka* is carried out periodically at many of the temples and it is clear, once the list of *abhiseka* ingredients and their resultant benefits is consulted, that this ritual is of considerable benefit, not only to the goddess in question, but to the devotee as well.

The decoration of the goddess, primarily with sandal paste (in Tamilnadu), is also an important part of the larger *abhiseka* ceremonies, particularly those in temples (large and small). Making the deities look beautiful (male and female) and, therefore, worthy of worship is a ritual performed on a daily basis in the temple, and to a lesser extent in the home. Just as a king or queen might be woken, bathed and suitably dressed by their courtiers every morning, the priests' first job is to awaken the deities. They are then bathed and suitably dressed before their sanctum doors are opened and their worship can commence. In the larger, often wealthier temples the adornment might be elaborate, whereas in smaller temples and in the home the daily decoration may be very simple. However, having said that, there are many shops and market stalls that sell a vast array of beautifully crafted garments and decorations, such as crowns and necklaces, specifically for the adornment of the small statues that are installed on the home shrine.

Bengali *devotional* bhakti

An important aspect of goddess worship is evident in Bengal, but may also be found elsewhere. This form of devotional *bhakti* worship was influenced by the *Vaisnava bhakti* tradition, which centred on Radha-Krsna, but in contrast is largely based on oral tradition. The bond between the devotee and the goddess is based mainly on two types of relationship; the goddess as mother or mistress with the devotee as child or servant and the goddess as child/daughter and the devotee as parent. The relationship is a very close one which is described by June McDaniel as being personal, intimate and passionate in nature.[7] Devotees spend their time in contemplation of the goddess and pour out their love in a variety of ways. What makes this devotional relationship different to some of those examined so far is its predominantly unselfish nature, prompting McDaniel to claim: "Supreme devotion is unselfish, for the devotee does not seek boons from the goddess. He or she recites the goddess's names and attributes, fixes the mind on her, has no desire to get rewards, and does not seek liberation."[8]

Gaining popularity in the second half of the eighteenth century many were inspired to write songs and poetry dedicated to the goddess that was then consumed by her devotees. What might be unexpected in this form of worship is the principal goddess to whom many beautiful poems and songs were written. Kali might not seem the obvious recipient of tender words, but those who were instrumental in this form of worship envisaged her as the primal source of their joy. Kali worship had become widespread in Bengal by mid-late eighteenth century[9] with wealthy, upper-class patrons being instrumental in commissioning poetry and accommodating her rituals, in part to "articulate their social and economic status".[10]

One of the foremost *bhakti* poets of this age was Ramprasad Sen (*c*.1718–75) who often lapsed into meditational trances that resulted in a wide range of poems, mostly devoted to Kali.

> O Ma Kali, wearing a garland of skulls,
> What an experience (*bhava*) you have shown me.
> You taught me how to call you,
> And at the moment I chanted "Ma"
> You drove me to ecstasy!
> Ma Tara, please tell me the source (of your sweetness) –
> Where did you get this name full of nectar?
> When worldly people look at me
> They call me mad from love;
> The members of my family
> Hurl curses and insults at me.
> But whatever people say, dark Mother,
> My faith will not waver.
> Let people say what they want
> I will chant the name of Kali forever.
> If you get rid of this illusory world,
> Insults and egotism are unimportant.
> I have made your red feet my goal.
> I am no longer concerned with worldly opinions. *Ramparasad Sen*[11]

Ramprasad was "credited with being the first to compose Sakta lyrics on Kali"[12] and these are still available in a collection of Ramprasad's poetry (*Ramprasadi Sangit – Songs of Ramprasad*) that is sold in Western Bengal.[13] However, he was not the only *bhakti* poet as his work inspired others to follow his lead. What he and those who have followed him have done is not to ignore Kali's darker aspects, but to reinterpret them in terms of their own devotion. This idea is evident in the following poem.

Because you love cremation grounds
I have made my heart one
so that You
Black Goddess of the Burning Grounds
can always dance there.
No desires are left, Ma, on the pyre
for the fire burns my heart,
and I have covered everything with its ash
to prepare for Your coming.
As for the Conqueror of Death, the Destructive Lord,
He can lie at Your feet. But You, come Ma,
dance to the beat; I'll watch You
with my eyes closed. *Ramlal Dasdatta*[14]

However, the interpretation of this poetry has prompted debate among scholars as to whether it is based on *Tantra* or *bhakti*. The question to be answered is: Are the poets *bhaktas* (lovers of god) or *sadhakas* (seekers)? David Kinsley argues that there is "a salvific tension between the two, creative and destructive, aspects of Kali's nature".[15] Kinsley states: "Kali's boon is won when man confronts or accepts her and the realities she dramatically conveys to him."[16] Other scholars, such as Malcolm McLean, attribute a *Tantric* context (based on opposites) to Kali worship in Bengal at the time when Ramprasad was composing his poetry and sees it as "radically tantric".[17] However, others, such as Arunkumar Basu, view Ramprasad and his poetry as "devotional outpouring[s]" . . . "heavily influenced by the Vaisnava mood of love and sweetness (*madhur rasa*)".[18]

Rachel Fell McDermott hesitates to support either side, apart from drawing our attention to the ideas it has stimulated, but does conclude that Ramprasad, and later, Ramakrishna who was influenced by his poetry, were probably both *bhaktas* and *sadhakas*, being influenced by both forms of religious ideas.

Ramakrishna – Kali's ultimate devotee

Perhaps the most famous devotee of Kali was Sri Ramakrishna

Paramhansa (1836–86). He had a position as a priest at the Daksinesvar temple in Kolkata, where he had a unique relationship with the goddess. Ramakrishna desperately sought a vision of Kali. "He began to spend long periods in solitary meditation and sometimes neglected his formal duties while he lost himself in singing ecstatically before the temple image of Kali."[19] However, no matter how much he longed to see Kali he was unable. The turning point came one day when, in desperation, he grabbed a sword and was about to kill himself. Finally, Kali appeared to him:

> Her scintillating Black Form rising out of a golden ocean, with gigantic waves rushing at me from all sides – I remained in a constant visionary state. It was impossible for me to tell any difference between night and day, so brilliant was Her Radiance, permeating my entire mind and senses.[20]

Ecstatic visions of Kali dominated the rest of Ramakrishna's life in which she appeared in many forms including as child or mother. Since Ramakrishna was a priest at the temple he had access to her sanctum and consequently her image. His relationship with Kali was unique.

> As priest, he saw her statue as *alive*, and he would laugh and dance with it, joke with the statue and hold its hands, and lie down next to it at night. Sometimes he identified himself with Kali, and he would decorate himself with flowers and sandal paste.[21]

As time progressed, Ramakrishna often lapsed into deep meditational states (*samadhi*) during which he had visions of Kali. He described one encounter:

> "I put the palm of my hand near her nostrils and felt that the Mother was actually breathing. I watched very closely, but I could never see her shadow on the temple wall in the light of the lamp, at night. I used to hear from my room how Mother ran upstairs, as merry as a little girl, with her anklets jingling. I wanted to be sure that she'd really done this, so I went outside. And there she was, standing on the veranda of the second floor of the temple, with her hair flying."[22]

This vision is interesting as Kali is clearly seen as a benevolent force and indeed she often appeared, either as a child who was happy to play or as a nurturing Mother. Seldom did the visions highlight Kali's fierce and destructive tendencies. In this respect Ramakrishna's visions mirror the attitude and feeling toward Kali of many ordinary Bengalis who, according to the research of McDermott, fail to notice or be impressed by Kali's overtly fierce iconography.[23] This they put down to familiarity, to most she is simply Mother or Ma and as such is often the object of loving devotion, as was evident in the *bhakta* poetry of Ramprasad Sen and others.

In the early days, Ramakrishna's visions were concrete in nature, but as his relationship with Kali deepened his visions became increasingly abstract. Carl Olson points out that the states leading to the visions (*samadhi*) were of two types:

> Ramakrishna distinguished between two types of *samadhi*: *sthira* or *jada* and *bhava*. The seeker attained the former type of *samadhi* by following the path of knowledge, which entailed the destruction of the ego. In contrast, *bhava samadhi* is gained by pursuing the path of *bhakti* (devotion). With relation to the play of the Goddess, the second type of *samadhi* was to be preferred because in this type of *samadhi* a trace of ego remained in the individual.[24]

Ramakrishna experimented with many forms of Hindu ritual practice and thought including *Vedanta* and *Tantrism*, and he willingly embraced different religions. Although he readily embraced and experimented with other ways of experiencing the divine, *bhakti* remained his definitive tool. Ramakrishna spent three days in meditation on Allah and believed that he had experienced this form of God. He also spent four days with a picture of the Madonna and child and again experienced Divinity. This leads Neeval to claim: "In both cases, he had visionary realizations that he held to be the same as those he had of various Hindu divinities."[25] However, this enquiry never led him far from Kali as eventually he came to see "the presence of the Mother at play in all things".[26] Ramakrishna was considered, by many, to embody divinity himself. He now appears on posters of Daksinesvar Kali, accompanied by his wife Sarada Devi, who he viewed as an incarnation of the Mother, and with Swami Vivekananda, his most ardent devotee. There is no doubt that he was a great mystic that inspired others, not by writing poetry, not necessarily by his teachings, although admittedly they are important and inspirational, but perhaps more by simply living his life. In this respect he is described thus:

> A great saint of modern times. He exemplified with his own life the union

with the Divine through the mystic experience. He did this, not only by following the path of his own tradition, but by following the paths of all major religions of the world.[27]

Local worship of the goddess[28]

Local or village worship, as it is sometimes referred to, is the most diverse and dramatic form of goddess worship. By local worship I am generally referring to the non-orthodox patterns of worship that are evident in many villages, towns and even small cities throughout India. However, the majority of local worship is most evident in the many small shrines that are prolific throughout the Indian sub-continent with worship at them being an integral aspect of religious practice for the majority of the population who still live in rural settlements or small towns.

In contrast to the large and towering temples discussed previously, it is the shrines and small temples that are found most extensively punctuating the rural landscape of India though towns and cities also have their share of individually placed, small shrines dedicated to one of the many Hindu gods and goddesses. Many of these shrines are situated in and associated with the countryside, such as rice fields, groves of trees, etc. and the worship undertaken at them is generally representative of the simpler acts of devotion. Many of these goddesses are approached for their protective powers, especially those situated at the side of a road, near a pond or at the edge of a rice field. Those located at the base of a tree or within a grove of trees demonstrate their connection with nature and in particular with fertility or the life-giving power that is often symbolized with tree sap. It is this form of goddess worship that is most prolific in India and which provides Hinduism with its colourful character. It is impossible to travel very far in India (particularly in the south) without being confronted by the aroma of sandal-paste and the heady perfume of jasmine – curled in fragrant white strands and contrasting sharply with the mounds of bright yellow sandal-paste. This pungent cocktail signifies that daily worship (*puja*) is the most prolific form of religious activity.

The form and construction of local shrines and the deities who inhabit them are numerous and very individual. Many are dedicated to goddesses but certainly not all of them. While most local shrines are small, commonly a three-sided house type of structure installed under a tree, others, particularly in Tamilnadu, are large and imposing. They rise out of the often-featureless landscape, their outer walls painted with the characteristic red and white stripes that indicate a sacred place, perhaps with an enormous garishly painted horse carrying a local hero turned god. In contrast and often overlooked to any but the keen observer, are the often-deified red earth termite mounds that also dot the south Indian landscape. Their only decoration might be a faded flower garland. More simply still, other local deities have no shrine, but are simply represented by a stone that may be carved, or as many are, without feature, which nevertheless has some symbolic meaning for someone. Whether large or small, they all receive periodic worship from the people who have adopted them as their own, or from people passing by them. As India is a sacred land to the Hindus, it seems natural that its landscape should contain an unlimited amount of sacred places.

The regular worship that is directed towards local goddesses is commonly confined to simple acts of devotion, such as offering a few flowers, incense, or a camphor flame. Local goddesses are intimately linked with the settlement they inhabit and are often thought to protect the inhabitants. However, a variety of previous scholars have labelled the independent local goddesses as malevolent, mainly due to their links with disease.[29] Later studies have cast doubt on this position, showing that the so-called malevolent goddesses have more complex characters than was previously envisaged.[30] Similarly, the relationship between deity and devotee is now seen in a more positive light as originally there appears to have been an opinion that the goddesses demanded painful acts of devotion from their devotees. This is an idea that is explored more fully in the discussion on the fire-walking associated with the goddess Mariyamman, in chapter 6.[31]

One of the least orthodox aspects of local goddess worship is the rituals that transcend caste distinctions, in some cases reversing them. One such example is when the goddess takes possession of a low caste woman called Matangi:

As she rushes about spitting on those who under ordinary circumstances would almost choose death rather than to suffer such pollution from a Madiga [the low caste from which the woman comes], she breaks into wild, exulting songs, telling of the humiliation to which she is subjecting the proud caste people. She also abuses them all thoroughly and . . . they appear to expect it and not to be satisfied without a full measure of her invective.[32]

Generally the different castes of a town or village would have their own deities that they would worship in ways appropriate to the particular social group. However, there are specific times when normal distinctions do not apply. The reversal of the norms of society seems to be a common feature of goddess worship, particularly in the local context. For instance, blood is normally avoided at all costs, but a common feature of many local festivals is a blood sacrifice. At this time only, the blood becomes sacred and those attending may try to obtain a drop which might be applied to the forehead as would normally be done with *kumkum* (red powder).

Clearly, the acceptance of animal sacrifices and the overturning of caste distinctions do not readily fit with the views of orthodox Hinduism. Consequently, many local deities have undergone a process of Brahmanization, Hinduization or Sanskritization, a process of alteration of their inherent characteristics, bringing them more into line with the values of Brahmanical Hinduism. Since it is most often the local goddesses who transgress rules of acceptability, it is often they who are targeted first. One way in which the character of a local goddess is altered is through a process that Lynn Gatwood had termed "spousification".[33] Independent goddesses often undergo a ritual marriage, either temporarily, annually, or if fully Brahmanized, permanently to an established god, often Siva. Michael Moffatt in his study of an untouchable community in south India provides an example of a temporary ritual of spousification for the goddess Selliyamman (a form of Mariyamman) who is invoked in her unmarried form at her field temple, her usual abode, and ceremonially married to Siva. Images of Siva and Parvati are then carried through the village streets, which are understood to represent Siva and Selliyamman. However, once the festival is over Selliyamman reverts to her un-spousified form and returns to her temple in the fields.[34] The regional goddess Minaksi, on the other hand, has her own sanctum, but is reunited with her husband Sundaresvara (Siva) each evening in an elaborate ceremony, during which he is taken to join the goddess in their bedchamber. Although Sundaresvara is represented by "a pair of feet embossed on a metal stool",[35] referred to as Cokkar, the pair are considered to have marital relations. During this time the goddess is subordinate to her husband, but during the daytime she is worshipped alone in her own sanctum. Their marriage is also central to the temple's most important yearly festival (*Cittrai*), which is celebrated over a twelve-day period. The marriage of Minaksi and Sundaresvara is re-enacted and celebrated on the tenth day.[36]

Snake worship

The worship of local goddesses takes all forms and varies from state to state. In south India, and Tamilnadu in particular, the veneration of snakes (*nagas*) is a common feature of local worship although it is not unknown in other parts of India. In particular, a snake goddess called Nakamal is often installed within the temple complex, most probably because a snake resides there already. (See plate 6). Snakes occupy an ambiguous position in Indian culture, having both sacred and profane associations. On one hand, they are feared (not surprisingly as many people die each year from snakebites) yet, conversely, they are also deified as the power of fertility. Many shrines, not just those dedicated to snakes, are known for their power in granting children and are visited, mostly by women hoping for offspring. These shrines are immediately obvious as the women tie red and yellow threads to the tree, if there is one, or simply to the edge of the shrine. Often little wooden cribs are also offered and tied, in the hope that the goddess will provide the baby to occupy them. (See plate 7). In this capacity, snakes are inextricably linked both to trees and to the netherworld (*patala*), to which they were assigned guardianship. Most snake or *naga* stones are placed, often at the base of trees where they are frequently worshipped. These stones are stylized depictions of the cobra, associated with *nim* trees in particular. The *naga* resting place and doorway to this world is very often among the roots of trees, or in the case of some Nakamal shrines, via a specially made snake house. Snakes are considered powerful creatures and are offered milk and eggs in order to divert their potential to cause trouble, or to persuade them to offer their help in matters of infertility.

In Bengal the most important regional goddess associated with snakes is Manasa. Her worship places her originally among the tribal or folk traditions of the area. Despite attempts at Brahmanization, Manasa has never really been accepted into the Hindu pantheon of pan-Indian deities. In the medieval period, especially in Bengal, she became very popular and the subject of numerous *mangal-kavyas* (glorification poems) which were read out during festivals.[37]

Many local goddesses are worshipped on an ad hoc basis or when needed. This is particularly the case for those who are famous for their healing powers, evident from the offerings of small pottery or silver foil arms and legs, which are presented in the hope that the deity will heal the devotee. Yet more offer various sorts of protection or pubic services, such as finding lost cattle. Therefore, they may only be approached when a particular need arises. However, all deities, is seems, are approached for help in securing desirable jobs and marriage partners. A significant number of local shrines are situated at the sides of many roads and may offer protection to those who travel through their territory. These goddesses are most regularly offered incense, perhaps a camphor flame or some flowers by travellers who wish for protection during their journey. Some deities have been installed specifically at locations where many accidents have occurred. One goddess in rural Tamilnadu, a form of Kali (Kaliyamman), was installed by the local community next to a particularly dangerous road bend after a spate of accidents. This goddess, who is installed in the open at the top of a set of concrete steps, is now worshipped, bathed, and decorated once a month by the local population. They claim that since her installation, there have been no accidents on her stretch of road. Periodically worshipped for their protection of the town or village water supply, many deities occupy shrines that are situated next to ponds or water tanks.

Particular types of goddess appear to proliferate in different areas of India. For instance, in Rajasthan, a number of local shrines and temples are dedicated to local *satis* (virtuous wives), as discussed in chapter 3. Sati-Matas were once wives that ended their lives on their husband's funeral pyre and were subsequently deified. They are considered to be very powerful and are generally offered worship for their protective powers. The importance of *sati* seems more prevalent in Rajasthan than elsewhere in India and occasionally women still end their lives this way. However, there is considerable debate about whether they were coerced or whether their mode of death was of their own choosing.[38]

It is often unclear what specific function individual goddesses have as some shrines are situated away from any obvious feature. Even here, evidence of worship is clear in the garlands of dried flowers and the smoke blackened pedestal, where camphor tablets have obviously been lit. This worship is usually undertaken on an individual basis, rather than communally. Since the deities are generally in the open, rather than in a closed temple, and are not attended by a priest, the devotee interacts directly with the god or goddess. Therefore, worship, which may simply entail the lighting of an incense stick or might involve offerings that are more lavish, may take place at any time and serve many needs.

Tantric worship of the goddess

Tantrism is essentially a practical and experiential method to gain liberation. In direct contrast to other paths towards liberation, in particular asceticism, in which the adherent withdraws from life, *Tantrism* encompasses the fullest acceptance of the desires and feelings encountered in the manifest world. This worship or *sadhana* (spiritual discipline) might be divided into two types, ritual worship or *puja* and meditation or yoga, with both being of equal importance.[39] Apart from this rather generalized observation it is very hard to provide a concise definition of what *Tantric* worship is. There is no "definitive form of Tantric ritual" with practitioners having a "non-exclusive allegiance to various streams of tradition".[40] They tend to use and blend *Tantric* and non-*Tantric* rituals using them as they are appropriate. However, there are statements and trends that can be identified within *Tantric* practice, such as the central use of seed-*mantras* (sacred syllables), *mudras* (hand gestures) and *yantras* (mystical diagrams) associated with various goddesses. But, that is not to say that use of these is not also evident in orthodox worship. Perhaps a more uniquely *Tantric* aspect of worship is the context in which it may be performed, for instance:

> Tantric ritual seeks to overcome all socially based distinctions, enabling one to realize in a direct, experiential manner that *all* aspects of existence are manifestations of the Divine Mother, the Sakti, the divine productive power.[41]

Tantric practice offers practical techniques for attaining its ultimate goal of self-enlightenment. In this respect "ritual assumes the status of much more than mere obeisance to the deity; it calls for unification, an internalization of the personal and specific towards the timeless, abstract and universal."[42]

Tantric ritual can also be divided into three groups, *nitya-puja*, the purest type of worship which is performed every day. Of a more complex nature is *naimittika-puja*, essentially a more detailed version of *nitya-puja*, it is performed five times a month and on special occasions such as the guru's birthday and festivals of the goddess. The final type of worship is *kamya-puja*, which has worldly motivations and is performed to fulfil a wish or to avert calamity. It is only those who are capable of performing the other types of worship that can attempt *kamya-puja*. It is the most advanced and dangerous because it endeavours to mobilize divine power and "verges on magic", therefore the practitioner must be "embedded in his tradition"[43] and divine power must have previously been awakened in them for the ritual to be successful. What is of vital importance in all types of ritual practice is that their performance should be flawless – there is no room for

1 Sixty-four *Yogini* temple at Hirapur, Orissa. *Lynn Foulston*

2 Mahamaya Durga and her priest at Sixty-four *Yogini* temple at Hirapur, Orissa. *Sian Michael*

3 *Yoginis* and offerings at Sixty-four *Yogini* temple at Hirapur, Orissa. *Lynn Foulston*

4 Auto-rickshaw *puja* at Sixty-four *Yogini* temple at Hirapur, Orissa. *Lynn Foulston*

5 One of the *gopurams* at Minaksi temple in Madurai, Tamilnadu. *Judith Stephenson*

6 *Naga* shrine within Minaksi temple in Madurai, Tamilnadu. *Julia Edwards*

7 Offering in order to gain children at the *naga* shrine within Minaksi temple in Madurai, Tamilnadu. *Jamie Foulston*

8 A craftsman paints in the eyes of a traditional Durga image, Kumartuli, Kolkata. *Jayanta Roy*

9 A *pandal* decorated with old records, at *Durga Puja* 2002, Kolkata. *Lynn Foulston*

10 FIFA world Cup inspired *pandal* at *Durga Puja* 2002, Kolkata. *Lynn Foulston*

11 A *ghata* representing the goddess at *Durga Puja* 2002, Kolkata. *Lynn Foulston*

12 The immersion of the deities at the conclusion of *Durga Puja*, Kolkata. *Jayanta Roy*

13 *Arti* tray with images of Laksmi and Ganesa made specifically for *Divali*, purchased in New Delhi, 2000. *Lynn Foulston*

14 Laksmi *sara* used during *Laksmi Puja*, Kolkata. *Jayanta Roy*

15 Saumya Kali in preparation for *Kali Puja* 2002, Kolkata. *Jayanta Roy*

16 A painting of Santosi Ma that decorates the outer temple wall in Khurdapur, Orissa. *Lynn Foulston*

mistakes.[44] Therefore, a guru is of vital importance, as practitioners do not operate by themselves, but learn gradually with the help of the guru and in this respect perhaps the first and most important ritual for the *Tantric* practitioner is formal initiation or *diksa*. It is on this occasion that the guru imparts the personal *mantra* to the *sadhaka* "seeker" (if female *sadhika*) and identifies his or her *istadevata* (personal deity).

Nitya-Puja

Nitya-puja commences with various, quite complex, purification rituals of the practitioner, the place where *puja* is to take place and the equipment and substances used for the ritual. The next step is to take various precautionary measures to eliminate any negative forces that might disrupt the practice. Finally, the main aspects of the *puja* can be undertaken. Since this *puja* is quite lengthy and involved it will often be carried out in the evening when the practitioner or *sadhaka* has more time. One distinguishing feature of *Tantric* worship is the belief that to worship the divine one must first *be* divine. Therefore, many of the rituals at the heart of *nitya-puja* are performed to make this possible. For instance, once the purification rituals are complete the *sadhaka* will envisage the dissolution of each element of the self into the cosmic source.[45] Then the reverse is carried out as the individual is re-created, but made of pure substance. In this state the *sadhaka* is in a position to invite the goddess to enter his or her body. The next set of rituals centre on the identification of the goddess with the body of the *sadhaka*.

The use of *mantra* plays a central role in *Tantic* worship. *Bija* or seed *mantras* symbolize each deity. They represent the innate power of the deity and when recited, generally in repetitions, their vibrations activate certain desirable states within the *sadhaka*. For instance, the seed *mantra* for the goddess Bhuvanesvari (Mistress of the World) is *Hrim* which symbolises H – Siva, R – Sakti, I – transcendental illusion, and M – progenitor of the universe.[46] Mookerjee and Khanna go on to explain that: "The main function of the *mantra* is identification with or internalization of the divine form or its energy."[47] *Nyasa* is used in conjunction with the utterance of *mantras* to direct the power of the divine into the body. *Nyasa* is a ritual that consists of the practitioner touching certain points of the body, such as the heart, the forehead, the chest, etc. with the fingers or the palm of the right hand. By uttering an accompanying *mantra* the body is sensitized to the power of the deity, by which the practitioner "accommodates the divine form, limb by limb in his own body".[48]

In conjunction with *mantra* and *nyasa* is the use of *mudras* or hand gestures. "Both mudras and nyasas are external expressions of 'inner resolve' suggesting that such non-verbal communications are more powerful than the spoken word."[49] There are said to be 108 different *mudras* according to the *Kalika Purana* (70. 33). *Mudras* are such an important aspect of *Tantric* practice that without their use, other forms of worship are considered useless.[50]

Kundalini Yoga

In order to realize the fundamental unity between the self and Siva-Sakti the *Tantric* adept must tap into the energy source within the subtle body, Kundalini-Sakti (envisaged as a coiled serpent). The *Tantric* adept is encouraged, through metaphysical questioning, ritual practice, yoga and personal conduct, to realize and activate the individual inherent spiritual power within called Kundalini-Sakti. Therefore, *Tantrism* is not the detection of the unknown, but the cognizance of what is known within, but veiled. Kundalini-Sakti is envisaged as coiled-up energy at the base of the spine, which unless activated through *hathayoga* or ritual practices, remains unmanifest and dormant. "When the Kundalini sleeps, man is aware of his immediate earthly circumstances only. When she awakens to a higher spiritual plane, the individual is not limited to his own perception but instead participates in the source of light."[51]

A variety of practices are used by the *sadhaka* in order to activate Kundalini-Sakti and draw this power, envisaged as "a flash of red lightning"[52] up through the *susumna* channel (subtle channel in the spinal column) through the *cakras* (centres of cosmic consciousness within the body) towards a growing realization of the unity between the self and Ultimate Reality or Siva-Sakti, which is symbolized by the *sahasrara cakra*, an imagined thousand-petalled lotus at the top of the head. The use of breath control (*pranayama*), the utterance of *mantras* and the visualization of magical diagrams (*yantras*) and meditation are a few of the ways by which the Kundalini-Sakti can be stirred. As an indirect result of activating the force within, the *sadhaka* attains various magical powers or *siddhis* such as *anima*, the power to become as small as an atom or *vasitva*, the power to control others. One of the more advanced and less ambiguous *siddhis* is *pratyaksa*, the power of God-vision when desired, which would help the *sadhaka* towards their ultimate goal of liberation. However, there are those to which the acquisition of these powers is more important than others.

Since the manifest world is suffused with power or energy it is rational to assume that liberation entails the use of that power. However, the ultimate aim of the *sadhaka* is to bring Kundalini-Sakti through the *cakras* of the body and out through the top of the head where Siva and Sakti unite, symbolizing full realization or cosmic consciousness and its consequent liberation. The misuse of power is believed to have very serious consequences for the *sadhaka*.

Use of the panca-makaras

In order to transcend the ego and sense attachments one must work on a different level. In the case of *Tantrism* it is by subjecting oneself to practices which would normally be regarded as causing defilement, such as contact with death, menstrual fluid, sexual fluid, low castes, meat, liquor, and faeces. So, instead of avoiding sex or polluting situations, the *Tantric* adept faces them head on and in so doing hopes to transcend the particular desires and aversions that are stimulated by the proximity of such situations. The *panca-makaras* are five forbidden substances, *mamsa* meaning 'meat', *matsya* meaning 'fish', *madhu* or 'alcohol', *mudra* a kind of psychoactive parched grain and finally *maithuna* literally meaning 'sexual intercourse', in this case intercourse was usually with a polluted low-caste female, the mingled sexual fluids produced by the pair understood as the power substance. Due to their transgressive nature (i.e. they directly opposed orthodox moral codes of conduct and were considered strongly *adharmic*), the ritual ingestion of the five substances was deemed an exceptionally powerful and transformative act. In transgressing *Vedic* purity values, the participant sought to transcend their limited individual ego through the manipulation of divine *sakti*. *Tantrism* proposes that such rituals aid a participant in achieving liberation and the attainment of *siddhis*; they are felt to empower the *sadhaka* with divine energy faster than would normally be achieved through non-*Tantric* religious practice. The *Kularnava Tantra* asserts:

> Drinking wine, eating flesh, carrying out the practices of one's own initiatory teaching, contemplating of the unitive experience of both "I" and "That," so the Heart yogin dwells in true happiness. (9. 52)

> Valuing what is devalued in the world and devaluing what the world values, this the Terrifying Lord who is the supreme Self has pointed out is the path of the Heart. (9. 55)

> There are no commands; there are no prohibitions. There is neither merit

nor fall; no heaven and truly no hell for the followers of the heart, O
Goddess of the Heart. (9. 59)[53]

Although sexual practices are part of *Tantric puja*, this act is carried out
under strict conditions. The partners represent Siva–Sakti and both have
been made divine by *dhyana or cakra* visualization, *mantra*, and *mudra*
or hand gestures, but especially by *nyasa* (to form a micro/macrocosmic
relationship). Sexual union or *maithuna* celebrates the unity of Ultimate
Reality and ends with the male retaining his seed in order to build up
inner power or *tapas*. What is often neglected to be mentioned by the
critics is that these practices must be performed without any sense
attachment, and in so doing, the devotee transcends his or her ego. What
they fail to perceive when they accuse *Tantrism* of being base and
orgiastic is that these practices are not performed by *any* one. Only a
devotee who has reached an advanced level of training, the *vira-bhava*
or heroic stage (one who is in control of their senses), and has proved
his or her commitment and understanding is allowed to participate in
the *panca-makara* rites.

Some say that those with superior qualities, i.e. those who are capable
of performing the 5 Ms are hard to find. Accordingly, *Tantrism* divides
sadhakas into three types; *pasu-bhava* (animal), *vira-bhava* (heroic),
and *divya-bhava* (divine) and the guru would prescribe practices appropriate to each type. The *sadhaka* who is categorized as embodying
pasu-bhava is instructed to "avoid all objects of temptation as far as he
can and engage himself in *japam* [repetition of the Lord's name] and
such other practices with strict regard for purity".[54] The next group of
Tantric practitioner (*vira-bhava*) are considered "comparatively
advanced" and in this *sadhaka* "devotion to God supersedes the crav-
ings of the senses, and the sense-attractions only heighten their longing
for God".[55] They are charged with the task of living "in the midst of
these temptations and try to concentrate their mind on the Lord,
unshaken by those jarring elements in the outside world".[56] The *divya-
bhava*, the most advanced practitioner, is described as "far above the
reach of the, sense impulses – which have been swept away from him by
a tidal wave of yearning for God-realization – and to whom the practice
of truth, forgiveness, compassion, contentment, and such other attributes has become natural like respiration".[57] Therefore, the *vira* and the
divya sadhakas are the only ones who should attempt the more extreme
Tantric practices for it is only when the practitioner has reached a certain
level of self-control that he or she is deemed advanced enough to rise
above the danger that is inherent in performing rituals without the ego

fully controlled. Consequently Madhavananda claims "the practices of the Tantras will bear fruit if only the aspirant makes self-control the bed-rock of his endeavours, and in default of this he will be no better –if not worse –than an ordinary man".[58]

Cremation ground rituals

What is the significance of the cremation ground? It is a place of fear and dread for most Hindus, but is also the location for many *Tantric* practices, particularly those of the left-handed path. Kinsley, in his analysis of the *Dasamahavidyas*, the ten goddesses that represent forms of transcendent knowledge, states that "worship of nearly all of them is said to be most effective if undertaken in a cremation ground".[59] Why should this be? Taken at face value, the cremation ground is simply a place of overwhelming pollution where the dead are cremated. It is, therefore, superficially a place of sadness. However, as a place of extreme pollution it represents the ultimate challenge for the *Tantric* practitioner. Just as the ego must be suppressed in order to partake of the five forbidden substances (*panca-makara*), so to undertake rituals in the cremation ground – among the remnants of the dead – without fear or revulsion, the ego must be conquered.

The cremation ground is the most potent symbol of the transience of the manifest world. It is a constant reminder that the bodies that we all inhabit are impermanent. It is, therefore, the place of ultimate transformation, for although it is a place of death, from another perspective the cremation ground becomes a place of rebirth, where the soul is finally released from its gross human body to be reincarnated in another form. If we follow this line of reasoning, the cremation ground could be seen as a place of liberation, since in its purifying flames the liberated soul is finally freed from the bonds of *samsara*, the cycle of birth, death and rebirth.

The cremation ground is, not surprisingly, considered to be a place of great power since, like the more conventional places of pilgrimage, it too is considered to be a crossing place between two worlds. Kinsley beautifully illustrates this idea when he states:

> The cremation ground . . . represents a more-or-less-permanent "opening" to the spirit world and the beings that inhabit it. It is a place of spirit traffic, of coming and going from one world to another. It is a liminal place, betwixt and between worlds, where radical transformations take place and contact between worlds is relatively common.[60]

Therefore, by the performance of rituals in such close proximity to the divine spirit world, the adherent is perhaps able to draw more easily on, and amplify the power underlying this place of absolute opposition. The *Tantric sadhaka* goes one step further as many of the rituals performed in the cremation ground are aimed at crossing the barrier between the two worlds of, either becoming immersed in the world of the spirits, or drawing the spirits to the human world.

At least one *Tantric* group, the *Aghoris*, spend protracted periods living in the cremation ground, breaking all attachments to the material world. They are reputed to scavenge all their needs from the cremation ground. However, while they might make use of shrouds, wood from the funeral pyres and smear themselves with the ashes of the newly cremated, it is doubtful how many of them are sustained by the flesh of corpses. *Aghori* ascetics carry a skull bowl, which they are supposed to acquire from a "putrid and bloated corpse fished out of the river", although one of Jonathan Parry's informants sheepishly revealed that his skull had come from the local mortuary.[61] The path of the *Aghori* is the most difficult form of *Tantrism*, with very few adherents able to fully embrace its ideology that completely transposes the opposites of purity with pollution and morality with immorality in an effort to fully subdue the ego and to transcend, *even* the order of *dharma*. *Tantric* worship then, it seems, takes many forms ranging from the most complex purification and visualization techniques to the most extreme sexual and potentially polluting practices. While it offers liberation in one lifetime to those who master its esoteric rituals, those who misuse the power generated by its practices can expect to reap very serious karmic consequences.

Clearly, the worship directed towards Hindu goddesses is as diverse as the goddesses themselves. While many of the rituals bring the devotee closer to the divine in accordance with the law of *dharma*, others remain on the margins of acceptability, while some clearly go beyond. What seems clear in all of these forms of worship is that Sakti, Power and Energy, in all her forms plays a crucial and immediate part. The Goddess, in whatever form she is approached, is there with the worshipper, accessible in a tangible form. She is not distant, but instead embodies the rituals themselves and this is never more apparent than in festival rituals that will be examined in the following chapter.

6 Goddess Festivals

A brief look at the Hindu religious calendar immediately alerts the reader to the importance of festivals and ceremonial days. There are very few months when festivities of some description do not take place. Some festivals are the celebration of an individual deity's birthday – such as Ganesa whose birthday is celebrated at *Ganesa Caturthi*, and Krsna at *Krsna Janamastami* – whereas many others are undoubtedly associated with nature, the changing seasons and fertility. The stories recounted in the epic and *puranic* texts often provide the context for a particular festival. The festivals celebrated each year can be separated into two loose categories: orthodox pan-Indian festivals and local festivals that may only be celebrated in one particular state or perhaps by a specific community. The orthodox festivals are celebrated across India and in other countries too, and many are known all over the world, particularly *Holi* and *Divali*.

The pan-Indian festivals, while they may differ in name from state to state, are legitimized by textual sources, often celebrating an important religious event. For instance, perhaps the most popular Hindu festival, *Divali* (the festival of lights), celebrating the return of Rama and Sita to Ayodhya after their ordeal with the demon Ravana, is a story related in the epic text, the *Ramayana*. Celebrated at the beginning of winter, *Divali* or *Dipavali*, as it is sometimes called, is a time when darkness is dispelled. All the houses are cleaned and decorated. Then they are filled with lights in order to encourage Laksmi to visit them, to bring prosperity for the coming year. Many orthodox festivals are centred on a period of devotion to deities in the temple or to specially made images of a particular god or goddess, which are worshipped in temporary buildings, called *pandals*. Although animal sacrifice is still a part of some traditionally celebrated festivals, generally, orthodox festivals are characterized by the offering of fruit, food and flowers.

In contrast, local festivals are celebrated in a very different manner to the majority of orthodox festivals. In many parts of India, possession, animal sacrifice and potentially harmful acts of devotion such as fire-walking and hook swinging are central elements of local festivals, the majority of which are in honour of goddesses, in contrast to the orthodox festivals that honour a variety of deities. Festivals celebrated in a local setting may be centred on pan-Indian goddesses but their ritual content is generally very different. What follows is an examination of just a few of the most important goddess festivals, some popular in many parts of India and others celebrated only in a particular location.

Orthodox goddess festivals

Durga Puja[1]

Durga Puja is the most popular annual festival celebrated in Bengal and is at its most magnificent in Kolkata. This is perhaps because there are "almost no permanent temples to Durga" so "only once a year do Bengali devotees get to gaze upon the Goddess's face".[2] While other parts of India celebrate *Navaratri* (Nine Nights), commemorating the nine nights that Lord Rama invoked the goddess Durga to help him conquer the demon Ravana, and *Dussehra* (Glorious Tenth) on which he destroyed the demon, Bengal celebrates the victory of good over evil in its own special way. For much of India *Divali* is the biggest and most important festival of the year, but in Kolkata, *Durga Puja* is the most eagerly awaited festival of the year.

To visit Kolkata at the time of *Durga Puja* is to step into a different world. As darkness descends, the grubby streets and dilapidated buildings that once spoke of the opulence of this city are replaced by a wonderland of lights and sound. Excitement fills the air as thousands of people throng the streets. Dressed in their finest clothes and decked in gold, they wander from one magnificently decorated *pandal* (temporary pavilion housing huge tableaux of Durga and her children) to the next. The community face of the festival consists of hundreds of temporary buildings constructed of bamboo, cloth or other materials, some of which are replicas of famous temples or places of pilgrimage or simply famous buildings. These *pandals* are constructed solely to house the huge, fantastically decorated clay images of the ten-armed Durga slaying the buffalo demon, Mahisasura, and the other deities, Ganesa, Laksmi, Sarasvati and Karttikeya, who surround her on either side.

Traditionally, the Durga image has a triangular-shaped face with large and expressive almond-shaped eyes. One style, referred to as *bangla*, represents her with a hooked, beak-like nose and dark arched eyebrows that extend towards the sides of her face. More common among the family *pujas* are the *do-bhasi* style images whose eyebrows and nose are less severe but they retain the large almond-shaped, red-rimmed eyes. (See plate 8). Both of these traditional styles are coloured a deep golden yellow and are striking because they appear otherworldly. In recent years, many of the community *pujas* have incorporated images that have become rather humanized and life-like. Durga is often represented with a pale pink, benevolent-looking face though in some images her eyes seem to flash angrily as she thrusts her trident into the demon's shoulder. There have also been changes in the appearance of the other deities, who appear more humanized in the community *pujas*. By tradition, the body of Ganesa is coloured a deep red, Laksmi and Karttikeya should be golden coloured in contrast to Sarasvati who should be white and Mahisasura who is traditionally coloured green. Durga's mount, the lion, has also undergone significant changes since its earliest conception in which it looked more like a horse than a lion. In the modern *pujas*, the realistic appearance of the lion, which snarls and lunges at Mahisasura, is often one of the most impressive aspects of the tableaux. What has not changed so much is the elaborate decoration of deities and the back piece (*cal-citra*) against which they stand. Every conceivable type of material has been used to make the deities look spectacular. Most traditional are the decorations made of pith and the gold and silver shiny ornamentation. The community *pujas* have become very inventive and often decorate their deities in the same style that has been used for the *pandal*. For instance, in 2002 one *pandal* was decorated with old vinyl 'LP' and '78' records, and another decorated its *pandal* and deities with biscuits.

The streets of Kolkata during the *pujas* are alive and vibrant with the ubiquitous presence of Durga and the sheer spectacle (*tamasa*) surrounding her worship. Although sight (*darsana*) of the deities is important, on a more worldly level the crowds go to have fun at the fairs (*melas*) that have become attached to the biggest *pujas*, and to see what delights the *pandal* designers have in store for them this year. The sheer creativity and skill of the *pandal* makers, who produce ever more realistic and inventive ideas each year, are for many the highlight of the festival. *Durga Puja* in Kolkata has become, more than any other Indian festival, an amalgamation of sacred and secular. While the foundation of this festival is religious, much of its outward appearance is now secular. For example, although a number of the *pandals* are wholly concerned with religion – in 2002 representing sacred places such as the eleventh-century Brihadesvara temple in Tamilnadu, or the Pagala Baba temple in Mathura – others are rather more secular. Their theme might be political, such as one *pandal* at Santosh Mitra Square that portrayed the contentious division of the Eastern Railway, represented by the Headquarter building split apart. Its political theme extended to the deities, who all wore garlands in the colours of the Indian flag. Interestingly, some *pujas* managed to cater for all tastes as the Singhi Park *pandal* on Dover Lane recreated scenes from the *Mahabharata*, which were illuminated by a 400 kg soccer ball, floating in the air, described by one newspaper as: "celebrating a World Cup hangover".[3]

The community *pujas* that are now funded by business sponsors compete with each other to draw in the crowds and to win awards. In doing so, many of the designs have less to do with religion and more to do with what might capture the imagination of the public. Evidently in 2002 the World Cup was prominent in the *pandal* designers' minds as it also featured in another *puja* where Durga was housed in a giant football, which was clearly marked FIFA World Cup. (See plate 10). In 1998, one of the *pandals* housing some of Hinduism's most celebrated deities was a replica of the *Titanic*, inspired by the popularity of the film of the same name. This trend continues as in 2007 one of the *pandals* was a replica of Hogwarts castle complete with the Hogwarts Express and characters from the Harry Potter books. This caused quite a stir as J. K. Rowling and Warner Bros attempted to sue the community group for infringing copyright.[4] While some *pandals* are clearly of novelty value, there is, nonetheless, an artistry to many that cannot fail to impress even the most cynical westerner. The work that had gone into the decoration of some *pandals*, for instance, the Bosepuktur Talaban community *puja* in 2002, whose *pandal* and deities were decorated with over 60,000 old vinyl records, is truly astounding. (See plate 9). Similarly, the Mudiali Club decorated their huge *pandal*, both inside and out, with buttons and broken bangles, lining the street leading to it with 180 peacocks on pedestals, their magnificent tails also made with buttons, bangles and vibrantly coloured blue and green feathers. Pradip Ghosh (president of one of the biggest *puja* committees) commented in a newspaper article: "Earlier people would come to see the goddess. Later, lighting came in focus. Now the pandals are what draw people." He goes on to say that: "grandeur has transformed Durga Puja into a secular festival".[5] It is the multi-national sponsors like Coca Cola that have enabled the *pujas* to become more extravagant, and on this point Ghosh comments: "Till [sic] the Eighties, the mainstay of every pujas [sic] was door-to-door collection. Now it accounts for barely 0.1 per cent of our capital. Whatever collection the boys do is to keep the locals happy."[6]

Perhaps one of the most significant changes to the *Durga Puja* festival is the emphasis on the role of the goddess. The textual sources, and indeed, the imagery of the goddess herself suggests that this festival is a celebration of Durga's victory over the demon, Mahisasura – in other words a victory of good over evil or light over dark. However, though the victory, related in the *Devi-Mahatmya*, is still celebrated in part, the goddess is treated more overtly as a daughter returning to her parental home. In this context, the other deities that make up the *Durga Puja* tableaux – Ganesa, Laksmi, Sarasvati and Karttikeya – are described as her children. *Puranic* mythology does provide evidence for Ganesa and Karttikeya being the offspring of Siva and Parvati, but Laksmi and Sarasvati have always been considered goddesses in their own right. The law books (*sastras*) do not mention the worship of other deities during this festival, though the tradition has prevailed for some time, since Ghosha comments that in 1871 the other deities were worshipped widely as the children of Parvati.[7] He goes on to say that the *Tantras* describe the above deities as the children of Durga, but that no texts say they should be worshipped at the autumnal festival with Durga.[8] Whatever the texts say, they have, to a certain extent, been replaced in importance by the many devotional songs that reinforce the idea of Durga as a returning daughter, for as David Kinsley points out: "These songs contain no mention whatsoever of her roles as battle queen or cosmic saviour."[9] Kinsley goes on to say:

> The dominant theme in these songs of welcome and farewell seems to be the difficult life the goddess/daughter has had in her husband's home in contrast to the warm, tender treatment she receives from her parents when she visits them. This theme undoubtedly reflects the actual situation of many Bengali girls, for whom life in their husband's village can be diffi-cult in the extreme, particularly in the early years of their marriage when they have no seniority or children to give them respect and status in the eyes of their in-laws.[10]

Therefore, the common feeling that Durga, as the wife of Siva, has returned to her parental home with her children appears to be the most evident cause for celebration during this festival. Durga mirrors the pattern adopted by her devotees, many of whom are also returning to their family homes, especially those who originated from Kolkata. However, there are other, more ancient layers of meaning, that are still apparent if the iconography and rituals of the *Durga Puja* festival are examined. Quite probably the *Durga Puja* festival originally had more to do with crops, harvest and fertility than it did with homecoming relatives.

One of Durga's former names is Sakambhari, the goddess of vegetation, who, according to one myth in the *Devi-Bhagavatam* (VII. 46–80), became known as Durga when she slew the demon Durgamma. Since the goddess at the centre of *Durga Puja* was created by the gods for the sole purpose of slaying the demons that threatened the stability of the cosmos, the Sakambhari evidence might seem rather flimsy support that this was a festival of fertility. However, there is other, more compelling evidence found when the festival rituals are scrutinized. According to Rachel Fell McDermott, a scholar who has studied the *pujas* for many years, two of the most important rituals of the entire festival, without which it cannot proceed, are the installation of the pot (*ghata*) and the bundle of nine plants (*navapattrika*).[11] The installation of the *ghata*, a wide-bodied earthen pot with a narrow neck and a wide, open top is the first ritual of importance. (See plate 11). Throughout the festival, this pot represents the goddess.[12] Before the main deities are established in their place of worship, the *ghata* is ritually placed on a lump of river clay that has been sprinkled with five different types of grain. The pot is filled with a variety of constituents such as sacred water from the Ganges and twigs from five different trees – mango, *pipal*, *bata*, *asoka*, and jackfruit.[13] On its open mouth are placed two betel leaves with a stalk, and a shallow earthen dish filled with rice on which is put a coconut with its husk and stalk. The *ghata* is then decorated with a yellow cloth dyed with turmeric, to symbolize purity, and the belly of the *ghata* is painted with vermilion and ghee depicting the symbol of a god. Clearly there is much here to suggest that the *ghata* has some relationship to fertility, especially since the earthen pot, an important component of many goddess festivals, also represents a symbolic womb.

Another important component of the *Durga Puja* festival is the *navapattrika* (lit. nine leaves). The priest constructs a bundle of nine plants tied together around a plantain stalk, thereafter referred to as the *navapattrika*. The *navapattrika* consists of a plantain or banana stalk, turmeric, *sesbania*, *bilva*, pomegranate, *arum*, *asoka*, paddy and *mana*. It is anointed with various substances and then, on the first day of the main *puja*, *Saptami* (the seventh day after the new moon), the *navapat-*

trika is taken to the river to be bathed. Once it has been bathed, anointed, and dressed in a new sari, the *navapattrika* is taken back to the place of worship where it is installed on the right of the deities, next to Ganesa, and is henceforth regarded as an incarnation of the goddess. To many devotees, the symbolism of the *navapattrika* seems unclear as when asked, many claimed that the *navapattrika* was the bride of Ganesa. However, the priests of the family *pujas*, who follow the ancient traditions most closely, confirmed that the *navapattrika* does represent Durga. After the installation of the *navapattrika*, two *ghatas* are placed before it and the image of Durga. Then each *ghata* is circled with thread tied around upright arrows, which acts as a protective enclosure. It seems significant that each of these symbolic representations of the goddess is clearly concerned with vegetation and fertility, signifying her power, not just over nature, but also perhaps as the power sustaining all life – an idea expressed in the (*Devi-Mahatmaya* 11. 4): "You are the sole substratum of the world, because you subsist in the form of earth. By you, who exist in the shape of water, all this (universe) is gratified, O Devi of inviolable valour!"[14] Durga's early associations with fertility have been superseded by her role as a warrior goddess, praised for her martial capability or, more recently, her identity as a daughter returning to her parent's home.

Durga's military might led to her association with the epic battles in the Indian classics, the *Ramayana* (the slaying of Ravana) and in the *Mahabharata* (the battle between the Pandavas and the Kurus). In both epic narratives, Durga was propitiated before the battle and petitioned to bestow victory on Lord Rama in the *Ramayana*, and the Pandavas in the *Mahabharata*. In turn, her role as the goddess of martial victory led to her association with the Indian kings who, in all likelihood, started her worship. According to one newspaper article, *Durga Puja* began in the sixteenth century, apparently organized by a Maharaja, though there seems to be no unanimous agreement as to the identity of this king.[15] Other kings followed suit, in all likelihood trying to outdo one another and, consequently, *Durga Puja* became widespread. The land-owning *zamindars* also established *pujas* and, as the article goes on to say: "By mid-18th century, the national festival of the Bengalis had become the occasion for the nouveaux riches babus of Kolkata to flaunt their wealth."[16]

The wealthy families of Kolkata still maintain their own *pujas* and, whereas in the past they might have been a show of wealth, they now preserve the traditional *puja* rituals and iconography. The majority of family *pujas* actively seek to replicate the *pujas* of their forefathers' time so there is very little change in the ritual formulas used by the priests and the style of the deities themselves. The most traditional iconography portrays Durga's lion with a fierce horse-like face. Durga herself bears no relationship to many of the community *puja's* Durga images, who often have very pale skin and realistic faces. There was a trend at one time for the faces of the deities to resemble famous film stars though traditionally, Durga does not look human but, as mentioned, has a very stylized, yellow face with large, fierce-looking eyes. Although the family *pujas* preserve tradition, some of them have created it in their own style. For instance, many families are *Vaisnavas* (worshippers of Visnu) whose normal pattern of worship is peaceful and contemplative. Consequently, some find the warrior goddess Durga, who traditionally accepts animal sacrifices at her yearly festival, at odds with their customary religious practices. At least two family *pujas* have replaced the image of Durga slaying the demon Mahisasura, for an image of Parvati (a gentler form of the goddess) seated on Siva's knee. In all other respects, the traditional style of depicting the goddess and the ceremonies, which make *Durga Puja* what it is, are adhered to, except for animal sacrifice, of course.

As many of the community *pujas* welcome change, seeking innovation and awards, their ritual aspect is being reduced, whereas the family *pujas* stick rigidly to a tradition that they have maintained for decades. The texts say that: "The hall in which the goddess is to be worshipped should be quadrangular, regular, secluded, decorated with svastica [swastika] and other auspicious articles, beautifully canopied and screened."[17] The old houses of Kolkata are able to fulfil these requirements fully as they are arranged around a central courtyard with a huge pillared space at one end. This is where the deities of the house are usually kept but, as was the case at one traditional family *puja* that I visited, their primary deities, Gopinath Jiu (Radha and Krsna), were moved to an upper room during the festival period, where they were worshipped daily by a specially hired priest. Traditionally *Durga Puja* is to be celebrated with animal sacrifices; therefore, vegetarian deities such as Radha and Krsna need to be shielded from such rites.

Festival proceedings

The *Durga Puja* festival, based on the lunar calendar, begins on the *mahalaya* (the new moon day) in the month of *Asvin* (September/October). On this day a ceremony called *tarpana* is performed, in which offerings are made to one's ancestors. Lamps are lit to guide the souls of the departed to earth to receive their offerings. It is also on this day that the eyes of the Durga images are painted.

The festival rituals start on the day following the new moon, referred to as *pratipada*. On this day, those who will be involved in the festival purify themselves and undertake any rituals that are pre-requisite to the start of the festival. Various priests are chosen for an assortment of tasks and they, too, must ritually purify themselves. Once this is done, it is their responsibility to make sure that the area where the ceremonies are to take place is purified and that any negative forces are dispelled and any unwanted spirits are propitiated. As already mentioned, the first and perhaps the most important ceremony is the installation of the *ghata* in the ritually purified place. It is interesting to note that a number of the rituals that accompany the installation of the *ghata* are *tantric* in nature, for instance, the performance of various *nyasas*. A *nyasa* is the projection or awareness of divinity in various parts of the body, awakened by touching the body part and uttering a sacred formula (*mantra*). Finally, rituals for the protection of the *ghata*, a representative of the goddess, are performed, such as the scattering of mustard seed and its enclosure by a sacred thread. Ghosha explains:

> Then on the four sides of the Ghata fix four arrows with the mantras, Om from Kandas (arrow) Om from Kandas (arrow) grow hardness upon hardness, may he [who dares trespass within sacred precincts] be pierced as if by a thousand blades of Durva,[18] which grow one over the other. Encircle the same with three threads with the following mantra, Om with the thread the heavens and the earth are encircled, by me similarly this place is encircled, may the serpents protect this place from all impurities &c.[19]

The goddess, as the *ghata*, is then offered flowers, incense, water and fruits. After this *puja* is completed, an offering is made into a fire (*homa*) sacrifice of *ghee* and various types of grass and wood might be undertaken, and offering of lights (*arti*) is performed. These rituals take place daily until *Navami* (the ninth day after the new moon) that, along with *Saptami* (seventh day), *Astami* (eighth day) and *Dasami* (tenth day) make up the four main festival days that are celebrated by everyone. Although the ritual proceedings start from the new moon day, the goddess, once she is installed in her *pandal*, is worshipped for four days until her immersion in the river on the last day, *Dasami*. In the past, some families may have made animal sacrifices every day from *pratipada*, whereas today only the most traditional families carry on this custom during three or four of the main festival days.

On the sixth lunar day after the new moon, the goddess is awakened in a ceremony known as *bodhana*. The *Kalika Purana* 60. 8 says: "On the sixth day the worshipper should invoke the goddess on the branches of the *bilva*-tree (*Aegle Marmelos*) and on the fruits of the bigger variety *bilva* (*sriphala*). On the seventh day he should collect the branches of the *bilva*-tree and worship the goddess on them." [20] By touching the *bilva* branch and reciting *mantras*, the priest awakens the goddess; the *bilva* branch is then transferred to the previously mentioned *navapattrika*.[21] The images of the deities have been installed by this time in their respective *pandals* and the final changes are made to their decorations. The day finishes with *arti* offered to the deities.

Saptami (seventh day) is the first day of the main *puja* during which a variety of important rituals take place, proceeding in the following order.

- Bathing the *navapattrika*
- Invoking the deities into the *murtis* (images)
- Anointing the *murtis* with various substances
- Worship of the principle gods
- Sacrifice, animal or a substitute
- Institution of the *homa* fire
- *Homa* offerings
- *Kumari* (virgin) worship

The bathing of the *navapattrika* has already been explained but suffice it to say its importance is apparent because it is the first ritual undertaken on this day. In this respect, it is a pre-requisite to the invocation of the main deities. Most importantly, the *navapattrika* clearly represents the divine warrior of the *Devi-Mahatmya*, Durga, as the priest says: "Om you were born gold-coloured on the earth for the success of the Devas, oh Mahesvari I bathe you with this divine water"[22] and "concludes by saying, I salute thee, oh Durga".[23]

During many festivals, the deities involved are asked to grace the festival with their presence, most commonly in the form of a pot, but also in the form of an image. At *Durga Puja*, the goddess is invoked when the priest uses *mantras* and by touching the *murti*. According to Ghosha, the priest says: "I invoke thee goddess in the earthen idol, and in the Sripala twig; descend Devi from the peaks of Kailasa, Vindya, and the Himalya Mountains."[24] The three eyes of the goddess are given life through *mantras* and the *murti* is finally brought to life by a series of *tantric mantras*. Once this is completed, *puja* is given to the goddess

with various offerings, including water, incense, milk, sweets, ornaments, and vermilion. The deities, including the *navapattrika* and the
ghatas (one in a side room and two before Durga and the *navapattrika*),
are worshipped with offering of flowers (*puspanjali*).

At traditional *pujas*, generally those organized by individual families,
animal sacrifices may be performed at this point. A small, black, male
goat is the traditional sacrifice though on *Navami* (ninth day), the day
when the most animals are sacrificed; at least one family still sacrifice a
buffalo, even though the Indian Government prohibited it in 1947. At
the 2002 *puja* of Sabarna Choudhury – claimed to be the oldest *puja* in
Bengal, which started in 1610 – one goat was sacrificed on *Saptami*, two
on *Astami*, and on *Navami*, nine goats and one buffalo were sacrificed
along with sugarcane and a sweet gourd.

The sacrifice commences with the purification of the goat, which is
positioned so that it faces towards the east (the most auspicious direction). Various parts of it are thought to be the residences of a number of
deities – these are worshipped before the sacrifice takes place. Finally,
the animal is addressed by the following words:

> "Om goat, blessed be my star that thou hast appeared as a sacrificial
> animal, I salute thee and all such forms of sacrifice, Om salutation to thou
> object of sacrifice. Om all misfortunes of the donor are removed by the
> gratification of Chandika. I salute thee, oh Vaishnavi in the form of sacri-
> fice. Om the animals are created by the Self-born Himself [Brahma I
> assume] for sacrifice, and therefore I do kill thee in this yajna though thou
> art unkillable. Om thou art born in the womb of animal for the sacred
> purposes of puja, homa, and other ceremonies. Be the goddess propitiated
> with thy flesh mixed with blood."[25]

Mantras are whispered into the goat's ear and it is granted salvation for
selflessly giving its life. It is then killed with a single stroke of the sword
that is addressed as the tongue of Candika (another name for Durga).
Some of the blood is offered to the goddess. At one family *puja* I
attended, the head was also offered. The goddess took her share of the
sacrifice behind a screen and the sacrificial area was quickly cleaned up.
The body of the goat was given to the man who performed the sacrifice,
as the family who usually worship Radha and Krsna are vegetarian
during the *puja*. None of the family *pujas* that I visited during the 2002
Durga Puja festival kept the bodies of the sacrifices, they all remained
vegetarian throughout the festival. Animal sacrifice does not take place
at the community *pujas*.

The institution of a small fire pit for making sacrifices is a remnant from the *Vedic* period. Nevertheless, the inclusion of the *homa* sacrifice is still an important Hindu ritual during festivals and, in particular, at weddings, where the couple circle the fire seven times – an act that seals their marriage and is witnessed by the god of fire, Agni. During the *Durga Puja* festival, various items are put into a small fire, for instance, *ghee*, sacred *kusa* grass and *bilva* leaves, which are taken to the goddess by Agni.

On *Saptami* night, or in some cases, *Astami* or *Navami* morning, *kumari puja* takes place. A young Brahman girl of about nine years old is worshipped as a representative of the goddess. She is dressed up in new clothes, given sweets and offered *puja*. This is a *tantric*-influenced ritual, which some families do not observe. As a pure and chaste virgin, the *kumari* symbolizes living divinity,[26] a belief clearly held in Nepal where there is a permanently worshipped, living *kumari*, as detailed in chapter 8.

Astami or *Mahastami* as it is sometimes called is considered the most auspicious day of the festival. It was on this day that Durga fought against and killed the buffalo demon Mahisasura. They are depicted locked in mortal combat, with many festival images depicting the final deathblow. While her other nine arms wield the weapons given to her by the gods who created her, the trident held in her tenth hand pierces the evil demon. Traditionally on this day, the priests recount the valorous deeds of the goddess that are detailed in the *Devi-Mahatmya*, an account of which was detailed in chapter 2. In addition, on *Astami*, nine small *ghatas* are installed before the deities and decorated with coloured flags. These pots are said to represent either nine forms of Durga, or the nine goddesses that are associated with the different plants that make up the *navapattrika*.[27]

Navami (ninth day) corresponds with *Navaratri* (nine nights) celebrated in other parts of India. During *Navaratri* and the nine nights preceding it, the story of the *Ramayana* is enacted, referred to as *Ramlila* (the play of Rama). During each of the nights preceding Rama's battle with the ten-headed demon Ravana – who had taken Sita away to his home in Lanka (modern-day Sri Lanka) – Rama prayed to the goddess Durga asking her to grant him victory in the coming battle. In Bengal and Kolkata, *Navami* is the last full day of the festival. At some family *pujas* that I attended, a greater number of animals are sacrificed and, in the case of this *puja*, they include a buffalo calf. One senior member of the family said that goats symbolize lust and the buffalo is a symbol of anger. By ceremonially sacrificing them, the family's unwanted passions are destroyed. This particular family *puja* also sacrifices a gourd or pumpkin, said to represent desire, and a bundle of sugarcane, the symbol of greed. Once the sacrifices are completed, a grand *arti* is performed, after which many family members prostrate themselves before Durga.

The last day of the festival is on *Dasami* (the tenth day), which coincides with the festival of *Dusshera* celebrated in other parts of India. *Dusshera* is a celebration of Rama's victory over the demon Ravana. On this night, huge papier-mâché images of Ravana are made and filled with fireworks. A bowman dressed as Rama ignites these. He fires a flaming arrow through the image's navel.

This final day of *Durga Puja* is bittersweet as it marks the end of the festival when all the clay images of the deities are immersed in the river. Through this act, Durga returns to her home with her husband Siva on Mount Kailasa. Consequently, most of the rituals performed on *Dasami* are in preparation for Durga's departure. In the morning, married women offer sweets and the red powder that married women put along their hair parting (*sindur*). At the large community *pujas* such as Bagbazar in northern Kolkata, women waited in line for hours for a chance to make their offerings to the goddess. At the smaller family *pujas* the idols (*pratima*) are brought into the courtyard of the house and the married women circle the deities seven times. In a ritual known as playing with the vermilion (*khela sindur*), they press sweets to the mouth of the Durga image and anoint her with *sindur*. If the images are very large, the women use a stepladder to reach her mouth. They then whisper into Durga's ear the plea that she should come back next year. At the community *pujas*, whose images are often gigantic, the women must content themselves with anointing Durga's feet with *sindur* and offering their sweets before her. When the women have finished, they anoint each other's faces with *sindur*, emerging from the *pandal* very colourfully decorated with red patches across their cheeks and foreheads. Although this causes a good deal of fun and laughter, the women are nevertheless sad that the goddess will soon be leaving them. *Vijaya* poems are recited at this time that expresses this sadness and ambivalent feelings about her departure, for example:

Am I afraid of the tenth day?
    Go, Ma, back home to Hara [Siva].
I'll see you off with a smiling face;
    that'll make your jaw drop.
Even though you leave me in the form of Durga,
you stay here surrounding me,
as Kali.

So why should I worry?
    I won't try to keep you back,
    clutching the end of your sari.
Just the opposite: I'm happy
knowing that Siva will break into smiles
as the light of the full moon streams
    into the darkness of Kailasa city.
The ninth day hasn't come merely to go away again;
it has come to take you
Can you avoid it?
It has forsaken all else, Ma,
    for you.   *Kalyankumar Mukhopadhyay*[28]

Eventually, it is time to take the goddess and the other deities to a nearby river, or pond if there is no river close by. Kolkata is situated on the banks of the Hoogly River (a tributary of the Ganges), so all the images are taken to *ghats* along the riverbank. (See plate 12). Because there are so many *pujas* in Kolkata they cannot all immerse their deities on *Dasami* day. In 2002, an estimated 1,900 images were immersed on *Dasami*, and 2,100 the day after, with still more to be immersed the following day. The largest images are loaded into the back of colour-fully painted trucks, which are then crammed with people, many of whom dance to the beat of the large drums (*dhaks*). Many more people accompany the images to the banks of the river with a great deal of chanting and music. The *dhakkis* beat their drums and, as the streets of Kolkata fill with hundreds of processions – some in trucks others on foot – a carnival atmosphere spreads through the city. Formerly, the images were taken out into the river, suspended between two boats; the boats would part and Durga would drop into the water. However, this practice is not allowed any more and all immersions must take place from the shore. When the smaller *ekcalas* (all deities attached to one *cal* or back piece) reach the riverbank, they are turned around three times before the men carry the deities to the water's edge. The larger deities are taken to the water separately. In some of the most traditional family *pujas*, a *nilkantha* (blue-throated bird) is released before the deities' immersion. The devotees believe that it flies to Mount Kailasa to tell Siva that Durga will soon be coming home.

    The ritual of immersion is a feature of many festivals, both orthodox and local. Although devotees believe that the river will carry Durga back to Mount Kailasa, this ceremony is also carried out in order to dissipate the immense power built up during the festival. Once the various rituals have been performed to invoke the power of the goddess into her clay image, it cannot simply be dismissed or left unattended. While the power built up during festivals is beneficial, there is also a belief that if the power were left unchecked it might build to such a level that it would threaten the cosmos. Therefore, immersion in water of all representations of the deity, such as the *ghatas* and the *navapattrika*, is necessary so that their power can be dissipated naturally and safely.

The women wait on the bank with sorrowful expressions on their faces as they silently bid goodbye to the goddess whose homecoming has seemed so short. As she is cast into the water, along with the *ghatas* and the *navapattrika*, all those assembled shout a victory salute. One brass pot of water, the water of peace (*santi jal*) is brought back and its water is sprinkled on the assembled devotees. This final act of purification and the distribution of well-being marks the end of the festival.

Laksmi Puja

Laksmi is worshipped throughout the year, particularly in shops and by businessmen, but is honoured most widely at *Divali*. Although *Divali* (the festival of lights) is a celebration of the return of Rama, Sita and Laksmana from their exile in the forest, it is most overtly celebrated to encourage Laksmi, the goddess of wealth and prosperity, to visit. In the days preceding *Divali*, houses are cleaned and repainted because Laksmi will not visit a dirty house. This is also the beginning of the new financial year so businessmen, in particular, close their books and start fresh ones. Offices are decorated with beautifully coloured floor patterns and customers are often given gifts at this time of year. Images of Laksmi and Ganesa are seen everywhere, adorning *arti* plates and many other items that are sold especially to celebrate the festival. (See plate 13). The most important and prolific are of course lights, since this is a festival of light. Celebrated on the new moon night, the darkest night of the dark fortnight of *Kartik* (October/November), an important aspect of the festival is the lighting of many lamps.

Divali is generally based round the home and so statues of Laksmi, as well as Rama, Sita and Laksman, are given pride of place. The worship of Laksmi starts at dusk when she is offered incense, puffed rice and flowers. Since Laksmi is not only the goddess of wealth and prosperity, but is also closely associated with fertility, five types of grain are used in her *puja* – paddy, maize, linseed, mustard seed and *daal*. Finally, *arti* is offered and the family receive her blessing in the form of *prasada* (some of the puffed rice that was offered to the goddess). Now many small clay lamps called *deep* are lit from the lights offered to Laksmi during her *puja*. In a party atmosphere, fireworks are let off. It is hoped that by cleaning the house and making it bright and inviting, Laksmi will be encouraged to enter and bring with her prosperity for the coming year.

In Bengal, Orissa and other parts of northern India Laksmi is also worshipped at the full moon after *Durga Puja* or *Dusshera*. In Bengal, this is the most important *Laksmi Puja* of the year. Many people worship Laksmi at home, using small images purchased from a stall or in the form of an earthen lid or plate (*sara*) painted with an image of Laksmi seated on a lotus attended by two females and her owl vehicle. (See plate 14). The *sara*, or image, of Laksmi is installed in the house and rice flour patterns of her feet are drawn on the floor. As with other goddess festivals in Bengal, Laksmi is also represented as a *ghata* filled with different types of grain and river water. Alaksmi (ill-fortune) is driven out of the back door at night in the hope Laksmi will enter through the front. During this day, Bengali families traditionally recite the legend of Kojagari Laksmi, in which a king has his adherence to righteousness (*dharma*) tested by the goddess Laksmi.[29] The goddess is worshipped with lights, incense, flowers and songs during the night. In the morning, her image is immersed in a nearby river.

As well as worship of Laksmi in the home, many beautifully decorated clay statues of Laksmi are installed in *pandals* for community worship. Sometimes a lighted lamp is left on the spot where the image of Durga was installed for *Durga Puja*. The image of Laksmi is then installed on the same place, although the *Durga Puja pandals* are dismantled and smaller, less elaborate ones are constructed to house the images of Laksmi. The Laksmi images are generally two-armed, sometimes with a cornucopia in her left hand while her right is held in a boon-granting gesture with the palm facing towards the devotee and the fingers pointing downwards. She is usually pink or golden coloured wearing a red sari and decorated with tinsel or pith. In Bhubaneswar, the capital of Orissa, the most predominant form of Laksmi in 2002 was of Gaja Laksmi. The Gaja Laksmi images represent Laksmi's associations with fertility as two elephants on either side of her pour water on her with their trunks. The showers of water, according to David Kinsley: "most likely represent fertilizing rains".[30] This image is widespread, and is often found carved on temple walls and on posters and pictures. The priests bring the images to life in the morning by performing the eye-opening ceremony (in which the eyes are repainted) and, using *mantras*, they ask the goddess to occupy the image. After one day, *Laksmi Puja* is over and the numerous images of the goddess of prosperity are consigned to the waters of a nearby river or pond.

Kali Puja

Laksmi is not the only goddess worshipped during *Divali*. In Bengal, the goddess Kali is very popular, with two of her most important temples (Kalighat and Daksinesvar) being located in Kolkata. Although Kali is not usually worshipped in the home, she is worshipped on the new moon night of *Kartik*, the same night as *Divali*. Community worship of Kali is said to have started when Maharaja Krsnacandra of Nadia ordered his subjects to install and worship images of Kali otherwise he would punish them. Consequently, over ten thousand images were worshipped in Nadia, a tradition that became accepted and was continued by his grandson.[31] Now the worship of Kali is prevalent all over Bengal and beyond.

There are various clay images of Kali worshipped at her yearly festival in Kolkata. The most popular is the *Daksina* (Generous) black-coloured images depicting her most common iconography. She stands naked, except for a garland of skulls, with her right foot on the prone body of Siva. A blood-red lolling tongue protrudes from her mouth, and around her waist is a girdle of arms. Her upper left hand holds a sword and her lower left holds a severed head. The hand gestures (*mudras*) of her right hands offer benevolence to the devotee. The upraised palm of her upper right hand advises the devotee not to fear her and the outstretched palm of the lower left, suggests her boon-granting power. The images of Kali are decorated with a stylized tinsel breastplate, armbands, anklets and a crown. Her red-painted palms, feet and red-rimmed eyes contrast sharply with the inky blackness of her body. Although traditionally the temporary festival images were black, some are now painted in various shades of blue. (See plate 15). As well as the *Daksina* images there are also *Raksa* Kali images that have only two arms, which hold a skull and a bowl of wine. Raksa Kali, whose power is the protection from misfortune, is portrayed without a lolling tongue or the garland of skulls. The most feared incarnation of Kali is *Smasana* Kali, who is worshipped in, and presides over, the cremation ground, a place of fear and dread for most Hindus. Her image is black and very similar to the *Daksina* image, the most significant difference being that it is her left foot that rests on Siva's chest rather than the right. The difference between these two images has led James Robinson to surmise that they may represent left-handed and right-handed *Tantra*.[32] The *Smasana* Kali images must be made and decorated on the same day as they are worshipped, being consigned to the Hoogly River before dawn the following day.[33] According to one scholar, Cynthia Bradley, who attended a *Smasana Kali Puja* conducted somewhere behind the Kalighat temple, the image had a rather terrifying appearance with the addition of red flashing light-bulb eyes.[34] She was shocked that around the *pandal* were white-wrapped, apparently dead, bodies. In sharp contrast to the images of death was a woman dressed in wedding finery, who appeared to be possessed by the goddess. Cynthia described the atmosphere at the *puja* as one of hysterical fun at which there was singing and dancing, but the participants were rather uneasy. However, the majority of *pujas* celebrated are rather less sensational than that of *Smasana* Kali. Also during *Kali Puja* the *pandals* tend to be much less ornate, being created simply to house the images of Kali, which are the focus of this festival.

The rituals that accompany the worship of Kali are in essence similar to those already discussed for *Durga Puja* though during *Kali Puja* they are concentrated into one day and night. After purifying himself and the area where the rituals will take place, the priest welcomes the goddess. Through the use of *mantras* and other rituals he draws the energy and power into the goddess *murti*. This ritual is referred to as the "gift of eyes" (*cakkhudan*). As the priest repaints the eyes, the power enters the image and it is only at this point that it becomes worthy of worship.[35] The main rituals are conducted after midnight and include various offerings of light, incense, fruit and flowers. However, the climax of the festival rituals is the animal sacrifice, which is followed by hymn (*bhajan*) singing and dancing. Some family and community *pujas* no longer sacrifice the traditional goat, but instead, substitute a red-fleshed pumpkin. The goddess may be given a meal of fish, rice and lentils (*khicuri*) and a sweet rice pudding. The night is finally ended with *arti*, before the clay images of Kali are taken to the river for immersion. Traditionally this ritual should be performed before dawn, but there are now so many Kali images in Kolkata that some must perform the immersion ceremonies during the following day.

Kali Puja seems a curious mix of devotion and danger. As it is celebrated alongside *Divali*, during which the main goddess worshipped is Laksmi, in Bengal at least, the duality of *sakti* worship is brought together and amalgamated. The horror of *Smasana Kali Puja*, though attended by a minority rather than a majority, on the one hand appears more powerful, but on the other is softened by its juxtaposition to the lights and flowers attendant to the worship of Laksmi and the fireworks and gift-giving that for many are now the main focus of *Divali*.

The festival procession

So far, this chapter has examined discrete festivals of individual goddesses, however before looking at a selection of local festival rituals I would now like to examine an aspect of festival celebration that is not specific to any one goddess or festival. A core ritual of many festivals (both pan-Indian and local) is the decoration and procession of the temple deities around the streets that surround the temple. In order that this might happen the deities must have a suitable vehicle on which to ride. All deities are depicted with an animal companion who often acts as their vehicle (*vahana*). Some of these vehicles have taken on a status and personality of their own; for instance, Nandi, Siva's bull, is much loved and receives a share of the worship. Sometimes referred to as Nandi-Isvara (Lord Nandi), he is often garlanded and honoured during festivals.

The procession of the elaborately decorated deities is a religious spectacle that is eagerly awaited by the local inhabitants. Many of these events do not just draw community crowds but also those from the surrounding area as well. On many occasions, the ritual decoration by the temple priests is the precursor to this procession. This is a time when barriers are broken down as those who might normally be excluded from the temple have a chance to receive *darsana* (sight of the deity and consequently their blessing). During the procession there is clearly a blurring of the normal distinctions between sacred temple and the profane town or city, most noticeable in the removal of the participants' shoes during the procession, during which the area outside becomes a sacred extension of the temple. The most elaborate festival processions are generally confined to the larger temples that have the finances and the accommodation necessary to acquire and store the festival image, and one or sometimes many suitable vehicles on which to carry the movable image, a ritual that is not solely confined to goddess worship. The vehicle is typically a wooden representation of the animal that the deity is usually depicted with.

A good example of the ritual of procession is evident in the fifteen-day Car (vehicle) festival of Jenakai Mariyamman's (in Colavandan), which is celebrated each year during *Vaikaci* (May/June). Although this festival is strictly speaking local the events related here are not significantly different from those performed at the large orthodox temples and hence its inclusion here. In a pattern that is repeated at many large temples, the daily decoration of the goddess's festival image and her subsequent procession around the streets surrounding the temple is repeated each morning and evening from the second day of the festival to the eighth. At 9 a.m., the festival image of the goddess is installed in a canopied car-like vehicle (*capparam*), used for carrying deities, and is taken around the temple. In the evening, at 7 p.m., a similar ritual is performed as the moveable image of the goddess is taken in procession around the streets of Colavandan. However, in the evening procession the goddess is seated on a different animal vehicle each day, including a lion, a *yali* (a mythological lion-faced animal with elephantine proboscis and tusks), a lotus, Kamadhenu (the wish-fulfilling cow), a bull, a swan, a horse, and an elephant. Between the eleventh and the fifteenth days of the festival, there is only one procession per night, but on days eleven and twelve a special ritual bathing or (*abhiseka*) and decoration of the goddess is carried out. After the evening procession, various programmes of dance, music, folk songs, and religious discourse are presented each night. These festival proceedings readily correspond to those of the Brahmanical or Sanskritic deities.

While the festival procession of Jenakai Mariyamman is undoubtedly a central and important aspect of her annual festival, it is the fire-walk that represents the festival's climax (discussed below). The fire-walk, of course, is clearly not a festival ritual in which Sanskritic deities generally participate. Consequently, the festival of Jenakai Mariyamman emphasizes the fact that she has not been fully Brahmanized or Sanskritized, since important aspects of her local character remain. Although the details of the ritual procession recounted might vary, it is not unique to this location. Temples all over India draw crowds to them in the same way and perhaps once a year gods and goddesses leave the confines of their home and move about among their devotees. This is one occasion when there is a perceptibly close relationship between humanity and divinity.

Local goddess festivals[36]

Possession, fire-walking and animal sacrifice are generally not a part of orthodox worship, although as we have already seen, in the worship of Durga and Kali in Bengal, some orthodox worship does include animal sacrifice. However, the goddesses Kali and Durga are not typically orthodox since their iconography and ritual worship places them on the margins of acceptability. More often, the devotees of an orthodox goddess might sing devotional songs or read the sacred texts defining her exploits rather than testing their faith by walking across a pit of hot coals or venturing into the cremation ground late at night. While an atmosphere of religious devotion certainly accompanies orthodox worship, it is somewhat supplanted by the vibrant and dynamic atmosphere of many local festivities. Local rituals, which often propel the devotee into differing states of consciousness, are by their very nature open to misunderstanding. A case in point is the nature of the more remarkable rituals, such as hook swinging and fire-walking, which may well have encouraged the belief that local goddesses *demand* such sacrifices from their devotees. Such practices, which are in fact gifts to the goddess rather than penances, have contributed, to some degree, to the erroneous label "malevolent" being attached to some local goddesses. One such south Indian goddess is Mariyamman. Particularly popular in Tamilnadu, Mariyamman – whose name (*mari*) as well as meaning "water" or "rain", is also defined as "death" and "smallpox" in the *Tamil Lexicon* – presides over an annual festival, the climax of which is a fire-walk.

Mariyamman festivals and fire walking

The practice of piercing the tongue or cheeks with metal skewers or hook swinging[37] often accompanied the fire-walking ceremony, especially for the south Indian goddess Mariyamman. Despite the British outlawing this custom it is, nevertheless, occasionally performed in India today. The practice is not evident in Colavandan nowadays, though in the past, according to Elmore, this town was "famous for the ceremony".[38] Oppert, writing in 1893, remarked on the prevalence of the ritual in Colavandan as he commented: "it is a pity that this detestable custom has been of late revived, as is proved by the hook-swinging festival at Colavandan which took place the other day."[39]

In Tamilnadu, two goddesses are the main recipients of fire-walking festivals, Mariyamman and Draupadiyamman, a divinized form of Draupadi, the wife of the five Pandavas in the *Mahabharata*.[40] Since I was unable to attend the fire-walk in Colavandan, I offer a detailed account of the fire-walking ritual that I did attend for Mariyamman in the nearby town of Natham. This particular festival took place in the Tamil month of *Maci* (February/March). The nearby Mariyamman fire-walking festival in Natham is in essence very similar to that in Colavandan though the Natham festival is on a much larger scale with an estimated 50,000 people attending the festival and reportedly as many as 10,000 undertaking the fire-walk.[41]

The Tamil term for the fire-walking pit is *pu-k-kuli*, meaning "pit of flowers", which the devotees claim is the feeling they get when they walk across the hot coals. According to the Natham non-brahman priest (*pujari*) the fire pit should be ten feet in length, five feet wide, and five feet deep. It is situated before the entrance to the temple, in the centre of town. The following represents my experience and interpretation of a unique event, albeit one that is replicated across India in a variety of forms.

On approaching the centre of town, the estimated crowds became a nightmarish reality. Being swept along by a tide of people all intent on reaching one small temple was in itself a unique experience. This huge body of like-minded souls moved together like the waves of the sea or a tightly packed shoal of fish. In these situations, no one is able to act individually, so what would happen if this fast-flowing river encountered an obstacle? One of the truly amazing events of that day happened as this vast crowd suddenly parted. For a moment, the world stood still as my eyes met the gaze of a small willow-like creature covered from head to toe in yellow turmeric paste and draped in yellow garments. Through her tongue and cheeks there protruded intricately decorated metal skewers, tipped with small lemons. For a second we occupied the same world, unaffected by time and space. But, all too soon, I was torn from the place, though she remained – motionless – in the midst of the rushing tide.

The fire-walkers came from many of the surrounding villages, with the spectators coming from some considerable distance away to witness the great spectacle.[42] The area for the fire-walk was set up directly in front of the temple and the yellow-clad devotees filed through the temple on their way to it. Yellow is a colour of purity, with the cloth being dyed using turmeric, also symbolically pure. Yellow is also a colour especially associated with the goddess Mariyamman.

Many had been waiting, probably for five hours or more, before they reached the temple and the goal they must have been preparing for, for so long. As they were ushered through the temple by anxious temple personnel, they made their last supplications to the goddess, who must have looked on approvingly at such a massive demonstration of faith in her. The huge number of people walking across the fire pit is also an affirmation of the power of the goddess, not because she compels her devotees to honour her in such a ritual, but because she must have used her power constructively and benevolently to help them: her reward is their act of self-sacrifice. The final walk through the temple was particularly chaotic as marshals tried to keep some semblance of order, and those participants who had waited for so long were anxious to complete their task. Apparently, during the previous year's festival, the fire-walk had not been controlled in this way and there was complete chaos with some people lying on the coals and others finding themselves being pushed over. In 1997, the organizers were determined to keep command of the situation with the police out in force to keep the over-excited crowd at bay.

The gamut of facial expressions among the fire-walkers expressed more than words could ever say. These devotees consisted of men and women, ranging from the very old to the very young. There was a tremendous feeling of emotion there. Some were jubilant when, after waiting so long to face the fire, their spiritual goal, the fire pit finally came into view. A few seemed to be in a trance-like state, barely aware of their surroundings, completely rapt in a devotional stupor. A number of devotees of this type, mainly men, were already displaying the outward symbols of their devotion as they had long skewers forced through their tongue or cheeks. The tide of mutual devotion bore them towards the climactic conclusion of their consecration. One young yellow-clad girl had a look of terror on her face as she walked through the temple and she found it impossible to hold back her tears. A small boy who seemed to be with her looked equally frightened. Many of the women uttered prayers or *mantras* as they proceeded towards the fire pit, many clutching small bunches of *margosa* leaves that are especially associated with Mariyamman. They all wore the garlands that are normally given to the goddess and as they passed under the flag-tower erected for the festival, they threw the garlands over its many struts. By mid-afternoon the bottom portion was thick with flowers, a testament to those who had already undergone this baptism of fire, their faith and purity of heart tested and revitalized anew.

Every available rooftop or vantage point was occupied by thousands more people who were content to observe the spectacle from a distance. The whole area seemed charged with emotional tension, from the devotees themselves to the spectators, who could not possibly remain unmoved by the show of mass dedication to the goddess. Especially significant was the surprising number of children attempting the fire-walking feat. For some, the experience of the intense heat of the coals at the last moment was more than they could bear. Understanding adults plucked them up and they were carried across on the shoulders of those undaunted by the potential threat the fire pit represented. However, many children did walk across the coals unaided and it was to them that the crowd gave special adulation and encouragement. The general feeling was of intense admiration for all whose faith had brought them before the goddess on this day. From some distance away, the heat of the coals could be felt over and above the intense heat of the afternoon sun.

Having walked through the pit of hot coals the devotees walked to a sacred pool for a ritual bath. There was an air of the conquering hero about the jubilant devotees, who were then surrounded by admiring crowds, probably those who had come with them, many from far away. They had been reborn in a more sacred and pure state by putting their trust in the goddess. In many cases, the devotees were probably feeling the relief of having finally fulfilled a vow that they had previously made to Mariyamman – their pact with the goddess was now complete. The honour and the exhilaration felt by those who had undertaken the fire-walk was plain to see, in their facial expressions, and in the way they were treated by the spectators. There was no sense among the devotees that they had undertaken a penance or punishment exacted by a wrathful goddess: rather, they had publicly proved their faith and devotion. More importantly, the goddess had acknowledged and reciprocated that faith through her protection. The fire-walk was seen as an honour and a privilege rather than a punishment, an offering of thanks for the beneficence of the goddess rather than an act to deter her anger. This climax of the yearly festival was a celebration of the bond between deity and devotee that re-established their close relationship as well as strengthening community ties.

A local festival in Orissa

Fire-walking is also the climax of the most popular goddess festival in Khurdapur, a village settlement in Orissa. In Khurdapur, the fire-walk represents the climax of the *Pana Sankranti* festival. This festival is celebrated in two separate ceremonies, one involving several goddesses – Ma Mangala belonging to the *Bhois* of Sarasvatipur, Ma Khanduala, Baghei, Dulladei, and Ma Jagesvari; the other in worship of just one goddess – Ma Mangala belonging to the *Bhois* of Bandanapur. The festival of *Mahabisuba Sankranti* or, more commonly in Orissa, *Pana Sankranti*, is so called because of the sweet *pana* drink specially prepared and distributed on this day. Celebrated on the first day of the Oriya month of *Baisakh* (April/May) – in 1997 it was on April 14, the start of the solar New Year – it is the major festival in the Khurdapur settlement.

Related here are the preparations that were deemed necessary by the inhabitants of Khurdapur for walking across the fire. Although the festival lasts only one day, the preparations commence six days before, with the priests and those who wish to take part in the climax of the festival, the fire-walk, moving to the Ma Khanduala temple enclosure, where they eat and sleep until the day of the festival. The participants take only one meal a day, which is prepared within the confines of the sacred area and is purely vegetarian, containing no garlic or onion. One of the food items that is consumed is a very white, pure rice called *arua*, which is not boiled but cooked in the sun and considered to be a sacred foodstuff. The participants sleep at the Ma Khanduala enclosure until the night before the festival when they move to the Ma Jagesvari temple/shrine. This practice symbolizes their move from their ordinary secular environment to the sacred world of the divine, enabling them to purify themselves in preparation for their close encounter with the goddess, in particular during the fire-walk.

On the day of the festival, everyone bathes and puts on new clothes, and those who are to walk on the fire, fast. At midday the priests representing Ma Khanduala, Ma Mangala from Ma Khanduala shrine, Baghei, and the priest of Ma Mangala belonging to the *Bhois* of Sarasvatipur, become possessed by the goddesses and come to Ma Jagesvari's temple/shrine in a procession round Sarasvatipur and Jatesvar, accompanied by a band. Meanwhile the fire-walkers wait at Ma Jagesvari temple and as the possessed priests arrive, the fire-walkers roll along the hot ground in a preliminary act of faith.[43] The possessed priests or, as they are now regarded, the goddesses, hit the rolling fire-walkers with their canes as a sign that they are pleased with their devotion and that they may now stop.

When the possessed priests and the fire-walkers are assembled at the Ma Jagesvari temple/shrine, *puja* is performed for Ma Jagesvari. During this time, the villagers prepare a large pit of charcoal in front of Ma Jagesvari's sanctum, where the main festivities will take place. After ritual bathing, the priests, possessed by whichever goddess they represent, are the first to walk on the burning hot coals, followed by the other people who, by this time, have also become possessed. In essence, the goddesses walk on the fire first, in an act that perhaps establishes the sacredness of the fire and sanctions the ritual for their devotees. The informants clearly stated that it is crucial to become possessed by a goddess before the fire can be safely traversed, thereby indicating that the power of the goddess sanctions the devotee's participation and, consequently, protects him or her from harm.

It seems clear that the preparations that the festival participants must undergo facilitate their movement from one world to another. They leave the everyday world of the village, including their families, and immerse themselves in the sacredness of the temple.[44] Everything must change – their clothes, their food, their normal habits and, perhaps most importantly, their state of mind. In order to retain the level of purity and resultant sacredness required to walk across the fire pit without being burned, the participants must physically and spiritually remove themselves from their profane or secular surroundings. Furthermore, the concentration of the participants during the period of preparation is wholly directed towards the divine world, which they will fully enter when they cross the fire of the goddess. As the period of preparation continues, the devotees become increasingly infused by the sacred, and a transformation takes place. This is crucial, as when they step onto the fire pit, or in the case of the priests, when they accept the communal blood sacrifice on behalf of the goddess, they are exposed to a super-abundance of divine power. They become the channels through which this power is safely transferred to the settlement.

The importance of possession in local festivals

The possession of a mortal by a deity is a central and often pivotal part of many of the local festivals.[45] It is a significantly local phenomenon, as in general there is no place for possession in Brahmanical religion. It is also a ritual most commonly associated with local goddesses rather than gods, though occasionally male deities possess people too. Considered either a blessing or a curse, depending on whether the possession is insti-gated by a deity or by an evil spirit, possession is entirely dependent on the will of the deity. Therefore, as Diehl explains, to be possessed is often an indication that a person has been specially chosen. For instance, the selection of a new *pujari* might depend on the goddess possessing him.[46] While possession by a deity is viewed as an honour, possession by an evil spirit is considered highly undesirable, and many ritual practices are performed specifically to guard against it. This negative possession is also generally dependent on the will of the evil spirit, though the action or inaction of the person possessed might have made it possible. For instance, certain actions or places are to be avoided because they are considered inhabited by, or attractive to, evil spirits.

Possession takes place at various times and in a variety of situations during a festival. Or, in some cases, it may be the very focus of the festival, as is recorded by Peter Claus in south Kanara District,

Mysore.[47] At this festival, the goddess Siri and her descendants possess the variety of caste groups that have assembled for the festival, with those who are more experienced being possessed by Siri herself. This particular example, as far as I am aware, is rare since at most festivals possession is only one ritual among many and it only happens to a select few, most commonly to the attendant *pujari*. Nonetheless, possession does, it seems, happen at important moments during the festival. It is particularly prominent at three main occasions. First, during a ritual performed to infuse the power of the goddess into a *sakti karakam* (ceremonial pot) and on the occasion of its procession back to the temple or shrine; secondly, at the time of the main procession, if there is one; thirdly, and perhaps most importantly, at the climax of the festival, for example the sacrifice, fire-walk or other central ritual. The beating of the drum *(pampai)* or of a metal gong most often brings on the possessed state. Possession is clearly an important facet of local ritual, but why is it necessary?

When a possessed *pujari* accepts the blood of the sacrificial victim on behalf of the goddess, he represents her dual personality in much the same way as a festival image does. It is generally the festival image, if there is one, which is presented with the blood offering, thereby avoiding any pollution to the essential form of the goddess that remains in her sanctum. In Khurdapur, at the *Pana Sankranti* festival, the possessed *pujaris*, having completed the fire-walk, suck the blood of sacrificed fowl straight from their necks, on behalf of the goddess they represent.[48] This act represents the literal draining of the life's blood of the sacrificial victim by the goddess, an act that the *pujaris* might be incapable of performing if they were acting under their own volition. The relationship between the possessor and the possessed is a very intimate one, and one that is mutually beneficial.[49] Without a mortal body, the sacred goddess would not be able to leave her sanctum nor have such a closely interactive relationship with her devotees. Furthermore, the secular receptacle for the spirit of the goddess is protected by his or her newly endowed sacredness from the pollutants of the outside world.

The possession of a mortal has a number of benefits to the goddesses; perhaps the most obvious is as a way of communication. Most commonly, the possessed *pujari* or other representative is able to make the wishes and concerns of the goddess known to the devotees. If the goddess is angry or pleased with her worship during the year, she will make it apparent through the mouth of her representative who, during the period of possession, is addressed as, and considered to be, the goddess in question. The possession of a mortal can also be beneficial to the goddess in revealing her power. Often the main function of the possessed person is to give advice and to heal those who have sought the goddess's help. In many cases, those in need of help have been possessed by a "bad soul" or evil spirit, which the goddess is able to dispel by her superior power. Nowhere is this more apparent than in the local worship of Santosi Ma (Mother of Satisfaction) who regularly possesses a local woman, the details of which are given in chapter 8.

Festivals, both orthodox and local, are social occasions when deity and devotee meet. However, clearly there is a considerable difference between orthodox, pan-Indian festivals and those dedicated to the local goddesses who abound in India. While the orthodox festivals may have textual support, many of them appear to be changing, often becoming more commercialized. Conversely, the local festivals that are replete with ritual and symbolism preserve their traditions more closely. To a certain extent, this is necessary to carry on a tradition that has no written form but is passed on from one generation to the next. There appears to be a closer relationship between the goddesses and her devotees in the context of local festivals that often include possession and rituals such as fire-walking. However, perhaps most importantly, festivals represent a renewal of community ties, where all are brought together in the name of the goddess.

While the celebration of festivals is a regular and visible aspect of goddess worship, the need to visit the places sacred to her is also another great motivating force. Sometimes the two are combined as the lengthy and expensive undertaking of possibly travelling vast distances to take *darsana* of an individual goddess can be integrated into taking part in a particularly powerful festival. In this way the devotee is able to maximize their religious experience by tapping into the increased sacredness of a particular place and time.

7 Pigrimage to the Temples of the Goddess

Setting out on a pilgrimage – whether it is to the nearest large temple, to a sacred city or the source of a river that may be many miles away – is an integral part of what it means to be a Hindu. Millions of people save for many years in order to undertake a significant pilgrimage such as to the source of the Ganges or to visit the cave of Vaisno Devi, high in the Jammu hills. But pilgrimage in India is not exclusively for people with money. Those who have no money may also undertake such a religious journey, travelling the whole distance on foot and begging their food along the way. Fortunately India respects and looks after those who make such sacrifices, so ordinary people feel it is not only their duty but also a meritorious act to help such people. It never ceases to amaze me that when travelling along the roads in India one is sure to come across a number of small parties of pilgrims with their red or orange flag proudly held aloft. The distances that these people have travelled on foot are unthinkable to westerners who are so used to getting around in trains, cars and aeroplanes. Wandering *sadhus*, holy men who have given up all their possessions and attachments to a material life, are on a constant pilgrimage as they walk from one temple to another. Others who undertake a pilgrimage, no matter how near or far it is, are momentarily united, and become part of the world inhabited by India's *sadhus*. They, too, abandon their ordinary attachments to the material world, focusing instead on the sacredness of their final destination.

The land of India is considered sacred, especially with regard to the goddess. The power of the goddess infuses the land and her mythology records the places where this power is most potent. To travel to such a place, called a *tirtha*, literally a "ford" or a "crossing", place is to tap into that power.[1] *Tirthas* were originally associated with crossing places at rivers, or where rivers met, but the term now applies to many places that are considered sacred. The *tirtha* is a place where two worlds meet, the human and the divine. By physically going to a *tirtha*, the pilgrim is able to access the sacred power that is abundant there. Although there are *tirthas* and many sacred places associated with male deities, the central importance of those associated with the divine feminine is most evident. Many goddess temples visited by pilgrims are at the top of hills. The pilgrims must ceremonially leave the human world behind them as they ascend towards the realm of the goddess. The climb in itself is often arduous, especially in the hot Indian sun, for all but the very fittest. However, the sense of achievement and exhilaration felt when the top is reached, only adds to the feeling of entering the divine realm of the goddess. Because the pilgrim has had to struggle, the final "sight" *darsana* of the goddess is all the more potent and meaningful.

The importance of the River Ganges

The river Ganges, or Ganga Ma as she is affectionately known, cuts a swathe across northern India between the southern Himalayas and the Bay of Bengal. Beginning as a rushing torrent, she eventually becomes more sedate as she passes through the pilgrimage city of Haridwar, past the burning *ghats* of Varanasi, and on through the rice bowl of Patna as she makes her way to the sea. Ganga provides the source of nourishment for the millions of people who depend on the crops that are fertilized by her waters and is a source of spiritual nourishment for many millions more. The life-giving and purifying properties are what make the river Ganges an object of veneration. The power and majesty of so important a river is symbolized in the designation Ganga Ma or Mother Ganges. In a land that is full of holy rivers, Ganga is the holiest of all. She is the epitome of sacredness and purity, representing the quintessence of divinity in all India's rivers. Consequently, as Diana Eck points out: "The River Ganga is not confined to the course she takes across the plains of North India but participates in that spatial transposition that is so typical of Hindu sacred topography, pervading the sacred waters of all India's great rivers."[2] For instance, to visit any river in the right frame of mind is, to a certain extent, to visit Ganga Ma. She is called the River of Heaven, described as the Milky Way[3] and now flows through the three worlds: heaven, earth and the netherworld (*patala*).

Her earthly source is in an ice cave at the foot of the Gangotri glacier, a place of modern-day pilgrimage, but only for the most determined pilgrims. Those who do endure the sub-zero temperatures to visit the place where Ganga makes her descent from heaven to earth are rewarded by the definitive sight of (*darsana*) the goddess. For at that place there are no temples or statues, nor are there any priests to intervene between the goddess and the devotee – consequently, contact there is at its most intimate. Some have never returned from Ganga Ma's side. High in the Himalaya Mountains, Ganga provides a place of solace for holy men who have left the material world behind. Sheltering in rock caves, these hardy *sadhus* spend their lives in meditation and prayer in constant contact with the purifying waters of this most sacred of rivers.

One drop of her water is more precious to the spiritually-minded Hindu than any amount of gold or precious stones. She is 'purity in liquid form' (Eck) and her very touch has the power to purify the most sinful person; her waters, according to the *Ramayana*, "destroy all sin"[4] and: "If one takes the holy dip in Ganga in accordance with the injunctions with devotion and faith, one shall become purified even if one is a Brahmana-slayer. [The worst crime one might commit] What to say of other sinners."[5]

Whereas some Brahmanical temples still exclude those without class (scheduled castes or *dalits*) Ganga discriminates against no one. Ganga is the definitive Mother of All, and it is easier to receive her blessing than any of the other gods or goddesses. Loved by every one, Ganga Ma accepts, without question, the hopes and dreams of all who come to immerse themselves in her icy waters. She turns no one away, not even the most miserable wretch. While the rest of society may shun them, Ganga Ma will not reject them. In her eyes, all are equal, the sinner and the saint, the beggar and the king. Thus, welcoming all to her bosom, Ganga Ma is naturally popular among all forms of society.[6]

During the current age, the *kali yuga*, when liberation from the seemingly endless cycle of reincarnation is too difficult for most to attain through meditation or renunciation, it can be achieved, it is said, by being cremated on the banks of Mother Ganga.[7] Consequently, the greatest wish of many Hindus is to die within the sight of the river, ideally at Varanasi or Kasi, as it was formerly known, Siva's City of Light. Death here assures the devotee of liberation, when his or her ashes are scattered in the salvific waters of Ganga Ma. Fundamentally, since there are no rules or restrictions to her succour, Ganga is the epitome of mercy and compassion. At one time, Ganga Ma was a goddess dwelling in heaven where she had a reputation for mischief and mayhem. But as a goddess on earth she is regarded as wholly beneficent, her initial anger

and destructive intent at being summoned to earth being "utterly purified and calmed in the hair of Siva".[8]

The *Sakta pithas*

The belief in the sacredness of the land that is India is doubtless very
ancient. In many Indian texts, the importance of various places as being
particularly sacred is reiterated. As Eck points out: "India's myths are
living in the geography of the land, and conversely India's geography is
alive with mythology."[9] However, the unification of the sites associated
with goddesses is relatively recent (late medieval period) in India's long
tradition. These sacred sites are referred to collectively as the *Sakta
pithas* "seats of the goddess". The culmination of the *pitha* tradition is
represented by a list of fifty-one sites in a text called the *Pithanirnaya*
or *Mahapithanirupana*, listing the locations of the sites, the goddess and
the form of Bhairava (a fierce form of Siva) that resides with the goddess
at each place.[10] However, this list is by no means authoritative for it
seems that no agreement has ever been reached on the number of sites –
ranging from four in the *Hevajra Tantra* to one hundred and eight in
the *Devi-Bhagavatam* – nor their exact location. To make matters more
complicated one text may provide different numbers of sacred goddess
pithas. The *Kalika Purana*, for example, lists seven sites in (18. 42–51)
and only four sites, that have already been included in the previous
verses, in (64. 43–45). To a certain extent, this is irrelevant since all of
India is considered sacred and, as such, is inextricably linked to the
divine feminine. Therefore, anywhere has the potential to be a sacred
goddess site.

Mythologically, the *Sakta pithas* originated and are linked by one
particular incident, the death of the goddess Sati, which was examined
in chapter 3. Although there are numerous sacred sites of the goddess
and, indeed, other deities mentioned in early texts such as the
Mahabharata – "Tour of the Sacred Fords"[11] – it was not until the myth
of Sati's death and subsequent dismemberment was fully developed that
the *Sakta pithas* became a cohesive idea. In each of the sacred seats of
the goddess, Siva is also found as a *linga* or, according to some texts, as
a form of Bhairava, his fierce aspect.

> O twice borns! wherever the pair of feet and the other parts of the dead
> body of Sati had fallen, Mahadeva being attracted and out of deep attach-
> ment to her stayed Himself, in all those places, assuming the shape of a
> *linga* (male organ). (*Kalika Purana* 18. 46)[12]

According to the *Kalika Purana* (18. 41–3 and 48–50), Sati's feet fell at Devikuta, where the goddess is called Mahabhaga. At Uddiyana her thighs fell and the goddess there is Katyayani. Perhaps the most important of the *Sakta pithas* is at a mountain called Kamagiri in Kamarupa where the *yoni* (vagina) and the navel of Sati fell and is now known as Kamakhya. This particular goddess is important in the *Kalika Purana*, which is said to have been written at Kamarupa. The goddess Candi now resides at Jalandhara where the breasts (adorned with gold chain) of Sati fell. Sati's arms and neck fell on a mountain called Purnagiri, now the home of the goddess Purnesvari. Finally, according to the *Kalika Purana*, the goddess Dikkaravasini or Lalita-Kanta can be found beyond the east end of Kamarupa, where Sati's head fell. However, the one hundred and eight *Sakta pithas* mentioned in the later *Devi-Bhagavatam* (7. 30. 53–102) do not include those mentioned here. Perhaps this is because the names of the goddess given in the *Devi-Bhagavatam* are reminders of the orthodox side of the power of the goddess, such as Mahadevi (Great Goddess). The variation in the names and location of the *Sakta pithas* may also reflect orthodox opposition to the abodes of originally local goddesses. Narendra Bhattacharyya claims that the myth of Sati's death was used to connect many local goddesses to the *Sakta* Devi.[13] Many of the lists of the *Sakta pithas* seem fanciful and Bhattacharyya points out that some writers leave out important sites or seem unfamiliar with the places they are writing about.[14] It seems more than likely that Bhattacharyya's assertions are correct for though they may not be mentioned in any textual sources, local centres of goddess worship do claim ownership of a part of Sati's body. However, if the central beliefs concerning the nature of goddesses as the personification of divine power or energy (*sakti*) are remembered, then it is not paradoxical to have any number of *Saka pithas*.

Important goddess temples

India abounds with temples both grand and humble. Many temples are famous because of the acts of deities that dwell within or because they are unique in some way. For instance, the richest temple in India is said to be the Venkatesvara temple in Andhara Pradesh, the home of the more commonly named Lord Tirupati (a form of Visnu). Every day thousands of pilgrims are fed and, perhaps more famously, women from all over India sacrifice their long, beautiful, black hair. Some temples outline the spirituality of the land, often called Bharat Mata, Mother

India. Located in each of the four compass directions, the four holy *dhams* define the sacred geography of India. In the north is Badrinath, the source of the Ganges; in the south is Ramesvaram, the town where Rama brought Sita after he rescued her from Lanka, and worshipped Siva in the form of a *linga*. To the east is Dvarka where Krsna had his palace, and to the west is Puri, the site of the *Vaisnava*, Jagannath temple. As well as the important temples that are significant to male deities, many are particularly important in goddess worship. They are found in all regions of India, north and south. Some are magnificent and draw worshippers and tourists alike whereas others are particularly significant to *Sakta* and *Tantric* adherents.

Kanchipuram, in south India, is a famous place of pilgrimage for the devotees of Visnu, Siva and Sakti. The Goddess appears here as Kamaksi who, rather than residing in Siva's temple, has her own huge temple complete with a golden-domed roof; clearly a measure of her importance. She is worshipped as an incarnation of Parasakti (Supreme Power), and is said to have Sarasvati, Laksmi, and Parvati as her eyes. Legend states that originally, Kamaksi came to Kanchipuram and, seated under the shade of a mango tree, she offered worship to a Siva *linga* made of sand. Through her austerities and devotion, she won Siva as her husband. Kamaksi is depicted in a *padmasana* (lotus posture) indicating her majesty and beneficence. However, she was not always so approachable. Tradition states that originally she was considered a fierce incarnation of Sakti (*ugra svarupini*) but, after the great Indian religious teacher, Sankaracarya, had installed a *Sri cakra* (a mystical diagram representing the benign goddess Sri or Laksmi) before her image, Kamaksi became a peaceful goddess (*santa svarupini*). Kamaksi is worshipped in temples across Tamilnadu, but sight of (*darsana*) her in her temple in Kanchipuram is considered particularly beneficial.

Temples associated with one particular goddess may be significantly different in their iconography, layout and forms of worship. Dissimilarity is nowhere more evident than in two important temples for the goddess Kali in Kolkata. While arguably the most important and popular Kali temple, Kalighat is in the heart of old Kolkata, another important temple is situated on the outskirts of the city. At the other side of the Hoogly River (a tributary of the Ganges) stands a large temple called Daksinesvar, meaning the "Lord of the South". The main deity is Kali who is depicted standing on top of the prone body of Siva. This temple is unique because it also encompasses a series of twelve shrines containing Siva *lingas* that line the riverbank. Daksinesvar is situated on the outskirts of Kolkata and is consequently more spacious than Kalighat. Although Kalighat and Daksinesvar are both dedicated to the worship of Kali, the atmosphere at each temple is perceptibly different. Animal sacrifice is rarely carried out at Daksinesvar whereas it is a daily occurrence at Kalighat. Nevertheless, the sacrificial post does draw devotees during their worship. Instead of bringing an animal to sacrifice, devotees touch their head to the post, symbolically sacrificing themselves. The practices at the temples may be one reason for the difference in atmosphere at the two places. Kalighat has rather a brooding air about it, perhaps because some of the people who loiter there are less religiously minded than they might be, perhaps seeking the opportunity to make money out of unsuspecting tourists by providing a quick tour of the temple. However, having said that there is also a perceptible accumulation of power at Kalighat, which is hard to describe but is noticeable in the charged atmosphere that seems to pervade the temple, especially during evening *puja*. In contrast, the atmosphere at Daksinesvar seems much lighter and might best be described as contemplative, possibly because of its open construction or perhaps because of the influence of Ramakrishna, who made this temple his home (see chapter 5). The presence of Ramakrishna and the intensity of his relationship with Kali is possibly the main reason why this particular temple is famous. Pilgrims come to see the place where Ramakrishna lived and died as much as to receive *darsana* of Kali.

Among all the sites sacred to the goddess, a few are more popular and famous than the rest. Some are important because they are included in the *Sakta pithas*, others are famous for other reasons. The following represents a selection of the most famous Indian goddess temples, but they are by no means the only ones.

Kamarupa, abode of the goddess Kamakhya

Assam, formerly known as Kamarupa, is the location of perhaps the most famous, and arguably one of the oldest, *Sakta pithas*. An early reference to the *pithas* is found in the *Hevajra Tantra, circa.* seventh century, in which four sacred sites are mentioned; Kamarupa is included among them.[15] Perched on top of a hill known as Nilacala or Nilakuta (Blue Mountain), with the holy Brahmaputra River flowing beneath it, the temple of the goddess Kamakhya draws pilgrims and visitors from all over India:

> The Yonimandala Kamakhya, the place of Srimati Tripura Bhairavi, the excellent of all places in this earth, where the Devi Maha Maya always

dwells. There is no other place better than this on the earth. Here the Devi becomes every month in Her course of menstruation and where the virtuous men are seen. Here all the Devas remain in the form of mountains and where on the mountains the excellent Devas inhabit. The sages say: That all the places there are of the nature of the Devi; there is no better place than this Kamakhya Yonimandala. (*Devi-Bhagavatam* 7. 38. 15–18)[16]

The temple itself is not particularly spectacular; it has no ornate towers or intricately carved decoration as some temples do. Similarly, there is no magnificent image of the goddess Kamakhya to draw in the crowds. So why, you might ask, is this particular temple so important? Although from the outside the temple may look relatively uninteresting, it has at its very heart an unusual and unique representation of the divine feminine. There is no statue because down a flight of steps, "in the depths of the shrine there is a yoni-shaped cleft in the rock, adored as the Yoni of Sakti. A natural spring within the cave keeps the cleft moist."[17] Since this represents the genitals of the goddess, referred to as the *yoni-pitha* or *yoni-mandala*, it is partly covered with a cloth and garlands of flowers.[18] The goddess Kamakhya, represented simply by her *yoni* (vagina), expresses the creative aspect of the power or energy that is an integral element of *sakti*. The *Kalika Purana* often refers to Kamakhya as the Mother of the World, or Ambika (38.149); her representation as a *yoni* indicates her role as Earth Mother.

In many texts, Kamarupa is mentioned as the place where the *yoni* of Sati fell. It is, therefore, considered the most important *Sakta pitha*, the source of the goddess's creative power. In the *Kalika Purana* Siva says of Kamakhya:

On this most sacred seat, named Kubjika-pitha, which is Nilakuta, and there the goddess reside [sic] with me in secret. The female organ of Sati, which had fallen on this most sacred place (hill) was broken into pieces, and then the pudendum of Sati turned to stone, in which the goddess Kamakhya herself resides. Should a mortal being ever touch that stone (in the shape of a female organ) attains [sic] immortality. Being immortal he resides in the abode of Brahma, and if he stays there attains liberation (moksa).[19]

An interesting episode in the *Kalika Purana* brings together the goddess Kamakhya who is worshipped in Assam, and Mahamaya, whose actions illustrate her over-riding power. In chapter seventy-two, the Glory of

Kamakhya, a strange tale is related in which Visnu (referred to as Kesava) approaches Kamakhya's mountain home but does not pay her due reverence. Visnu finds himself stuck in the air; for he is riding on his mount Garuda who is part bird, part man. In his efforts to free himself, Visnu tries to move the mountain, a deed that angers the goddess, causing her to cast him into the ocean.

> Then Mahamaya with her (divine) power restrained the movement of Kesava, who reached the bottom of the ocean, and thus pinned him down to the ocean rock. Even with all his effort Hari [Visnu] was unable to come up to the surface of the water; he kept on making even still greater efforts to float himself.[20]

The other gods go to try and rescue Visnu but they, too, are also held at the bottom of the ocean by the power of the goddess. Eventually Siva comes to the stricken gods and advises them that they are in need of the armour (*kavaca*) of the goddess, a sort of prayer or *mantra* that will free them from the water. The *kavaca* starts with assigning various aspects of the goddess to different parts of the devotee's (god's) body, followed by an acknowledgement of the power of the goddess: "I salute the goddess Kamesvari, Mahamaya, the embodiment of the world, who is the Primordial Force of the world and, who as such, causes the world to emerge."[21] There is then a meditation or visualization (*dhyana*) of the goddess:

> The goddess Kamakhya stands on a white ghost, wears a rosary, and a siddha-sutra in her two hands, her other two hands are boon-granting and safety providing postures; she is of saffron-yellow colour, bedecked with gems and ornaments, she resides in the wisdom and meditation (of devotees), adequately manifested she is worshipped by Brahma, Indra and others, she is engaged in sexual intercourse, her favourite *mantra* is preceded by *candra* and *bindu*: I pay my obeisance to this goddess.[22]

The gods are released from their bondage and offer worship to the goddess. Visnu says:

> Thou art the Primordial Force, the goddess, thou art, the earth and water, thou art the matter of the world, thou art the embodiment of the world. The entire world is created by you, thou art superior wisdom, who cause liberation. O great goddess! thou art essence of both remote and proximate, thou art the soul of the subtle and gross elements, be pleased to us.

O auspicious goddess; when thou art propitiated all gods become pleased.
O auspicious one! thou fulfillest the four-fold aims of life.[23]

The reply made by the goddess brings her worship back to its earthly
realm as she advises the gods to, "take the bath in my vaginal-water and
sip from that water without delay".[24] The allusion made here is to the
temple of Kamakhya in Assam, in which the goddess is represented by
a cleft in the rock, signifying the vagina (*yoni*) of the immolated body of
Sati, examined in chapter 3. In these references the cosmic and earthly
powers of the goddess meet, clearly revealing her dualistic nature. This
strange tale ends with the goddess promising that anyone who sips the
water from her *yoni* will attain liberation, freedom from reincarnation.

The temple of Kamakhya is both famous as an important centre of
goddess worship and infamous as a centre of *Tantric* practices. One
unusual feature of this temple is the inclusion, both in the temple itself
and in various shrines outside, of the *Dasamahavidyas* (ten goddesses
of transcendent knowledge). The *Mahavidyas* are rarely represented
other than in pictorial form on some temple walls and are firmly linked
with *Tantric* modes of worship and appear in *Tantric* texts. According
to Ajit Mookerjee, the temple of Kamakhya is "a stronghold of tantric
tradition . . . regarded as a living centre of her immeasurable power".[25]
Various *Tantric* texts – the *Yogini Tantra*, the *Kamakhya Tantra* and
the *Maya Tantra* – express the importance and benefits of *yoni*
worship.[26] Although Kamakhya draws many non-*Tantric* pilgrims and
worshippers, it is also associated with magical practices and is an important place to attain magical powers (*siddhis*). It is thought by many to
be inhabited by ghosts and demons. Folk tales perpetuate the myth that:
"Only magicians and *tantriks*, riding enchanted flying trees, could go
there at night."[27] The *Yogini Tantra* provides the worshipper with directions on how the temple and its goddesses should be approached.

The introduction of worship of Kamakhya is attributed to Naraka
the king of Kamarupa. The story of Naraka and the instruction to
worship the goddess Kamakhya, given to him by Visnu, are related in
the *Kalaika Purana* (chapter 38). However, while the mythology of
Kamakhya explains the nature of the *yoni*-shaped stone, it provides no
specific origins of this goddess. Bhattacharyya concludes that she was
probably a tribal goddess, "the Khasi tribal mother ka-me-kha who",
through Sanskritization, "later came into the fold of Sakta-Tantric
cults".[28] That she is clearly a *Sakta-Tantric* goddess is evident in the
Kamakhya-tantra that ascribes five different forms to the goddess –
Kamakhya, Tripura, Kamesvari, Sarada and Mahamaya – all of whom

are *Tantric* in nature.[29] The evidence of animal and even human sacrifice also supports the view that she is a *Tantric* goddess who has possible tribal origins. According to one commentator: "When the new temple of Kamakhya was opened, the occasion was celebrated by the immolation of no less than a hundred and forty men, whose heads were offered to the goddess on salvers made of copper."[30]

The site is most sacred at one particular time of year, between the seventh and eleventh day of *Asadha* (June/July), when the goddess has her annual period of menstruation. At this time, the monsoon rains swell the Brahmaputra River flowing under the temple. Because of the composition of the underlying rock it oozes out of the fissure in the *yoni* in a reddish stream. For the first three days, the temple is closed but is reopened on the fourth day, when it attracts huge numbers of pilgrims and tourists alike. The identity between Kamakhya and Mother Earth is unmistakable at this time. The menstrual blood of the goddess is considered especially sacred, able to cure any illness and, according to Bhattacharyya, an "artificially prepared red liquid is sold to devotees as her blood".[31] Devotees also seek red clothes, representing Devi's blood-stained garments. Animal sacrifices, an ancient part of fertility rituals, are offered to the goddess during this festival. The fact that the menstruation of the goddess is such a sacred event again signifies a *Tantric* element of her worship. In ordinary terms, although a girl's first menstruation might be a cause for celebration, thereafter its defiling presence excludes her from temple worship and other activities. Kamakhya's power is so strong as to produce sacredness from an event that is usually profane.

The goddess Vaisno Devi in Jammu

Punjabi oral or local tradition claims that Sati's arms fell at the site of Vaisno Devi's shrine and, in so doing, legitimized this as a place of pilgrimage. The cave shrine of Vaisno Devi, in northwest India, is not generally found in the many lists of *Sakta pithas*, but it is one of the fastest growing pilgrimage sites in India. To claim that a part of Sati fell at a particular place of goddess worship is a device used at many regional sites, and since there is no definitive list of *Sakta pithas*, hence theoretically any number might exist. It is simply a method of legitimizing local goddesses. In the case of Vaisno Devi, though the contention that her shrine is a genuine *Sakta pitha* is asserted in local tradition, this particular connection is not evident in the goddess's mythology or iconography.

Local pamphlets explain the nature of Vaisno Devi's birth and provide the mythology of her appearance in her cave shrine. An extended account of the following mythology can be found in Kathleen Erndl's comprehensive study on Vaisno Devi and a number of other goddesses in the Punjab region.[32] The pamphlet myths commence by firmly establishing that Vaisno Devi is one of the forms of the Mahadevi that she promised would appear in times of danger:

> Thus whenever trouble arises due to the advent of the danavas (demons), I shall incarnate and destroy the foes.[33]

The Mahadevi, in the form of the three goddesses – Mahakali (Great Kali), Mahalaksmi (Great Laksmi) and Mahasarasvati (Great Sarasvati) – present in the form of stone outcrops (*pindis*) – create a beautiful virgin who was originally called Trikuta. Born in the silver age (*treta yuga*), the second of the four degenerating ages, she was an extraordinary woman who attracted many holy men by her supernatural powers. Her greatest desire was to win the hand of Lord Rama. Unfortunately for her, he had made a vow to remain faithful to his wife, Sita. When Rama could not dissuade Trikuta from her purpose he promised to return and set her a test. If she recognized him when she met him again, he would marry her. Sadly, she did not identify him disguised as an old man. However, Rama did promise that when he returned at the end of the fourth age, the *kali yuga*, in his Kalkin incarnation (*avatara*), she could be his consort. Rama told the woman that she should go and practise austerities in "a cave on Trikut Mountain in North India where the three Mahasaktis live", where, he told her, "she would become famous as Vaisno Devi".[34] This episode in Vaisno Devi's mythology clearly explains why she resides in a cave on the aptly named Trikut (three peaks) Mountain, perhaps mirroring the three *pindis*, or rock outcrops that symbolize the three goddesses within. Other episodes establish her great power and lead the devotee through the important places along her pilgrimage route, explaining why they are sacred.

The acceptance of Vaisno Devi as a powerful goddess in her own right is established in the myth of Sridhar, a Brahman devotee who lived nearby, seven hundred years ago. Kathleen Erndl once again provides a detailed account.[35] Sridhar was feeding some young girls during a virgin worship (*kanya puja*) when Vaisno Devi appeared among the girls. She requested that Sridhar should organize a grand feast for the next day. Sridhar complied with her wishes and started inviting the local people to the feast, including a party of mendicants that he happened to meet.

The leader of the mendicants, Bhaironath, disputed that Sridhar would be able to satisfy the hunger of himself and the rest of his group. The following day, when the goddess served vegetarian food to Bhaironath he complained that no meat was being served, despite the fact that he was in a Brahman house. When Bhaironath angrily tried to seize the goddess, she disappeared. Gripped by anger and desire, Bhaironath set off to find the goddess. The pilgrimage route to the cave shrine of Vaisno Devi is marked by the places where Bhaironath stopped or the goddess rested. One of the most important sites along the pilgrimage route is a small cave referred to as Adikumari (Primeval Virgin) or Garbha (Womb) *yoni* because Vaisno Devi hid inside the cave for nine months. When Bhaironath eventually caught up with her she made an opening in the back of the cave and escaped from him. Devotees mimic her actions by crawling through the twenty-foot cave, an action that symbolizes their spiritual rebirth. Vaisno Devi travelled on up the Trikut Mountain until she reached the entrance to her cave dwelling. Here she posted her companion, Langur Vir (a form of Hanuman the monkey god), to protect her. However, Bhaironath was completely undeterred and attacked and seriously wounded the goddess's guard. Vaisno Devi became angry at Bhaironath's dogged pursuance of her and appeared before him in a fierce form as Candi. As Bhaironath tried to enter her cave, the goddess attacked him, cutting off his head, which rolled down the mountain. His body remains at the entrance to the cave in the shape of a huge boulder. At the moment of his death Bhaironath realized the mistake he had made and called out:

"O Adi Sakti [Primeval Energy], O Generous Mother, I am not sorry to meet death, because it is at the hands of the Mother who created the world. O Matesvari [Mother Lord], forgive me. I was not familiar with this form of yours."[36]

Vaisno Devi offered him forgiveness. Consequently, Bhaironath's head is worshipped by devotees descending from Vaisno Devi's shrine. Erndl asserts that there are clear parallels between Vaisno Devi and Durga, and Bhaironath and Mahisasura, the buffalo demon of the *Devi-Mahatmya*.[37] The name *Bhairo* also points towards a fierce form of Siva (Bhairava), who has been identified with the buffalo demon and, in particular, with decapitation.[38]

Local mythology has established the reason behind Vaisno Devi's appearance in a cave on the side of a mountain. This particular shrine is considered special because it houses the three cosmic forms of *sakti* –

Mahakali (Great Kali), Mahalaksmi (Great Laksmi) and Mahasarasvati (Great Sarasvati). It is claimed that this is the only shrine in India to house natural forms of the three cosmic goddess. But the question arises as to why we are discussing Vaisno Devi if the three main goddesses are Mahakali, Mahalakshmi and Mahasarasvati? The name Vaisno is an indication that this goddess is allied with the *Vaisnava* ideal, particularly with purity. Vaisno Devi is renowned for her purity and her strict vegetarian diet and so is identified with the middle *pindi* representing Mahalaksmi. The mythology presented in local pamphlets also strengthens her association with Laksmi, since Vaisno Devi is waiting for the tenth *avatara* of Visnu to make her his consort, indicating that Vaisno Devi is in reality an incarnation of Laksmi. There appears to be a certain ambiguity about Vaisno Devi's identity,[39] whether as an incarnation of Lakshmi or as the Mahadevi, encompassing the power of the three goddesses represented by the *pindis*. Poster art identifies Vaisno Devi as a Durga-type figure, seated on a tiger, brandishing various weapons in her eight hands. Rohe eventually comes to the conclusion that Vaisno Devi can be many things to many people. The *Vaisnavite* devotee might see her as an incarnation of Laksmi, the *Saivite* may see her as a form of Durga and the *Sakta* may simply see Vaisno Devi as the Mahadevi, personified in many forms. Rohe finally concludes:

> Simultaneously distinct and ambiguous, Vaisno Devi is Mahadevi. She contains all *saktis*, all beings, and all creation; she is broadly inclusive, connecting deities, sects, times, places, and a diversity of devotees. Through her blessings, Vaisno Devi recreates the lives of her devotees, and they continually recreate her according to their own beliefs. Hence, the construction of Vaisno Devi as Mahadevi remains an ongoing process.[40]

Perhaps this is why Vaisno Devi's shrine is arguably the fastest growing pilgrimage site in India.

Tewari claims that the pilgrimage to Vaisno Devi's shrine starts in the mind and goes on to say that only those who have been called by the goddess will arrive at her shrine.[41] Certainly, only the most determined will reach the shrine of Vaisno Devi since it requires a climb of about fourteen kilometres before the mouth of her cave-abode is reached. On reaching the cave, the devotee must crawl through a ninety-foot tunnel:

> A pilgrim entering the ancient cave must squeeze through a narrow opening over a smooth boulder that is considered to be the petrified,

headless body of Bhairo, a *sadhu* whom the goddess is said to have killed after he pursued her up the mountain. . . . Past the boulder, a pilgrim can stand only at an angle in the ankle-to-calf-deep stream, the Charan Ganga, which flows from the covered base of the *pindis*. Proceeding forward in the stream for about one hundred feet and after a few turns and steps, the pilgrim stands in front of a platform where priests are seated. Ahead and to the right is the goddess herself, who is *svayambhu* (self-manifest) as three stone *pindis*, which are surrounded by other small images.[42]

Sources record that since the far end of the cave was opened up, an estimated twenty thousand devotees pass through the cave each day.[43] While the actual cave where the goddess resides may be ancient, the effort and planning that has gone into making the site available to many is decidedly modern. After 1986 the pilgrimage was transformed "from a physically difficult and dangerous path managed on the basis of greed into what appears to be currently one of the most efficiently run temples in India".[44] This, it seems, is a pilgrimage site for the modern age, with plentiful accommodation and food, all the facilities a pilgrim might need and, in the days of e-commerce, even an Internet site.[45] Although this may not be an "official" *Sakta pitha*, it is certainly a very important and sacred site of the power that pervades the sacred geography of India.

Kalighat in Bengal

Kalighat, the seat of the most well-known incarnation of Kali, gives its name to the modern city of Calcutta. The city was founded in 1690 and its name, Calcutta, is an anglicized version of Kalighat. Calcutta, as noted earlier, has recently reverted to its Indian name Kolkata. The temple complex of Kalighat is a world within itself.[46] In one of the oldest areas of Kolkata where the streets are narrow and the houses dilapidated, the temple of Kali stands proudly, drawing crowds from all over India and, indeed, the world. During the hours when Kali's doors are open, the narrow passageways that circle her sanctum are thronged with devotees, *dhoti*-clad priests, beggars hoping for a meal, and those making a quick rupee by showing visitors around. The outside of the temple is often as busy as the inside, for many people bring their new vehicles, especially taxis and auto rickshaws, to be blessed by the priests. The various parts of the engine are anointed with vermilion and ceremonially garlanded with red hibiscus flowers. Strings of lemons and chillies, shiny and green, contrast with the blood red of the hibiscus; the air is pungent with the mingled smells of exhausts, cooking and incense. The temple is vibrant and alive, though there is a slightly menacing air accompanying the fervent devotion of Kali's many worshippers. There is a constant coming and going since alongside Kali's sanctum there are four separately housed Siva *lingams* and a Sosthi Tala. This shrine houses an ancient cactus plant onto which small stones are tied with red string. The devotees hope that the goddesses of this shrine – Sastri, Sitala, Candi and Manasa – will answer their request for children. If their prayers are answered, they return to the shrine and make an offering of the child's hair. The shrine is unusual in that only priestesses officiate at it.

While the devotees go to take *darsana* of perhaps the most powerful incarnation of Kali, the large number of animals sacrificed daily attracts the tourists. One of the most incongruous sights I have encountered in India was a Japanese tourist party, with cameras at the ready, being led through the throngs of devotees at Kalighat. Almost certainly, they came to be shocked or titillated by the animal sacrifice that still happens daily. It is probably the last large urban temple still to perform animal sacrifice, which in itself is an indication that Kali has remained true to her unorthodox nature. Young black male goats are garlanded with red hibiscus flowers and doused with yellow turmeric water; if they shiver, Kali has accepted them as a suitable sacrifice. There is much excitement when a goat is sacrificed, announced by the rhythmical beat of a drum. As the sacrificial knife comes down on the goat's neck, the drum is silent. The crowd pushes forward hoping to receive a drop of the blood, which is now considered sacred, being charged with the blessings of the goddess. The goat, by giving its life, is released from the trials and tribulations of the *samsaric* world and, by the grace of the goddess, is liberated, being reborn on earth no more.

Kalighat is referred to in some texts as one of the *Sakta pithas*; the place where the big toe of Sati fell. The main sanctum of Kalighat is said to contain the toe, which had turned to stone. Legend recounts that in the Bhagirathi, an offshoot of the river Ganges, a Brahman named Atma Roy discovered the toe, which had turned to stone.[47] As he was sitting by the river one evening, he saw something sparkling in the water. The next morning he returned to the same spot and was amazed to see a glittering toe-shaped stone. He recovered the stone and took it into the forest where, strangely attracted to it, he sat and contemplated it for a long time. That night he had a dream that the toe belonged to the goddess Sati whose body parts (according to the Daksa myth) were scattered all over India. Atma Roy built a shrine for the stone and worshipped it regularly. At some time he must have built a more permanent structure and created an image of the goddess Kali. Santosh Roy Chowdhury, who happened upon the Kali shrine, immediately recognized the energy of the goddess within it and initiated the Kalighat temple that stands today.[48]

Minaksi, the fish-eyed goddess of Madurai

The name *Minaksi* means "fish-eyed" or "having the eyes of a fish". The fish was the emblem of the Pandyan rulers. It is said that: "Even as the mother fish has merely to gaze at her spawn in order to develop life in them, so also does spiritual life stir in the body of the worshippers the moment Goddess Meenakshi casts her eyes on them."[49] This popular south Indian goddess is situated at the heart of the oldest city in Tamilnadu, in a temple that draws people from all over India and beyond. The impressive Minaksi temple towering over the centre of the ancient city of Madurai is one of the wonders of Tamilnadu. The south Indian sun glitters on the golden domes that mark out the sanctums of Minaksi and her spouse. Above, countless gods, goddesses and other divine beings look down from the temple towers, watching the stream of pilgrims and tourists who enter the temple's hallowed halls to wonder at its splendour or to take *darsana* of the goddess on a daily basis. The majesty and splendour of the Minaksi temple are fitting for a goddess who was once considered the daughter of a king.

Legend states that Minaksi was born from a sacrificial fire to the Pandyan King Malayadhwajan. His wife, Kancanamala, was a devotee of Parvati and Siva, and in a previous life, as Vidyavati, Parvati had agreed to be born as her daughter. The queen was very happy when her daughter was born but the king was a little sad because he had hoped that his child would be a boy. The child was also unusual because she had three breasts. However, a divine voice spoke to the king, telling him to "name the child Thadadhagai and to bring her up as if she were a son. It also said that the third breast would disappear as soon as she saw her consort."[50] The king made her his successor and she became a supreme warrior. After her coronation, she fought many battles until she eventually came to the abode of Siva. Her mythology states that she was without equal until she met Siva. She destroyed his forces but when she came upon Siva himself, she was transformed.

The moment She saw him Her [third] breast disappeared.
She became bashful, passive, and fearful.
She leaned unsteadily, like the flowering vine

bending under the weight of its blossoms.
Her ancient love [for Him] was rekindled and stayed with Her.
Her heavy dark hair fell on Her neck.
She looked down toward her feet,
with collyriumed eyes like those of the kentai fish.
And there She stood, luminous as lightening,
scratching [shyly] in the earth with Her toes. (*The Story of Siva's Sacred Games*, 5. 43)[51]

Of course, she was not a mortal but an incarnation of the goddess Parvati and, therefore, the only man/god she could marry was Siva. After her marriage to Siva, the god and goddess entered the temple as Minaksi and Sundaresvara. In her goddess form in her huge temple in the centre of Madurai, her marriage ceremony to Siva in the form of Sundaresvara is celebrated annually at the full moon. As Chris Fuller states: "At the Citterai festival, Minaksi is crowned as the Pandyan Queen of Madurai on the eighth day, defeated by Siva in battle on the ninth, and married to him as Sundareswarar on the tenth."[52]

Although in some mythological accounts Minaksi is said to have originated in a sacrificial fire, it is likely that in reality Minaksi was a very popular regional goddess. It is perhaps through a process of Hinduization or Brahmanization that a local indigenous goddess is now considered an incarnation of the goddess Parvati. Minaksi is unusual in that, although she is the wife of Siva, she has her own sanctum. Devotees go first to take *darsana* of Minaksi, and then to Sundaresvara; they are not worshipped as a couple, except during their festival. It is for this reason that Lynn Gatwood describes her as "a temporarily spousified regional deity".[53] It is significant that after the seventeen-day *Cittirai* festival, Minaksi reverts to her independent character, which is more akin to the nature of local goddesses. However, she is attended by Brahman priests who enforce the strict purity rules that characterize her worship. Consequently, impure, non-Hindus are prohibited from entering her sanctum, contenting themselves with exploring her huge temple complex and, instead, taking their *darsana* of the lesser deities. Despite the show of ritual purity and orthodoxy, not all trace of Minaksi's local origins has been erased. It seems likely that animal sacrifice was once practiced, as periodically she is offered a melon or pumpkin smeared with a red paste (*kumkum*) that represents, when cut, a sacrificial head.[54]

Kanyakumari, the eternal virgin of Tamilnadu

At the southernmost tip of India, where the waters of the Bay of Bengal, the Indian Ocean, and the Arabian Sea meet and mingle, there resides the beautiful goddess Kanyakumari. Although this is not an official *Sakta pitha* it is nevertheless a very important place of goddess worship. As a holy place, it is very ancient as it is mentioned in the *Mahabharata* and written about by Herodotus, Ptolemy and Marco Polo. More recently, both Gandhi and Swami Vivekananda were drawn to this place and both are honoured there. Today, the Vivekananda memorial stands proudly on the rock lying off the coast, on which this renowned holy man regularly used to sit in meditation, facing towards the shrine of Kanyakumari. Every morning thousands of people come to Cape Cormorin, or Kanyakumari as it is known in India, to see the sun rise and to take *darsana* of the goddess.

From the outside, Kanyakumari's temple is not particularly spectacular. It does not have the huge *gopurams* of the Minaksi temple nor the arduous climb up a mountain that is a prerequisite for *darsana* of Vaisno Devi. However, the image of Kanyakumari in both poster art, and especially in her temple, is magnificent to behold. As the eternal virgin, Kanyakumari is depicted with two arms, a pleasing countenance, and is perpetually dressed in her wedding finery. In the temple, she is represented by a typically south Indian black stone image, beautifully dressed and holds a necklace or garland of sacred berries or nuts (*aksamala*) in her right hand, symbolizing time and the continuous pursuit of knowledge.[55] This particular image is famous for the nose ornament she wears. Legend has it that her diamond nose ring shone so brightly that ships, mistaking it for a marker light, crashed on the rocks. Devotees to the temple approach the goddess through a side door in an atmosphere of semi-darkness, for nowadays the eastern door to her sanctum is only opened five times a year. The temple of Kanyakumari is also unusual in that there is no image of Siva. Whereas many independent goddess temples or shrines include some representation of a god, usually Siva, Kanyakumari's temple is solely dedicated to the goddess as a virgin (*kanya*).

Another significant feature of Kanyakumari's temple is a cleft in the rock containing fresh water. Legend states that the gods asked her to produce some fresh water with which they could honour her image. She responded by splitting the earth with her spear, which produced a great flood. The gods then prayed that she would stem the water flowing from the netherworld (*patala*), which was threatening to engulf the earth.

Kanyakumari complied, and the water remains in the cleft, available for use but controlled by the goddess. It is referred to as Mulaganga and symbolizes the ability of the goddess to bring order from chaos, the latter represented by *patala*.[56] The story of how the goddess came to reside in this temple is one of the most tragic origin myths of a Hindu goddess.[57]

As she has done many times before, the goddess incarnated herself as a human. Born as the daughter of a local king, her mission on earth was to destroy a powerful demon called Vanasura/Banasura.[58] Time passed and the little princess grew into a beautiful woman. Quite naturally, her father's thoughts turned to finding a suitable husband for his daughter. Since she was no ordinary woman but the divine mother herself, there could only be one husband for her, the god Siva, whom she had married in many other incarnations. With her thoughts firmly fixed on him she meditated on Siva, eventually rousing him from his own meditation on Mount Kailasa and requesting that he come and marry her. Siva of course agreed and an auspicious time and date was set for their marriage. However, the other gods grew increasingly concerned. How could they let the goddess marry Siva? If the pair did marry, they would return to their sacred home on Mount Kailasa and the goddess's task on earth would remain unfulfilled. Furthermore, the goddess would only have enough power to kill the demon if she remained a virgin. Kinsley comments:

> In the context of Tamil culture a woman's virginity, through which she withholds her sexual energy, is more or less equivalent to the building up of *tapas* in males when they retain their semen, which is magically transformed into powerful heat. Quite simply, Kanniyakumari is much more powerful as an unmarried maiden than she would be as a married woman.[59]

Therefore, the gods felt that they must intervene.

Extensive preparations were made for this most auspicious of marriages. All the streets were hung with garlands, the princess was dressed in the finest bridal wear, her hair fragrant with the perfume of jasmine buds and her body adorned with jewels. Huge plates of coloured rice were made ready to shower the happy couple. All was ready and everyone eagerly waited for the auspicious time, midnight, when Siva would arrive to marry the princess. Meanwhile, Siva had set off in plenty of time to make the journey to the Land's End of India. Nevertheless, as he neared Cape Cormorin, he heard a cockerel crow, signifying the arrival of the dawn. This meant that the auspicious time for the marriage had passed; Siva was too late. What Siva did not know was the crowing of the cockerel was made by the sage Narada who had been sent by the gods to somehow stop the wedding. The gods' plan worked and Siva in his despair sat down and immediately entered a deep trance. A form of him remains in this place in the nearby temple at Sucindrum.

While the princess waited for Siva to appear, Vanasura arrived and demanded to marry her. When he was refused, he tried to take the princess by force. The goddess fought with the demon and eventually killed him, which of course was her purpose on the earth. Sadly, the goddess waited for Siva for so long that she turned to stone and there she remains as Kanyakumari and a perpetual virgin. Eventually, the wedding feast of coloured rice and other delicacies turned into the coloured sand and pebbles that litter the beach outside her temple. It is of interest that the coloured sand, known as monozite, has been found to contain uranium, which is now extracted.[60] Therefore, as an ancient power, Kanyakumari could be said to preside over a very modern form of power.

Some versions of Kanyakumari mythology do provide a happy conclusion of sorts. According to the *Kanyaksetramahatmya* 4, Kanyakumari waits for the end of the current age, the *kali yuga*, for "the *pralaya* [great flood or periodic cosmic dissolution], when Siva will appear and make her his bride".[61] Therefore, Kanyakumari, the valiant and ever watchful virgin goddess faces towards the east, towards the rising sun, protecting the land but also representing eternal hope.[62]

The cosmic power that the myriad Hindu goddesses represent infuses the land in many ways and in innumerable places. Although certain temples and natural features are popular places of pilgrimage, conferring on the pilgrim a boost of divinity, any place might be a sacred site. Similarly, to bathe in a local river is equivalent, to a degree, of bathing in the sacred waters of the Ganges – an idea that expresses the interconnectedness of the cosmos. For, according to Hindu belief, all that is visible and, indeed, all that is invisible is simply a manifestation, an expression of Brahman or Ultimate Reality.

8 The Goddess in Contemporary Hindusim

Many of the goddesses that have so far been examined have their origins in the past, although their worship is still current. The goddesses that we will meet in this final chapter are somewhat different in various ways. The connection between the land and a maternal goddess might be an ancient idea, but India worshipped as a mother goddess did not appear in concrete form until the conception of Bharat Mata (Mother India), inspired largely by the hugely important national song *Vande Mataram* (Hail to the Mother or I bow to Thee Mother), which has remained closely connected with Indian and later Hindu nationalism. More recently the goddess Santosi Ma (Mother of Satisfaction) attained prominence after a film about her worship was released in the mid-1970. Since then other goddesses have been 'manufactured' and worshipped, though the scale of their impact is as yet unclear. Also included in this chapter is an examination of the continued worship of the living goddess of Nepal, the Kumari (Virgin). Although she is not a 'new' goddess her worship is interesting as it represents an ancient tradition that is still alive in the twenty-first century, but because of it very nature (the deification of a living girl as a goddess), we might well wonder how long it will continue.

Bharat Mata – Mother India

One of Bharat Mata's earliest appearances was in "a satirical piece titled *Unabimsa Purana* ('The Nineteenth Purana'), by Bhudeb Mukhopadhyay, first published anonymously in 1866".[1] Here she is known "as Adhi-Bharati, the widow of Arya Swami, the embodiment of all that is essentially 'Aryan'".[2] Shortly after, she appeared as "the dispossessed motherland . . . in Kiran Chandra Bandyopadhyay's play, Bharat Mata, first performed in 1873".[3] However, her most significant and enduring appearance was in Bankim Chandra Chatterjee's nationalistic novel *Anandamath* (*Abbey of Bliss* or *The Sacred Brotherhood*), which was originally serialized in Chatterjee's journal *Bangadarshan* between 1881 and 1882 with the novel published afterwards.[4]

In *Anandamath*, retrospectively "set in Bengal . . . at the time of the famine of 1770 and its aftermath",[5] a Mother goddess[6] is introduced as the primary deity of a group of renouncer warriors called the Order of Children. This struggling community of warrior monks, whose monastery (*asram* or *math*) is located in the heart of a forest, strive to free themselves and their Mother, from the yoke of their oppressors. The lower, uninitiated strata of the Order of Children, was loosely based on the itinerant renouncers that roamed Bengal in the aftermath of the famine[7] who, at the time, were described as "lawless banditti . . . known under the name of Sanyasis or Faquirs" who included "Bands of cashiered soldiers, the dregs of the Mussulman armies".[8] The Muslim element of the Children is missing in *Anandamath* and a higher, middle class, initiated, Hindu renouncer group who have a "patriotic purpose" have been added.[9] This short novel became a seminal work in influencing the growing national identity and furthering the nationalistic cause. Lise McKean attributes *Anandamath*'s success in capturing the imagination of subsequent thinkers and politicians, to its strong characterizations:

> Characters, their relationships and actions serve to evoke a range of emotions in the audience: sorrow and anger, fear, disgust and revenge. Bankim Chandra's expressive powers reach their greatest intensity in his elaboration of the religious devotion of Bharat Mata's children, a devotion so powerful that it purifies and librates the mother and her children.[10]

June McDaniel takes this idea further in her characterization of Bharat Mata when she asserts:

> The land is the Mother, and frequently she is in distress because of political difficulties. Her children (usually her sons) are her rescuers, who will save this damsel in distress. She calls upon them through the words of the poets and writers . . . The poets glorify her, asking her children to serve and protect her, and her children follow their exhortations.[11]

McDaniel characterizes the devotion of the Goddess as Nation as "political Shakta bhakti or Shakta nationalism"[12] in which patriotism becomes a religious experience.[13]

One of the most important and poignant scenes in the novel is when Mahendra, one of the central characters, is taken inside the Order's temple by Satyananda, the chief monk. Here, he shows Mahendra three forms of the Mother. As India of the past she is Annapurna the goddess of plenty. In her current state she is in the form of a naked and dishevelled Kali: "Blackened and shrouded in darkness. She has been robbed of everything; that is why she is naked. And because the land is a burning-ground, she is garlanded in skulls."[14] Bengal was under British rule at the time the novel was written, but also set during the Bengal famine. The depiction of the Mother reflects both the suffering caused by the famine and that imposed by British taxation. Chatterjee has adapted Kali's usual iconographic symbolism (i.e. nakedness and skulls) for his own purposes as her nakedness generally represents unveiled reality and the garland of skulls her domination over evil or form. Nevertheless, the depiction of Kali as used by Chatterjee does provide an evocative depiction of India subdued by her Muslim and British oppressors. However, Mahendra, who has just joined the Order of Children, is also shown how the Mother could be if she was liberated:

> Mahendra saw a golden ten-armed image of the Goddess in a large marble shrine glistening and smiling in the early morning rays. Prostrating himself, the monk said, "And this is the Mother – as-she-will-be. Her ten arms reach out in the ten directions, adorned with various powers in the form of the different weapons she holds, the enemy crushed at her feet, while the mighty lion who has taken refuge there is engaged in destroying the foe."[15]

Clearly this description of the Goddess draws inspiration from the image of Durga as the supreme warrior, who is very popular in Bengal where the novel was conceived. According to Bhakat, cited by Lipner, the three forms of the goddess were based on Bankim Chandra Chatterjee's experiences at three temples in Lagola forest. The three goddesses that he encountered were Jagaddhatri (World Protectress), Mahakali and Durga.[16]

Mahendra then asks "When will we be able to see the Mother in this form?" The monk replied, "When all the Mother's children recognise her as the Mother, she will be gracious to us".[17] This statement has clear parallels with modern Hindu nationalistic rhetoric that suggests that anyone who wants a place in India should view India as their sacred land and their Mother. It is Bankim Chandra Chatterjee's depiction of the Mother, but also the stirring lyrical quality of the poem/song *Vande Mataram* that is perhaps the genesis of the later conceptualizations of Bharat Mata or Mother India, particularly those associated with Hindu nationalism.

Vande Mataram

As well as the strong and lasting depictions of the Mother as goddess, *Anandamath* has also provided India, but especially the nationalists, with a national song in the hymn of praise offered to the goddess in the novel; *Vande* (Ben. *Bande*) *Mataram* (I revere the Mother, Hail to the Mother or I bow to Thee Mother). There are various translations of the song, one of which is attributed to Sri Aurobindo, an early nationalist, activist and scholar, who later devoted his life to spiritual pursuits, establishing an *asram* at Pondicherry. In the novel, *Vande Mataram* was taught to Mahendra as a hymn in praise of the goddess.

(I revere the Mother!)[18]

I revere the Mother! The Mother
Rich in waters, rich in fruit,
Cooled by the southern airs,
Verdant with the harvest fair.

The Mother – with nights that thrill
in the light of the moon,
Radiant with foliage and flowers in bloom,
Smiling sweetly, speaking gently,
Giving joy and gifts in plenty.

Powerless? How so, Mother,
With the strength of voices fell,
Seventy millions in their swell!
And with sharpened swords
By twice as many hands upheld!

To the Mother I bow low,
To her who wields so great a force,
To her who saves,
And drives away the hostile hordes!

You our wisdom, you our law,
You our heart, you our core,
In our bodies the living force is thine!

Mother, you're our strength of arm,
And in our hearts the loving balm,
Yours the form we shape in every shrine!

For you are Durga, bearer of the tenfold power,
And wealth's Goddess, dallying on the lotus flower, [Laksmi]
You are Speech, to you I bow, [Vak]
To us wisdom you endow.

I bow to the Goddess Fair,
Rich in waters, rich in fruit,
To the Mother,
Spotless – and beyond compare!

I revere the Mother! the Mother
Darkly green and also true,
Richly dressed, of joyous face,
This ever-plenteous land of grace.

Vande Mataram, written before the novel in a mixture of Sanskrit and Bengali, alludes to various goddesses who have been amalgamated into this praise of the Mother India. The conception of the Motherland and the stirring nature of her anthem have been attractive to many seeking their own identity. It also became a sacred *mantra* or rallying cry for those who sought to establish India's independence from the British. The song and particularly the slogan *"Vande Mataram"* was adopted outside of the novel soon after it was published. According to Lipner, Chatterjee considered Bengal as the Mother of the composition and her children included the Muslim population of Bengal, pointing to his "seventy million voices" that according to the 1871 census approximated the inclusive Bengali population.[19] The first political use of the slogan was in 1905 at demonstrations at the proposed partition of Bengal and at the time it was shouted by Hindus and Muslims alike.[20] However, by 1921 during the Calcutta riots, *Vande Mataram* "was used as a slogan by Hindu rioters against Muslims for the first time" and later became the "war cry of the Hindu fanatic".[21] Not surprisingly, many Muslims now see *Vande Mataram* as anti-Muslim, even though it is only the first two stanzas (verses 1–4) that constitute the national song, thereby excluding any verses that might be interpreted as idolatrous, a criticism commonly made by Muslims.

The compulsory singing of *Vande Mataram* in schools and other public buildings on 7 September 2006 has more recently caused conflict in government and between different religious groups. This date supposedly marked its centenary and the Hindu nationalist BJP party pushed for its singing to be compulsory to commemorate the event.[22] The underlying debate appears to centre on whether it should simply be construed as patriotic or whether – because of its context in *Anandamath* which contains anti-Muslim sentiments and its subsequent adoption by right-wing groups such as the Rashtriya Swayamsevak Sangh, National Volunteer Corps/Union (RSS) – it is now a Hindu nationalistic anthem.[23] A similar shift has happened in the representation of Bharat Mata, which initially, due to her conceptualization in *Anandamath*, associated her with Indian nationalism, in earlier times directly related to freeing India from British influence. However, since the 1980s she has become firmly embedded into the Hindu nationalist movement.

Bharat Mata and Hindu Nationalism

The first temple dedicated to Bharat Mata was built in Benaras (Varanasi) in 1936. The temple was unique in that all it contained was a very detailed relief map of undivided India, since Independence and Partition had not taken place at that time. Charu Gupta comments: "Here Bharat Mata is not a distinct personality in her own right but a metaphor for a fixed, bounded space. It is different from the images one associates with a temple, or even of Bharat Mata."[24] The temple was inaugurated by Mahatma Gandhi, who said:

> "In this temple there are no statues of gods and goddesses. Here there is only a map of India raised on marble. I hope that this temple will take the form of a worldwide platform for all religions, along with Harijans, and of all castes and beliefs, and it would contribute to feelings of religious unity, peace and love in this country."[25]

The temple and its image was shaped by good intentions as "an attempt at creating a composite religious and national identity"[26] where anyone was welcome to worship. However, alongside Gandhi's sentiments and the communal feast that followed, attended by Muslims and low castes, the temple was inextricably Hindu in character. On its gates was inscribed *Vande Mataram*, which by that time was seen as idolatrous and anti-Islamic by many Muslims. It is, therefore, questionable just how inclusive the temple could ever be. Gupta sees the temple "as a mark of the basic confusion and conflation between Hindu/Indian/nation. . . . The symbol of Bharat Mata, and that too enclosed in a temple, expressed Hindu nationalism, alienating the Muslims further".[27]

While the temple at Varanasi might have been an honest attempt to unite the nation, the later construction of a Bharat Mata temple at Haridwar, another important Hindu pilgrimage city, is firmly linked with Hindu nationalism. It was built by Swami Satyamiterand Giri, leader of the Vishva Hindu Parishad (World Hindu Council or VHP), one wing of the Sangh Parivar (family of political parties) who support and propagate Hindu nationalistic sentiments. The temple at Haridwar, consecrated in 1983, is an eight-storey building that dominates the surrounding area. In contrast to the Varanasi temple, Bharat Mata here is represented in anthropomorphic form majestically standing on a map of India, holding stalks of grain in one hand and an auspicious pot of milk in the other. While she might simply be viewed as personifying the abundant nurturing vision of the Mother espoused in *Vande Mataram*, McKean suggests that they may also be a reminder of less inclusive symbolism such as "cow protection movement, gifts to Brahmins – as well as recalling ritual vessels like the ones filled with Ganga water that were worshipped and sold during the VHP's Sacrifice for Unity",[28] discussed below. The goddess dominates the ground floor of the temple whereas the other floors glorify a variety of deities, national heroes and virtuous women *satis*, some of whom burned themselves on their husband's funeral pyre (as discussed in chapter 3). The Bharat Mata temple in Haridwar promotes Hindu nationalist ideology, not just in terms of its glorification of deities adopted by the movement and national martyrs, but is also a "means to popularize Hindu nationalist ideology and to raise money for the movement".[29] The Vishva Hindu Parisad promoted the worship of Bharat Mata prior to the consecration of the temple during a six-week tour of India earlier in 1983. The *Ekatmata Rath Yatra* (One Mother Chariot Procession) was organized by the VHP and intended as a ritual of integration in which 400 litres of Ganga water (most sacred to Hindus) from Gangotri (source of the Ganges) was taken all over India, as were images of Ganga Ma, Siva and a temporary shrine to Bharat Mata. While Bharat Mata received worship, religious leaders and Hindu nationalists warned that Hinduism was under threat due to the government's pampering of religious minorities, especially the Muslims. According to McKean: "The Bharat Mata cult propagated by contemporary Hindu nationalists combines the devotional heroic imagery of *Anandamath* with a set of elements defining Hinduness (Hindutva) formulated in 1922 by Savarkar."[30]

Santosi Ma – Mother of Satisfaction

Santosi Ma or Santosi Mata, the Mother of Satisfaction, is a relatively new goddess popular in north India. This obscure goddess is particularly interesting as she was catapulted to fame after the release of a low budget film about her in 1975. Her worship has since become widespread across north India, but who is she and why she (among other goddesses who appear in mythological films) became so popular, remains a subject of debate.

My first encounter with Santosi Ma was when, during some research, a foreword written by Arthur Basham in 1985 drew my attention.

> That the myth-making propensities of Hinduism are far from extinct has been shown in recent years by the appearance of a new goddess, Santosi Mata, whose cult has appeared during the last twenty years over the whole of Northern India, and who is not unknown in the South. This friendly goddess, who bestows practical and material benefits in return for a comparatively easy *vrata*, has already been given a genealogy, as the daughter of Ganesa, and a ritual of her own. Where she comes from and how and why her cult began are quite unknown to the best of my present knowledge, and might form the subject of much further research.[31]

It seems that there are three important aspects to any examination of this goddess. First, there is her genesis and early worship which resulted in pamphlet stories and possibly some iconography. I say possibly, because there is no conclusive evidence of when the poster image, which is still popular, was produced. Christopher Pinney tracked down a poster of the goddess produced by Sharma Picture Publications, which they originally claimed had been commissioned in 1964. However, in a subsequent interview (1994) the publisher stated that the picture was probably completed around the same time as the film was released.[32] Secondly, there is the film, *Jai Santosi Maa*, released in 1975 and directed by Vijay Sharma. It was the incredible success of the film that propelled Santosi Ma, a relatively minor goddess, to popularity all over north India and gradually some notoriety in the south as well. A key question would be, why was the film and its goddess such a success? Lastly, there is the current worship and propagation of this goddess since the film.

Early knowledge of Santosi Ma

It is still unclear what Santosi Ma's genesis is and where she first originated. However, it does seem clear that there were a number of pamphlets detailing her *vrata katha* (votive tale), often recited during her worship, circulating prior to the making of the film about her. They may have appeared as early as 1962 according to Stanley Kurtz.[33] It appears that Santosi Ma's early worship was in a temple at Jodhpur from about 1967 according to John Stratton Hawley.[34] She must have had a strong following at that time because the temple that she was installed into was previously occupied by another goddess. However, she is not simply an incarnation of the original goddess who received animal sacrifices, because Santosi Ma is strictly vegetarian.[35] Hawley goes on to report that the wife of Vijay Sharma visited the Jodhpur temple and persuaded her husband to make a film about the goddess.[36] This would suggest that Santosi Ma had considerable influence, albeit on a small scale, before the film's release. What is not known is whether Jodhpur was where she originated, since none of the pamphlets connect her to any specific location in India.

Although the pamphlets may not tell us much about Santosi Ma's place of origin they do contain valuable information about the goddess and her worship. Before going on to look at the *vrata-katha* contained in the pamphlets, mention must be made of their form and availability. The stories contained in the pamphlets might have been given greater authentication and status, simply by their shape. For as Michael Brand points out, the pamphlets mimic the shape of ancient palm leaf manuscripts. This, he claims, may have "imbued" them "with an air of ancient religious wisdom" even among those who were illiterate.[37]

There have been claims that Santosi Ma is mentioned in the *Puranas* and the *Devi-Mahatmya*. In the *Devi-Mahatmya* the goddess is referred to as "Tusti", contentment. There are two episodes where this name of the goddess is used, in the myth of Kaitabha and the myth of Sumbha-Nisumbha.

You are *Sri*, you are the queen, you modesty, you intelligence, characterized by knowing; Modesty, well-being, contentment, too, tranquillity and forbearance are you. (*Devi-Mahatmya* 1. 60)[38]

The use of the term *tusti*, contentment as an aspect of the goddess, seems weak here, but in a later verse the evidence is a little more convincing.

The Goddess . . . contentment, Hail to her, hail to her, hail to her: hail, hail!" (*Devi-Mahatmya* 5. 30)[39]

This link with Santosi Ma is still tenuous although as Kathleen Erndl points out, " . . . most worshippers identify her as an aspect of the Great Goddess"[40] because of the examples mentioned above. The only other clue, which seems somewhat unconvincing, is "a single reference in one of the Puranas to an unnamed mind-born daughter of Ganesa".[41] Since she is now widely acknowledged to be the daughter of Ganesa, this provides an example of the authentication of some goddesses by association. This is not particular to Santosi Ma as it is often claimed that other local or regional goddesses appear in textual source material.

Brand was perhaps the first scholar to translate and study the devotional pamphlets about Santosi Ma. He notes an interesting anomaly in the way that Santosi Ma is presented. Generally the pamphlets, written in praise of many different goddesses, start by placing their chosen deity within the Hindu pantheon, most commonly associating them with Parvati. However, Santosi Ma "is added to the pantheon as the daughter of the elephant-headed god Ganesha and his wife Riddhi-Siddhi".[42] This "humble position" Brand sees as "a great advantage" since, he claims, the established goddesses may have started "to appear increasingly aloof and out of touch with modern problems."[43] This is a point that I will return to later in the chapter.

The pamphlets narrate the story of a woman who is ill treated by her in-laws after her husband leaves the family home in search of work.[44] One day the woman, who is often sent into the forest to collect wood, encounters a group of women performing Santosi Ma's worship. On enquiring what the benefits of this worship are, she is told:

By the performance of this *vrata* poverty and destitution are destroyed. Fortune enters the house. The burden of the mind's worries is driven away. The mind finds peace and happiness as joy comes to the home. The childless woman will bear a child. If your husband has gone far away he will return quickly. The unmarried maiden will find a pleasing bridegroom.[45]

This worship will also combat illness, lead to the accumulation of wealth and heal rifts. The nameless woman then asks how the worship should be performed. She is told that she should offer a small amount of chickpeas (*cana*) and unrefined sugar (*jaggery* or *gur*), to fast on Friday and to recite the story of Santosi Ma. This should be undertaken consecutively until her wishes have been fulfilled (usually sixteen consecutive weeks). A completion ceremony should then be organized in which eight boys are fed. During this time no one in the household should eat anything sour.[46]

The woman commences her *vrata* to Santosi Ma and money starts to arrive from her husband; however, she is still badly treated by the family. Santosi Ma appears to the husband to precipitate his return. The grateful woman organizes the *udyapana* ceremony required at the fulfilment of her *vrata*, but it is sabotaged by her nephews at the request of their mothers. Santosi Ma is angry and punishes the woman, but later relents and the whole family eventually takes up her worship and is rewarded.

In the pamphlet story, we are told of her powers, but not where she has come from. In trying to ascertain the origin of Santosi Ma, an important clue is that the first encounter with Santosi Ma takes place in the jungle or forest where a group of women are performing her *vrata*, fast. Brand has an interesting comment to make about this fact.

> The rural setting of this *katha* and the fact that the first group of women were performing the Santosi Mata *vrata* in the forest, where the heroine also came across a Santosi Mata temple, might suggest some unexpected aboriginal influence in the origin of this goddess.[47]

Could Santosi Ma's link with the forest perhaps indicate that she was a village goddess, whose origins have been lost? She is presented as a goddess who is independent and is capable of inflicting punishment on the innocent if she is angered, two features of the character of the local or village goddesses. However, this is doubtful as these tenuous threads seem to be the only pieces of evidence that would suggest this. The majority of evidence, detailed below, suggests that Santosi Ma's origins lie elsewhere.

The importance of Jai Santosi Maa

Santosi Ma's popularity became widespread after the release of the 1975 film, *Jai Santosi Maa*, directed by Vijay Sharma. This was very surprising as the film, classified by Rachel Dwyer as a "mythological", was produced on a low budget and did not include any 'A' list stars. Incredibly, it topped the ratings that year alongside *Sholay* and *Deewaar* that both starred Amitabh Bachchan[48] who was probably at the height of his career. Mythologicals and Devotionals, that featured the gods or their devotees, had been instrumental in the early days of Indian cinema, but "had virtually disappeared by 1950s."[49] This makes the success of the film all the more poignant. Philip Lutgendorf describes it as a "word of mouth hit" at which women were the primary audience.[50] In it, Santosi Ma appeared as the saviour of her long-suffering devotee, Satyavati, who endures cruelty at the hands of her in-laws. Santosi Ma made a dramatic and immediate impact on the audiences.

> Anita Guha, who played the role of Santosi Maa, remembers . . . "Audiences were showering coins, flower petals and rice at the screen in appreciation of the film. They entered the cinema barefoot and set up a small temple outside the cinema. In Bandra, where mythological films aren't shown, it ran for fifty weeks. It's a miracle."[51]

The film version of Santosi Ma's *vrata-katha* is loosely based on the pamphlets, but there are some important differences. The intervention of established gods and goddesses and their subsequent struggle with Santosi Ma is entirely missing from the pamphlets. Veena Das, in her analysis of the film, provides a synopsis of the important aspects of the story:

> The three great gods, Brahma, Visnu and Siva, come in the garb of ascetics to receive the *prasada* of jaggery and roast chick-peas (*gur* and *cana*) offered to Santosi Ma, at Satyavati's doorstep. This act of the three gods enrages their wives Brahmani, Laksmi and Parvati; they vow to punish Satyavati if she persists in her devotion to Santosi Ma. . . . This leads to a great conflict between the principles of *Sakti*, represented by the three goddesses, and *sati*, represented by Satyavati. . . . In heaven, the three goddesses reveal that they were only putting Satyavati to the test. They bless Santosi Ma and pray that her worship may be established throughout the world.[52]

The film has had a great deal to do with the very fast acceptance of Santosi Ma, for a number of reasons. This medium by its very nature is certain to reach many more people than the pamphlets would although they are cheap and written in Hindi. They would still be inaccessible to the illiterate in a way that the film would not. Das comments:

Jai Santosi Ma is directly accessible to the vast majority of illiterate people and is regularly given a re-run around the time of major Hindu festivals. Unlike the printed versions of a myth which might still need to be interpreted through the mediation of a priest, film as a medium does away with the necessity of all mediation.[53]

The film is first and foremost in the minds of most Indians, as those that I have asked about Santosi Ma have immediately mentioned "the film", no one has mentioned the pamphlets. It is significant that the story in the film has been made more appealing to a mass audience as woven into it is the classic love story and the devout battling against cosmic forces.

It seems clear that the accessible nature and wide coverage of the film has been instrumental in Santosi Ma's recent popularity, but this is not the only factor. Santosi Ma must also have something special to offer her prospective devotees. She was almost certainly popular to a degree before the film was made, in order to have come to the film makers' notice. It would seem that one of the most important aspects of the film and the pamphlet accounts is that Santosi Ma can give hope to women mistreated by their husband's family, which is, if one listens to the media, a very common occurrence. This point is illustrated in numerous documentaries, books and news footage. In one such account, Anees Jung, in her book on women in India, relates a tragic tale of the precarious position women *can* find themselves in at the mercy of their in-laws.

> Make my daughter happy first; let her have a child and then I will try to give you the scooter, I had told her husband. How did I know that two days later my daughter, big with child, would be burnt to death? I had never seen anything like it ... there were no eyes, no mouth ... one could not tell whether the body was that of a man or woman; it was just a twisted, black bundle lying in the corner. The mother-in-law refused to give me even a *kafan* (white shroud) to cover the body. She told me to pick up my rubbish and clear her courtyard. *Satyarani Chandha, New Delhi.*[54]

This is perhaps an extreme account of the way that women may be mistreated, but it is by no means unique. New wives may find themselves in a precarious position and generally do not move up the family hierarchy until they become mothers themselves, preferably of a son.

Santosi Ma, the Mother of Satisfaction, is worshipped on Fridays by her devotees who perform a fast in return for their wishes granted by the goddess. The offerings and ceremony associated with her fast are very simple and cheap. She requires only a small amount of brown sugar and chickpeas held while listening to her story. This is then fed to a cow and the remainder taken as *prasada*. This ceremony is carried out on consecutive Fridays until one's wish is fulfilled, usually within three months. There is often a direct relationship between the devotee and the goddess; a mediator, such as a priest is unnecessary. This makes Santosi Ma very accessible to all people. All castes and classes are welcome to worship her and very few would be deterred by elaborate rituals or expensive offerings.

It seems that Santosi Ma is a goddess who is appropriate for the present age and this is almost certainly one reason why she became so popular so quickly. Brand comments: "Perhaps one reason behind Santosi Mata's astonishing rise to fame is that it was simply felt inappropriate to ask an ancient goddess for such modern appliances as radios and refrigerators."[55] As well as the capacity to grant wishes in an increasingly materialistic society, Santosi Ma has something else to offer her devotees. She is perhaps more in touch with modern demons than the more traditional goddesses. Kali and Durga fight epic battles against the forces of evil whereas Santosi Ma fights the more mundane demons that may plague her devotees daily. In this respect, perhaps the traditional goddesses seem to be on another, higher, plane more concerned with cosmic disorder than that of the person in the street. On this matter, Das makes an astute observation:

> . . . one fails to identify any specific villain in the film to whom one may attribute Satyavati's sufferings. This fact, it seems to me is itself significant, for it suggests that the everyday tensions of existence have themselves become shapeless demons against whom the existing gods and goddesses are helpless.[56]

It seems clear that although the film version of the Santosi Ma story has had a great deal to do with making the goddess accessible to many people, the very nature of this goddess is appropriate for the age in which we are living. This, perhaps, has more to do with her popularity. However, where she has come from is still to be discovered. One might suspect that she was created by the pamphlet writers, but to what end? As Brand has pointed out no one person or body stands to benefit from her worship as monopolies on her story are not held by any one company.[57] However, what is clear is that her popularity has continued to increase at the expense of the older, traditional goddesses to a certain degree, for as Das points out, many city temples, and even those in "pilgrim cities like Varanasi" have been "reconsecrated in the name of Santosi Ma".[58]

Jai Santosi Maa continues to be screened periodically and a new version of the film has recently been released on DVD (2006) directed by Ahmed Siddiqui, who has retold the story in an updated version. This version follows the ethos of the original version and has retained two of the principle songs. The DVD can be purchased in a gift set that is accompanied by a variety of ritual implements, an *arti* book, a small *murti*, a *diya* (lamp), a *puja* bell, a *puja thali* (tray), Mata's *cunnari* (veil), incense sticks, and a garland. The film's tag line encourages its viewers to rediscover their faith, which along with devotion and sacrifice is a quality stressed in the film. This version excludes the involvement of deities from the Hindu pantheon, but does mention them at the start of the film.

Present-day worship of Santosi Ma

Santosi Ma is worshipped across north India, but seems particularly popular in Orissa. Worshipped in Bhubaneswar and in the surrounding villages, this essentially orthodox goddess is sought out for her ability to heal devotees by taking possession of local women, a form of religion generally confined to local deities. The following account is based on my encounter with one such incarnation of Santosi Ma, but this form of human–goddess interaction happens in other locations as well.[59]

A few miles outside of Bhubaneswar, the state capital of Orissa, is the small village settlement of Khurdapur.[60] Each Friday morning people stream into the village because, for them, this place represents hope, a light at the end of their dark and dismal tunnel. A small hand-painted sign in Oriya and English is the only indication that here, the Mother of Satisfaction, Santosi Ma, is waiting to offer them solace and comfort. By around 10 a.m. an assorted group collects around the small temple in the hamlet of Bandanapur, generating an air of expectancy. Some have arrived in cars, others on bikes, but many have made this pilgrimage on foot. All who are present have fasted this morning, temporarily removing garlic, onion and lemon from their diet, for this is the only restriction imposed in the worship of Santosi Ma. The goddess is appealing to many types of people in various life situations. While the people wait patiently the priests bustle round preparing the offerings of bananas, chickpeas and flowers that they sell on to the devotees. In such a small hamlet, there are none of the shops that line the streets surrounding the large temples, selling flower garlands and all that is needed to honour the deities.

Bananas are very important in this particular Santosi Ma ritual as they are used by her as part of her cure and made into her special drink. Her close connection with bananas – the simple staple of many poor Indians – emphasizes her accessibility and lack of exclusivity, and again she seems to be a goddess appropriate for the modern-day Indian. The approachability of Santosi Ma, as Michael Brand points out, is one reason for her growing popularity:

> [I]f the older goddesses were seen as increasingly aloof and unapproach-able there would have been a definite need for a more humble goddess in whom women in particular could confide, and whom they could ask for assistance away from grand temples and their academic or haughty priests.[61]

An unassuming woman dressed in a red and green cotton sari strolls in a leisurely manner towards the temple. She appears unaffected by anything happening around her, perhaps lost in thought. Although she is not immediately apparent, the crowd spot her and on her approach, they silently part to allow her access to the temple. As she enters, many follow her. This is the woman who, in a short time, will be transformed into the goddess, Santosi Ma. The woman sits cross-legged in medita-tion before the image of the goddess, her lips moving as she offers her own obeisance and supplications. By now the sanctum is thick with fragrant blue *dhuha* smoke. As soon as her prayer is finished the priest starts beating a large metal gong. The deep, booming, metallic sound reverberates, filling the temple with almost unbearable noise. This is a heady cocktail. After what seems like an eternity, the woman lets out a strange unearthly cry. Instantly the noise stops for the spirit of Santosi Ma has entered the woman's body. She is helped up, anointed with a *tilak* of red paste and garlanded with hibiscus flowers. Now she is Santosi Ma.

When the woman emerges from the temple there is no doubt that a transformation has taken place. Her whole appearance, demeanour, and especially her voice is different, although it is difficult to say exactly how. Accompanying the goddess are two Brahman priests car-rying water, a tray with wood-apple leaves, some chickpeas, some bananas and a small, lighted dish. The goddess herself carries a bundle of canes and a small, tightly rolled up cloth. The canes represent her weapon against evil, which she uses to dispel any evil spirits that sometimes possess her devotees. The cloth is used to demonstrate her power, being periodically lighted and the goddess proceeding to take the fire into her mouth.

A constant stream of people presents themselves before the goddess, all of them sharing the common bond of having some burden that needs lifting. Some have come from as far away as Bengal with the conviction that *this* goddess will be able to help. She talks to the supplicants in a different voice, occasionally tapping them with her canes, making her special, sacred noise, and eating fire. The goddess blows on the devotees, rubbing the afflicted area with her hand or putting her sari over the part of the body that is ailing. She offers the devotees water stirred with her canes, flowers from her garland or small bananas that have to be eaten unpeeled and whole. These are all ways in which the goddess offers her blessing and healing to the devotees. Periodically the goddess is brought a special drink, *sarabat*, containing mashed banana, coconut milk, ginger, pepper and sugarcane juice. At one point, a smoking tray with burning teak sap is wafted over her, and a small dish containing camphor, which she blows out and which is then re-lit. This she does repeatedly until she has had enough: this is considered her food.

There are numerous problems presented during any particular morning. Among the medical problems are throat cancer, blindness, failure of menses, and paralysis. All of these people claim that they have been helped considerably with these problems by the intervention of the goddess and are now regular attendees. Among the other problems, a son who has gone missing and a woman whose husband has left. The woman has come all the way from Bengal in the hope that the goddess could help her. People are sometimes very distraught, especially, on one occasion, a man who had committed some unspecified misdeed. He had not followed the advice given to him on a previous visit and so further ill fortune had befallen him; he was now ready to repent. In a very touching display the old man stood alone, singing a devotional song to Santosi Ma, even though the tears were streaming down his cheeks.

By about 12.30 p.m. the goddess returns to the temple. She re-enters the inner sanctum and turns around, again accompanied by the *dhuha* smoke and the beating of a gong. As the goddess again faces her temple image, as suddenly as it had come, the spirit of the goddess leaves the woman, causing her to fall to the floor. There she remains unmoving for a while. On coming round, she is given a drink and she removes the flower garlands and the *tilak* from her forehead, signifying that she has returned to her mortal state. A place is prepared for her outside the sanctum where she lies down and is massaged by a number of women. Apparently, she is very stiff and tired for the rest of the day. Throughout the morning, assistants prepare cooked *prasada*, which is ready at about 3.00 p.m. and is distributed to everyone there. It consists of plain rice, cow butter, *dalma* (a type of lentil mixed with vegetables), *sag* (spinach) and *khiri*, a type of sweet rice pudding.

The pivotal ritual of Santosi Ma's Friday worship is most clearly her possession of the woman. The establishment of the power of Santosi Ma, channelled through this woman, is the reason that this goddess is so popular. On one hand, the goddess is able to leave the confines of the temple, gaining direct contact with her devotees. Possession is one of only two ways in which a goddess may emerge from her sanctum and engage more fully with the inhabitants of her settlement. In order for a goddess to be physically brought out of her sanctum, there must be a moveable image and a suitable vehicle on which to transport her. As local goddesses are in the main located in small shrines or temple/shrines, the goddesses of Khurdapur invariably only leave their shrines in the form of a possessed person.

The other benefit to Santosi Ma in possessing a human representative is that she is able to demonstrate her power more overtly. However, perhaps more important is the ability of her devotees to develop a meaningful relationship with the goddess via her possessed representative. Initially a few people had heard of the great power of this goddess and came to see for themselves whether what they had heard was true. This is a more direct method of communication as the goddess is able to give voice to her approval or disapproval of the devotee, and direct him or her towards a solution of problems or towards a more meaningful religious experience.

Although this goddess continually reasserts her great power during her Friday worship, it was also clear from the observation of Santosi Ma's interaction with her devotees, and subsequent interviews, that at no time is this goddess considered angry or unpredictable. It is important to note that those who approach her believe that she will give them assistance; they have no fear of her, only love and gratitude were evident in their eyes. Interviews with those present attest that Santosi Ma has healed or given assistance to many people – many who now regularly come to pay homage to her. The most poignant example that fully confirms the lack of anger in Santosi Ma's character is the old man who had confidence enough to return to Santosi Ma even though he had ignored her advice on his first visit. She did not vent her spite on him but gently comforted him, promising him help once more. It is clear, then, that Santosi Ma, for her devotees, is a stable, constant force in an ever-changing and unpredictable world.

The character of this particular incarnation of Santosi Ma is hard to categorize; should she be seen as Brahmanical or local. What seems to be the most important element of this particular Santosi Ma's character is that, despite her numerous Brahmanical characteristics – her new white temple image, the Brahman priests that serve her, and her purity – her worship and her mode of interaction still retain a distinctly local character. The most important and dominating feature of Santosi Ma's worship is her regular possession of a local woman. Possession by a deity, most often a goddess, is most clearly a feature of local religion; it is not normally a part of Brahmanical worship. However, Santosi Ma could not be simply labelled a local goddess, since in this particular incarnation the two strands of tradition, Brahmanical and local, complement each other rather than being antagonistic. (See plate 16). Santosi Ma combines the purity and beneficence of a Brahmanical goddess with the power, dynamism, and affinity with her devotees, more characteristic of the local goddesses. In this way she appeals to those who seek immediacy and those to whom orthodoxy is important.

More new goddesses?

Since power and energy have no limit, it is surely legitimate that new forms of the goddess should appear. Similarly, power and energy are not static, so why should 'the Goddess', as an all encompassing divine entity, be firmly defined and frozen in time. The fluidity of conceptualising 'the Goddess' is perceptible in goddesses whose function and role changes and, more radically perhaps, in the appearance of new goddesses. Established goddesses often undergo change, particularly those who are associated with smallpox, a disease that was eradicated in 1970s.[62] Since that time, Sitala, popular in north India and Mariyamman, popular in the south, have diversified; they now protect their devotees against measles, chickenpox and other illnesses. As one devastating disease is eradicated, another rears its ugly head. HIV/AIDS, one of the most insidious diseases of the twenty-first century, is now prevalent in India with an estimated 5.1 million (at the end of 2005) suffering from the disease.[63] Consequently, Sitala, and quite probably other goddesses as well, has become associated with the disease. However, her association with the disease is not wholly desirable as some devotees believe that her worship will protect them from infection.[64] While Sitala perpetuates tradition, albeit adapted, the appearance of new goddesses have fashioned a more modern approach to contemporary social issues. In the case of AIDS-amma and Manushi Swachha Narayani, a deliberate attempt was made to manufacture new goddesses who would address some of the problems inherent in twenty-first century life.[65]

AIDS-amma

AIDS-amma has been installed in a small shrine in the village of Menasikyathana Halli, in rural Karnataka. She was "created by an idealistic, civic-minded schoolteacher as part of an AIDS awareness campaign".[66] The local Science teacher, Mr H. H. Girish, built the shrine and installed the goddess on World AIDS Day (1 December 1997).[67] He did this in response to the village's first encounter with AIDS. Girish was told about a local couple who had died of starvation when it was discovered that they had AIDS. They were effectively ostracized from their community as people thought that they, too, would contract the disease if they had any contact with them. Girish learned that the couple may have also been denied proper cremation rites.[68] This enterprising teacher then decided that he might use fear that is sometimes thought to accompany local goddess worship to help raise awareness of AIDS. According to Anna Portnoy, he said, "Just to create phobia, I started AIDS-amma".[69] Accordingly, Girish has since given lectures at the shrine, which he has named a "Temple of Science", and has urged the villagers to ask for information rather than seek protection from the goddess. This, of course, is a real danger as commonly local goddesses are seen as controlling disease. Critics of this endeavour have cited this as a problem with the shrine and its goddess. However, this shrine is significantly different from other local shrines, particularly in terms of its contents. AIDS-amma is represented by a "whitewashed stone featured solid black silhouettes of a man's and a woman's torso. The figures were standing back-to-back. In the middle of their merging heads was a large red circle."[70] The acronyms AIDS and HIV are written in English along with informative WHO slogans in Kannada the local language.[71] When Portnoy visited AIDS-amma she reported that the villagers were not visiting the shrine regularly and, indeed, some were purposely avoiding it.[72] There are inherent problems in associating AIDS or sex with religion and it remains to be seen whether this new goddess will help or hinder the effort to raise awareness of, and hopefully the avoidance of, AIDS in the future.

A rather more conventional but equally artificially created goddess is Manushi Swachha Narayani, who occupies a shrine in Sewa Nagar hawker market in Delhi. Her role is to protect the street traders of this area from abuse.[73] *Manushi*[74] had taken up the cause of the street traders or hawkers who are seen as "sources of squalor and chaos"[75] and are often victims of extortion and abuse. It raised money and sought to change the archaic laws that allowed such victimization. *Manushi* recognized that the vendors represent a vital need to supply cheap goods and food to the poorest members of the community. They are often the first to be targeted when city beautification initiatives are launched as their small street stalls are considered by many to be unsightly and a hindrance to the smooth running of the city. Those campaigning on their behalf recognized that the vendors themselves needed to show that they could be responsible for keeping the market clean.[76] On 19 December 2001, in an effort to encourage the traders of Sewa Nagar to keep the areas where they work clean and tidy, a *jhadu puja* (worship of the cleaning broom) was performed.[77] The *puja* was offered to Ganesa, Laksmi, Sarsvati and Durga and marked the start of a campaign aimed at stopping the harassment and extortion that the street vendors were currently subject to.[78] The secular cleaning broom was at the centre of the ritual, used to "drive home the message that ensuring cleanliness and hygiene of our immediate, physical environment are sacred duties of every citizen".[79] This ritual was also an analogy for *Manushi*'s efforts to cleanse rotten government systems. By raising money, *Manushi* hoped to create a model market that would demonstrate that the marginalized traders could be successfully integrated into society.

Over time, the regular worship of the *jhadu* (cleaning broom) evolved until eventually a goddess took shape. Manushi Swachha Narayani (Goddess of Cleanliness), who represents more than physical cleanliness, was installed at Sewa Nagar on 12 March 2005. This was earlier than originally planned in an effort to halt the continued violence against the vendors and those constructing the new model market.[80] In iconographic terms, Manushi Swachha Narayani incorporates the lotus on which she stands from Laksmi, her white dress, an indication of purity, from Sarasvati and her ten arms from Durga. This is truly a modern goddess, for instead of brandishing swords, clubs and other weaponry in her hands, Manushi Swachha Narayani holds a broom and a video camera among other things. These are the weapons she and the vendors are using in order to win their fight. Manushi comments:

While our goddess has Durga like ability to battle tyrants, none of the weapons and symbols associated with her have violent or bloody overtones. While the foremost symbol of Swachha Narayani is the broom representing her creative energy to cleanse wrong doing, she is as much the goddess of self discipline – the power of the individual as a member of a group to create order and withstand chaos.[81]

Manushi Swachha Narayani also holds a clock, a coin, a weighing balance, a *diya* (lamp), account book, a pen, a conch shell and a stalk of barley.[82] Interestingly, it has been the video camera that has proved the most effective weapon, particularly in preventing violence, according to Kishwar. On occasion, just by turning up with a video camera has managed to avert the violence that was about to be meted out on the vendors; it has also been instrumental in gathering evidence.[83] In 2007, according to a video report,[84] the market is now hailed as a success with traders legalized and protected and the local government collecting rent. However, the video does not include any information about Manushi Swachha Narayani and her ongoing worship. It seems that she perhaps mobilized the vendors at a particularly difficult time, providing a focus and inspiration for them.

While some aspects of goddess worship are new, the following section examines the worship of living goddesses, but questions whether this form of worship will continue indefinitely.

The Raj Kumari of Nepal – A living goddess: But for how long?

Kumari worship in Hinduism

Kumari puja or the worship of a young virgin girl is an important and common ritual within Hinduism generally. Typically, it plays an important part in the *Durga Puja* festival in Kolkata, as described in chapter 6. It is a *Tantric* ritual, one of many that has been incorporated into orthodox forms of Hinduism. However, the worship of a living goddess, as is central in Nepal, especially the Kathmandu Valley, is uncommon in India. Religion in Nepal is directly influenced by *Tantrism*, in both Hinduism and Buddhism, the predominant religions there. According to Michael Allen there are only three temples in India dedicated to Sakti as a virgin, the most famous being Kanyakumari at the southernmost tip of India, encountered in chapter 7. The other two are Kanya Devi who resides in the Kangara Valley in the Punjab and Karani Mata who is located in Bikaner, Rajasthan.[85] According to Hindu mythology goddesses are at their most potent when they remain virgins, hence the subterfuge necessary to stop Kanyakumari's wedding to Siva. There is an important difference between Kumari worship in India and of that in Nepal. In India, though the rite is important it is usually temporary and often periodic, i.e. performed on a yearly basis. In contrast, Kumari worship in Nepal is continuous and widespread. The worship of the Raj Kumari (in the form of a living goddess) is a nation-wide phenomenon, not simply regional or localized.[86] Even today this young girl with her dramatically applied blood-red make up intrigues or disgusts those who are lucky enough to catch a glimpse of her. While many rely heavily on her presence, others feel that her life as a living goddess is barbaric, calling for a ban on this outdated tradition.

Selection of the Raj Kumari

It is not certain when the practice of choosing and installing a young girl, between 3–5 years old, as the living incarnation of the Nepali goddess Taleju started. It has been claimed that the first incarnation of Taleju was in the form of a Sri *yantra* (powerful mystical diagram).[87] There are other stories that relate the king of Nepal's relationship with the goddess. She acted as his adviser, but when she was offended (by him or his wife or some other mortal) she withdrew. In response to the king's extended petitions, the goddess agreed to manifest herself in the person of a young virgin girl of the Newari Sakya caste who showed the thirty-two signs of perfection.[88] These are listed by Allen who was given the information by a *Vajracarya*.[89]

Feet well-proportioned	Teeth white and nicely shaped
Spiralling lines on the soles of the feet	No gaps between the teeth
Nails well-proportioned	Tongue small and sensitive
Long and well-formed toes	Tongue moist
Feet and hands like those of a duck (with netlike lines)	Voice clear and soft like duck's
Feet and hands soft and firm	Eyes blue/black
The body broad at the shoulders and narrow at the waist	Eyelashes like those of a cow
Thighs like those of a deer	A beautiful complexion with white lustre
Small and recessed sexual organs	A gold-coloured complexion

Chest like a lion	Skin-pores small and not too open
Well spread shoulders	Hair whorls stiff and turning to the right
Long arms	Hair black
Pure body	Forehead large and well proportioned
Neck like a conch-shell	Head round with cone-shaped top
Cheeks like a lion	Body shaped like a banyan tree
Forty teeth	Robust body

A former Kumari, Rashmila Shakya (1984-91), claims that many of these "improbable" requirements are related to the girl's horoscope rather than her physique, and that it is more important that her horoscope must not be in conflict with that of the king.[90] There must be no inter-caste marriages in the ancestry of the family and the girl must not have undergone either of two mock marriage ceremonies (rites of passage). If she has, then she cannot be considered a true virgin.[91] Much speculation surrounds the rituals carried at the selection process of a new Kumari who, it is sometimes claimed, must endure frightful sights and experiences without showing any emotion.[92] Once chosen, the goddess Telaju is invited to enter the girl and from that time on she is regarded as the goddess. She remains in place until she sheds blood or her perfection is tainted by illness, such as smallpox when it was prevalent. Since the Kumari is protected at all times, this generally means that she remains as the Kumari until puberty. Once signs are detected by her caretaker that menstruation is immanent, the search will start for a new Kumari. In this way, the unbroken succession of the living goddess tradition has been preserved in Nepal.

In Nepal there is a great deal of integration of Hinduism and Buddhism, with Hindus and Buddhists worshipping at the same temples. This is perhaps in part due to the influence of *Tantrism* that pervades both Hinduism and Buddhism in Nepal. Another way in which the two traditions are brought together is in the form of the Kumari. Although the king is Hindu and the practice of Kumari worship is also Hindu, each of the Raj Kumaris is chosen only from the Newari Sakya caste who are Buddhists.[93]

There are a number of Kumaris worshipped as the personification of the goddesses in the Kathmandu area. While the other Kumaris are worshipped primarily by a particular caste, the Raj or Royal Kumari is worshipped by the king and the whole nation. The Raj Kumari is the living incarnation of Taleju, a fierce form of Kali. Although the critical aspect of the living goddess is her purity, it is interesting that Taleju is predominantly approached for her fierce and protective powers, with her festivals including animal sacrifices.[94] It is clear that this aspect of the goddess has not been erased or glossed over within the character of the Raj Kumari, and is still evident in various symbolic aspects and in her worship. Allen has pointed out that rather than wearing white, a pure, *sattvic* colour, that might be more fitting for a virgin goddess, the Kumari wears only red clothes and has vermillion paste applied to her forehead surrounding the third eye. Red is a colour associated with fertility and generally worn by married women who have had children.[95]

The function of the Raj Kumari is also associated with earthly power, which she bestows on the king, rather than for her *sattvic* purity, associated with enlightenment or salvation. Similarly, this living goddess is approached on a daily basis by worshippers seeking solutions to worldly problems and many women who approach her suffer from menstrual problems, rather than in the hope of salvation. On the other hand, in terms of the Kumari's treatment, purity is paramount in terms of eating arrangements (her food is cooked in a separate kitchen) and if she leaves her house (*Kumari che/ghar*) her feet must not touch the ground. Once again two key aspects of the personality of Sakti are brought together. Chapter 1 explored the dual nature of Sakti; in the Kumari, duality of character is again visible in the pure-impure, worldly-salvific dichotomy apparent in her worship and iconography.

Although the Kumari lives segregated in her house she is expected to make herself available for worship each day to receive *nitya-puja* (daily *puja*) from those who wish to bring her offerings or seek her help with a variety of problems. In addition to these relatively uncomplicated acts of worship, the Kumari must also take part in more elaborate ritual activities; predominantly the various festivals in which she takes a part. The most important is *Indra Jatra* which lasts for nine days and during which the Kumari is paraded round the streets of Kathmandu three times in her chariot. This festival is particularly important to the king because at the end of the festivities the Kumari places a *tika* (red mark of blessing) on his forehead, which symbolizes her blessings for the coming year. The blessing of the Kumari is of vital importance to the king as local mythology provides examples of changes of the monarchy when the *tika* was given to the wrong person. In particular this applied to the change in royal dynasty from Malla to Shah, when the Gorkhas conquered the Kathmandu Valley and Prithvi Narayan Shah received a *tika* from the Raj Kumari, instead of Jaya Prakash Malla.[96]

The current Kumari was installed on 10 July 2001, a little over a month after the massacre of the Nepali royal family. It is unclear whether this was a coincidence or whether there was any connection between the two events. According to *The Kathmandu Post*: "The royal priests and officials responsible for the affairs of the Kumari had spent the past few months looking for the new Kumari."[97] The search for suitable candidates to become a Kumari appears to getting harder, for as the article reports, "they hit a lot of snags with many families not ready to give their daughter away to become the living goddess with most parents opting for their daughters to take up careers like engineer or doctors".[98] Another reason for the ambivalent attitude of parents to their child becoming Kumari is that much speculation surrounds her life during and after her term as a living goddess. The life of a Kumari is certainly an unusual one as she may be taken from her family home at a young age and installed in a palace in the capital, Kathmandu. There her every need is supplied and all her whims and fancies indulged. However, she no longer has her family including any siblings around her, nor does she attend school or play outside with other children. She is protected in whatever she does in an effort to ensure that she does not spill a drop of blood. After a number of years of being carried everywhere, being adorned with jewelry and dressed up each day, she is one day expected to return to her family and the old life that she never had. It is no wonder that many ex- Raj Kumaris find it difficult to adjust. Speculation also surrounds the fate of any man who is brave enough to marry an ex-Kumari as they will reputedly die within the first year of marriage. Nevertheless, many ex-Kumaris have found husbands and some have managed some semblance of normality.[99] Added to the apparent change of attitude among the parents of prospective Kumaris are the recent developments in Nepal. In 2006 the king gave power back to the people after mass demonstrations and the ongoing struggle with the Maoists. Will this have an impact on the life of the Kumari? It remains to be seen how long these customs will prevail and, if they do, how much will change in the life of future Kumaris.

It is hoped that by now the reader of this book will have gained an appreciation of the richness and diversity of Hindu goddesses and their associated worship. Rather than being an archaic tradition, goddess worship adds vibrancy and colour to the profusion of gurus, gods and philosophies that have been conveniently termed Hinduism. What is also clear is that Hindu goddess worship is not static. Just as it has shifted and developed over many centuries it is still developing and changing. New goddesses still appear and only time will tell whether AIDS-amma, for instance, becomes popular on a wider scale and actually helps in the fight against the disease she is named after. Conversely, will the living goddess tradition in Nepal survive for much longer? Its critics might argue that it is an outdated practice that is detrimental to the development of the girls who are temporarily encapsulating divinity. However, for many this ongoing tradition provides stability in a country that was recently faced with the uncertainty surrounding the massacre of the royal family.

Whatever changes may take place with respect to the character of individual goddesses, it is clear that the underlying nature of Hindu goddess worship will be unchanged. For Devi will still pervade the world and everything in it. She will remain an integral part of every living being, in the rivers that water the land, in the land itself, in the smallest blade of grass or the tiniest insect. Beyond and above, within and without, nothing will exist or stir in the cosmos that does not remain infused with the power of the Goddess. This is perhaps the original and most potent form of "girl power". *Jai Mata di.*

Notes

Introduction

1   P. Kolenda, "Pox and the Terror of Childlessness: Images and ideas of the smallpox goddess in a North Indian village" in J. J. Preston (ed.), *Mother Worship: Themes and variations* (North Carolina: University of North Carolina Press, 1982), pp. 227–50.

2   C. J. Fuller, *The Camphor Flame: Popular Hinduism and society in India* (Princeton, New Jersey: Princeton University Press, 1992), p. 128.

3   *Brihadaranyaka Upanishad*, 4.2.6.

4   Rosemany Radford Ruether, *Goddesses and the Divine Feminine: A western religious history* (Berkeley, Los Angeles and London: University of California Press, 2005).

5   A. L. Basham, *The Wonder That Was India* (London: Sidgwick and Jackson, 1982 reprint of 1967 third revised edn), p. 16.

6   P. K. Agrawala, *Goddesses in Ancient India* (New Delhi: Abhinav Publications, 1984), p. 29.

7   N. N. Bhattacharyya, *The Indian Mother Goddess* (New Delhi: Manohar Book Service, 1977, 2nd revised edn), pp. 8–9.

8   Basham, *The Wonder That Was India*, p. 22.

9   J. D. Fowler, *Hinduism: Beliefs and practices* (Brighton & Portland: Sussex Academic Press, 1997), p. 90.

10 N. N. Bhattacharyya, *History of the Sakta Religion* (New Delhi: Munshiram Manoharlal, 1996, 2nd revised edn), pp. 15–16.

1 Sakti – The Divine Feminine

1   Monier Monier-Williams, *A Sanskrit–English Dictionary* (Delhi: Motilal Banarsidass, 1993 reprint of 1899 edn), p. 1044.

2   *Kena Upanisad* 3. 12 and 4. 1.

3   P. Olivelle, translator, *Upanisads* (Oxford: Oxford University Press, 1996).

4   This text is referred to by a number of names with a variety of spellings,

e.g. *Devi-Mahatmyam, Devi-Mahatmya, Sri Durga Saptasati,* or *Candi Path.* In order to aid clarity, I shall refer to this text throughout as *Devi-Mahatmya.*

5   *Kurma Purana* 1. 1. 30, translator, V. G. Tagare, *Kurma Purana,* vol. 1 (Delhi: Motilal Banarsidass, 1981).
6   *Ibid., Kurma Purana,* 1. 1. 34.
7   T. B. Coburn, *Encountering the Goddess: A translation of the Devi Mahatmya and a study of its interpretation* (Delhi: Sri Satguru Publications, 1991), p. 8.
8   T. B. Coburn, "Consort of None, Sakti of All: The vision of the *Devi-Mahatmya*" in J. S. Hawley and D. M. Wulff (eds), *The Divine Consort: Radha and the goddesses of India* (Boston: Beacon Press, 1986 reprint of 1982 edn), p. 153.
9   Translator, Swami Jagadiswarananda, *Devi-Mahatmyam (Glory of the Divine Mother): 700 Mantras on Sri Durga* (Madras: Sri Ramakrishna Math, 1969).
10   *Devi-Mahatmya,* 12. 36.
11   Cheever Mackenzie Brown, *The Triumph of the Goddess: The canonical models and theological visions of the Devi-Bhagavata Purana* (Albany: SUNY, 1990), p. x.
12   *Ibid.*
13   Cheever Mackenzie Brown, "The Tantric and Vedantic Identity of the Great Goddess in the *Devi Gita* of the *Devi-Bhagavata Purana*" in T. Pintchman (ed.), *Seeking Mahadevi: Constructing the identities of the Hindu great goddess* (Albany: SUNY, 2001), p. 21.
14   Translator, Swami Vijnanananda, *The Srimad Devi-Bhagavatatam* (New Delhi: Munishiram Manoharlal, 1986, 3rd edn).
15   *Devi-Bhagavatam* 3. 6. 2, translator, Swami Vijnanananda.
16   T. Pintchman, "Creation and the Great Goddess in the Puranas" in *Purana,* 35/2 (1993), pp. 152–3.
17   *Kurma Purana* 1. 1. 34–5.
18   J. D. Fowler, *Perspectives of Reality: An introduction to the philosophy of Hinduism* (Brighton, Sussex and Portland, Oregon: Sussex Academic Press, 2002), p. 250.
19   Translator, Cheever Mackenzie Brown, *The Devi Gita – The Song of the Goddess: A translation, annotation, and commentary* (Albany: SUNY, 1998). My inclusion is in square brackets.
20   *Ibid.,* p. 15.
21   *Ibid.,* p. 87.
22   *Ibid.,* p. 17.
23   K. Guru Dutt, "Shakti Worship in India", *Religion and Society (Bangalore),* 22 (1975), p. 49.
24   *Ibid.*
25   Klaus, K. Klostermaier, *Hindu Writings: A short introduction to the major sources* (Oxford: One World, 2000), p. 96.

26 *Brahmavaivarta Purana* PKh 1.12–13. This verse is translated and given in Cheever Mackenzie Brown, *God as Mother: A feminine theology in India* (Hartford, Vermont: Claude Stark, 1974), p. 142.

27 *Prakrti* in this particular text is not a negative term denoting the impermanence of life, but is considered one aspect of the Adisakti's unmanifest character.

28 *Kurma Purana*, 1. 11. 6.

29 Tracy Pintchman, *The Rise of the Goddess in the Hindu Tradition* (Albany: SUNY, 1994), p. 108.

30 V. S. Guleri, *Female Deities in Vedic and Epic Literature* (Delhi: Nag Publishers, 1990), p. 151.

31 Stella Kramrisch, "The Indian Great Goddess", *History of Religions*, 14/ 4 (1975), pp. 263–4.

32 Translator, Cheever Mackenzie Brown.

33 Translator, Cheever Mackenzie Brown. My inclusions are in square brackets.

34 Translator, Swami Jagadiswarananda.

35 S. Jaiswal, *The Origin and Development of Vaisnavism from 200 BC to AD 500* (Delhi: Munshiram Manoharlal, 1967), p. 95.

36 P. P. Kumar, *The Goddess Laksmi: The divine consort in South Indian Vaisnava tradition* (Atlanta, Georgia: Scholars Press, 1997), p. 14.

37 Upendra Nath Dhal, *Goddess Laksmi: Origin and development* (New Delhi: Oriental Publishers and Distributors, 1978), p. 2.

38 *Shri Shukta*, translated by Upendra Nath Dhal, *Goddess Laksmi*, pp. 51–2. My inclusions are in square brackets. Another commentary and translation of the *Shri Shukta* is found in Thomas B. Coburn, *Devi Mahatmya: The crystallization of the goddess tradition* (Delhi: Motilal Banarsidass, 1988 reprint of the 1984 edn), pp. 258–64.

39 *Shantiparvan* 12. 228. 26, *The Mahabharata (translated literally from the original Sanskrit text)* translator M. N. Dutt (Calcutta: H. C. Dass, Elysium Press, 1896).

40 J. Gonda, *Aspects of Early Visnuism* (Delhi: Motilal Banarsidass, 1969 2nd edn of 1954 edn), p. 220

41 D. R. Kinsley, *Hindu Goddesses: Visions of the divine feminine in the Hindu religious tradition* (Berkeley, Los Angeles and London: University of California Press, 1986), p. 30.

42 *Laksmi Tantra*, 4. 51–4, translator, Sanjukta Gupta, *Laksmi Tantra: A Pancaratra text* (Leiden: E. J. Brill, 1972).

43 Kinsley, *Hindu Goddesses*, p. 58.

44 A. Daniélou, *The Myths and Gods of India* (Rochester, Vermont: Inner Traditions International Ltd., 1991), p. 260.

45 Kinsley, *Hindu Goddesses*, p. 62.

46 *Ibid.*, p. 54.

47 *Ibid.*, p. 47.

48 Wendy Doniger O'Flaherty, "The Shifting Balance of Power in the

Marriage of Siva and Parvati" in Hawley and Wulff (eds), *The Divine Consort*, p. 134.

49 *Kurma Purana* 1. 12. 53–9.
50 W. J. Wilkins, *Hindu Mythology* (Calcutta: Rupa and Co., 1991 reprint of 1882 edn), p. 296.
51 N. N. Bhattacharyya, *The Indian Mother Goddess* (New Delhi: Manohar, 1977 2nd edn), p. 61.
52 *Devi-Mahatmya* 13. 11, translator, Swami Jagadiswarananda.
53 *Ibid.*, 11. 4.
54 *Devi-Mahatmya* 2. 9 – 12, translator Coburn, *Encountering the Goddess*.
55 *Devi-Mahatmya* 12. 36, translator, Swami Jagadiswarananda.
56 Kinsley, *Hindu Goddesses*, p. 97.
57 *Ibid.*, p. 105.
58 *Devi Mahatmya* 11. 5, translator, Swami Jagadiswarananda.
59 *Ibid.*, 3. 34.
60 E. Osborn Martin, *Gods of India: A brief description of their history, character & worship* (London: Dent; New York: Dutton, 1914), p. 185.
61 *Ibid.*, p. 180.
62 Rachel Fell McDermott, "Popular Attitudes Towards Kali and Her Poetry Tradition" in A. Michaels, C. Volgelsanger, and A. Wilke (eds), *Wild Goddesses in India and Nepal: Proceedings of an international symposium, Berne and Zurich, November 1994* (Studia Religiosa Helvetica, Jahrbuch Vol. 2, Bern: Peter Lang, 1994), p. 385.
63 Daniélou, *The Myths and Gods of India*, p. 273.
64 D. R. Kinsley, *The Sword and the Flute: Kali and Krsna, dark visions of the terrible and the sublime* (Berkeley, California: University of California Press, 1975), p. 95.
65 *Ibid.*, p. 82.
66 *Ibid.*, p. 97.
67 Translator, Swami Jagadiswarananda.
68 *Ibid.*
69 A. Mookerjee, *Kali: The feminine force* (London: Thames and Hudson, 1988), p. 61.
70 A. Avalon (trans.) *Hymn to Kali (Karpuradi-stotra)* (Madras: Ganesh and Co., 1965), p. 71.
71 Daniélou, *The Myths and Gods of India*, p. 268.
72 *Ibid.*, p. 274.
73 Kinsley, *Hindu Goddesses*, p. 129.
74 David R. Kinsley, "Blood and Death Out of Place: Reflections of the goddess Kali" in Hawley and Wulff (eds), *The Divine Consort*, p. 152.
75 I prefer to use the term "goddess collective" to refer to the range of goddesses in one settlement rather than the term "pantheon", since the latter has hierarchical connotations.
76 H. Whitehead, *The Village Gods of South India* (Calcutta: YMCA Association Press, 1921 3rd rev. edn), p. 29.

77 O. Lewis, *Village Life in Northern India: Studies in a Delhi village* (New York: Random House, 1965), chapter 7.

78 P. Kolenda, "Pox and the Terror of Childlessness: Images and ideas of the smallpox goddess in a north Indian village", in J. J. Preston (ed.), *Mother Worship: Themes and variations* (North Carolina: University of North Carolina Press, 1982), p. 235 and R. W. Nicholas, "The Goddess Sitala and Epidemic Smallpox in Bengal", *Journal of Asian Studies*, XLI/1 (Nov. 1981), pp. 21–44; and "The Village Mother in Bengal", in Preston, *Mother Worship*, pp. 192–209.

79 *Devi-Bhagavatam* 9. 1. 58, translator, Swami Vijnanananda.

80 *Kurma Purana* 1. 12. 64.

81 A term coined by Lynn E. Gatwood, *Devi and the Spouse Goddess: Women, sexuality and marriage in India* (New Delhi: Manohar Publications, 1985), p. 2.

2 Goddesses in Textual Sources

1 L. E. Gatwood, *Devi and the Spouse Goddess: Women, sexuality and marriage in India* (New Delhi: Manohar Publications, 1985), p. 33.

2 V. S. Guleri, *Female Deities in Vedic and Epic Literature* (Delhi: Nag Publishers, 1990), pp. 6–7.

3 N. N. Bhattacharyya, *History of the Sakta Religion* (New Delhi: Munshiram Manoharlal Publishers, 1974), pp. 27–8.

4 Gatwood, *Devi and the Spouse Goddess*, p. 35.

5 *Rg Veda* 7. 75. 1.

6 *Rg Veda* 1. 113. 7.

7 Guleri, *Female Deities in Vedic and Epic Literature*, p. 32.

8 Sacrifice was the main form of communication between humans and the Vedic deities at that time.

9 *Rg Veda* 1. 113. 13.

10 D. R. Kinsley, *Hindu Goddesses: Visions of the divine feminine in the Hindu religious tradition* (Berkeley, Los Angeles and London: University of California Press, 1986), p. 8.

11 N. N. Bhattacharyya, *The Indian Mother Goddess* (New Delhi: Manohar Book Service, 1977, 2nd revised edn), p. 97.

12 R. T. H. Griffith, translator, *The Hymns of the Rg Veda* (Delhi: Motilal Banarsidass, 1991 reprint of 1973 revised edn). My inclusion is in square brackets.

13 *Rg Veda*, 2. 15. 6.; 10. 73. 6.; and 10. 138. 5.

14 Bhattacharyya, *The Indian Mother Goddess*, pp. 97–8.

15 *Ibid*.

16 Gatwood, *Devi and the Spouse Goddess*, p. 35.

17 *Ibid*.

18 *Rg Veda* 4. 30. 8–9.

19 H. H. Wilson, translator, *Rig-Veda Sanhita: A collection of ancient Hindu Hymns*, Vol. 1 (London: N. Trübner and Co., 1866 2nd edn).

20　Renate Söhnen, "Rise and Decline of the Indra Religion in the Veda" in Michael Witzel (ed.), *Inside the Texts Beyond the Texts: New approaches to the study of the Vedas*, proceedings of the International Vedic Workshop Harvard University, June 1989 (Cambridge, Mass: Dept. of Sanskrit and Indian Studies, Harvard University, 1990), pp. 236–7.

21　*Rg Veda* 1. 32 and 4. 30. 12.

22　Kinsley, *Hindu Goddesses*, p. 9.

23　Guleri, *Female Deities in Vedic and Epic Literature*, p. 34.

24　*Rg Veda* 10. 5. 7, translator Griffith.

25　P. K. Agrawala, *Goddesses in Ancient India* (New Delhi: Abhinav Publications, 1984), p. 60.

26　Kinsley, *Hindu Goddesses*, p. 10.

27　Agrawala, *Goddesses in Ancient India*, p. 49.

28　*Ibid.*, p. 57.

29　J. D. Fowler, *Hinduism: Beliefs and Practices* (Brighton, Sussex & Portland, Oregon: Sussex Academic Press, 1997), p. 100.

30　Guleri, *Female Deities in Vedic and Epic Literature*, p. 134.

31　Bhattacharyya, *History of the Sakta Religion*, p. 32.

32　Translator Griffith.

33　Guleri, *Female Deities in Vedic and Epic Literature*, p. 48.

34　Translator Griffith. My inclusion is in square brackets.

35　Guleri, *Female Deities in Vedic and Epic Literature*, p. 131.

36　Kinsley, *Hindu Goddesses*, p. 17.

37　Bhattacharyya, *History of the Sakta Religion*, p. 32.

38　S. K. Lal, *Female Deities in Hindu Mythology and Ritual* (Pune: University of Poona, 1980), p. 123.

39　Translator Griffith.

40　Kinsley, *Hindu Goddesses*, p. 14.

41　Thomas B. Coburn, *Devi-Mahatmya: The crystallization of the goddess tradition* (Delhi: Motilal Banarsidass, 1988 reprint of 1984 edn), p. 265.

42　Guleri, *Female Deities in Vedic and Epic Literature*, pp. 136–7.

43　Translator Griffith.

44　G. Sastri, "The Cult of Sakti" in D. C. Sircar (ed.), *The Sakti Cult and Tara* (Calcutta: University of Calcutta, 1967), p. 13.

45　Bhattacharyya, *The Indian Mother Goddess*, p. 99.

46　Coburn, *Devi-Mahatmya*, p. 255.

47　Kinsley, *Hindu Goddesses*, p. 13.

48　*Ibid.*

49　Bhattacharyya, *The Indian Mother Goddess*, p. 99.

50　*Rg Veda* 10. 159.

51　Griffith, *The Hymns of the Rg Veda*, p. 644.

52　*Ibid.*, *Rg Veda* 10. 159. 6. My inclusion is in square brackets.

53　*Ibid.*, 10. 159. 2.

54　S. K. Das, *Sakti, or Divine Power: A historical study based on original Sanskrit texts* (Calcutta: University of Calcutta, 1934), p. 12.

55 Kinsley, *Hindu Goddesses*, p. 17.
56 Das, *Sakti, or Divine Power*, p. 14.
57 *Ibid.*
58 *Rg Veda* 10. 59. 1–4, translator Griffith.
59 Lal, *Female Deities in Hindu Mythology and Ritual*, p. 109.
60 *Ibid.*
61 *Atharva Veda* 9. 84. 2. See notes in Guleri, *Female Deities in Vedic and Epic Literature*, p. 67.
62 *Atharva Veda* 7. 63. 1.
63 *Atharva Veda* 5. 7. 9. Maurice Bloomfield, translator, *Hymns of the Atharva-Veda: Together with extracts from the ritual books and commentaries*, Sacred Books of the East, vol. 42, general ed. M. Müller (Delhi: Motilal Banarsidass, 1987 reprint of 1897 edn).
64 Guleri, *Female Deities in Vedic and Epic Literature*, p. 140.
65 Lal, *Female Deities in Hindu Mythology and Ritual*, p. 119. A point supported in Stella Kramrisch, "The Indian Great Goddess", *History of Religions*, 14/4 (1975), p. 253.
66 Alf Hiltebeitel, "*Mahabharata*" in Mircea Eliade (ed.), *Encyclopedia of Religion*, vol. 9 (New York: Macmillan Publishing Company, 1987), p. 118.
67 W. J. Johnson, translator, *The Sauptikaparvan of the Mahabharata: The massacre at night* (Oxford and New York: Oxford University Press, 1998), p. ix.
68 *Mahabharata*, 1 (7) 91–92, J. A. B. Van Buitenen, translator and ed., *The Mahabharata: 1. The book of the beginning*, vol. 1 (Chicago and London: University of Chicago Press, 1973).
69 *Ibid., Mahabharata*, 1 (7) 91. 1, p. 216.
70 *Ibid., Mahabharata*, 1 (7) 91. 27, p. 219.
71 *Ibid., Mahabharata*, 1 (7) 91. 35, p. 219.
72 *Ibid., Mahabharata*, 1 (7) 91. 44–5, p. 219.
73 Alf Hiltebeitel, "The Indus Valley "Proto-Siva", Reexamined through Reflections on the Goddess, the Buffalo, and the Symbolism of *vahanas*", *Anthropos*, 73 (1978), p. 783.
74 M. N. Dutt, translator, *The Mahabharata (translated literally from the original Sanskrit text)*, vol. VI (Calcutta: H. C. Dass, Elysium Press, 1896), p. 83.
75 *Ibid.*, p. 84.
76 Hiltebeitel, "The Indus Valley", p. 784.
77 *Drona Parva*, 53. 23, translator, Dutt.
78 *Drona Parva*, 54. 38, *ibid.*
79 *Drona Parva*, 54. 50, *ibid.*
80 Madeleine Biardeau, "The Sami Tree and the Sacrificial Buffalo", *Contributions to Indian Sociology* (n.s.), 18/1 (1984), p. 3.
81 *Ibid.*, p. 22.
82 *Ibid.*

83 Klaus K. Klostermaier, *Hindu Writings: A short introduction to the major sources* (Oxford: One World, 2000), p. 86.
84 *Bhishmaparva* 23, translator P. C. Roy, , *The Mahabharata of Krishna-Dwaipayana Vayasa*, vol. 5 (Calcutta: Oriental Publishing Co., 1955 2nd revised edn of 1925 edn).
85 *Ibid.*
86 *Ibid.*
87 Biardeau, "The Sami Tree and the Sacrificial Buffalo", p. 23.
88 Translator, Johnson, *The Sauptikaparvan of the Mahabharata*, pp. 39–40.
89 Guleri, *Female Deities in Vedic and Epic Literature*, p. 175.
90 Jacques Scheuer, *Siva dans le Mahabharata* (Paris: Presses Universitaires du France, 1982), p. 316.
91 R. C. Hazra, *Studies in the Upapuranas, Vol. II: Sakta and non-sectarian Upapuranas* (Calcutta: Calcutta Sanskrit College, 1979 reprint of 1963 edn), p. 1.
92 C. Mackenzie Brown, *The Triumph of the Goddess: The canonical models and theological visions of the Devi-Bhagavata Purana* (Albany, New York: SUNY, 1990), p. ix.
93 *Devi-Mahatmya*, 1. 53, translator, Swami Jagadiswarananda, *Devi-Mahatmyam (Glory of the Divine Mother): 700 Mantras on Sri Durga* (Madras: Sri Ramakrishna Math, 1969).
94 Thomas, B. Coburn, *Encountering the Goddess: A translation of the Devi-Mahatmya and a study of its interpretation* (Delhi: Sri Satguru Publications, 1992 reprint of 1991 edn), pp. 22–3.
95 Translator, Thomas, B. Coburn, *Encountering the Goddess*, pp. 37–8.
96 *Devi-Mahatmyam (Glory of the Divine Mother): 700 Mantras on Sri Durga*, 2.32–3, translator Swami Jagadiswarananda (Madras: Sri Ramakrishna Math, 1969).
97 The heavens, the earth and *patala* the netherworld.
98 Translator Coburn, *Encountering the Goddess*, p. 42.
99 Cynthia Anne Humes, "Is the *Devi-Mahatmya* a Feminist Scripture?" in Alf Hiltebeitel and Kathleen M. Erndl (eds), *Is the Goddess a Feminist?: The politics of South Asian goddesses* (Sheffield: Sheffield Academic Press, 2000), p. 127.
100 Translator Jagadiswarananda.
101 *Ibid.*, p. 43.
102 Translator Jagadiswarananda.
103 The slaying of Mahisasura originally appeared in the *Mahabharata* in which the warrior was Skanda, the son of Siva. For Skanda it was an important victory, which was described as his first glorious deed. *Mahabharata* 3 (37) 221, J. A. B. Van Buitenen, translator and ed., *The Mahabharata:3. The book of the forest*, vol. 2 (Chicago and London: University of Chicago Press, 1975), pp. 661–4.
104 Translator Jagadiswarananda.
105 Translator Coburn, *Encountering the Goddess*, p. 47.

106 *Devi-Mahatmya* 13. 18 and 24–5, translator Jagadiswarananda.
107 Usha Dev, *The Concept of Sakti in the Puranas* (Delhi: Nag Publishers, 1987), pp. 43 and 44 respectively.
108 Hazra, *Studies in the Upapuranas, vol. II*, p. 16.
109 *Ibid.*, p. 20.
110 *Ibid.*, p. 77.
111 *Ibid.*, pp. 28–9.
112 *Ibid.*, p. 261.
113 *Mahabhagavata Purana* 8. 77, my inclusion in square brackets, given in Hazra, p. 283.
114 Passage from the *Mahabhagavata Upapurana*, translated by Elisabeth Anne Benard and presented in her book, *Chinnamasta: The aweful Buddhist and Hindu tantric goddess* (Delhi: Motilal Banarsidass, 1994), p. 2.
115 B. Shastri, translator, *Kalika Purana (text, introduction and translation in English)*, vol. 1 (Delhi: Nag Publishers, 1991), p. 10.
116 *Kalika Purana*, 1. 2, *ibid.* My inclusion is in square brackets.
117 *Ibid.*, p. 3.
118 *Ibid.*
119 Translator Shastri.
120 *Ibid.*
121 *Kalika Purana*, 58. 65, *ibid.*
122 Brown, *The Triumph of the Goddess*, p. ix.
123 *Ibid.*, p. x.
124 *Ibid.*, p. ix.
125 Dev, *The Concept of Sakti in the Puranas*, pp. 39–40.
126 David Kinsley, "The Image of the Divine and the Status of Women in the *Devi-Bhagavata-Purana*", *Anima*, 9/1 (1982), p. 53.
127 P. G. Lalye, "The Incarnations of Devi, as Described in the Devi Bhagavata Purana" in K. C. Mishra, T. Mishra, and R. K. Mishra (eds), *Studies in Saktism* (Bhubaneswar: Institute of Orissan Culture, 1995), p. 29.
128 Kinsley, "The Image of the Divine and the Status of Women in the *Devi-Bhagavata-Purana*", p. 50.
129 *Devi-Bhagavatam* 1. 5. 58, translator, Swami Vijnanananda, *The Srimad Devi-Bhagavatatam* (New Delhi: Munishiram Manoharlal, 1986, 3rd edn). My inclusion is in square brackets.
130 *Devi-Bhagavatam* 12. 8. 81. *Ibid.* My inclusion is in square brackets.
131 C. Mackenzie Brown, *The Devi Gita – The Song of the Goddess: A translation, annotation, and commentary* (Albany, New York: SUNY, 1998), p. 41.
132 *Ibid.*, pp. 42–3.
133 *Ibid.*, p. 43.
134 For a detailed index of the names of the Goddess in the *Devi Gita* see the appendix, *ibid.*, pp. 325–33.
135 Lalye, "The Incarnations of Devi, as Described in the Devi Bhagavata Purana", p. 29.

3 Goddess Mythology

1   The wives of Sagara are called Kesini and Sumati in the *Ramayana* and Saibya and Vaidarbhi in the *Mahabharata*.

2   The horse sacrifice was a huge affair that started the year before the actual sacrifice. A white stallion was allowed to roam free for a year being watched and followed by protectors. After a year, it was returned to the king and, along with many other animals, it was ritually sacrificed. The queen simulated copulation with the dead horse, since this was a fertility ritual, generally performed in spring.

3   This is the version in the *Mahabharata, Vanaparvan* 107. 14 in J. A. B. van Buitenen (translator and ed.) *The Mahabhartata: 3. The book of the forest*, vol. 2 (Chicago: University of Chicago Press, 1975), p. 429.

4   This is why Siva is often depicted with water spouting out of his hair.

5   B. Walker, *Hindu World: An encyclopaedic survey of Hinduism*, vol. II M–Z (New Delhi: Munishiram Manoharlal Publishers Pvt. Ltd., 1983), p. 328.

6   D. L. Eck, "Ganga: The Goddess Ganges in Sacred Geography" in J. S. Hawley and D. M. Wulff, (eds), *Devi: Goddesses of India* (Berkeley, California: Universiy of California Press, 1996), p. 145.

7   *Padma Purana* 4. 6b–7, vol. 5, translator N. A. Deshpande (Delhi: Motilal Banarsidass, 1990).

8   *Skanda Purana* II. 9. 18–20, translator Tagare.

9   *Bhagavata Purana* 8. 8. 8, vol. 3, translator G V. Tagare (Delhi: Motilal Banarsidass, 1994 reprint of 1976 edn).

10 D. C. Sircar, "The Sakta Pithas". *Journal of the Royal Asiatic Society of Bengal*, 16/1 (1948), p. 5.

11 *Kalika Purana* 8. 9–11, translator B. Shastri (Delhi: Nag Publishers, 1991–2).

12 *Kalika Purana* 8. 32–34, translator Shastri. My inclusions are inserted in square brackets.

13 The nine doors of the body (*dvarani sarvani*) are the nine orifices, the eyes, ears, nostrils, mouth, anus and vagina.

14 The tenth door (*dasama dvaram*) is at the top of the skull called the *bhramarandhara*.

15 *Kalika Purana* 16. 47–50, translator Shastri.

16 This is not the actual name of the settlement, but has been used to provide anonymity at the request of some of the residents.

17 These and other local myths can be found in L. Foulston, *At the Feet of the Goddess: The divine feminine in local Hindu religion* (Brighton & Portland: Sussex Academic Press, 2002).

18 Since the eradication of smallpox this goddess is now associated with chickenpox, measles and other such diseases.

19 *Vanaparvan (Book of the Forest)*, 116. 1–19 in J. A. B. van Buitenen (translator and ed.), *The Mahabharata: 2. The book of the assembly hall, 3. The book of the forest* (Chicago and London: The University of Chicago Press, 1975), pp. 445–6.

20 H. Whitehead, *The Village Gods of South India* (New Delhi: Cosmo, 1983 reprint of 1921 edn), p. 116. See also, R. L. Brubaker, "The Ambivalent Mistress: A study of south Indian village goddesses and their religious meaning", unpublished Ph.D thesis, University of Chicago, 1978, pp. 99–105, who provides a synopsis of a number of versions of the Renuka myth.

21 K. Nanacampantan, "Colavantan Jenakai Mariyamman Kovil Valipatum Tiruvilakkalum", unpublished M.Phil. dissertation, Madurai Kamaraj University, 1982–3, p. 24. Translated by Dr P. Sarveswaran, Professor of History at Madurai Kamaraj University, with my inclusions in square brackets. According to Nanacampantan, this myth originally appeared in an anonymous poem of ancient composition, *Apitana Cintamani* (n.d.), cited from A. Sinkanavelu Mutaliyar, *The Encyclopedia of Tamil Literature* (New Delhi: Asian Education Services, 1981 reprint of 1899 edn). However, another version in the *Brahmanda Purana*, chapter 86, is cited by Vettam Mani, *Puranic Encyclopaedia: A comprehensive dictionary with special reference to the epic and puranic literature* (Delhi: Motilal Banarsidass, 1989 reprint of 1975 edn), p. 341. In this version, Renuka is burnt on her husband's funeral pyre, perhaps indicating that the south Indian version has been embellished to accommodate the connection between Renuka and Mariyamman, the south Indian goddess of smallpox.

22 N. N. Bhattacharyya, *The Indian Mother Goddess* (New Delhi: Manohar Book Service, 1977 2nd revised edn of 1970 edn), pp. 55–6.

23 This story is apparently related in the south Indian version of the *Markandeya Purana.*

24 Sweat is an amalgamation of fire and water and generally has a creative quality. See W. D. O'Flaherty, *Siva: The erotic ascetic* (London and New York: Oxford University Press, 1981 reprint of 1973 edn), p. 24. This creative quality gives rise to demons (p. 31), sages (pp. 118–9) and goddesses (p. 119) alike.

25 A. Aiyappan, "Myth of the Origin of Smallpox", *Folklore*, 42 (1931), p. 292.

26 *Ibid.*

27 *Ibid.*

28 Mangala is also one of Durga's *saktis* in an Orissan account of part of the Durga/Mahisasura myth, given by Frédérique Apffel Marglin, *Wives of the God-King: Rituals of the Devadasis of Puri* (New York: Oxford University Press, 1985), pp. 214–15.

29 R. C. Hazra, *Studies in the Upapuranas, vol. II: Shakta and non-sectarian Upapuranas* (Calcutta: Calcutta Sanskrit College, 1979 reprint of 1963 edn), p. 73.

30 This myth of how Mangala originated was translated by Niranjan Mohapatra from Trinath Pattnaik *Ma Mangala Mahapurana* (Orissa: Sri Sarada Store, n.d., purchased in Kakatpur).

31 M. Stutley and J. Stutley, *A Dictionary of Hinduism: Its mythology, folklore and development 1500 B.C.–A.D. 1500* (London: Routledge and Kegan Paul, 1977), p. 177.

32 These stories can be found in "The Cycle of Snake Tales" Sister Niverdita, *Cradle Tales of Hinduism* (Calcutta: Adaita Ashrama, 1988).

33 W. L. Smith, *The One-Eyed Goddess: A study of the Manasa Mangal* (Stockholm, Sweden: Almqvist and Wiksell, Uppsala, 1980), p. 15.

34 The *Shakta* text the *Mahabhagavata Upapurana* is one such example, outlined in Elisabeth Anne Benard, *Chinnamasta: The aweful Buddhist and Hindu Tantric goddess* (Delhi: Motilal Banarsidass, 1994), p. 2 and in the *Linga Purana* I. 106, translator J. L. Shastri (Delhi: Motilal Banarsidass, reprint 1990).

35 This idea is explored by S. H. Blackburn, "Death and Deification: Folk cults in Hinduism", *History of Religions*, 24 (1985), p. 272.

36 Many people in India chew a digestive called *paan*. It is made of betel nut, which turns the saliva, and eventually the teeth, red.

37 L. Harlan, "Perfection and Devotion: Sati tradition in Rajasthan" in J. S. Hawley (ed.), *Sati, the Blessing and the Curse* (New York and Oxford: Oxford University Press, 1994), p. 86.

38 J. Leslie, "Suttee or *Sati*: Victim or victor?" in J. Leslie (ed.), Roles and Rituals for Hindu Women (New Delhi: Motilal Banarsidass, 1992), p. 185.

39 J. S. Hawley (ed.), *Sati, the Blessing and the Curse* (New York and Oxford: Oxford University Press, 1994), p. 13.

40 P. B. Courtright, "Sati, Sacrifice and Marriage: The modernity of tradition" in L. Harlan, and P. B. Courtright (eds), *From the Margins of Hindu Marriage: Essays on gender, religion and culture* (New York, Oxford: Oxford University Press, 1995), p. 189.

41 P. B. Courtright, "The Iconographies of Sati" in J. S. Hawley (ed.), *Sati, the Blessing and the Curse* (New York and Oxford: Oxford University Press, 1994), pp. 31–3.

42 Harlan, "Perfection and Devotion", pp. 84–5.

43 V. T. Oldenburg, "The Roop Kanwar Case: Feminist responses" in J. S. Hawley (ed.), *Sati, the Blessing and the Curse* (New York and Oxford: Oxford University Press, 1994), p. 113.

44 Hawley, *Sati, the Blessing and the Curse*, pp. 7–8.

45 J. Leslie, "Suttee or *Sati*" , p. 190.

46 "Sati: women's panel calls for stern action", *The Hindu* (13 August 2002).

47 "It was 'sati' in M.P., says report", *The Hindu* (18 August 2002)

48 Luke Harding "The Ultimate Sacrifice" *The Guardian* (Friday, August 23, 2002) <http://www.guardian.co.uk/gender/story/0,11812,779265,00.html> (11/02/08); "Kuttu Bai Didn't Commit Sati; She Was Murdered" *People's Democracy* (XXVI, 37, September 22 2002) <http://www.cpim.org/pd/2002/sept22/09152002_mp_sati.htm> (11/02/08)

49 Suchananda Gupta "Woman's death sparks 'sati' row" *The Times of India* (23 August 2006) <http://timesofindia.indiatimes.com/articleshow/1917392.cms> (10/06/08)

50 "Woman attempts 'sati' in Madhya Pradesh" *The Times of India* (13

September 2006) <http://timesofindia.indiatimes.com/articleshow/ 1988228.cms> (10/06/08).

4 Tantrism and Hindu Goddesses

1   Andre Padoux, "What Do We Mean by Tantrism?" in K. A. Harper and R. L. Brown (eds), *The Roots of Tantra* (Albany: SUNY, 2002), p. 17.
2   N. N. Bhattacharyya, *History of the Tantric Religion* (New Delhi: Manohar, 1999 2nd revised edn), p. 1.
3   *Vijnanabhairava* 18 & 19 in J. Singh (trans), *Vijnanabhairava or Divine Consciousness* (Delhi: Motilal Banarsidass, 1979), p. 16.
4   Tracy Pintchman, *The Rise of the Goddess in the Hindu Tradition* (Albany: SUNY, 1994), p. 108.
5   *Kularnava Tantra* 13. 64–5 Douglas Renfrew Brooks, translator "The Ocean of the Heart: Selections from the *Kularnava Tantra*", in: David Gordon White (ed.), *Tantra in Practice* (Princeton: Princeton University Press, 2000), p. 359.
6   Brian K. Smith, "Tantrism: Hindu Tantrism" in L. Jones (ed.), *Encyclopedia of Religion*, 2nd revised edn, vol. 13 (New York: Macmillan Reference USA, 2005), p. 8991.
7   *Kularnava Tantra* 9. 41 *ibid.*, p. 357.
8   *Kularnava Tantra* 9. 52 *ibid.*, p. 357.
9   David Gordon White, "Tantrism" in D. Cush, C. Robinson and M. York (eds), *Encyclopedia of Hinduism* (London and New York: Routledge, 2008b), p. 857.
10 *Kularnava Tantra* 15. 19 and 15. 113 translator Brooks, "The Ocean of the Heart", p. 360.
11 *Kularnava Tantra* 6. 85–87 *ibid.*, p. 356.
12 White, "Tantrism", p. 854.
13 Ernest A. Payne, *The Saktas: An introductory and comparative study* (New Delhi: Munshiram Manoharlal Publishers, 1997 reprint of 1993 edn), p. 72.
14 Bhattacharyya, *History of the Tantric Religion*, p. 200.
15 White, "Tantrism", p. 854; Geoffrey Samuel, *The Origins of Yoga and Tantra: Indic religions to the thirteenth century* (Cambridge: Cambridge University Press, 2008), pp. 248–9.
16 Bhattacharyya, *History of the Tantric Religion*, p. 249.
17 *Ibid.*, p. 199; Samuel, *The Origins of Yoga and Tantra*, pp. 255–7.
18 Katherine Anne Harper, *Seven Hindu Goddesses of Spiritual Transformation: The iconography of the Saptamatrikas* (Lewiston: Edwin Mellen Press, 1989), pp. 153–4.
19 Fabrizio M. Ferrari, "Saktism" in D. Cush, C. Robinson and M. York (eds), *Encyclopedia of Hinduism* (London and New York: Routledge, 2008), p. 735; Elizabeth Chalier-Visuvalingam, "Bhairava and the Goddess: Tradition, gender and transgression" in A. Michaels, C. Vogelsanger and A. Wilke (eds), *Wild Goddesses in India and Nepal: Proceedings of an international symposium* (Berne and Zurich: Peter Lang, 1994), pp. 253–8.

20   Alexis Sanderson, "Purity and Power among the Brahmans of Kashmir" in
      M. Carrithers, S. Collins and S. Lukes (eds), *The Category of the Person*
      (Cambridge: Cambridge University Press, 1985), pp. 198–200.
21   David N. Lorenzen, "Saivism: Kapalikas" in M. Eliade (ed.), *Encyclopedia
      of Religion*, vol. 13 (New York: Macmillan, 1987), p. 19.
22   David N. Lorenzen, *The Kapalikas and Kalamukhas: Two lost Saivite sects*
      (Delhi: Motilal Banarsidass, 1991 2nd revised edn), pp. 88–92.
23   Alexis Sanderson, "Saivism and the Tantric Traditions" in F. Hardy (ed.),
      The World's Religions: The Religions of Asia (London: Routledge, 1988),
      pp. 146–50.
24   *Ibid.*, p. 147.
25   June McDaniel, *Offering Flowers, Feeding Skulls: Popular goddess worship
      in West Bengal* (Oxford: Oxford University Press, 2004), p. 89.
26   For a useful account of the relationship between *Matrikas* and
      Saptamatrikas see Harper, *Seven Hindu Goddesses of Spiritual
      Transformation*; For an insightful explanation of the development of
      Yogini figures from *Matrika* goddesses see David Gordon White. *Kiss of
      the Yogini: "Tantric Sex" in its South Asian context* (Chicago: University
      of Chicago, 2003)
27   David Gordon White, "Saptamatrkas" in D. Cush, C. Robinson and M.
      York (eds), *Encyclopedia of Hinduism* (London and New York: Routledge,
      2008a), p. 764.
28   David Kinsley, *Hindu Goddesses: Visions of the divine feminine in Hindu
      religious tradition* (Berkeley, Los Angeles and London: University of
      California Press, 1986), pp. 154–5.
29   *Ibid.*, pp. 151–2; Harper, *Seven Hindu Goddesses of Spiritual
      Transformation*, pp. 55–6.
30   Harper, *Seven Hindu Goddesses of Spiritual Transformation*, p. 155.
31   *Mahabharata* 9. 46 translator P. C. Roy cited in Harper, *Seven Hindu
      Goddesses of Spiritual Transformation*, pp. 57–8.
32   *Ibid.*, p. 58.
33   Kinsley, *Hindu Goddesses*, p. 155.
34   David N. Lorenzen, "Early Evidence for Tantric Religion" in K. A. Harper
      and R. L. Brown (eds), *The Roots of Tantra* (Albany: SUNY, 2002), p. 29.
35   Samuel, *The Origins of Yoga and Tantra*, p. 249.
36   Kinsley, *Hindu Goddesses*, p. 156.
37   M. C. Joshi, "Historical and Iconographic Aspects of Sakta Tantrism" in
      K. A. Harper and R. L. Brown (eds), *The Roots of Tantra* (Albany: SUNY,
      2002), p. 47.
38   *Devi-Mahatmya* 8. 12–23 translator Thomas C. Coburn. *Encountering the
      Goddess: A translation of the Devi-Mahatmya and a study of its interpre-
      tation* (Delhi: Sri Satguru Publications, 1991), pp. 63–4.
39   Kinsley, *Hindu Goddesses*, p. 158, Harper, *Seven Hindu Goddesses of
      Spiritual Transformation*, p. 94.
40   Kinsley, *Hindu Goddesses*, p. 158.

41 Harper, *Seven Hindu Goddesses of Spiritual Transformation*, p. 161.
42 *Ibid.*, p. 158.
43 *Ibid.*, p. 167.
44 White, "Saptamatrkas", p. 764.
45 Harper, *Seven Hindu Goddesses of Spiritual Transformation*, pp. 156–8; Samuel, *The Origins of Yoga and Tantra*, p. 297.
46 Harper, *Seven Hindu Goddesses of Spiritual Transformation*, p. 163.
47 Vidya Dehejia, *Yogini Cult and Temples: A Tantric tradition* (New Delhi: National Museum, New Delhi, 1986), pp. 13–15.
48 McDaniel, *Offering Flowers, Feeding Skulls*, p. 83.
49 Dehejia, *Yogini Cult and Temples*, p. 2.
50 White, *Kiss of the Yogini*, pp. 35–63.
51 Dehejia, *Yogini Cult and Temples*, p. 36; White, *Kiss of the Yogini*, pp. 63–6.
52 Kedarnath Mahapatra, "A Note on the Hypaethral Temple of the Sixty-four Yoginis at Hirapur" in *Orissa Historical Research Journal*, 11 (1953), pp. 23–40 who discovered the temple provides a description of each of the sixty-four *Yoginis*.
53 *Kalika Purana* 63. 37–44 translator B. Shastri, *Kalika Purana (text, introduction and translation in English)*, vol. 2 (Delhi: Nag Publishers, 1991), p. 934. My inclusion in square brackets.
54 Sanderson, "Saivism and the Tantric Traditions", p. 139; Samuel, *The Origins of Yoga and Tantra*, p. 246.
55 White, "Tantrism", p. 859.
56 McDaniel, *Offering Flowers, Feeding Skulls*, p. 83.
57 Dehejia, *Yogini Cult and Temples*, p. 32.
58 *Kularnava Tantra* 17. 102 translator Brooks, "The Ocean of the Heart", p. 360.
59 Dehejia, *Yogini Cult and Temples*, pp. 31–5.
60 David Gordon White, "Transformations in the Art of Love: Kamakala practices in Hindu Tantric and Kaula traditions". *History of Religions*, 38/2 (1998), pp. 172–3; White, *Kiss of the Yogini*, p. 114.
61 H. C. Das, *Tantricism: A study of the Yogini cult* (New Delhi, Bangalore, Jullundur: Sterling Publishers Private Ltd, 1981), p. 3.
62 Mahapatra, "A Note on the Hypaethral Temple of the Sixty-four Yoginis at Hirapur", p. 24.
63 *Ibid.*
64 Das, *Tantricism: A study of the Yogini cult*, p. 4.
65 Kinsley, *Hindu Goddesses*, p. 161.
66 *Kularnava Tantra* 16. 40 explicitly identifies the term *vidya* as meaning a *mantra* of a female deity. See Brooks, "The Ocean of the Heart", p. 360.
67 David Kinsley, *Tantric Visions of the Divine Feminine: The ten Mahavidyas* (Delhi: Motilal Banarsidass, 1998), pp. 58–9.
68 *Ibid.*, pp. 46–7.
69 *Ibid.*, pp. 47–8.
70 *Ibid.*, p. 1.

71 Kinsley, *Hindu Goddesses*, p. 161.
72 For example the killing of Mahisasura in which Durga manifests from within herself her own army of goddesses in order to slay a demon king.
73 Kinsley, *Tantric Visions of the Divine Feminine*, p. 20.
74 K. P. Goswami, *Kamakhya Temple: Past and present* (New Delhi: A. P. H Publishing Corporation, 1998), pp. 77–87.
75 Kinsley, *Tantric Visions of the Divine Feminine*, p. 57.
76 *Ibid.*, p. 9.
77 Bhattacharyya, *History of the Tantric Religion*, p. 321.
78 Kinsley, *Tantric Visions of the Divine Feminine*, p. 80.
79 *Ibid.*, p. 103.
80 *Ibid.*, pp. 103–4.
81 Translator Alain Daniélou, *The Myths and Gods of India* (Rochester, Vermont: Inner Traditions International 1991), p. 277.
82 *Ibid.*, p. 275.
83 Kinsley, *Hindu Goddesses*, p. 166; Kinsley, *Tantric Visions of the Divine Feminine*, p. 105.
84 Kinsley, *Tantric Visions of the Divine Feminine*, p. 112.
85 *Ibid.*, p. 119.
86 *Ibid.*, p. 120.
87 *Ibid.*, p. 122.
88 *Ibid.*, p. 131.
89 Translator Daniélou, *The Myths and Gods of India*, p. 279.
90 Kinsley, *Tantric Visions of the Divine Feminine*, p. 141.
91 *Ibid.*, p. 143.
92 Translator Daniélou, *The Myths and Gods of India*, p. 281.
93 Kinsley, *Tantric Visions of the Divine Feminine*, pp. 159–61.
94 *Ibid.*, p. 170.
95 *Kalika Purana* 74. 124–125a translator B. Shastri, *Kalika Purana (text, introduction and translation in English)*, vol. 3 (Delhi: Nag Publishers, 1991), p. 1125.
96 Kinsley, *Tantric Visions of the Divine Feminine*, p. 172.
97 *Ibid.*, p. 175.
98 *Ibid.*, p. 176.
99 Translator Daniélou, *The Myths and Gods of India*, p. 282.
100 Kinsley, *Tantric Visions of the Divine Feminine*, pp. 182–3.
101 *Ibid.*, p. 184.
102 *Ibid.*, p. 199.
103 *Ibid.*, p. 206.
104 *Ibid.*, p. 216.
105 *Ibid.*, p. 232.
106 *Ibid.*, p. 228.
107 *Ibid.*, p. 229.
108 *Ibid.*, p. 232.
109 Annette Wilke, "Sankara and the Taming of Wild Goddesses" in A.

Michaels, C. Vogelsanger and A. Wilke (eds), *Wild Goddesses in India and Nepal: Proceedings of an international symposium* (Berne and Zurich: Peter Lang, 1994), pp. 130–1.

110 Douglas Renfrew Brooks, *Auspicious Wisdom: The texts and traditions of Srividya Sakta Tantrism in south India* (Albany: SUNY, 1992), pp. xv–xvi.

111 Brooks, *Auspicious Wisdom*, p. 60; Wilke, "Sankara and the Taming of Wild Goddesses", pp. 123–7.

112 Brooks, *Auspicious Wisdom*, p. 64.

113 *Ibid.*, pp. 64–5.

114 Andre Padoux, "The Sricakra According to the First Chapter of the Yoginihrdaya" in G. Buhnemann (ed.), *Mandalas and Yantras in the Hindu Traditions* (New Delhi: D. K. Printworld, 2007 revised Indian edn), pp. 239–40.

115 Brooks, *Auspicious Wisdom*, p. 98.

116 Kathleen M. Erndl, "Sakta" in S. Mittal and G. Thursby (eds), *The Hindu World* (New York and London: Routledge, 2004), p. 155.

117 Brooks, *Auspicious Wisdom*, p. 118.

118 Brooks, *Auspicious Wisdom*, p. 115.

119 B. Walker, *Hindu World: An encyclopedic survey of Hinduism* vol. II M-Z (New Delhi: Manoharlal Publishers Pvt. Ltd., 1983), p. 484.

5 Goddess Worship

1 For a detailed study of Kalighat see I. B. Roy, *Kalighat: Its impact on socio-cultural life of Hindus* (New Delhi: Gyan Publishing House, 1993) and also Sanjukta Gupta, "The Domestication of a Goddess: *Carana-tirtha Kalighat, the* Mahapitha of *Kali*" In Rachel Fell McDermott and Jeffrey J. Kripal (eds), *Encountering Kali: In the margins, at the center, in the west* (Berkeley and Los Angeles: University of California Press, 2003), pp. 60–79.

2 G. Michell, *The Hindu Temple: An introduction to its meaning and forms* (Chicago and London: University of Chicago Press, 1988 reprint of 1977 edn), p. 70.

3 The temple is situated in the ancient town of Colavandan, near Madurai in Tamilnadu.

4 *Calendar Informing the Pradosham Festival Days of the Arulmiku Sudeshvarar Thirukoil* – Nalattinputhoor (Thirunelveli District), 1995–96. I am grateful to Dr P. Sarveswaran, Professor of History at Madurai Kamaraj University, for this translation. The authority for the ritual was said to come from *Vedic* texts although the informants, Brahman priests, could not say which texts.

5 Although this is where my main informant regularly worships, he did not know what significance the various *abhiseka* ingredients had, until I showed him the pamphlet loaned to me by the temple priests.

6 At the Draupadiyamman temple in Colavandan the *pujari* said that the *kumbhabhiseka* is an injection of power for the goddess.

7   June McDaniel, *Offering Flowers, Feeding Skulls: Popular Goddess Worship in West Bengal* (Oxford and New York: Oxford University Press, 2004), p. 156.

8   *Ibid.*, p. 159

9   Rachel Fell McDermott, "Popular Attitudes Towards Kali and Her Poetry Tradition" in A. Michaels, C. Volgelsanger, and A. Wilke (eds), *Wild Goddesses in India and Nepal: Proceedings of an international symposium, Berne and Zurich, November 1994* (Studia Religiosa Helvetica, Jahrbuch vol. 2, Bern: Peter Lang, 1994), p. 386.

10   *Ibid.*, p. 387.

11   Ramprasad Sen, *Ramprasadi Sangit* (Cacutta: Rajendra Library, n.d.), p. 47 cited in McDaniel, *Offering Flowers, Feeding Skulls*, p. 163.

12   McDermott, "Popular Attitudes Towards Kali and Her Poetry Tradition", p. 388.

13   McDaniel, *Offering Flowers, Feeding Skulls*, p. 162.

14   Rachel Fell McDermott, *Singing to the Goddess: Poems to Kali and Uma from Bengal* (Oxford and New York: Oxford University Press, 2001), pp. 74–5.

15   Summarised by McDermott, "Popular Attitudes Towards Kali and Her Poetry Tradition", p. 384, in reference to David R. Kinsley, *The Sword and the Flute: Kali and Krsna, dark visions of the terrible and the sublime* (Berkeley, California: University of California Press, 1975).

16   Kinsley, *The Sword and the Flute*, p. 144.

17   McDermott, "Popular Attitudes Towards Kali and Her Poetry Tradition", p. 388.

18   *Ibid.*, p. 389.

19   Swami Nikhilananda (trans.) *Selections from the Gospel of Sri Ramakrishna* (Woodstock, Vermont: Skylight Paths Publishing, 2002), p. xxii.

20   Lex Hixon, *Great Swan: Meetings with Ramakrishna* (Burdett, New York: Larson Publications, 1996 [1992]), p. 85.

21   McDaniel, *Offering Flowers, Feeding Skulls*, p. 189.

22   Christopher Isherwood, *Ramakrishna and his Disciples* (Kolkata: Advaita Ashrama, 2001 reprint of 1965 edn), p. 66.

23   McDermott, "Popular Attitudes Towards Kali and Her Poetry Tradition" pp. 383–415.

24   Taken from M. *The Gospel of Sri Ramakrishna.* Translated by Swami Nikhilananda (New York: Ramakrishna-Vivikananda Center, 1973) p. 812 and cited by Carl Olson, *The Mysterious Play of Kali: An interpretive study of Ramakrishna* (Atlanta, Georgia: Scholars Press, 1990), pp. 112–13.

25   W. G. Neevel, "Ramakrishna" In M. Eliade (ed.), *The Encyclopedia of Religion* vol. 12. (New York: Macmillan, 1987), p. 210.

26   Nikhilananda, *Selections from the Gospel of Sri Ramakrishna*, p. xxiii.

27   Vedanta Society, Berkeley, <http://www.vedantaberkeley.org/ toppage1. htm>.

28   For a detailed discussion of local goddesses and their worship see Lynn

Foulston, *At the Feet of the Goddess: The divine feminine in local Hindu religion* (Brighton, Sussex and Portland, Oregon: Sussex Academic Press, 2002).

29 W. T. Elmore, *Dravidian Gods in Modern Hinduism* (New Delhi: Asian Educational Services, 1984 reprint of 1913 edn); L. A. Babb, "Marriage and Malevolence: The uses of sexual opposition in a Hindu pantheon", *Ethnology*, 9/2 (1970), pp. 137–48; H. Whitehead, *The Village Gods of South India* (New Delhi: Cosmo, 1983 reprint of 1921 edn); Brenda E. F. Beck, "The Vacillating Goddess: Sexual control and social rank in the Indian pantheon" (unpublished paper presented at the Association of Asian Studies meeting, Chicago, 1969); and S. S. Wadley, *Shakti: Power in the conceptual structure of Karimpur religion* (New Delhi: Munishiram Manoharlal, 1985 reprint of 1975 edn).

30 K. M. Erndl, *Victory to the Mother: The Hindu goddesses of northwest India in myth, ritual, and symbol* (New York: Oxford University Press, 1993) and Foulston, *At the Feet of the Goddess*.

31 An analysis of this point is also made in Foulston, *At the Feet of the Goddess*.

32 Elmore, *Dravidian Gods in Modern Hinduism*, p. 25.

33 Lynn E. Gatwood, *Devi and the Spouse Goddess: Women, sexuality, and marriage in India* (New Delhi: Manohar Publications, 1985).

34 Michael Moffatt, *An Untouchable Community in South India: Structure and consensus* (Princeton, New Jersey: Princeton University Press, 1979), pp. 276–89.

35 C. J. Fuller, "The Divine Couple's Relationship in a South Indian Temple: Minaksi and Sundaresvara at Madurai." *History of Religions*, 19/4 (May, 1980), p. 323.

36 *Ibid.*, pp. 343–5.

37 McDaniel, *Offering Flowers, Feeding Skulls*, p. 21.

38 V. T. Oldenburg, "The Roop Kanwar Case: Feminist responses". In J. S. Hawley (ed.), *Sati, the Blessing and the Curse: The burning of wives in India* (New York and Oxford: Oxford University Press, 1994), pp. 101–30 and also M. Kishwar, and R. Vanita. "The Burning of Roop Kanwar." *Manushi* 42–3 (1987) pp. 15–25.

39 Sanjukta Gupta "Tantric Sadhana: Puja" In Sanjukta Gupta, T. J. Hoens and Teun Goudriaan (eds), *Hindu Tantrism* (Leiden: E. J. Brill, 1979), p. 121.

40 *Ibid.*

41 Neevel, "Ramakrishna", pp. 209–10.

42 A. Mookerjee, and M. Khanna, *The Tantric Way* (London: Thames and Hudson, 1977), p. 126.

43 Gupta, "Tantric Sadhana", p. 126.

44 *Ibid.*, p. 125.

45 *Ibid.*, p. 136.

46 Mookerjee and Khanna, *The Tantric Way*, p. 134.

47 *Ibid.*
48 Gupta, "Tantric Sadhana", p. 136.
49 Mookerjee and Khanna, *The Tantric Way*, p. 142.
50 Usha Dev, *The Concept of Sakti in the Puranas* (Delhi: Nag Publishers, 1987), p. 92.
51 Mookerjee and Khanna, *The Tantric Way*, p. 21.
52 Gupta, "Tantric Sadhana", p. 130.
53 Translator Douglas Renfrew Brooks, "The Ocean of the Heart: Selections from the *Kularnava Tantra*", in: David Gordon White (ed.), *Tantra in Practice* (Princeton: Princeton University Press, 2000), p. 357.
54 Madhavananda et al. *Studies on the Tantras* (Calcutta: The Ramakrishna Mission Institute of Calcutta, 1989), pp. 3–4. My inclusion in square brackets.
55 *Ibid.*
56 *Ibid.*
57 *Ibid.*
58 *Ibid.*
59 David Kinsley, *Tantric Visions of the Divine Feminine: The Ten Mahavidyas* (Berkeley: University of California Press, 1997), p. 234.
60 *Ibid.*, p. 237.
61 Jonathan P. Parry, *Death in Benaras* (Cambridge: Cambridge University Press, 1994), p. 88.

6 Goddess Festivals

1 This section is based on various written sources and my own research at the *Durga Puja* festival in 2002. During this time I was assisted by Ms Hena Basu, whose help was invaluable in data collection and interpretation.
2 Rachel Fell McDermott, *Singing to the Goddess: Poems to Kali and Uma from Bengal* (Oxford and New York: Oxford University Press, 2001), p. 123.
3 "Pandal Picks", *The Telegraph*, Saturday 12th October 2002.
4 <http://news.bbc.co.uk/1/hi/world/south_asia/7040191.stm> (14-02-08) and <http://www.timesonline.co.uk/tol/news/world/asia/ article2648418.ece> (14-02-08).
5 "The deity down the decades", *The Telegraph*, 28th September 2002 (Kolkata issue).
6 *Ibid.*
7 The detail of the festival rituals has been taken largely from P. Ghosha, *Durga Puja: With notes and illustrations* (Calcutta: Hindu Patriot Press, 1871), fn. 3, p. ix. The latest account of the *Durga Puja* festival rituals can be found in H. P. Rodrigues, *Ritual Worship of the Great Goddess: The liturgy of the Durga Puja with interpretations* (Albany: SUNY, 2003). However, this research is based on the festival as celebrated by Bengali families in Varanasi.
8 Ghosha, *Durga Puja*, p. x.

9   D. R. Kinsley, *Hindu Goddesses: Visions of the divine feminine in the Hindu religious tradition* (Berkeley, Los Angeles and London: University of California Press, 1986), p. 114.

10 *Ibid.*

11 Verbal communication.

12 In a number of festivals, both orthodox and local, the power of the goddess is invoked into a pot (*kalasam*) which then represents her. For details of some local festival where this is the case see L. Foulston, *At the Feet of the Goddess: The divine feminine in local Hindu religion* (Brighton, Sussex & Portland, Oregon: Sussex Academic Press, 2002), pp. 114, 129, 162, 164, 168–9.

13 The mango is symbolized as a wish-granting tree according to M. Gandhi and Y. Singh, *Brahma's Hair: The mythology of Indian plants* (New Delhi: Rupa and Co., 1989), p. 99. The *pipal*, the *bata* and the *ashoka* are all sacred trees and the jackfruit is a tree that produces huge fruit.

14 *Devi-Mahatmyam (Glory of the Divine Mother): 700 Mantras on Sri Durga*, translator Swami Jagadiswarananda (Madras: Sri RamaKrsna Math, 1969).

15 "The deity down the decades" *The Telegraph*, 28 September 2002. Although this article states that Raja Kangshanarayan of Taherpur started the *puja*, Pranab Bandyopadhyay, *Mother Goddess Durga* (Calcutta: United Writers, 1993), p. 121, claims that Maharaja Krsna Chandra of Krsnanagar was the first.

16 "The deity down the decades" *The Telegraph*, 28th September 2002.

17 Ghosha, *Durga Puja*, fn. 1, p. vii. My inclusion in square brackets.

18 A type of grass said to be the hairs of Visnu that were torn off when he was rubbed by the serpent Vasuki during the churning of the milk ocean, *ibid.*, fn. 17, p. xxvi.

19 *Ibid.*, p. 38.

20 *Kalika Purana*, vol. 2, translator B. Shastri (Delhi: Nag Publishers, 1991–2).

21 The *bilva*, *vilva* or wood-apple tree is sacred to Siva as well as the goddess. It has groups of three leaves that mimic a *trisula*, a three-pronged spear that is symbolic of Siva and the goddess, especially Kali.

22 Ghosha, *Durga Puja*, p. 49.

23 *Ibid.*, p. 51

24 *Ibid.*, p. 53.

25 *Ibid.*, pp. 62–3.

26 Bandyopadhyay, *Mother Goddess Durga*, p. 132.

27 The nine goddesses associated with the *navapattrika* are; Brahmani, Durga, Kartiki, Siva (female form of the god of the same name), Raktadantika, Kalika, Camunda, Sokarahita and Laksmi.

28 McDermott, *Singing to the Goddess*, pp. 149–50. my inclusion is in square brackets.

29 B. Mohanty, "Laksmi and Alaksmi: The Kojagari Laksmi *vrat katha* of Bengal", *Manushi*, 104 (1998), pp. 9–11.

30 Kinsley, *Hindu Goddesses*, p. 22.
31 C. Chakravarti, "Kali Worship in Bengal", *Adyar Library Bulletin*, 21/3–4 (1957), p. 301.
32 J. D. Robinson, "The Worship of Clay Images in Bengal", unpublished Ph.D. thesis, Oxford University, 1983, p. 133.
33 *Ibid.*
34 Verbal communication.
35 S. Samata, "Cognition and Experience: The goddess Kali in the lives of her Bengal devotees", unpublished Ph.D. thesis, University of Virginia, 1990, p. 102.
36 For a more detailed discussion of local goddess festivals see chapter 6 of Foulston, *At the Feet of the Goddess.*
37 This ritual entails placing metal hooks in the skin of the back, and either being suspended from a pole or pulling a festival car attached to the hooks.
38 W. T. Elmore, *Dravidian Gods in Modern Hinduism* (New Delhi: Asian Educational Services, 1984 reprint of 1913 edn), p. 32, fn. 2.
39 G. Oppert, *The Original Inhabitants of Bharatavarsa or India* (Delhi: Oriental Publishers, 1972 reprint of 1893 edn), p. 482. Although I did not personally encounter any hook swinging, from conversations with people in various parts of India, I believe that it is still a common practice in many places.
40 For a detailed study of Draupadi and her worship see Alf Hiltebeitel, *The Cult of Draupadi, 1, Mythologies: From Gingee to Kuruksetra* (New Delhi: Motilal Banarsidass, 1991 reprint of 1988 edn). Alf Hiltebeitel, *The Cult of Draupadi, 2, On Hindu Ritual and the Goddess* (Chicago and London: University of Chicago Press, 1991).
41 In Colavandan, it was estimated that the fire-walkers numbered hundreds rather than thousands.
42 The majority of goddess festivals that include a fire-walk are on a much smaller scale, with dozens of walkers being typical rather than thousands.
43 The ground at this time is scorching hot; therefore, this feat is not one to be taken lightly.
44 It is vital for them to become segregated from the polluting influence of their family.
45 For the most recent (at the time of writing) and probably the most extensive study of possession see Frederick M. Smith, *The Self Possessed: Deity and spirit possession in South Asian literature and civilization* (New York and Chichester, West Sussex: Columbia University Press, 2006).
46 C. G. Diehl, *Instrument and Purpose: Studies on rites and rituals in south India* (Lund: C. W. K. Gleerup, 1956), p. 40.
47 P. J. Claus, "The Siri Myth and Ritual: A mass possession cult of south India", *Ethnology*, 14/1 (1975), pp. 47–58.
48 This is not an isolated incident since the same manner of accepting the sacrifice is mentioned by Brenda E. F. Beck, "The Goddess and the Demon: A local south Indian festival and its wider context", *Purusartha*, 5 (1981), p.

88, in her research of a festival for Mariyamman in Tamilnadu. Freeman, "Trial by Fire", p. 58, also mentions this form of sacrifice at the celebration of the *Pana Sankranti* festival elsewhere in the Bhubaneswar area.

49 Beck goes as far as to suggest that this relationship is a form of marriage. Beck, "The Goddess and the Demon", pp. 110–11.

7 Pilgrimage to the Temples of the Goddess

1 D. L. Eck, "India's *Tirthas*: 'Crossings' in sacred geography", *History of Religions*, 20/4 (1981), pp. 323–44.

2 D. L. Eck, "Ganga: The goddess Ganges in Hindu sacred geography", in J. S. Hawley, and D. M. Wulff, *Devi: Goddesses of India* (Berkeley, California: University of California Press, 1996), p. 138.

3 *Vayu Purana*, 1. 47. 28, translator G. V. Tagare (Delhi: Motilal Banarsidass, 1987).

4 *The Ramayana of Valmiki*, vol. 1, translator H. P. Shastri (London: Shanti Sadan, 1952), p. 74.

5 *Skanda Purana* 10.27.133, translator G. V. Tagare (Delhi: Motilal Banarsidass, 1996). My inclusions are inserted in square brackets.

6 William Dalrymple, *Indian Journeys: Shiva's Matted Locks* (Hugh Thompson, Icon Films, 2000).

7 See *Skanda Purana*, part 10, "Kashi Khanda" 27. 134, translator Tagare.

8 Eck, Ganga, pp. 148–9.

9 Diana L. Eck, *Darsan: Seeing the divine image in India* (New York: Columbia University Press, 1998 reprint of 1981edn), p. 68.

10 D. C. Sircar, "The Sakta Pithas". *Journal of the Royal Asiatic Society of Bengal*, 16/1 (1948), p. 3.

11 *Mahabharata, Vanaparvan* in *The Mahabhartata: 3. The book of the forest*, vol. 2, translator and (ed.), J. A. B. van Buitenen (Chicago: University of Chicago Press, 1975).

12 *Kalika Purana* 18. 46, translator B. Shastri (Delhi: Nag Publishers, 1991–2).

13 N. N. Bhattacharyya, *The Indian Mother Goddess* (New Delhi: Manohar, 1977 reprint of 1970 edn), p. 247.

14 *Ibid.*, pp. 247ff.

15 K. M. Erndl, *Victory to the Mother: The Hindu goddess of northwest India in myth, ritual, and symbol* (New York: Oxford University Press, 1993), p. 33.

16 *Devi-Bhagavatam* 7. 38. 15–18, translator Swami Vijnanananda (New Delhi: Munishiram Manoharlal, 1986, 3rd edn).

17 A. Mookerjee, *Kali: The feminine force* (London: Thames and Hudson, 1988), p. 30.

18 K. P. Goswami, *Kamakhya Temple: Past and present* (New Delhi: A. P. H. Publishing Corporation, 1998), p. 69.

19 *Kalika Purana* 62. 73b–5b. translator Shastri.

20 *Kalika Purana*, 72. 10–11, *ibid*. My inclusion is in square brackets.

21 *Kalika Purana*, 72. 62, *ibid*.

22   *Kalika Purana*, 72. 63, *ibid*.
23   *Kalika Purana*, 72. 74–6, *ibid*.
24   *Kalika Purana*, 72. 78, *ibid*.
25   A. Mookerjee and M. Khanna, *The Tantric Way* (London: Thames and Hudson, 1993 reprint of 1977 edn), p. 13.
26   D. R. Kinsley, *Tantric Visions of the Divine Feminine: The ten Mahavidyas* (Berkeley, Los Angeles and London: University of California Press, 1997), p. 248.
27   M. Das, *Legends of India's Temples* (Mumbai: Neve, 1999), p. 81.
28   N. N. Bhattacharyya, *History of the Tantric Religion (A historical, ritualistic and philosophical study)* (New Delhi: Manohar, 1982), p. 307.
29   Bhattacharyya, *The Indian Mother Goddess*, p. 236.
30   *Ibid.*, p. 65.
31   Bhattacharyya, *History of the Tantric Religion*, p. 133.
32   Erndl, *Victory to the Mother*, pp. 40–3.
33   *Devi Mahatmayam (Glory of the Divine Mother): 700 Mantras on Sri Durga*, 11. 55, translator Swami Jagadiswarananda (Madras: Sri Ramakrishna Math, 1969). My inclusion is in brackets.
34   Erndl, *Victory to the Mother*, p. 41.
35   *Ibid.*, pp. 40–3.
36   *Ibid.*, p. 42.
37   K. M. Erndl, "Rapist or Bodyguard, Demon or Devotee?" in Alf Hiltebeitel (ed.), *Criminal Gods and Demon Devotees: Essays on the guardians of popular Hinduism* (Albany: SUNY, 1989), p. 247.
38   *Ibid.*, p. 246. For more information on the connection between Siva and the buffalo demon see D. D. Shulman, "The Murderous Bride: Tamil versions of the myth of Devi and the Buffalo-Demon", *History of Religions*, 16/2 (1976), pp. 120–46. For the connection between Bhairava and decapitation see W. D. O'Flaherty, *Siva: The erotic ascetic* (London and New York: Oxford University Press, 1981 reprint of 1973 edn), pp. 123–7.
39   This is a point examined specifically by Mark Rohe in "Ambiguous and Definitive: The greatness of the goddess Vaisno Devi", in T. Pintchman (ed.), *Seeking Mahadevi: Constructing the identities of the Hindu great goddess* (Albany: SUNY, 2001), pp. 55–76.
40   *Ibid.*, p. 74.
41   N. Tewari, *The Mother Goddess Vaishno Devi* (New Delhi: Lancer International, 1988), pp. 6 and 51.
42   Rohe, "Ambiguous and Definitive", p. 58.
43   *Ibid.*, p. 61.
44   *Ibid.*, p. 58.
45   Shri Mata Vaishno Devi Shrine Board – official website. <http://maavaishnodevi.org/new1/index.html> (30/03/08).
46   For a detailed study of Kalighat see I. B. Roy, *Kalighat: Its impact on socio-cultural life of Hindus* (New Delhi: Gyan Publishing House, 1993).

47   Das, *Legends of India's Temples*, p. 74.
48   *Ibid.*, p. 75.
49   R. K. Das, *The Temples of Tamilnad* (Bombay: Bharatiya Vidya Bhavan, 1964), p. 58.
50   T. G. S. Balaram Iyer, *History and Description of Sri Meenakshi Temple* (Madurai: Sri Karthik Agency, 1994 reprint of 1984 edn), p. 11.
51   Translated by William P. Harman, *The Sacred Marriage of a Hindu Goddess* (New Delhi: Motilal Banarsidass, 1992 reprint of 1989 edn), p. 175.
52   C. J. Fuller, *The Camphor Flame: Popular Hinduism and society in India* (Princeton, New Jersey: Princeton University Press, 1992), p. 190.
53   Lynn E. Gatwood, *Devi and the Spouse Goddess: Women, sexuality and marriage in India* (New Delhi: Manohar Publications, 1985), p. 155.
54   Fuller, *The Camphor Flame*, p. 97.
55   D. R. Rajeshwari, *Sakti Iconography* (New Delhi: Intellectual Publishing House, 1989), p. 87.
56   D. D. Shulman, *Tamil Temple Myths: Sacrifice and divine marriage in the south Indian Saiva tradition* (Princeton, New Jersey: Princeton University Press, 1980), pp. 60–1.
57   Das, *Legends of India's Temples*, pp. 17–20. K. Marathe, *Temples of India: Circles of stone* (Mumbai: Eeshwar, 1998), pp. 111–3.
58   There are other versions of this myth that can be found in Shulman, *Tamil Temple Myths*, pp. 144–8, and Das, *The Temples of Tamilnad*, pp. 1–4.
59   D. R. Kinsley, *Hindu Goddesses: Visions of the divine feminine in the Hindu religious tradition* (Berkeley, Los Angeles and London: University of California Press, 1986), p. 202.
60   Das, *The Temples of Tamilnad*, p. 3.
61   Shulman, *Tamil Temple Myths*, p. 145. My inclusion is in square brackets.
62   Das, *Legends of India's Temples*, p. 20.

8 The Goddess in Contemporary Hinduism

1   Sadhan Jha, "The Life and Times of Bharat Mata: Nationalism as invented religion", in *Manushi*, 142 (2004), p. 35.
2   *Ibid.*
3   *Ibid.*
4   *Anandamath* was translated as *Abbey of Bliss* by B. K. Roy (trans.) *Anandamath: a novel by Bankim Chandra Chatterji* (Delhi: Oriental Paperbacks, 2005 reprint of 1992edn) and as *The Sacred Brotherhood* by Julius J. Lipner, *Anandamath, or The Sacred Brotherhood Bankimcandra Chatterji Translated with an Introduction and Critical Apparatus* (Oxford and New York: Oxford University Press, 2005), p. 5.
5   *Ibid.*, p. 28.
6   I refrain from calling her Bharat Mata at this point because Lipner claims that the term was not used by Chatterjee, *ibid.*, p. 100.

7 *Ibid.*, p. 29.
8 Sir William Wilson Hunter, *Annals of Rural Bengal* (London: Smith, Elder, 1897 7th edn of 1860 edn), pp. 69–71, cited by Lipner, *ibid.*, p. 27.
9 *Ibid.*, p. 29.
10 Lise McKean, *Divine Enterprise: Gurus and the Hindu Nationalist movement* (Chicago and London: University of Chicago Press, 1996), p. 114.
11 June McDaniel, *Offering Flowers, Feeding Skulls: Popular goddess worship in West Bengal* (Oxford and New York: Oxford University Press, 2004), p. 180.
12 *Ibid.*
13 *Ibid.*, p. 146.
14 Lipner, *Anandamath,* p. 150.
15 *Ibid.*
16 *Ibid.*, pp. 37–8.
17 *Ibid.*, p. 151.
18 *Ibid.*, pp. 144–6. Lipner's translation. My inclusions in square brackets.
19 *Ibid.*, p. 66.
20 *Ibid.*, p. 75.
21 *Ibid.*, p. 79.
22 *The Hindu*, reporting on 8th September 2006 claimed that "Historians have pointed out that nothing of relevance happened to the song on September 7, 1906 to warrant its public singing precisely 100 years later." Siddharth Varadarajan, "Parties mark centenary that was not" The Hindu Online, 8th September 2006, <http://www.hindu.com/2006/09/08/ stories/ 2006090823000100.htm> (06/04/08)
23 See Irfan Ahmed, "Contextualising *Vande Mataram.*" In *Manushi*, 111 (March/April 1999), pp. 29–30 and the response to this article D. V. Gokhale, "Judge the Song on Merit." In *Manushi*, 113 (July/August 1999), p. 2.
24 Charu Gupta, "The Icon of Mother in Late Colonial North India: 'Bharat Mata', 'Matri Bhasha' and 'Gau Mata', *Economic and Political Weekly* 36/45 (November 10, 2001), p. 4291.
25 Cited in *Ibid.*, p. 4292. Taken from Mahatma Gandhi, 'Bharat Mata Mandir', in Tiwari and Krishnanath (eds), *Kashi Vidyapeeth Hirak Jayanti Abhinandan Granth* (Varanasi, 1983), p 387.
26 *Ibid.*, p. 4292.
27 *Ibid.*, p. 4293
28 Lise McKean, "Bharat Mata: Mother India and Her Militant Matriots". In J. S Hawley and D. M. Wulff (eds.), *Devi: Goddesses of India* (Berkeley, Los Angeles and London: University of California Press, 1996), p. 269.
29 *Ibid.*, pp. 257–8.
30 McKean, *Divine Enterprise*, p. 147.
31 A. L. Basham 'Foreword' in J. N. Tiwari, *Goddess Cults in Ancient India with Special Reference to the First Seven Centuries AD* (Delhi: Sundeep Prakasham, 1985).

32 Christopher Pinney, *'Photos of the Gods': The printed image and political struggle in India* (London: Reaktion Books, 2004), n. 9, p. 220.
33 S. N. Kurtz, *All the Mothers are One: Hindu India and the cultural reshaping of psychoanalysis* (New York: Columbia University Press, 1992), p. 13.
34 J. S. Hawley "The Goddess in India" in J. S. Hawley and D. M. Wulff (eds), *Devi: Goddesses of India* (Berkeley, Los Angeles and London: University of California Press, 1996), p. 3.
35 *Ibid.*
36 *Ibid.*, p. 4.
37 M. Brand , "A New Hindu Goddess." *Hemisphere: An Asian Australian Magazine 26/6* (May/June 1982) p. 382.
38 T. B. Coburn, *Encountering the Goddess: A translation of the Devi Mahatmya and a study of its interpretation* (Delhi: Sri Satguru Publications, 1991), p. 37.
39 *Ibid.*, p. 54.
40 K. M. Erndl, *Victory to the Mother: The Hindu goddess of northwest India in myth, ritual, and symbol* (New York: Oxford University Press, 1993), p. 142.
41 *Ibid.*, footnote 17, p. 186.
42 Brand, "A New Hindu Goddess", p. 382.
43 *Ibid.*
44 I am using Brand's translation. M. Brand, Translation of anon. "Santosi Mata vrat-katha." (purchased 1969) in M. Brand "A New Hindu Goddess", unpublished BA dissertation [Appendix 'A' only] (Australian National University, 1979), pp. 79–89.
45 *Ibid.*, pp. 81–2.
46 *Ibid.*, p. 82.
47 *Ibid.*, fn 4, p 83.
48 Rachel Dwyer, *Filming the Gods: Religion and Indian cinema* (London and New York: Routledge, 2006), pp. 45–6.
49 Muni Nasreen, Kabir, *Bollywood: The Indian cinema story* (London: Channel 4 Books, 2001), p. 114.
50 Philip Lutgendorf, ""A Superhit Goddess: Jai Santosi *Maa* and caste hierarchy in Indian films, part one", *Manushi*, 131 (July/August 2002), p. 11.
51 Kabir, *Bollywood*, p. 115.
52 Veena Das, "The Mythological Film and Its Framework of Meaning: An analysis of *Jai Santosi Ma*." *India International Quarterly 8/1* (March 1980) pp 43–45.
53 *Ibid.*, p. 55.
54 Anees Jung, *Unveiling India: A woman's journey* (Calcutta: Penguin, 1987), p 117.
55 Brand, "A New Hindu Goddess", p. 384.
56 Das, "The Mythological Film and Its Framework of Meaning", p. 54.
57 Brand, "A New Hindu Goddess", p. 384.

58 Das, "The Mythological Film and Its Framework of Meaning", p. 55.

59 See <http://tagmeme.com/orissa/kalasis.html> for details of other women possessed by Santosi Ma in the Bhubaneswar area.

60 The name of the village settlement and of the woman possessed by Santosi Ma have been changed to ensure anonymity.

61 Brand, "A New Hindu Goddess", p. 384.

62 See M. T. Egnor, "The Changed Mother or What the Smallpox Goddess Did When There Was No More Smallpox." *Contributions to Asian Studies* XVIII (1984), pp. 24–45.

63 This is a World Health Organisation (WHO) estimate reported in Fabrizio F. Ferrari, "'Love Me Two Times.' From Smallpox to AIDS: Contagion and possession in the cult of Sitala", *Religions of South Asia*, 1.1 (June 2007), p. 95.

64 *Ibid.*, pp. 81–106.

65 See *Ibid.* and Madhu Purnima Kishwar, "Emergency *Avatar* of a Secular Goddess!: Manushi Swachha Narayani descends to protect street vendors." *Manushi*, 147 (March–April 2005), pp. 4–15.

66 Ken Gewertz, [WWW] "Undergraduate Witnesses Birth of a Goddess" *The Harvard University Gazette,* 24 February 24 2000, <http://www.hno.harvard.edu/gazette/2000/02.24/AIDS.html> (08-09-07)

67 Ferrari, "Love Me Two Times", p. 94.

68 Anna Portnoy, [WWW] "A Goddess in the Making: A very hard-to-find town in India builds a shrine to a goddess for AIDS." *Whole Earth* (Fall 2000) <http://www.wholeearthmag.com/ArticleBin/395.html> (08-09-07)

69 *Ibid.*

70 *Ibid.*

71 *Ibid.*

72 *Ibid.*

73 Kishwar, "Emergency *Avatar* of a Secular Goddess!", p. 4.

74 *Manushi* is a journal concerned with women and society, but also describes itself as "a non-profit venture, financed through subscriptions and donations from individuals." *Ibid.*, p. 1 Madhu Kishwar, its founding editor has campaigned to address many social injustices over the years.

75 *Ibid.*, p. 4.

76 The street vendors also have to pay bribes to the sweepers who may or may not do their job. Madhu Kishwar, "*Jhadu Pooja* at Sewa Nagar: Manushi's campaign for cleansing governance." In *Manushi*, 127 (2001), pp. 5–6.

77 *Ibid.*, p. 3.

78 *Ibid.*, p. 5.

79 *Ibid.*

80 Kishwar, "Emergency *Avatar* of a Secular Goddess!", p. 4.

81 *Ibid.*, p. 5

82 *Ibid.*

83 *Ibid.*

84 <http://www.youtube.com/watch?v=AB62Itu37eg> (09-09-07).
85 Michael R. Allen, *The Cult of Kumari: Virgin worship in Nepal* (New Delhi: Siddhartha Press, n.d. 2nd edn.), p. 2.
86 *Ibid.*, p. 3.
87 Patricia Roberts and Indra Manjupuria cited in Jnan Kaji Manandhar, *The Legends of Nepal* (Kathmandu: Sukhaveti Manandhar, 2002), p. 27.
88 Rashmila Shakya as told to Scott Berry, *From Goddess to Mortal: The true life story of a former royal kumari* (Thamel Kathmandu: Vajra Publications), p. 9.
89 Allen, *The Cult of Kumari*, note 7, p. 105.
90 Shakya and Berry, *From Goddess to Mortal*, p. 16.
91 *Ibid.* p. 15.
92 V. Carol Dunham, "Nepal's Virgin Goddesses." *Hinduism Today* (June 1997), p. 27.
93 *Ibid.*, p. 14.
94 Allen, *The Cult of Kumari*, p. 9.
95 *Ibid.*, pp. 8–9.
96 Allen, *The Cult of Kumari*, p. 18.
97 Chet Bahadur Singh, [WWW] "Four-year-old Shakya girl selected new 'Kumari'", *The Kathmandu Post* (11th July 2001) <http://www.nepalnews.com.np/contents/englishdaily/ktmpost/2001/jul/jul11/index.htm#5> (13-09-07)
98 *Ibid.*
99 Dunham, "Nepal's Virgin Goddesses", p. 29.

Glossary

abhiseka	'anointment', ritual bathing of deities.
Adiparvan	*Book of the Beginning* – book 1 of the *Mahabharata*.
Advaita Vedanta	monistic system of philosophy promoted by Sankara.
Adyasakti or *adi-sakti*	First or Primordial Power.
Aghoris	'terrible', 'fearful' *Tantric* ascetics that live in the cremation ground.
aksamala	garland of sacred berries or nuts.
Anandamath	lit. '*Abbey of Bliss*' nationalistic novel by Bankim Chandra Chatterjee.
anumarana	'following (one's husband) in death'.
apsarasas	divine nymphs.
Ardhanaisvara	image in which Parvati as Sakti occupies the left side of the body while Siva occupies the right side.
ardra	'moist'.
Arti, arati	offering of light to a deity.
arua	sacred sun dried pure rice.
Asadha	June/July.
asram	'monastery'.
astami	'eighth day' One of the important *Durga Puja* days.
asura (m) *asuri* (f)	'demon'/ 'demoness'.
asvamedha	horse sacrifice
Asvin	September/October
Atman	'Self', permanent essence in all life.
avatara	'incarnation'.
(a)vidya	'ignorance'.
Ayodhya	Birthplace of Rama.
Baisakh	Oriya: April/May.
bali	animal sacrifice.
bangala	One of the traditional styles of representing Durga during the annual *Durga Puja* festival in Kolkata.

Bhagavad Gita	*Song of the Lord* – dialogue between Arjuna and Krsna, contained in the *Mahabharata*
Bhairava	'terrible', a fierce form of Siva.
bhajan	hymn.
bhakta	devotee, one who practices *bhakti*.
bhakti	loving devotion.
bhava	'mood', 'emotion'.
Bhismaparvan	*Book of Bhisma*, book 6 of the *Mahabharata*.
Bhoi	Oriya: one of the higher scheduled castes – from the *Bauri* group.
bhukti	'enjoyment', path of worldly pleasures.
bija	'seed', 'seminal', seed syllable *mantra*.
bilva-tree	*bel* or *vilva*-tree, wood-apple, a tree sacred to Siva as its leaves are grouped in threes resembling Siva's trident.
bindu	'drop', seed or point from which creation starts.
BJP	Bharatiya Janta Party (Indian People's Party) – Hindu nationalist party.
bodhana	'awakening' the goddess, an important ritual in the *Durga Puja* festival.
Brahman	Ultimate Reality.
Brahmana	Priests – highest class.
Brahmanas	*sruti* texts – interpretations or commentaries on the *Vedas*.
Brahmanize, Brahmanization	to make unorthodox deities more orthodox.
brahma-vidya	knowledge of Brahman.
cakkhudan	'gift of eyes'.
cakra	'circle', energy centre within the body.
cakra-puja	*Tantric* ritual centred on the worship of *Yoginis* in which participants form a circle.
cal-citra	back piece on which *Durga Puja* images are erected.
cana	chickpeas.
capparam	Tamil: a canopied car-like vehicle used for carrying deities.
Cittrai	Tamil: festival celebrated, especially in Madurai.
cunnari	veil.
daityas	demons.
Daksa	father of Sati.
daksina	'generous'; also Right (-handed path of *Tantrism*).
Daksinesvar, Daksineswar	Kali temple in Kolkata, which is famous as the home of the mystic Ramakrishna.
dalits	'oppressed' adopted by those formerly referred to as untouchables.

dalma	lentils and vegetables.
danavas	demons.
darsana	'seeing' or 'auspicious sight of'; literally the act of seeing and being seen by a deity. *Darsana* is the main act of devotion where the devotee transmits their feelings of love and reverence by gazing at the deity. In return, the deity confers blessings on the devotee by looking at or seeing them.
dasami	'tenth day'. One of the important *Durga Puja* days.
Deva	God.
Devi	Goddess.
dhak	large drum used during *Durga Puja* in Kolkata.
dham(s)	holy places that define the sacred geography of India (north, south, east and west).
dharma	right conduct or duty (there is no literal translation).
Dharma sastras	Hindu law books.
dhoti	traditional cloth (usually white) worn by men, pleated and pulled between their legs. The traditional dress of priests.
dhuha	teak sap used to make cleansing smoke.
diksa	initiation ritual.
Dipavali	see *Divali*.
Divali	'row of lights' Festival of Lights celebrated in October/November.
do-bhasi	one of the traditional styles of representing Durga during the annual *Durga Puja* festival in Kolkata.
Dronaparvan	*Book of Drona*, book 7 of the *Mahabharata*.
Durga Puja	celebrating Durga's victory over Mahisasura. Most popular in Bengal.
Dusshera	'glorious tenth' celebrating the Rama's victory over the demon Ravana.
dvapara yuga	bronze age. See *yuga*.
ekcala	one back piece. *Durga Puja* deities are attached to one back piece.
Ganesa Caturthi	festival dedicated to Ganesa, which is most popular in Mumbai.
garbhagrha	'womb house', inner sanctum of a Hindu temple.
ghat	steps leading down to the river.
ghata	Bengali: ceremonial pot that represents the goddess, especially during *Durga Puja*.
gopuram	Tamil: 'temple tower'.
guna	'quality'; 'attribute'; 'constituent'. Three *gunas* (*sattva*, *rajas* and *tamas*) are the basis of the material world (*prakriti*). See also individual *gunas*.

gur	unrefined sugar, see jaggery.
guru	religious teacher.
Hara	Siva.
Hari	Visnu.
hathayoga	yoga of 'force' which utilises physical positions to manipulate energies within the body.
Hinduize, Hinduization	to make unorthodox deities more orthodox.
Hindutva	Hinduness.
Holi	Spring festival.
homa	sacrificial fire into which *ghee*, wood or grains are offered.
istadeva	personal deity.
Isvara	'Lord'.
itihasa	'history', and category of text which includes the Epics.
jaggery	unrefined sugar, see *gur*.
Jai Mata di	Victory to the Mother.
japa	repetition of a deity's name or *mantra*.
jhadu puja	worship of the cleaning broom'
jnana	'intuitive knowledge'.
kala	'fraction'.
kalasam	Oriya: ceremonial pot that represents the goddess.
Kali-kula	'lineage of Kali', a branch of *Tantric* practice centred on the worship of terrifying female deities.
kali yuga	iron or dark age. The most degenerate of the four *yugas* (ages). We are currently in the *kali yuga*, when *moksa* (liberation) is most hard to attain. At the end of this age the *krita yuga* (golden age) will be reinstated. See *yuga*.
Kailasa	Siva's mountain home.
Kamadhenu	the wish-fulfilling cow.
kanya-puja	virgin worship.
Kapalikas	'skull bowl bearers', heterodox Hindu tradition which practiced ecstatic cremation ground rites.
karakam	Tamil: ceremonial pot that represents the goddess.
karisini	cow dung.
Kartik	October/November.
Karttikeya	See Skanda.
katha	'story'.
Kaula	tradition of left handed *Tantric* practice known for its use of the *panca-makara*.
kavaca	'armour' symbolic, invoked through the use of *mantras*.

khela sindur	*Durga Puja* ritual known as playing with the vermillion, which happens on the last day of the festival.
khicuri	fish, rice and lentils.
khiri	sweet rice pudding.
Krsna Janmastami	festival celebrating Krsna's birthday.
Ksatriyas	Warriors – second highest class.
kula	'lineage', 'family'.
Kumari	'Virgin'.
Kumari che/ghar	house of the living goddess (Raj Kumari) in Kathmandu.
kumbhabhiseka	The renewal of a temple by anointing it from top to bottom.
kumkum	red powder, see *sindur*.
kundalini	'spiral'; 'winding', feminine spiritual energy which lies dormant within the human body but can be awakened and utilised in the pursuit of liberation.
kundalini yoga	A type of *Tantric* yoga which aims to awaken and utilise *kundalini* energy.
kurma	'tortoise', one of Visnu's incarnations.
Kurus, Kauravas	The cousins and later opponents of the Pandavas.
Laksmana	Rama's brother who followed him into exile.
Laksmi Puja	annual festival dedicated to the goddess Laksmi.
lila	'play', the divine game.
linga	'sign' but also refers to the phallic symbol of Siva.
lingam	*linga* and *yoni* combined.
Maci	Tamil: February/March.
madhu	'liquor'; 'wine'; 'alcohol', one of the *panca-makara*.
Mahabharata	Great Story of the Bharatas – Hindu epic.
Mahadevi	'Great Goddess'.
mahalaya	New moon day.
Mahamaya	'Great Illusion'.
Mahastami	See *astami*. Most auspicious day of the *Durga Puja* festival.
Mahavidyas	'Great knowledge' a group of ten *Tantric* goddesses.
Mahesvara	Siva.
Mahisasura	'buffalo demon'.
maithuna	'sexual intercourse', one of the *panca-makara*.
mamsa	'meat', one of the *panca-makara*.
mandala	'circle', visual representation of a deity used as a meditational aid.
mandapa	temple or hall.
mangala, Mangala	'auspicious' but also the name of a popular goddess in Orissa.
mangals	devotional poetry popular in Bengal.

mantra	'word'; 'formula', manifestation of a deity used as meditational aid or as part of *puja*.
Manusmrti	*Laws of Manu.*
margosa	sacred plant associated with Mariyamman.
math	monastery or *asram*.
Matrkas	'Mothers', a group of Hindu goddesses.
matsya	'fish', one of the *panca-makara*.
maya	'illusion'.
mela	'fair'.
moksa	'liberation', release from *samsara*
mudra	hand gesture.
mudra	'parched grain', one of the *panca-makara*.
mukti	'liberation', see *moksa*.
mula murti	central immovable image of a deity, as opposed to the *utsava murti* (festival image).
Mulaprakrti	Primordial Matter (title of the Goddess).
murti	image or statue of a deity.
naga (Tam. *naka*)	'snake', 'serpent', also a group of semi-divine serpent deities.
naimittika-puja	a more detailed version of *nitya-puja*, it is performed five times a month and on special occasions such as the *guru's* birthday and festivals of the goddess.
Nakamal	Tamil: snake goddess.
Nandi	Siva's bull and companion.
navami	'ninth day'. One of the important *Durga Puja* days.
navapattrika	'nine leaves', bundle of nine plants used during *Durga Puja*.
Navratri	'nine nights', celebrates the nine nights that Rama invoked the help of Durga. At the same time as *Durga Puja*.
nidra	'sleep'.
nilkantha	blue-throated bird that is released before the deities are immersed at *Durga Puja*.
nirguna	'without *gunas*'; 'without attributes, qualities'. Only Brahman is without *gunas* (the three strands that account for the individuality in the manifest world). When the world is unmanifest the three *gunas* are in equilibrium.
nitya-puja	daily worship.
nyasa	the feeling of the Divine in various parts of the body – invoked by *mantra* and *mudra*.
padmasana	lotus (*padma*) yogic posture (*asana*).
palipidam	Tamil: sacrificial altar outside the sanctum of south Indian deities.

pampai	Tamil: double drum used to summon the goddess.
pana	Oriya: sweet drink especially popular at the *pana sankranti* (1st day of *Baisakh*).
pana sankranti	1st day of *Baisakh*.
panca-makara	5 Ms, impure substances that begin with the letter 'M' used in *Tantric* ritual (meat, fish, alcohol, grain and sexual intercourse).
pandal	temporary pavilions constructed to house deities, especially Durga during the annual *Durga Puja* festival.
Pandavas	5 brothers (sons of Pandu) who were really descended from the gods in the *Mahabharata*. They are Yudhisthira, Bhima, Arjuna, Nakula and Sahadeva .
Parasakti	Supreme Power (title of Goddess).
pariah	south Indian untouchable caste.
patala	netherwold.
pindi	rocky outcrop.
pipal	sacred tree.
prakrti	'primal material nature'. It is personified as the active feminine principle.
pralaya	'dissolution'. The periodical dissolution of the cosmos, often symbolized by a great flood.
pranayama	yogic practice centred upon control of breath and breathing.
prasada	'grace', food and substances blessed by the deities that is then returned to worshippers at the end of *puja*.
pratima	*murtis* or images that are worshipped during *Durga Puja*. Durga, Ganesa, Laksmi, Sarasvati and Karttikeya.
pratipada	the first day after the new moon in the month of *Asvin* (September/October) and the start of the *Durga Puja* rituals.
puja	'ritual'; 'honor'; 'adoration'. Hindu worship.
pujari	non-*brahmana* priest.
pu-k-kuli	Tamil: 'pit of flowers' name for the fire-walking pit.
Purana(s)	'ancient' books – sectarian texts that contain the mythology of various gods and goddess.
purusa	cosmic person in *Vedas* and eternal spirit in Sankhya philosophy.
puspanjali	offering of flowers.
rajas (*guna*)	'activity'; 'passion'; 'energetic principle'. One of three *gunas*.
Raj Kumari	Royal Kumari.
raksa	'fierce'.

Raktabija	'Red seed', demon whose blood, once spilt, became replicas of himself. Kali vanquished him by drinking his blood.
Ramakrishna	famous mystic who frequently had ecstatic visions of Kali. He made his home at Daksinesvar temple in Kolkata.
Ramayana	*Tale of Rama* – epic.
Ramprasad Sen	writer of devotional poetry to Kali.
RSS	Rashtriya Swayamsevak Sangh (National Volunteer Corps/Union).
sadhaka	religious aspirant.
sadhana	'attainment', religious practice or discipline.
sadhu	Hindu holy man who has given up all his possessions and all family attachments. He wanders from place to place, his only concern being mediation on the divine.
saguna	'with *gunas*'; 'with attributes, qualities'. Only Brahman is *nirguna* without *gunas* (the three strands that account for the individuality in the manifest world).
sahagamana	'going together with (one's husband)' – in reference to widow immolation.
Saiva, Saivite	relating to Siva and his worship; a devotee of Siva.
Sakta	relating to the Goddess and her worship; a devotee of the goddess.
Sakta pithas	'seats of the goddess', places of pilgrimage.
sakti	'energy', 'power'. Sakti is an epithet of the Supreme Goddess.
samadhi	'absorption', state of deep spiritual concentration achieved through meditation.
samhita	collection of hymns i.e. *Veda Samhita*.
samsara	cycle of birth death and rebirth.
Sangh Parivar	Family of right wing parties including RSS, BJP, VHP and Shiv Sena.
Sankara or Sankaracarya	an influential nineteenth century philosopher of the *Advaita Vedanta* school of thought.
Sankhya	'enumeration' one of the six schools of thought which posits reality as *purusa* and *prakrti*.
Sanskritize, Sanskritization	To make unorthodox deities more orthodox.
santa svarupini	peaceful form of the goddess.
santi	'peace'.
santi jal	'water of peace' (pot of water used at *Durga Puja*).
Santiparvan	*Book of Peace* – book 12 in *Mahabharata*.
Santosi Ma or Mata	'Mother of Satisfaction'.

Saptamatrkas	'seven mothers', group of *Tantric* goddesses.
saptami	night' after the new moon. One of the important *Durga Puja* days.
sara	earthen lid or plate painted with an image of Laksmi (used during her festival in Bengal).
sarabat	special drink of Santosi Ma.
Sarada Devi	wife of Ramakrishna.
sat	'fiery power' indicating a woman's (esp. *sati*'s) inner purity.
sati	'good woman' used to describe a woman who ended her life on her husband's funeral pyre.
satimatas	Sati mothers, deified women who were burnt on their husband's funeral pyre.
sativrata	vow to become *sati*.
sattva (guna)	'purity'; 'goodness'; 'illuminating principle'. One of three *gunas*.
saumya	'benificent', refers to non-terrifying deities within Hinduism, particularly goddesses.
Sauptikaparvan	*Book of the Sleeping Warriors* - book 10 of the *Mahabharata*.
sava sadhana	*Tantric* worship and meditation performed on a corpse in a cremation ground.
Sesa	the cosmic snake.
siddhi	'accomplishment', superhuman power acquired through advanced religious practice.
sindur	red powder that married women put along their hair parting, see *kumkum*.
Siva-Sakti	The Absolute, understood as the unity of masculine and feminine aspects.
Skanda	Son of Siva, see Karttikeya.
skandha	book.
smasana	cremation ground.
smrti	remembered, tradition. Type of Hindu text. Includes Epics, Law books, and *Puranas*.
spousification	marriage of local, independent goddesses to tame their wild characteristics.
srap	'curse'.
sri cakra	*yantra* (geometric diagram) of the Goddess Sri.
Sri-kula	'lineage of Sri', a branch of *Tantric* practice centred on the worship of beneficent female deities.
Sri Sukta	*Vedic* hymn to the goddess that emphasises her power.
Sri Vidya	tradition of right-handed *Tantric* practice centred upon the worship of the goddess.
sruti	Heard, truth, revelation, most sacred type of Hindu text. It includes the *Vedas* and the *Upanisads*.

stotra	hymn of praise.
stridharma	women's duty.
Sudras	'servants', lowest class of people.
Sundaresvarar	local form of Siva at Minaksi temple in Madurai.
Svastica/swastika	auspicious symbol.
tamas (guna)	'darkness'; 'inertia'; 'dullness'. One of three *gunas*. The opposite of *sattva*.
tamasa	spectacle.
Tantras	scriptures representing dialogue between Siva and Parvati that inform *Tantric* belief and practice.
Tantric or *Tantrik*	pertaining to *Tantrism*.
tapas	'austerity'; 'penance' 'concentrated discipline' potential power or heat accumulated by ascetic practises.
tarpana	offerings to one's ancestors.
tejas	'fire'; spiritual heat or energy accumulated through ascetic practices, especially celibacy. Also one of the five elements.
tilak or tika	red mark on the forehead between the eyes that symbolises the third eye and is also a blessing.
tirtha	a 'ford' or 'crossing' place originally over a river but now indicative of a place of pilgrimage where there is a 'crossing' between the worlds of the human and the divine.
treta yuga	silver age. Follows on from the golden age. The second of four ages when *yajna* (sacrifice) is most effective. During this age, *dharma* stands on only three of its four legs. See also *yuga*.
trimurti	'three gods' the Hindu triad of Brahma, the creator, Visnu, the preserver, and Siva, the dissolver.
tusti	'contentment'.
udayapana	ceremony to conclude Santosi Ma's sixteen Fridays' fast. Food is given to eight *brahmana* boys.
ugra	'wrathful'; 'angry', refers to terrifying deities within Hinduism, particularly goddesses.
Upanisad	'to sit near to' group of texts that debate the nature of Brahman and its relationship to the *atman*.
utsava murti	festival image of a deity that is taken outside the temple during their main festival.
vac	'speech' also the name of a Vedic goddess.
vahana	vehicle of deities - animal companion
VHP	Vishva Hindu Parishad – World Hindu Council.
Vaikaci	Tamil: May/June.
Vaisnava, vaisnavite	relating to Visnu and his worship; a devotee of Visnu.
Vajracarya	teacher of a Buddhist *Tantric* sect.

vama	left (-handed path of *Tantrism*).
Vanaparvan	*Book of the Forest* - book 3 of the *Mahabharata*.
Vande Mataram	'Hail to the Mother' national song
Veda	'knowledge' there are four books of knowledge *Rg* (Royal), *Yajur* (Ritual), *Sama* (Songs), and *Arthava* (Incantations) – the earliest Hindu texts.
Vedagarbha	womb or source of the *Vedas*.
Vedanta	meaning 'end of the *Veda*'.
Venkatesvara	localized form of Visnu in Andhara Pradesh. He is the main deity of the richest temple in India.
vidya	'knowledge'.
viparitarati	sexual intercourse with the female in the dominant position.
vira	'hero'; 'victor', an advanced religious aspirant.
Virataparvan	*Book of Virata* - book 4 of the *Mahabharata*.
Visnumaya	Illusion of Visnu.
Vivekananda	disciple of Ramakrishna, accredited with bringing Hinduism to the West. He started the Ramakrishna Mission and Math.
vrata	'vow'.
yaksa(s)(m) *yaksini(s)* (f)	collective name of minor deities or sprites of vegetation.
yali	a mythological lion-faced animal with elephantine proboscis and tusks.
yantra	'machine', visual representation of a deity used as a meditational aid.
yogin (m) *yogini* (f)	practitioner of yoga.
Yogini	Goddesses usually in groups of 64.
yoni	female generative organ.
yuga	'age' The cyclical nature of Hinduism is organized in four progressively worsening ages, *krita yuga* (golden age), *treta yuga* (silver age), *dvapara yuga* (bronze age), and *kali yuga* (iron age) or dark age. We are presently in the *kali yuga*, the most degenerate of the four ages. One cycle of the four *yugas* is known as a *maha-yuga*, with 2000 *maha-yugas* (8,640,000,000 years) being equal to one *kalpa*. One *kalpa* is equal to a day and night of Brahma.
zamindar	land owner.

Bibliography

Primary Sources

Anon. 1995–96: *Calendar Informing the Pradosham Festival Days of the Arulmiku Sudeshvarar Thirukoil* – Nalattinputhoor (Thirunelveli District).

Avalon, A. (trans.) 1965: *Hymn to Kali (Karpuradi-stotra)*. Madras: Ganesh and Co.

Bloomfield, Maurice 1987 reprint of 1897 edn: *Hymns of the Atharva-Veda: Together with extracts from the ritual books and commentaries*. Sacred Books of the East, vol. 42, general ed. M. Müller. Delhi: Motilal Banarsidass.

Brooks, Douglas Renfrew (trans.) 2000: "The Ocean of the Heart: Selections from the *Kularnava Tantra*", in David Gordon White (ed.), *Tantra in Practice*. Princeton: Princeton University Press, pp. 347–60.

Brown, Cheever Mackenzie 1998: *The Devi Gita – The Song of the Goddess: A translation, annotation, and commentary*. Albany: State University of New York Press.

Coburn, T. B. 1991: *Encountering the Goddess: A translation of the Devi Mahatmya and a study of its interpretation*. Delhi: Sri Satguru Publications.

Deshpande, N. A. (trans.) 1990: *Padma Purana* vol. 5. Delhi: Motilal Banarsidass.

Dutt, M. N. (trans.) 1896: *The Mahabharata (translated literally from the original Sanskrit text)*. Calcutta: H. C. Dass, Elysium Press.

Griffith, R. T. H. (trans.) 1991 reprint of 1973 rev. edn: *The Hymns of the Rg Veda*. Delhi: Motilal Banarsidass.

Gupta, Sanjukta 1972: *Laksmi Tantra: A Pancaratra text*. Leiden: E. J. Brill.

Jagadiswarananda Swami (trans.) 1969: *Devi-Mahatmyam (Glory of the Divine Mother): 700 Mantras on Sri Durga*. Madras: Sri Ramakrishna Math.

Johnson, W. J. (trans.) 1998: *The Sauptikaparvan of the Mahabharata: The massacre at night*. Oxford and New York: Oxford University Press.

Lipner, Julius J. (trans.) 2005: *Anandamath, or The Sacred Brotherhood:*

Bankimcandra Chatterji translated with an introduction and critical apparatus. Oxford and New York: Oxford University Press.

Nikhilananda Swami (trans.) 2002: *Selections from the Gospel of Sri Ramakrishna*. Woodstock, Vermont: Skylight Paths Publishing.

Olivelle, P. (trans.) 1996: *Upanisads*. Oxford: Oxford University Press.

Roy, B. K. (trans.) 2005 reprint of 1992 edn: *Anandamath: a novel by Bankim Chandra Chatterji*, Delhi: Oriental Paperbacks.

Roy, P. C. (trans.) 1955: *The Mahabharata of Krishna-Dwaipanyana Vyasa*, vol. VI. Calcutta: Bharata Press.

Shastri, B. (trans.) 1991–2: *Kalika Purana*, vols 1–3. Delhi: Nag Publishers.

Shastri, H. P. (trans.) 1952: *The Ramayana of Valmiki*, vol. 1. London: Shanti Sadan.

Shastri J. L. (trans.) 1990 reprint: *Linga Purana* vol. 1 Delhi: Motilal Banarsidass.

Singh, Jaideva (trans.) 1979: *Vijnanabhairava or Divine Consciousness*. Delhi: Motilal Banarsidass.

Tagare, G. V. (trans.) 1981: *Kurma Purana*, vols 1–2. Delhi: Motilal Banarsidass.

Tagare, G. V. (trans.) 1987: *Vayu Purana*, vol. 1. Delhi: Motilal Banarsidass.

Tagare G V. (trans.) 1994 reprint of 1976 edn: *Bhagavata Purana* vol. 3, Delhi: Motilal Banarsidass.

Tagare, G. V. (trans.) 1996: *The Skanda Purana*, part 10. Delhi: Motilal Banarsidass.

Trinath Pattnaik, n.d.: *Ma Mangala Mahapurana*. Orissa: Sri Sarada Store (purchased in Kakatpur).

Van Buitenen, J. A. B. (trans. and ed.) 1973: *The Mahabharata: 1. The book of the beginning*, vol. 1. Chicago and London: University of Chicago Press.

Van Buitenen, J. A. B. (trans. and ed.) 1975: *The Mahabharata: 3. The book of the forest*, vol. 2. Chicago and London: University of Chicago Press.

Vijnanananda Swami (trans.) 1986, 3rd edn: *The Srimad Devi-Bhagavatatam*. New Delhi: Munishiram Manoharlal.

Wilson, H. H. (trans.) 1866 2nd edn: *Rig-Veda Sanhita: A collection of ancient Hindu hymns*, vol. 1. London: N. Trübner and Co.

Beliefs

Agrawala, P. K. 1984: *Goddesses in Ancient India*. New Delhi: Abhinav Publications.

Aiyappan, A. 1931: "Myth of the Origin of Smallpox". *Folklore*, vol. 42, pp. 291–3.

Bandyopadhyay, P. 1993: *Mother Goddess Durga*. Calcutta: United Writers.

Basham, A. L. 1982 reprint of 1967, 3rd revised edn: *The Wonder That Was India*. London: Sidgwick and Jackson.

Benard, Elisabeth Anne 1994: *Chinnamasta: The aweful Buddhist and Hindu Tantric goddess*. Delhi: Motilal Banarsidass.

Bhattacharyya, N. N. 1974: *History of the Sakta Religion*. New Delhi: Munshiram Manoharlal Publishers Pvt. Ltd.

Bhattacharyya, N. N. 1977, 2nd revised edn: *The Indian Mother Goddess*. New Delhi: Manohar Book Service.

Bhattacharyya, N. N. 1999, 2nd revised edn: *History of the Tantric Religion (A historical, ritualistic and philosophical study)*. New Delhi: Manohar.

Biardeau, Madeline 1984: "The Sami Tree and the Sacrificial Buffalo". *Contributions to Indian Sociology* (n.s.), vol. 18, no. 1, pp. 1–23.

Blackburn, S. H. 1985: "Death and Deification: Folk cults in Hinduism", *History of Religions*, vol. 24, pp. 255–74.

Brooks, Douglas Renfrew 1990: *The Secret of the Three cities: An introduction to Hindu Sakta Tantrism*. Chicago: University of Chicago Press.

Brooks, Douglas Renfrew 1992: *Auspicious Wisdom: The texts and traditions of Srividya Sakta Tantrism in South India*. Albany: State University of New York Press.

Brown, Cheever Mackenzie 1974: *God as Mother: A feminine theology in India*. Hartford, Vermont: Claude Stark.

Brown, Cheever Mackenzie 1990: *The Triumph of the Goddess: The canonical models and theological visions of the Devi-Bhagavata Purana*. Albany: State University of New York Press.

Brown, Cheever Mackenzie 2001: "The Tantric and Vedantic Identity of the Great Goddess in the *Devi Gita* of the *Devi-Bhagavata Purana*". In T. Pintchman (ed.), *Seeking Mahadevi: Constructing the identities of the Hindu great goddess*. Albany: State University of New York Press, pp. 19–36.

Chalier-Visuvalingam, Elizabeth, 1994: "Bhairava and the Goddess: Tradition, gender and transgression". In A. Michaels, C. Volgelsanger and A. Wilke (eds), *Wild Goddesses in India and Nepal: Proceedings of an international symposium, Berne and Zurich, November 1994*. Studia Religiosa Helvetica, Jahrbuch vol. 2, Bern: Peter Lang, pp. 253–301.

Coburn, T. B. 1986 reprint of 1982 edn: "Consort of None, Sakti of All: The vision of the *Devi-Mahatmya*" in J. S. Hawley and D. M. Wulff (eds), *The Divine Consort: Radha and the goddesses of India*. Boston: Beacon Press, pp. 153–65.

Coburn, Thomas B. 1988 reprint of 1984 edn: *Devi-Mahatmya: The crystallization of the goddess tradition*. Delhi: Motilal Banarsidass.

Courtright, P. B. 1994: "The Iconographies of Sati". In J. S. Hawley (ed.), *Sati, the Blessing and the Curse: The burning of wives in India*. New York and Oxford: Oxford University Press, pp. 27–49.

Courtright, P. B. 1995: "*Sati*, Sacrifice and Marriage: The modernity of tradition". In L. Harlan and P. B. Courtright (eds), *From the Margins of Hindu Marriage: Essays on gender, religion and culture*. New York, Oxford: Oxford University Press, pp. 184–203.

Daniélou, A. 1991: *The Myths and Gods of India*. Rochester, Vermont: Inner Traditions International.

Das, S. K. 1934: *Sakti, or Divine Power: A historical study based on original Sanskrit texts*. Calcutta: University of Calcutta.

Dehejia, V. 1986: *Yogini Cult and Temples: A Tantric tradition*. New Delhi: National Museum.

Dehejia, V. 1994: "Comment: A broader landscape". In J. S. Hawley (ed.), *Sati, the Blessing and the Curse: The burning of wives in India*. New York and Oxford: Oxford University Press, pp. 49–53.

Dev, Usha 1987: *The Concept of Sakti in the Puranas*. Delhi: Nag Publishers.

Dhal, Upendra Nath 1978: *Goddess Laksmi: Origin and development*. New Delhi: Oriental Publishers and Distributors.

Dowson, J. 1991 5th impression: *A Classical Dictionary of Hindu Mythology and Religion, Geography, History and Literature*. Calcutta, Allahabad, Bombay, Delhi: Rupa and Co.

Dutt, K. Guru 1975: "Shakti Worship in India". *Religion and Society (Bangalore)*, vol. 22, pp. 47–62.

Eck, Diana L. 1982: *Banaras: City of light*. Princeton, New Jersey: Princeton University Press.

Eck, D. L. 1996: "Ganga: The goddess Ganges in Hindu sacred geography", in J. S. Hawley, and D. M. Wulff (eds), *Devi: Goddesses of India*. Berkeley, California: University of California Press, pp. 137–53.

Eck, Diana L. 1998 3rd edn: *Darsan: Seeing the divine image in India*. New York: Columbia University Press.

Erndl, Kathleen M. 2004: "Sakta". In S. Mittal, and G. Thursby (eds), *The Hindu World*. New York and London: Routledge, pp. 140–61

Ferrari, Fabrizio. M. 2008: "Saktism". In Denise Cush, Catherine Robinson, and Michael York (eds), *Encyclopedia of Hinduism*. London and New York: Routledge, pp. 733–42.

Fowler, J. D. 1997: *Hinduism: Beliefs and practices*. Brighton, Sussex & Portland, Oregon: Sussex Academic Press.

Fowler, J. D. 2002: *Perspectives of Reality: An introduction to the philosophy of Hinduism*. Brighton, Sussex and Portland, Oregon: Sussex Academic Press.

Gatwood, Lynn E. 1985: *Devi and the Spouse Goddess: Women, sexuality and marriage in India*. New Delhi: Manohar.

Gonda, J. 1969 2nd edn of 1954 edn: *Aspects of Early Visnuism*. Delhi: Motilal Banarsidass.

Goswami, K. P. 1998: *Kamakhya Temple: Past and present*. New Delhi: A. P. H Publishing Corporation.

Guleri, V. S. 1990: *Female Deities in Vedic and Epic Literature*. New Delhi: Nag Publishers.

Harding, E. U. 1993: *Kali: The black goddess of Dakshineswar*. York Beach, Maine: Nicolas-Hays, Inc.

Harlan, L. 1994: "Perfection and Devotion: Sati tradition in Rajasthan". In J. S. Hawley (ed.), *Sati, the Blessing and the Curse: The burning of wives in India*. New York and Oxford: Oxford University Press, pp. 79–99.

Harlan, L. and Courtright, P. B. (eds) 1995: *From the Margins of Hindu Marriage: Essays on gender, religion and culture*. New York, Oxford: Oxford University Press.

Harper, Katherine Anne. 1989: *Seven Hindu Goddesses of Spiritual Transformation: The iconography of the Saptamatrikas*. Lewiston: Edwin Mellen Press.

Harper, K. A. and Brown, R. L. (eds) 2002: *The Roots of Tantra*. Albany: State University of New York.

Hawley, J. S. (ed.) 1994: *Sati, the Blessing and the Curse: The burning of wives in India*. New York and Oxford: Oxford University Press.

Hawley, J. S., and Wulff, D. M. (eds) 1986 reprint of 1982 edn: *The Divine Consort: Radha and the goddesses of India*. Boston: Beacon Press.

Hawley, J. S. and Wulff, D. M. (eds) 1996: *Devi: Goddesses of India*. Berkeley, Los Angeles and London: University of California Press.

Hazra, R. C. 1979 reprint of 1963 edn: *Studies on the Upapuranas, vol. 2: Sakta and non-sectarian Upapuranas*. Calcutta: Sanskrit College.

Hiltebeitel, Alf 1976: *The Ritual of Battle: Krishna in the Mahabharata*. Ithaca and London: Cornel University Press.

Hiltebeitel, Alf 1978: "The Indus Valley 'Proto-Siva', Reexamined through Reflections on the Goddess, the Buffalo, and the Symbolism of *vahanas*". *Anthropos*, vol. 73, pp. 767–97.

Hiltebeitel, Alf 1987: "Mahabharata". In Mircea Eliade (ed.), *Encyclopedia of Religion*, vol. 9. New York: Macmillan Publishing Company, pp. 118–9.

Hiltebeitel, Alf and Erndl, K. M. (eds) 2000: *Is the Goddess a Feminist? The politics of south Asian goddesses*. Sheffield: Sheffield Academic Press.

Humes, Cynthia Anne 2000: "Is the *Devi-Mahatmya* a Feminist Scripture?". In Alf Hiltebeitel and Kathleen M. Erndl (eds), *Is the Goddess a Feminist? The politics of south Asian goddesses*. Sheffield: Sheffield Academic Press, pp. 123–50.

Ions, V. 1967: *Indian Mythology*. London, New York, Sydney and Toronto: Paul Hamlyn.

Jaiswal, S. 1967: *The Origin and Development of Vaisnavism from 200 BC to AD 500*. Delhi: Munshiram Manoharlal.

Joshi, M. C. 2002: "Historical and Iconographic Aspects of Sakta Tantrism". In Katherine Anne Harper, and Robert L. Brown (eds), *The Roots of Tantra*. Albany: State University of New York, pp. 39–55

Kinsley, D. R. 1975: *The Sword and the Flute: Kali and Krsna, dark visions of the terrible and the sublime*. Berkeley, California: University of California Press.

Kinsley, David 1982: "The Image of the Divine and the Status of Women in the *Devi-Bhagavata-Purana*". *Anima*, vol. 9, no. 1, pp. 50–6.

Kinsley, D. R. 1986 reprint of 1982 edn: "Blood and Death Out of Place: Reflections on the goddess Kali". In J. S. Hawley and D. M. Wulff (eds), *The Divine Consort: Radha and the goddesses of India*. Boston: Beacon Press, pp. 144–52.

Kinsley, D. R. 1986: *Hindu Goddesses: Visions of the divine feminine in the Hindu religious tradition.* Berkeley, Los Angeles and London: University of California Press.

Kinsley, D. R. 1997: *Tantric Visions of the Divine Feminine: The ten mahavidyas.* Berkeley: University of California Press.

Klostermaier, Klaus K. 2000: *Hindu Writings: A short introduction to the major sources.* Oxford: One World.

Kramrisch, Stella 1975: "The Indian Great Goddess". *History of Religions*, vol. 14, no. 4, pp. 235–65.

Kumar, P. P. 1997: *The Goddess Laksmi: The divine consort in south India Vaisnava tradition.* Atlanta, Georgia: Scholars Press.

Lal, S. K. 1980: *Female Deities in Hindu Mythology and Ritual.* Pune: University of Poona.

Lalye, P. G. 1995: "The Incarnations of Devi, as Described in the *Devi Bhagavata Purana*". In K. C. Mishra, T. Mishra, and R. K. Mishra (eds), *Studies in Saktism.* Bhubaneswar: Institute of Orissan Culture.

Leslie, J. 1989: *The Perfect Wife.* Delhi: Oxford University Press.

Leslie, J. (ed.) 1992: *Roles and Rituals for Hindu Women.* New Delhi: Motilal Banarsidass.

Leslie, J. 1992: "Suttee or *Sati*: Victim or victor?". In J. Leslie (ed.), *Roles and Rituals for Hindu Women.* New Delhi: Motilal Banarsidass, pp. 175–191.

Lewis, O. 1965: *Village Life in Northern India: Studies in a Delhi village.* New York: Random House.

Lorenzen, David N. 1987: "Saivism: Kapalikas". In M. Eliade (ed.), *Encyclopedia of Religion*, vol. 13, New York: Macmillan, pp. 19–20.

Lorenzen, David N. 1991 2nd revised edn: *The Kapalikas and Kalamukhas: Two lost Saivite sects.* Delhi: Motilal Banarsidass.

Lorenzen, David N. 2002: "Early Evidence for Tantric Religion". In Katherine Anne Harper, and Robert L. Brown (eds), *The Roots of Tantra.* Albany: State University of New York, pp. 25–36

Mahapatra, Kedarnath 1953: "A Note on the Hypaethral Temple of the Sixty-four Yoginis at Hirapur" *Orissa Historical Research Journal*, vol. 11, pp. 23–40.

Mani, Vettam 1989 reprint of 1975 edn: *Puranic Encyclopaedia: A comprehensive dictionary with special reference to the epic and puranic literature.* Delhi: Motilal Banarsidass.

Marglin, Frédérique Apffel 1985: *Wives of the God-King: Rituals of the Devadasis of Puri.* New York: Oxford University Press.

Martin, E. Osborn 1914: *The Gods of India: A brief description of their history, character and worship.* London and Toronto: J. M. Dent and Sons Ltd.

McDaniel, June. 2004: *Offering Flowers, Feeding Skulls: Popular goddess worship in West Bengal.* Oxford: Oxford University Press.

McDermott, Rachel Fell 1994: "Popular Attitudes Towards Kali and Her Poetry Tradition". In A. Michaels, C. Volgelsanger and A. Wilke (eds), *Wild*

Goddesses in India and Nepal: Proceedings of an international symposium, Berne and Zurich, November 1994. Studia Religiosa Helvetica, Jahrbuch vol. 2, Bern: Peter Lang, pp. 383–415.

Michaels, A., Volgelsanger, C., and Wilke, A. (eds) 1994: *Wild Goddesses in India and Nepal: Proceedings of an international symposium, Berne and Zurich, November 1994.* Studia Religiosa Helvetica, Jahrbuch vol. 2, Bern: Peter Lang.

Mishra, K. C., Mishra, T. and Mishra, R. K. (eds) 1995: *Studies in Saktism.* Bhubaneswar: Institute of Orissan Culture.

Monier-Williams, Monier 1993 reprint of 1899 edn: *A Sanskrit–English Dictionary.* Delhi: Motilal Banarsidass.

Mookerjee, A. 1988: *Kali: The feminine force.* London: Thames and Hudson.

Narayan, R. K. 1986 reissue of 1964 edn: *Gods, Demons and Others.* London: Heinemann.

Nicholas, R. W. 1981: "The Goddess Sitala and Epidemic Smallpox in Bengal", *Journal of Asian Studies,* vol. XLI, no. 1 , pp. 21–44

Nicholas, R. W. 1982: "The Village Mother in Bengal". In J. J. Preston (ed.), *Mother Worship: Themes and variations,* North Carolina: University of North Carolina Press, pp. 192–209.

Niverdita, Sister 1988: *Cradle Tales of Hinduism.* Calcutta: Adaita Ashrama.

O'Flaherty, W. D. 1981 reprint of 1973 edn: *Siva: The erotic ascetic.* London and New York: Oxford University Press.

O'Flaherty, Wendy Doniger 1986 reprint of 1982 edn: "The Shifting Balance of Power in the Marriage of Siva and Parvati". In J. S. Hawley and D. M. Wulff (eds), *The Divine Consort: Radha and the goddesses of India.* Boston: Beacon Press, pp. 129–43.

Oldenburg, V. T. 1994: "The Roop Kanwar Case: Feminist responses". In J. S. Hawley (ed.), *Sati, the Blessing and the Curse: The burning of wives in India.* New York and Oxford: Oxford University Press, pp. 101–30.

Olsen, Carl (ed.) 1983: *The Book of the Goddess Past and Present.* New York: Crossroad.

Olsen, Carl 1983: "Sri Lakshmi and Radha: The obsequious wife and the lustful lover". In Carl Olsen (ed.), *The Book of the Goddess Past and Present.* New York: Crossroad, pp. 124–44.

Padoux, Andre, 2002: "What Do We Mean by Tantrism?" In Katherine Anne Harper, and Robert L. Brown (eds), *The Roots of Tantra.* (Albany: State University of New York, pp. 17–24

Padoux, Andre, 2007 revised Indian edn: "The Sricakra According to the First Chapter of the Yoginihrdaya". In G. Buhnemann (ed.), *Mandalas and Yantras in the Hindu Traditions.* New Delhi: D. K. Printworld, pp. 239–50

Payne, Ernest A. 1997 reprint of 1933 edn: *The Saktas: An introductory and comparative study.* New Delhi: Munshiram Manoharlal Publishers.

Pintchman, T. 1993: "Creation and the Great Goddess in the Puranas". *Purana,* vol. 35, no. 2, pp. 152–3.

Pintchman, Tracy. 1994: *The Rise of the Goddess in the Hindu Tradition*. Albany: State University of New York.

Pintchman, T. (ed.) 2001: *Seeking Mahadevi: Constructing the identities of the Hindu great goddess*. Albany: State University of New York Press.

Ruether, Rosemany Radford 2005: *Goddesses and the Divine Feminine: A western religious history*. Berkeley, Los Angeles and London: University of California Press.

Samuel, Geoffrey. 2008: *The Origins of Yoga and Tantra: Indic religions to the thirteenth century*. Cambridge: Cambridge University Press.

Sanderson, Alexis, 1985: "Purity and Power among the Brahmans of Kashmir". In M. Carrithers, S. Collins, and Steven Lukes (eds), *The Category of the Person*. Cambridge: Cambridge University Press, pp. 190–216.

Sanderson, Alexis, 1988: "Saivism and the Tantric Traditions". In F. Hardy (ed.), *The World's Religions: The religions of Asia*. London: Routledge, pp. 128–72.

Smith, Brian K. 2005 2nd revised edn: "Tantrism: Hindu Tantrism". In Lindsay Jones (ed.), *Encyclopedia of Religion*, vol. 13, New York: Macmillan Reference USA, pp. 8987–94.

Smith, W. L. 1980: *The One-Eyed Goddess: A study of the Manasa Mangal*. Stockholm, Sweden: Almqvist and Wiksell, Uppsala.

Sastri, G. 1967: "The Cult of Sakti". In D. C. Sircar (ed.), *The Sakti Cult and Tara*. Calcutta: University of Calcutta, pp. 10–16.

Scheuer, Jacques 1982: *Siva dans le Mahabharta*. Paris: Presses Universitaires du France.

Singh, V. 1994: *The River Goddess*. London: Moonlight Publishing.

Sircar, D. C. (ed.) 1967: *The Sakti Cult and Tara*. Calcutta: University of Calcutta.

Söhnen, Renate 1990: "Rise and Decline of the Indra Religion in the Veda". In Michael Witzel (ed.), *Inside the Texts Beyond the Texts: New approaches to the study of the Vedas*, proceedings of the International Vedic Workshop Harvard University, June 1989. Cambridge: Dept. of Sanskrit and Indian Studies, Harvard University, pp. 235–43.

Sorensen, S. 1963: *An Index to the Names in the Mahabharata*. Delhi: Motilal Banarsidass.

Stutley M. and Stutley, J. 1977: *A Dictionary of Hinduism: Its mythology, folk-lore and development 1500 B.C – A.D. 1500*. London: Routledge and Kegan Paul.

Walker, B. 1983: *Hindu World: An encyclopaedic survey of Hinduism*, 2 vols. New Delhi: Munishiram Manoharlal Publishers Pvt. Ltd.

White, David Gordon. 1998: "Transformations in the Art of Love: Kamakala practices in Hindu Tantric and Kaula traditions". *History of Religions*, vol. 38, no. 2, pp. 172–98.

White, David Gordon, 2000: "Introduction – Tantra in Practice: Mapping a tradition". In David Gordon White (ed.), *Tantra in Practice*. Princeton, New Jersey: Princeton University Press, pp. 3–38.

White, David Gordon (ed.), 2000: *Tantra in Practice.* Princeton, New Jersey: Princeton University Press.

White, David Gordon. 2003: *Kiss of the Yogini: "Tantric Sex" in its South Asian contexts.* Chicago: University of Chicago.

White, David Gordon 2008a: "Saptamatrkas". In Denise Cush, Catherine Robinson and Michael York (eds), *Encyclopedia of Hinduism.* London and New York: Routledge, p. 764.

White, David Gordon 2008b: "Tantrism". In Denise Cush, Catherine Robinson and Michael York (eds), *Encyclopedia of Hinduism.* London and New York: Routledge, pp. 853–63.

Whitehead, H. 1921 3rd rev. edn: *The Village Gods of South India.* Calcutta: YMCA Association Press.

Wilke, Annette, 1994: "Sankara and the Taming of Wild Goddesses". In A. Michaels, C. Volgelsanger and A. Wilke (eds), *Wild Goddesses in India and Nepal: Proceedings of an international symposium, Berne and Zurich, November 1994.* Studia Religiosa Helvetica, Jahrbuch vol. 2, Bern: Peter Lang, pp. 123–78.

Wilkins, W. J. 1991 reprint of 1882 edn: *Hindu Mythology: Vedic and puranic.* Calcutta: Rupa and Co.

Practices

Ahmed, Irfan 1999: "Contextualising *Vande Mataram.*" *Manushi*, vol. 111 (March/April), pp. 29–30.

Allen, Michael R. n.d. 2nd edn: *The Cult of Kumari: Virgin worship in Nepal.* New Delhi: Siddhartha Press.

Balaram Iyer, T. G. S. 1994 8th edn: *History and Description of Sri Meenakshi Temple.* Madurai: Sri Karthik Agency.

Bandyopadhyay, P. 1993: *Mother Goddess Durga.* Calcutta: United Writers.

Beck, Brenda E. F. 1969: "The Vacillating Goddess: Sexual control and social rank in the Indian pantheon" (unpublished paper presented at the Association of Asian Studies meeting, Chicago).

Beck, Brenda E. F. 1981: "The Goddess and the Demon: A local south Indian festival and its wider context." *Purusartha* vol. 5, pp. 83–136.

Bhattacharyya, N. N. 1977, 2nd revised edn: *The Indian Mother Goddess.* New Delhi: Manohar Book Service.

Bhattacharyya, N. N. 1999 2nd revised edn: *History of the Tantric Religion (A historical, ritualistic and philosophical study).* New Delhi: Manohar.

Brand, Michael. 1982: "A New Hindu Goddess." *Hemisphere: An Asian Australian magazine*, vol. 26, no. 6 (May/June), pp. 380–4.

Chakravarti, C. 1957: "Kali Worship in Bengal". *Adyar Library Bulletin*, vol. 21, pts 3 & 4, pp. 296–303.

Chatterjee, K. K. 1973: *The History of Dakshineswar Kali Temple.* Calcutta: Sabita Chatterjee.

Claus, P. J. 1975: "The Siri Myth and Ritual: A mass possession cult of south India", *Ethnology*, vol. 14, no.1, pp. 47–58.

Das, M. 1999: *Legends of India's Temples*. Mumbai: Neve.

Das, R. K. 1964: *The Temples of Tamilnad*. Bombay: Bharatiya Vidya Bhavan.

Das, Veena 1980: "The Mythological Film and its Framework of Meaning: An analysis of *Jai Santoshi Ma*." *India International Quarterly*, vol. 8, no. 1 (March), pp. 43–56.

Dev, Usha 1987: *The Concept of Sakti in the Puranas*. Delhi: Nag Publishers.

Diehl, C. G. 1956: *Instrument and Purpose: Studies on rites and rituals in south India*. Lund: C. W. K. Gleerup.

Dunham, V. Carol 1997: "Nepal's Virgin Goddesses." *Hinduism Today* (June), pp. 26–9.

Dwyer, Rachel 2006: *Filming the Gods: Religion and Indian cinema*. Abingdon, Oxon and New York: Routledge.

Eck, Diana L. 1981: "India's *Tirthas*: 'Crossings' in sacred geography". *History of Religions*, vol. 20, no. 4 (May), pp. 323–44.

Eck, D. L. 1996: "Ganga: The goddess Ganges in Hindu sacred geography", in J. S. Hawley, and D. M. Wulff (eds), *Devi: Goddesses of India*. Berkeley, California: University of California Press, pp. 137–53.

Eck, Diana, L. 1998, 3rd edn: *Darsan: Seeing the divine image in India*. New York and Chichester, West Sussex: Columbia University Press.

Egnor, M.T. 1984: "The Changed Mother or What the Smallpox Goddess Did When There Was No More Smallpox." *Contributions to Asian Studies*, vol. XVIII, pp. 24–45.

Elmore, W. T. 1984 reprint of 1913 edn: *Dravidian Gods in Modern Hinduism*. New Delhi: Asian Educational Services.

Erndl, K. M. 1993: *Victory to the Mother: The Hindu goddesses of northwest India in myth, ritual, and symbol*. New York: Oxford University Press.

Ferrari, F. M. 2007: "'Love Me Two Times.' From Smallpox to AIDS: Contagion and possession in the cult of Sitala." *Religions of South Asia*, vol. 1, no. 1 (June), pp. 81–106.

Foulston, Lynn 2002: *At the Feet of the Goddess: The divine feminine in local Hindu religion*. Brighton, Sussex and Portland, Oregon: Sussex Academic Press.

Freeman, James 1974: "Trial by Fire." *Natural History* (January), pp. 54–63.

Fuller, C. J. 1980: "The Divine Couple's Relationship in a South Indian Temple: Minaksi and Sundaresvara at Madurai." *History of Religions*, vol. 19, no. 4 (May), pp. 321–48.

Fuller, C. J. 1992: *The Camphor Flame: Popular Hinduism and society in India*. Princeton, New Jersey: Princeton University Press.

Gandhi, M., and Singh, Y. 1989: *Brahma's Hair: The mythology of Indian plants*. Calcutta: Rupa and Co.

Gatwood, Lynn E. 1985: *Devi and the Spouse Goddess: Women, sexuality and marriage in India*. New Delhi: Manohar.

Ghosha, P. 1871: *Durga Puja: With notes and illustrations*. Calcutta: Hindu Patriot Press.

Gokhale, D. V. 1999: "Judge the Song on Merit." *Manushi*, vol. 113 (July/August), p. 2.

Goswami, K. P. 1998: *Kamakhya Temple: Past and present*. New Delhi: A. P. H Publishing Corporation.

Gupta, Charu 2001: "The Icon of Mother in Late Colonial North India: 'Bharat Mata', 'Matri Bhasha' and 'Gau Mata', *Economic and Political Weekly*, vol. 36, no. 45 (November), pp. 4291–99.

Gupta, Sanjukta 1979: "Tantric Sadhana: Puja" In Sanjukta Gupta, T. J. Hoens and Teun Goudriaan (eds), *Hindu Tantrism*. Leiden: E. J. Brill.

Gupta, Sanjukta 2003: "The Domestication of a Goddess: *Carana-tirtha* Kalighat, the *mahapitha* of Kali" in Rachel Fell McDermott and Jeffrey J. Kripal (eds), *Encountering Kali: In the margins, at the center, in the west*. Berkeley and Los Angeles: University of California Press, pp. 60–79.

Gupta, Sanjukta, Hoens, T. J., and Goudriaan, Teun (eds) 1979: *Hindu Tantrism*. Leiden: E. J. Brill.

Harman, William P. 1992 reprint of 1989 edn: *The Sacred Marriage of a Hindu Goddess*. New Delhi: Motilal Banarsidass.

Hawley J. S. 1996: "The Goddess in India" in J. S. Hawley and D. M. Wulff (eds), *Devi: Goddesses of India*. Berkeley, Los Angeles and London: University of California Press, pp. 1–28.

Hawley, J. S. and Wulff, D. M. (eds), 1996: *Devi: Goddesses of India*. Berkeley, California: University of California Press.

Hiltebeitel, Alf 1991 reprint of 1988 edn: *The Cult of Draupadi, 1, Mythologies: From Gingee to Kuruksetra*, New Delhi: Motilal Banarsidass.

Hiltebeitel, Alf 1991: *The Cult of Draupadi, 2, On Hindu ritual and the Goddess*, Chicago and London: University of Chicago Press.

Hixon, Lex 1996 reprint of 1992 edn: *Great Swan: Meetings with Ramakrishna*. Burdett, New York: Larson Publications.

Isherwood, Christopher 2001 reprint of 1965 edn: *Ramakrishna and his Disciples*. Kolkata: Advaita Ashrama.

Jeyechandrun, A. V. 1985: *Madurai Temple Complex*. Madurai: Madurai Kamaraj University Publications Division.

Jha, Sadhan 2004: "The Life and Times of Bharat Mata: Nationalism as invented religion". *Manushi*, 142, pp. 34–8.

Jung, A. 1987: *Unveiling India: A woman's journey*, Calcutta: Penguin.

Kabir, Nasreen Munni 2001: *Bollywood: The Indian cinema story*. London: Channel 4 Books.

Kinsley, D. R. 1975: *The Sword and the Flute: Kali and Krsna, dark visions of the terrible and the sublime*. Berkeley, California: University of California Press.

Kinsley, D. R. 1986: *Hindu Goddesses: Visions of the divine feminine in the Hindu religious tradition*. Delhi: Motilal Banarsidass.

Kinsley, David R. 1993, 2nd edn: *Hinduism: A cultural perspective*. Englewood Cliffs, New Jersey: Prentice-Hall.

Kinsley, D. R. 1997: *Tantric Visions of the Divine Feminine: The ten mahavidyas*. Berkeley: University of California Press.

Kishwar, Madhu 2001: *"Jhadu Pooja* at Sewa Nagar: Manushi's campaign for cleansing governance." *Manushi*, vol. 127 (November/December), pp. 3–11.

Kishwar, Madhu Purnima 2005: "Emergency *Avatar* of a Secular Goddess!: Manushi Swachha Narayani descends to protect street vendors." *Manushi*, vol. 147 (March/April), pp. 4–15.

Kishwar, M. and Vanita, R. 1987: "The Burning of Roop Kanwar." *Manushi* vol. 42–3, pp. 15–25.

Kolenda, P. 1982: "Pox and the Terror of Childlessness: Images and ideas of the smallpox goddess in a north Indian village". In J. J. Preston (ed.), *Mother Worship: Themes and variations*. North Carolina: University of North Carolina Press, pp. 227–50.

Kurtz, S. N. 1992: *All the Mothers are One: Hindu India and the cultural reshaping of psychoanalysis*. New York: Columbia University Press.

Lutgendorf, Philip 2002: "A Superhit Goddess: *Jai Santoshi Maa* and caste hierarchy in Indian films". *Manushi*, vol. 131 (July/August), pp. 10–16.

Madhavananda et al. 1989: *Studies on the Tantras*. Calcutta: The Ramakrishna Mission Institute of Calcutta.

Manandhar, Jnan Kaji, 2002: *The Legends of Nepal.* Kathmandu: Sukhaveti Manandhar.

Marathe, K. 1998: *Temples of India: Circles of stone*. Mumbai: Eeshwar.

McDaniel, June 2004: *Offering Flowers, Feeding Skulls: Popular goddess worship in West Bengal*. Oxford and New York: Oxford University Press.

McDermott, Rachel Fell 1994: "Popular Attitudes Towards Kali and Her Poetry Tradition". In A. Michaels, C. Volgelsanger and A. Wilke (eds), *Wild Goddesses in India and Nepal: Proceedings of an international symposium, Berne and Zurich, November 1994*. Studia Religiosa Helvetica, Jahrbuch vol. 2, Bern: Peter Lang, pp. 383–415.

McDermott, Rachel Fell 2001: *Singing to the Goddess: Poems to Kali and Uma from Bengal.* Oxford and New York: Oxford University Press.

McDermott, Rachel Fell and Kripal, Jeffrey J. (eds) 2003: *Encountering Kali: In the margins, at the center, in the west*. Berkeley and Los Angeles: University of California Press.

McKean, Lise 1996: *Divine Enterprise: Gurus and the Hindu nationalist movement*. Chicago: University of Chicago Press.

McKean, Lise 1996: "Bharat Mata: Mother India and Her Militant Matriots". In J. S. Hawley, and D. M. Wulff (eds.), *Devi: Goddesses of India*. Berkeley, Los Angeles and London: University of California Press, pp. 250–80.

Michell, G. 1988 reprint of 1977 edn: *The Hindu Temple: An introduction to its meaning and forms*. Chicago and London: University of Chicago Press.

Moffatt, Michael 1979: *An Untouchable Community in South India: Structure and consensus.* Princeton, New Jersey: Princeton University Press.

Mohanty, B. 1998: "Lakshmi and Alakshmi: The Kojagari Lakshmi *vrat katha* of Bengal". *Manushi*, vol. 104 (January/February), pp. 9–11.

Mookerjee, A. 1988: *Kali: The feminine force.* London: Thames and Hudson.

Mookerjee, A. and Khanna, M. 1993 reprint of 1977 edn: *The Tantric Way.* London: Thames and Hudson.

Nagaswami, R. 1982: *Tantric Cult of South India.* Delhi: Agam Kala Prakashan.

Neevel, W. G. 1987: "Ramakrishna" In M. Eliade (ed.), *The Encyclopedia of Religion* vol. 12, New York: Macmillan, pp. 209–11.

Nikhilananda, Swami (trans.) 2002: *Selections from the Gospel of Sri Ramakrishna.* Woodstock, Vermont: Skylight Paths Publishing.

O'Flaherty, Wendy Doniger 1981 reprint of 1973 edn: *Siva: The erotic ascetic.* London and New York: Oxford University Press.

Oldenburg, V. T. 1994: "The Roop Kanwar Case: Feminist responses". In J. S. Hawley (ed.), *Sati, the Blessing and the Curse: The burning of wives in India.* New York and Oxford: Oxford University Press, pp. 101–30.

Olson, Carl 1990: *The Mysterious Play of Kali: An interpretive study of Ramakrishna.* Atlanta, Georgia: Scholars Press.

Oppert, G. 1972 reprint of 1893 edn: *The Original Inhabitants of Bharatavarsa or India.* Delhi: Oriental Publishers.

Parry, Jonathan P. 1994: *Death in Benaras.* Cambridge: Cambridge University Press.

Pinney, Christopher 2004: '*Photos of the Gods': The printed image and political struggle in India.* London: Reaktion Books.

Prasad, T. 1958: "How Fishermen Worship Goddess Kali". *Indian Folklore*, vol. 1, no. 4, pp. 70–2.

Rajeshwari, D. R. 1989: *Sakti Iconography.* New Delhi: Intellectual Publishing House.

Rodrigues, H. P. 2003: *Ritual Worship of the Great Goddess: The liturgy of the Durga Puja with interpretations.* Albany: State University of New York Press.

Rohe, M. E. 2001: "Ambiguous and Definitive: The greatness of the goddess Vaisno Devi". In T. Pintchman (ed.), *Seeking Mahadevi: Constructing the identities of the Hindu great goddess.* Albany: State University of New York Press, pp. 55–76.

Roy, I. B. 1993: *Kalighat: Its impact on socio-cultural life of Hindus.* New Delhi: Gyan Publishing House.

Shakya, Rashmila and Berry, Scott 2005: *From Goddess to Mortal: The true-life story of a former royal Kumari.* Thamel, Kathmandu: Vajra Publications.

Shulman, D. D. 1976: "The Murderous Bride: Tamil versions of the myth of Devi and the Buffalo-Demon". *History of Religions*, vol. 16, no. 2, pp. 120–46.

Shulman, D. D 1980: *Tamil Temple Myths: Sacrifice and divine marriage in the south Indian Saiva tradition.* Princeton, New Jersey: Princeton University Press.

Sircar, D. C. 1948: "The Sakta Pithas". *Journal of the Royal Asiatic Society of Bengal*, vol. 16, no. 1, pp. 1–108.

Smith, Frederick M. 2006: *The Self Possessed: Deity and spirit possession in South Asian literature and civilization.* New York and Chichester, West Sussex: Columbia University Press.

Tewari, N. 1988: *The Mother Goddess Vaishno Devi.* New Delhi: Lancer International.

Tiwari, J. N. 1985: *Goddess Cults in Ancient India with Special Reference to the First Seven Centuries A.D.* Delhi: Sundeep Prakasham.

Van Kooij, K. R. 1972: *Worship of the Goddess According to the Kalikapurana part 1, A translation with and introduction and notes of chapters 54 –69.* Leiden: Brill.

Wadley, S. S. 1985 reprint of 1975 edn: *Shakti: Power in the conceptual structure of Karimpur religion.* New Delhi: Munishiram Manoharlal.

Whitehead, H. 1983 reprint of 1921 edn. *The Village Gods of South India.* New Delhi: Cosmo.

Unpublished Dissertations

Brand, Michael 1979: "A New Hindu Goddess". BA dissertation (Appendix and Bibliography only), Australian National University.

Brubaker, R. L. 1978: "The Ambivalent Mistress: A study of south Indian village goddesses and their religious meaning". Ph.D. thesis, University of Chicago.

Logan, Penny 1980: "Domestic Worship and the Festival Cycle in the South Indian City of Madurai". Ph.D. thesis, Manchester University.

Nanacampantan, K. 1982–3: "Colavantan Jenakai Mariyamman Kovil Valipatum Tiruvilakkalum". M.Phil. dissertation, Madurai Kamaraj University.

Planalp, J. M. 1956: "Religious Life and Values in a North Indian Village". Ph.D. thesis, Cornell University.

Raja, P. 1996: "Janaka Perumal Temple – A Study". M.Phil. dissertation, Madurai Kamaraj University.

Robinson, J. D. 1983: "The Worship of Clay Images in Bengal". Ph.D. thesis, Oxford University.

Samata, S. 1990: "Cognition and Experience: The goddess Kali in the lives of her Bengal devotees". Ph.D. thesis, University of Virginia.

Websites

Bahadur Singh, Chet [WWW] "Four-year-old Shakya girl selected new 'Kumari'", The Kathmandu Post (11 July 2001) http://www.nepalnews.com.np/contents/englishdaily/ktmpost/2001/jul/jul11/index.htm#5 (13-09-07)

Gewertz, Ken [WWW]"Undergraduate Witnesses Birth of a Goddess" *The Harvard University Gazette*, 24 February 2000, http://www.hno.harvard.

edu/gazette/2000/02.24/AIDS.html (08-09-07)

Gupta, Suchananda "Woman's death sparks 'sati' row" *The Times of India* (23 August 2006) http://timesofindia.indiatimes.com/articleshow/1917392.cms (10/06/08)

Harding, Luke "The Ultimate Sacrifice" *The Guardian* (Friday 23 August 2002) http://www.guardian.co.uk/gender/story/0,11812,779265,00.html (11-02-08)

Much Ross, Nancy C. and Mahapatra, Manamohan [WWW] "Kalasis Introduction: The Santoshi Ma Kalasis" http://tagmeme.com/ orissa/kalasis.html (30-03-08)

Much Ross, Nancy C. and Mahapatra, Manmohan 2004: [WWW] "Kalasis Introduction: The Santoshi Ma Kalasis". http://tagmeme.com/orissa/ kalasis.html (30-08-07)

Portnoy, Anna [WWW] "A Goddess in the Making: A very hard-to-find town in India builds a shrine to a goddess for AIDS." *Whole Earth* (Fall 2000) http://www.wholeearthmag.com/ArticleBin/395.html (08-09-07)

Varadarajan, Siddharth "Parties mark centenary that was not" The Hindu Online, 8 September 2006, http://www.hindu.com/2006/09/08/stories/ 2006090823000100.htm (06/04/08)

Jai Santoshi Maa http://jaisantoshimaa.com (30-03-08)

Legal Empowerment of the Poor: Sewa Nagar http://www.youtube.com/ watch?v=AB62Itu37eg (30-03-08)

Shri Mata Vaishno Devi Shrine Board – official website. http:// maavaishn-odevi.org/new1/index.html (30-03-08)

"Kuttu Bai Didn't Commit Sati; She Was Murdered" *People's Democracy* (XXVI, 37, September 22 2002) http://www.cpim.org/pd/2002/sept22/ 09152002_mp_sati.htm(11-02-08)

http://news.bbc.co.uk/1/hi/world/south_asia/7040191.stm (14-02-08)

http://www.timesonline.co.uk/tol/news/world/asia/article2648418.ece (14-02-08)

Vedanta Society, Berkeley http://www.vedantaberkeley.org/toppage1.htm (01-04-08)

"Woman attempts 'sati' in Madhya Pradesh" *The Times of India* (13 September 2006) http://timesofindia.indiatimes.com/articleshow/1988228.cms (10/06/08)

http://news.bbc.co.uk/1/hi/world/south_asia/7040191.stm (14-02-08)

http://www.timesonline.co.uk/tol/news/world/asia/article2648418.ece (14-02-08)

Newspaper Articles

"Sati: women's panel calls for stern action", *The Hindu* (13 August 2002).

"The deity down the decades", *The Telegraph* (28 September 2002) Kolkata issue.

Films and Documentaries

Dalrymple, William, 2000: *Indian Journeys: Shiva's Matted Locks*, Hugh Thompson, Icon Films.

Jai Santosi Maa, 1975: Vijay Sharma

Jai Santoshi Maa, 2006: Ahmed Siddiqui

Index